when groups meet

ESSAYS IN SOCIAL PSYCHOLOGY

Series Editors:
Miles Hewstone, *University of Oxford*
Monica Biernat, *University of Kansas*

Essays in Social Psychology is designed to meet the need for rapid publication of brief volumes in social psychology. Primary topics will include social cognition, interpersonal relationships, group processes, and intergroup relations, as well as applied issues. Furthermore, the series seeks to define social psychology in its broadest sense, encompassing all topics either informed by, or informing, the study of individual behavior and thought in social situations. Each volume in the series will make a conceptual contribution to the topic by reviewing and synthesizing the existing research literature, by advancing theory in the area, or by some combination of these missions. The principal aim is that authors will provide an overview of their own highly successful research program in an area. It is also expected that volumes will, to some extent, include an assessment of current knowledge and identification of possible future trends in research. Each book will be a self-contained unit supplying the advanced reader with a well-structured review of the work described and evaluated.

PUBLISHED

Van der Vliert: *Complex Interpersonal Conflict Behaviour: Theoretical Frontiers*
Dweck: *Self-Theories: Their Role in Motivation, Personality, and Development*
Sorrentino & Roney: *The Uncertain Mind: Individual Differences in Facing the Unknown*
Gaertner & Dovidio: *Reducing Intergroup Bias: The Common Ingroup Identity Model*
Tyler & Blader: *Cooperation in Groups: Procedural Justice, Social Identity, and Behavioral Engagement*
Kruglanski: *The Psychology of Closed Mindedness*
Dunning: *Self-Insight: Roadblocks and Detours on the Path to Knowing Thyself*
Biernat: *Standards and Expectancies: Contrast and Assimilation in Judgments of Self and Others*
Pettigrew & Tropp: *When Groups Meet: The Dynamics of Intergroup Contact*

FORTHCOMING

Ambady & Weisbuch: *Shared Minds in Motion: Dynamic Nonverbal Behavior and Social Influence*
Monteith & Ashburn-Nardo: *The Self-Regulation of Prejudice*
Haslam: *Dehumanization: The Psychology of Humanness and its Denial*
Jost: *A Theory of System Justification*

For continually updated information about published and forthcoming titles in the *Essays in Social Psychology* series, please visit: **www.psypress.com/essays**

when groups meet
the dynamics of intergroup contact

THOMAS F. PETTIGREW
University of California, Santa Cruz

and

LINDA R. TROPP
University of Massachusetts Amherst

Psychology Press
Taylor & Francis Group
NEW YORK AND HOVE

Published in 2011
by Psychology Press
711 Third Avenue,
New York, NY 10017
www.psypress.com

Published in Great Britain
by Psychology Press
27 Church Road,
Hove, East Sussex BN3 2FA

Copyright © 2011 by Psychology Press

Psychology Press is an imprint of the Taylor & Francis Group, an Informa business

Typeset by RefineCatch Limited, Bungay, Suffolk, UK
Printed and bound by Sheridan Books, Inc. in the USA on acid-free paper

10 9 8 7 6 5 4 3 2 1

All rights reserved. No part of this book may be reprinted or reproduced or utilized in any form or by any electronic, mechanical, or other means, now known or hereafter invented, including photocopying and recording, or in any information storage or retrieval system, without permission in writing from the publishers.

Library of Congress Cataloging in Publication Data

Pettigrew, Thomas F.
　When groups meet : the dynamics of intergroup contact / Thomas F. Pettigrew and Linda R. Tropp.
　　p. cm. – (Essays in social psychology)
　　Includes bibliographical references and index.
　ISBN 978-1-84169-765-9 (hb)
　1. Intergroup relations. 2. Social groups. 3. Social interaction. I. Tropp, Linda R. II. Title. III. Series.

HM716.P48 2011
302.4–dc22

2010047888

ISBN: 978-1-84169-765-9 (hbk)

CONTENTS

Preface   vii

Acknowledgments   ix

Chapter 1   The Origins of Intergroup Contact Theory   1
Chapter 2   Does Intergroup Contact Typically Reduce
            Intergroup Prejudice?   13
Chapter 3   Do Intergroup Contact Effects Generalize?   29
Chapter 4   Are the Effects of Intergroup Contact Universal?   49
Chapter 5   When Does Intergroup Contact Reduce
            Prejudice?   61
Chapter 6   How Does Intergroup Contact Reduce
            Prejudice?   77
Chapter 7   Does Intergroup Contact Reduce All Aspects
            of Prejudice?   97
Chapter 8   Does Cross-Group Friendship Play a Special Role
            in Reducing Prejudice?   115
Chapter 9   Does Group Status Moderate Contact Effects?   131
Chapter 10 Intergroup Contact as One of Many Predictors
            of Prejudice   145
Chapter 11 Criticisms of Intergroup Contact Theory   161
Chapter 12 When Intergroup Contact Fails   185
Chapter 13 Summing Up and Looking to the Future   201

Appendix A	Bibliography of Research Papers in the Intergroup Contact Meta-Analysis	217
Appendix B	Item Wordings for Variables Used in Analyses of German Survey Data	247
References		255
Author Index		293
Subject Index		304

PREFACE

Intergroup contact theory has a central place in the social science discipline of social psychology. Since the field focuses on individuals and groups in their social contexts, contact between people from different groups is a fundamental concern.

Not only is intergroup contact of special theoretical importance, but it also has critical implications for many practical and applied issues. Affirmative action, immigration, neighborhood and school desegregation, and other major social policies necessarily entail widespread intergroup contact. This fact has led to considerable public speculation and controversy on the topic in North America as well as in Europe – from mass media chatter to US Supreme Court opinions. Unfortunately, most of this speculation has largely ignored the extensive research literature on the subject. Indeed, the overwhelming evidence presented in this book supports contact as a remedy to alleviate intergroup conflict and rebuts public discussion that regards intergroup contact as a cause of intergroup conflict.

Consequently, we wish to achieve two aims with this volume. First, we integrate the literally hundreds of research studies on the topic conducted by social scientists throughout the world. This integration forms a basis for establishing a more empirically based theory of intergroup contact for social science. In the following pages, we specify intergroup contact's typical effects, when and how these effects occur, and when and why it sometimes fails to lead to positive effects. We also consider at length the many criticisms that have been leveled at the theory. Second, hopefully, the volume will contribute to a more informed public debate on the subject.

This publication completes a lengthy 13-year project for the two authors. For the first author, it represents the attainment of a half-century ambition. The original formulation of intergroup contact theory was introduced by his graduate mentor, Gordon Allport of Harvard University, in his classic and influential volume, *The Nature of Prejudice,* in 1954. The first author, a native Virginian, was especially interested in ways to combat the racial prejudice and discrimination that he had witnessed throughout his childhood. Naturally intrigued by the potential of intergroup contact theory, he chose to take his doctoral specialty examination on the theory in 1955 under Allport himself – more than a half-century before the publication of this book.

The long time span between this initial interest in intergroup contact and the development of this book was caused by the absence of enough rigorous research on the topic to review. In addition, meta-analytic techniques for a rigorous, quantitative assessment of the research literature – a vast improvement over traditional qualitative, subjective reviews – were not introduced until the last quarter of the 20th century. By the 1990s, however, the time had come for him to implement what he had long wanted to accomplish – a rigorous and thorough quantitative review of the now vast social science research literature on the subject. He sought an answer to the long-debated questions: Does intergroup contact, as its critics claim, typically lead to enhanced prejudice and distrust? Or, as its advocates claim, does intergroup contact typically lead to reduced prejudice and distrust?

The meta-analysis itself proved to be an arduous task of 8 years made possible by a research grant from the National Science Foundation (SBR-9709519). And it might not have ever been accomplished were it not for the close collaboration between the two co-authors. While the first author had recently become an emeritus professor, the second author was a doctoral student in social psychology at the University of California, Santa Cruz, when the project began in 1998. Having grown up in Gary, Indiana – an industrial steel town in the Midwest – she wished to study how structural inequalities impact intergroup contact and how to bridge group differences in construals of intergroup relationships. Together, we analyzed and rated the many hundreds of possibly relevant studies, both published and unpublished. And we were importantly aided by a group of eager undergraduates who gathered many of the articles to be reviewed while learning about meta-analysis. Perhaps most importantly, we shared a mutual commitment to identifying a rigorous, scientific research foundation for intergroup contact theory and realizing its potential for improving relations between groups in real-world settings.

Thomas F. Pettigrew
University of California, Santa Cruz
Linda R. Tropp
University of Massachusetts Amherst

ACKNOWLEDGMENTS

We wish to thank the many people whose invaluable help made this book possible. The first author is especially indebted to the Social Psychology section of the Psychology faculty at Philipps University Marburg, Germany. For the past decade, this group – headed by Professor Ulrich Wagner – has allowed him to participate in its intensive program of intergroup contact research. Wagner and Professor Rolf van Dick (now at Goethe University at Frankfurt am Main, Germany), Dr. Oliver Christ, Dr. Jost Stellmaker, and Professor Andreas Zick (now at Bielefeld University in Bielefeld, Germany) became close friends as well as research colleagues. The results of this work will be seen by the reader in our many uses of German probability survey data.

We are also grateful for Professor Wilhelm Heitmeyer's kind permission to use his rigorous probability surveys of the German population reported throughout the book. Supported by major grants from the Volkswagen and Freudenberg Foundations, Heitmeyer (2002, 2003, 2005) at Bielefeld University heads one of the largest long-term studies ever conducted on intergroup prejudice in the social sciences. His 10-year project has regularly fielded national surveys with fresh probability samples as well as repeated surveys of the respondents from the first sample in 2002. Several of these studies focused on intergroup contact and are of special importance for our analyses. Heitmeyer's support made it possible for us to present new analyses on many critical aspects of contact theory discussed in the volume.

We are also grateful for the helpful comments provided for Chapter 11 by Professor Robert Putnam of Harvard University, Dr. Jonathan Rothwell of the Brookings Institute, and Professor Eric Uslaner of the University of Maryland.

The second author also wishes to thank the International Graduate College on Conflict and Cooperation at Friedrich Schiller University in Jena, Germany, for granting her a fellowship during which she wrote and revised several of the chapters included in this book. We would also like to thank Sue Duval, Blair Johnson, David Kenny, and Jack Vevea for their statistical advice and guidance, and Rupert Brown, Jack Dovidio, Samuel Gaertner, Miles Hewstone, Brian Mullen, Ulrich Wagner, and Stephen Wright for their thoughtful feedback and comments across the many stages of work on this 13-year project.

We also wish to extend thanks to Kristin Davies and Art Aron for compiling the meta-analytic data on friendship reported in Chapter 8, and to our many dedicated research assistants without whom we could not have completed this major project: Rebecca Boice, Geoffrey Burcaw, Susan Burton, Darcy Cabral, Robert Chang, Daniel Cheron, Vanessa Lee, Kimberly Lincoln, Peter Moore, Danielle Murray, Neal Nakano, Maxi Nieber, Rajinder Samra, Michael Sarette, Christine Schmitt, Amanda Stout, and Gina Vittori. Our meta-analysis cited throughout the volume was partially supported by the National Science Foundation (SBR-9709519), with the first author and Stephen Wright as co-investigators.

The Origins of Intergroup Contact Theory

One of the worst race riots in the history of the United States occurred in Detroit in 1943. But while Black and White mobs raged in the streets, Whites and Blacks who knew each other not only refrained from violence but often helped one another. Automotive workers and university students continued to work and study side-by-side. Families hid neighbors of the other race from threatening rioters, and those Blacks and Whites who were close friends were especially protective of each other (Lee & Humphrey, 1968).

Such interpersonal humanity in the face of intergroup strife is not uncommon. During the 1990s, for instance, the world watched in horror as "ethnic cleansing" unfolded in Bosnia-Herzegovina (Oberschall, 2001). The terror of genocide was widely reported from this region of the former Yugoslavia. But largely unnoticed were the many households of all ethnic groups who hid friends of rival ethnicities whose lives were threatened.

Similarly, a mixed Arab and Jewish street in Jaffa, Israel, witnessed repeated neighborhood tragedies in October 2000. Each group rioted against the other, followed by a sudden flood. A Jewish mother and her children were trapped in their apartment by the rising water. And an Arab family, neighbors in the same apartment building, braved the flood, broke down bars on the window, and rescued the mother and two of her children (Copans, 2000).

Consider also research by Oliner (2004) and Oliner and Oliner (1988) on the rescuers of Jews in the midst of the Holocaust. These tireless investigators interviewed more than 600 European Christians, and focused on more than 400 rescuers who had saved Jews during the war. Bystanders, who neither saved Jews nor participated in the resistance, served as the key comparison group. How do these two groups differ?

The rescuers do not fit the widespread Western image of the "hero" – the lone outsider facing off evildoers as in the classic motion picture, *High Noon*. More than bystanders, rescuers lived on farms or in small villages. Here there was a strong sense of community and hiding the hunted was easier. They benefited from more supportive networks, including family members; and the desperate more often asked them for help. After the war, the rescuers achieved higher status occupations and were more active in their communities than bystanders.

Intergroup contact played a crucial role in this behavior that extends far beyond mere reduced prejudice. Just as contact theory would predict, the rescuers had significantly more contacts than bystanders with Jews in a variety of roles prior to the war (Oliner & Oliner, 1988, p. 275). Thus, they more frequently had had Jews as friends ($p<.0001$), neighbors ($p<.006$), and coworkers ($p<.03$). In addition, the rescuers also had a significantly wider variety of friends beyond that of their greater contact with Jews. When asked, "While growing up, did you have any close friends different from you in social class," 62% of the rescuers, but only 36% of the bystanders, answered "yes" [1] (Oliner & Oliner, 1988, p. 304).

Such dramatic examples offer hope that intergroup contact can be a significant remedy for combating prejudice and hostility between groups. Many commentators have held optimistic views regarding the potential for intergroup contact to improve intergroup relations. A popular refrain among advocates of integration is "if only we could get people from different groups to come together," then we would be able to achieve improved relations between groups. Unfortunately, achieving positive effects of intergroup contact is not always so simple.

Think about it. African Americans and European Americans have had more contact in the southern United States than in other parts of the nation. Nonetheless, the South has witnessed the most severe racial oppression. In South Africa, people of Black African and White European descent have lived in close proximity more than in any other part of Africa, yet the country has endured intense racial conflict. From these examples, it almost appears as if the more contact between peoples, the *more* – not less – prejudice and conflict will result. Some observers have come to that conclusion (e.g., Baker, 1934), but this view would be just as fallacious as the assumption that contact by itself offers a panacea for prejudice and intergroup conflict (Hewstone, 2003).

In this volume, we will demonstrate that intergroup contact actually *does* typically decrease intergroup prejudice and hostility – but not always or under all conditions. While many of the social sciences share an interest in intergroup contact (e.g., Blake, 2003; Crain & Weisman, 1972; Mutz, 2002), it is social psychology that has intensely focused on studying its complex effects. And it is this work that we will be describing in particular detail.

☐ The Historical Development of Intergroup Contact Theory

Early Thinking and Practice

So, what happens when groups interact? Theorists and practitioners began to speculate about the effects of intergroup contact long before there was a research base to guide them. 19th Century thinking, dominated by Social Darwinism, was quite pessimistic. In particular, William Graham Sumner (1906), a Yale University sociologist and an Episcopal minister, held that intergroup contact almost inevitably led to conflict. He believed that hostility toward outgroups simply follows as a consequence of an ingroup's sense of superiority. Because Sumner also believed that most groups felt themselves to be superior to other groups, his theory viewed intergroup hostility and conflict to be natural and inevitable outcomes of contact. Some more recent perspectives make similar predictions (see Jackson, 1993; Levine & Campbell, 1972).

20th Century writers continued to speculate about intergroup contact without empirical evidence. Some persisted in believing that contact between races, even under conditions of equality, would only breed "suspicion, fear, resentment, disturbance, and at times open conflict" (Baker, 1934, p. 120). Many of these writers, like Sumner himself, were not-so-subtly defending the South's then-existing pattern of rigid racial segregation in schools, neighborhoods, and public facilities. But writers following World War II were more optimistic in their views. Hence, Lett (1945, p. 35) held that shared interracial experiences with a common objective led to "mutual understanding and regard." Instead, when groups "are isolated from one another," wrote Brameld (1946, p. 245), "prejudice and conflict grow like a disease."

The first major effort to achieve widespread intergroup contact followed World War II – after Adolf Hitler had given prejudice an exceedingly bad name. A popular crusade formed to condemn both racial and religious prejudice in the United States. Called the Human Relations Movement, it sought to end prejudice and correct negative stereotypes. Yet this attempt was as naïve as it was well-intentioned. The Movement placed its complete faith in educating racial groups about each other and having different groups interact. It avoided controversy by not directly seeking the institutional changes necessary to enhance intergroup contact and combat discrimination in jobs, housing, and education. Rather, it invested its energies in celebrating Brotherhood Week each February and hosting Brotherhood Dinners for all groups to come and meet each other once a year.

4 When Groups Meet: The Dynamics of Intergroup Contact

The Movement's guiding premise was that prejudice derived largely from ignorance. If only we could interact and come to know each other across group lines, went the reasoning, we would discover the common humanity we share. The Movement, noted Drake and Cayton (1962, p. 281), projected an "[a]llmost mystical faith in 'getting to know one another' as a solvent of racial tensions...."

To be sure, ignorance *is* a factor in intergroup relations (Stephan & Stephan, 1984). But this factor alone does not account for the many situational and institutional barriers that perpetuate prejudice between groups. Moreover, the Movement did not understand the complexity and variability of intergroup contact effects – issues that are the focus of this book.

Early Research on Intergroup Contact

Nonetheless, these initial efforts by the Human Relations Movement sparked early investigations of intergroup contact by social psychologists and sociologists. Research interest in the topic grew logically from these fields' emphases on intergroup relations, social interactions, and the power of situations to shape behavior. University of Alabama researchers were among the first to conduct a study that indirectly examined the effects of contact (Sims & Patrick, 1936). Their initial results were not encouraging, although it should be emphasized that their study did not measure intergroup contact directly. With each year that students from the North attended the tightly segregated southern university, their anti-Black attitudes increased. Because the university's faculty and student body were then exclusively White, Northern students were likely to have had little contact with Black peers and authorities, and more likely to have met only Blacks in lower status positions. They were also influenced by Alabama's extremely racist norms of that period.

Later studies investigated Black–White contact more directly and under more favorable conditions. After the desegregation of the Merchant Marine in 1948, close bonds developed between Black and White seamen on the ships and in the maritime union (Brophy, 1945). Consequently, the more voyages the White seamen took with Blacks, the more positive their racial attitudes became. But their racial prejudice did not evaporate with a single interracial voyage. What we see in Figure 1.1 is an almost linear effect – one by one, the more interracial voyages the White seamen took, the less anti-Black prejudice they expressed.

Similarly, Kephart (1957) found that White police officers in Philadelphia who had worked with Black colleagues differed sharply in their racial views from other White police officers. They offered fewer objections to teaming with a Black partner, having Blacks join their previously all-White police districts, and taking orders from qualified Black officers.

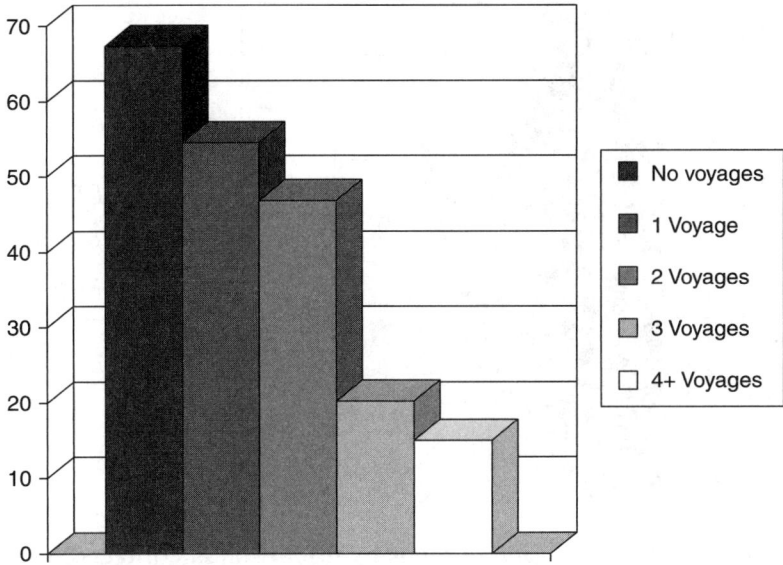

FIGURE 1.1 Prejudice percentages by interracial voyages. Adapted from Brophy (1945, table 9, p. 462).

Gordon Allport contributed to this early research (Allport & Kramer, 1946). Together with his then-graduate student, Bernard Kramer, he tested the effects of equal-status contact on the anti-Jewish attitudes of non-Jewish undergraduates at both Dartmouth College and Harvard University. As illustrated in Figure 1.2, an almost linear negative effect again emerges – the more equal-status contacts the non-Jewish students reported having had with Jews, the less they reported anti-Jewish prejudice.

As these early studies grew in number, the Social Science Research Council asked the Cornell University sociologist, Robin Williams, Jr., to review the research on intergroup relations. Williams' (1947) monograph, *The Reduction of Intergroup Tensions*, offers 102 testable "propositions" on intergroup relations that included the initial formulation of intergroup contact theory. He stressed that many variables would influence contact's effects on prejudice – such as the relative status of the participants, the social milieu, the level of prior prejudice, the duration of the contact, and the amount of competition between the groups in the situation. In particular, he stressed that contact's positive effects are maximized when: (1) the two groups share similar status, interests, and tasks; (2) the situation fosters personal, intimate intergroup contact; (3) the participants do not fit the stereotyped conceptions of their groups; and (4) the activities

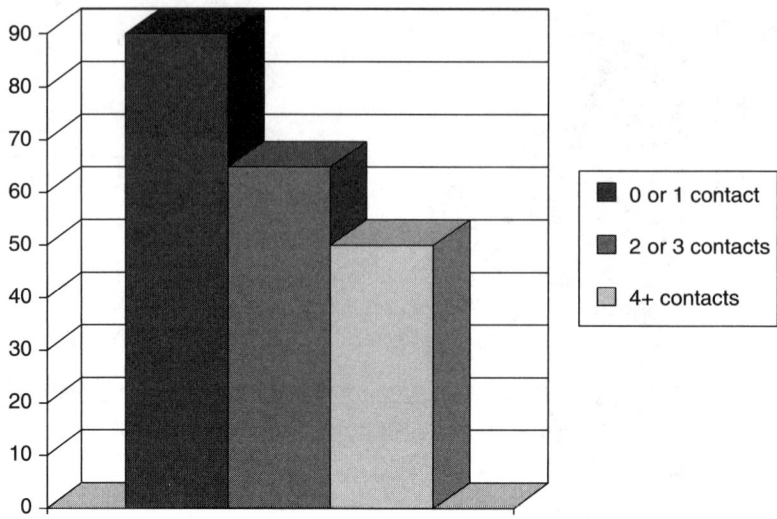

FIGURE 1.2 Prejudice percentages by equal-status contacts. Adapted from Allport and Kramer (1946, table 8, p. 23).

cut across group lines. This initial statement is apparently the first formal presentation of what has become intergroup contact theory. Though rudimentary, Williams shrewdly foresaw many of the findings of intergroup contact research that we will be discussing throughout this volume.

But there were potential problems involving self-selection and causal direction in these early studies. For example, it could have been that the more tolerant White seamen at the outset signed on for ships with Black seamen, that more tolerant White police initially chose to work with Black colleagues, and that White students who had had equal-status contact with Jews were already more tolerant before the intergroup contact. This problem of causal direction must always be kept in mind when judging intergroup contact effects. Did the contact cause the reduced prejudice, did the more tolerant seek the contact, or was it bidirectional? Longitudinal research reveals that both causal paths operate with roughly equal strength (Binder et al., 2009; Sidanius, Levin, Van Laar, & Sears, 2008), although some work suggests that the contact-to-prejudice path may be stronger (see Dhont, Van Hiel, & Roets, under review-b; Pettigrew, 1997a). This critical issue of causal direction will be discussed throughout the book.

In 1949, Samuel Stouffer and his colleagues' extensive study of *The American Soldier* provided the first massive field test of intergroup contact's effects. Using an ingenious quasi-experimental design, Stouffer showed that the experience of fighting side-by-side with African-American soldiers in the desperate Battle of the Bulge in eastern Belgium during the frozen winter of 1944–1945 sharply changed the attitudes of White American soldiers. These altered attitudes were found among Southerners as well as Northerners, and among officers as well as enlisted men. Unfortunately, however, these new attitudes were limited to the fighting situation and did not generalize to non-combat situations. We shall return to this important issue of generalization in Chapter 3.

Inspired by Williams' writings and Stouffer's results, research then began to test the theory more rigorously. Field studies of public housing provided the strongest evidence. This work marked the introduction of large-scale field research into North American social psychology. In the most notable example of this work, Deutsch and Collins (1951) interviewed White housewives across different public housing projects with a quasi-experimental design. Two housing projects in Newark assigned Black and White residents to apartments in separate buildings. Two comparable housing projects in New York City desegregated residents by making apartment assignments irrespective of race or personal preference. White women in the desegregated projects reported far more positive contact with their Black neighbors, and, in turn, they expressed higher esteem for their Black neighbors and greater support for interracial housing.

Further public housing research by Wilner, Walkley, and Cook (1955) replicated and extended these findings. They found the intimacy of interracial contact to be a critical factor for promoting positive effects. Favorable racial attitudes developed among only a third of the White tenants who did not interact with their African-American neighbors beyond casual greetings. However, favorable attitudes developed among half of those who had street conversations with their Black neighbors, and among three-quarters of those who engaged in many types of interactions with their Black neighbors. In short, those Whites who acted like neighbors, felt like neighbors. We shall see in Chapter 6 that this sequence of changed behavior leading to changed attitudes is a vital means by which optimal intergroup contact has positive effects.

Subsequent research by Works (1961) showed that similar patterns of contact effects can emerge for African Americans. He found that increased equal-status interracial contact in a public housing project related to more positive feelings and attitudes of the Black residents toward their White neighbors. However, in Chapters 9 and 11, we shall note some systematic differences in contact effects between majority and minority group members, as well as discuss some unintended consequences of contact that may emerge for minority groups.

Allport's Influential "Intergroup Contact Hypothesis"

The intellectual climate of the 1950s provided the foundation and context for Allport's thinking. Armed with these early investigations, in 1954 he introduced the most influential statement of intergroup contact effects in his renowned volume, *The Nature of Prejudice* (Allport, 1954). In a single chapter on intergroup contact (chapter 6), Allport set the agenda for social psychological research by presenting his "intergroup contact hypothesis." The 24 notes of this chapter reveal what directly shaped Allport's formulation. He was well aware of Williams' initial statement; and he cited the Brophy, Stouffer, and housing studies. But he also relied on the work of his doctoral students – Bernard Kramer (1950) and Barbara MacKenzie (1948). And, true to his belief in the richness of personal documents and idiographic methods, he also cited papers on personal intergroup contact experiences written for him by students in his annual graduate seminar on prejudice at Harvard University.

From the student papers especially, Allport noted the contrasting effects of intergroup contact – usually reducing but on occasion exacerbating prejudice. He therefore looked to features of the contact situation that could maximize the potential for prejudice reduction. Specifically, he proposed in part that:

> Prejudice (unless deeply rooted in the character structure of the individual) may be reduced by equal status contact between majority and minority groups in the pursuit of common goals. The effect is greatly enhanced if this contact is sanctioned by institutional supports (i.e., by law, custom, or local atmosphere), and provided it is of a sort that leads to the perception of common interests and common humanity between members of the two groups.
>
> (Allport, 1954, p. 281)

Inspired by Allport's contentions, investigators have continued to test contact theory across a variety of situations, groups, and societies. Indeed, as Figure 1.3 shows, the number of intergroup contact studies steadily increased in each decade since the publication of Allport's 1954 volume. In addition to having his guiding hypothesis shape these studies, this rapid increase in contact studies reflects two other trends: the field of social psychology and social science generally was expanding, and the contact hypothesis began to be tested in many areas beyond the ethnic and racial domain for which it was originally formulated.

Indeed, our extensive, multi-year search uncovered 515 studies that test the effects of intergroup contact (Pettigrew & Tropp, 2006). These investigations range from Chinese students studying in the United States (Chang, 1973) and interracial workers in South Africa (Bornman & Mynhardt,

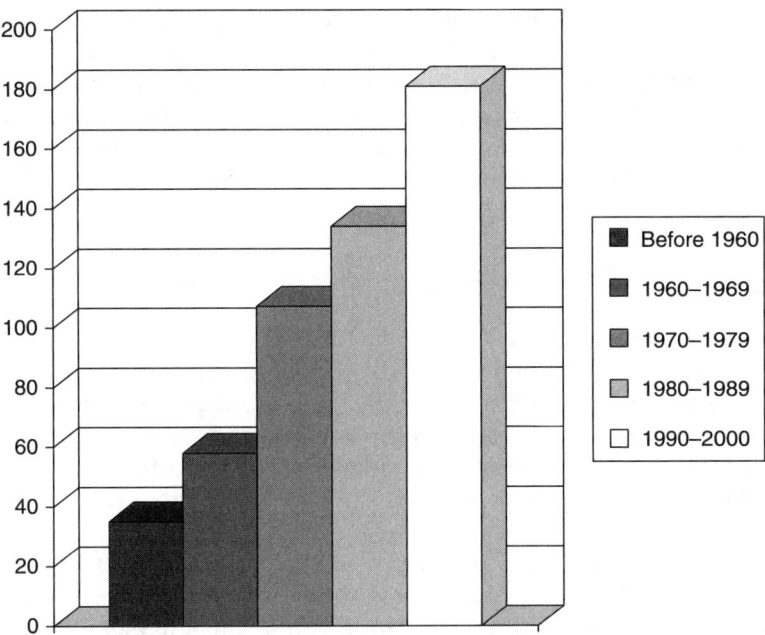

FIGURE 1.3 Number of intergroup contact studies by decade. Adapted from Pettigrew and Tropp (2006, pp. 771–783).

1991) to German children in school with Turkish children (Wagner, Hewstone, & Machleit, 1989) and Australians and Americans getting to know Vietnamese immigrants (McKay & Pittam, 1993; Riordan, 1978). This diverse set also includes studies of attitudes toward the elderly (Caspi, 1984), the mentally ill (Desforges et al., 1991), homosexuals (Herek & Capitanio, 1996), physically disabled persons (Amsel & Fichten, 1988), people with AIDS (Werth & Lord, 1992), and even computer programmers (McGinnis, 1990). Moreover, this work employs varied research methods, including field (Sherif et al., 1961), archival (Fine, 1979), survey (Pettigrew, 1997a; Sigelman & Welch, 1993), and laboratory (Cook, 1978, 1984; Desforges et al., 1991) techniques. Conducted in more than three dozen countries, these wide-ranging investigations greatly broaden our understanding of contact effects and the potential application of intergroup contact theory.

Despite the wealth and breadth of research on intergroup contact, some critics continue to view contact theory as naïve (e.g., McGarry & O'Leary, 1995; McGarty & de la Haye, 1997; Ray, 1983). It is sometimes mistakenly believed that intergroup contact theory simply holds that virtually all contact inevitably leads to a reduction of prejudice. But the theory has never made such a claim (Hewstone, 2003). The preliminary statements proposed by Williams and Allport more than a half-century ago have spurred generations of research that have led to many striking advances. Now we recognize that intergroup contact typically has positive effects and offers a promising approach, but also that its effects are highly complex (Brown & Hewstone, 2005; Pettigrew, 1998).

☐ Focus of This Book

Our goal in writing this volume is to summarize findings from this vast research literature on intergroup contact, based in part on our own meta-analytic investigation of intergroup contact effects. Further, we will describe how this work meshes with emergent perspectives in the broad field of intergroup relations. In so doing, we seek to provide readers with a more thorough and nuanced understanding of the nature of intergroup contact and the many important factors that contribute to its many effects.

First, we synthesize the results of literally hundreds of relevant studies that have been conducted on intergroup contact. In Chapter 2, we assess the overall effect of intergroup contact on prejudice based on all the obtainable and relevant studies, either published or unpublished, that were conducted during the 20th century. We discuss general patterns of relationships between intergroup contact and prejudice and present findings that address the many empirical and methodological complexities associated with intergroup contact's effects.

Chapter 3 considers the issue of generalization – an especially critical point for applications of contact research to social policy. In this chapter, we examine the many ways in which positive effects of contact with individual group members can generalize to new situations, unknown outgroup members, and even to outgroups not involved in the contact. Next, Chapter 4 considers a related question – how universal are intergroup contact's effects? We will see that significant effects of contact are found throughout the world and in a range of settings from the experimental laboratory to homes for the elderly, treatment centers for mental illness, and racially mixed schools and neighborhoods. In addition, extensive research reveals that positive effects of intergroup contact are found for many types of targets, extending far beyond the racial and ethnic contexts for which the theory was initially developed.

In Chapter 5, we ask: *When* does intergroup contact have positive effects? While the preceding chapters speak to generalities in intergroup contact effects, this chapter focuses on the precise conditions that promote positive contact effects. Specifically, we revisit in depth the situational conditions originally proposed by Williams and Allport and discuss the ways in which our meta-analytic findings and other empirical evidence do or do not support these earlier contentions.

Next we ask *how* and *why* does intergroup contact influence group attitudes. Chapter 6 discusses the processes by which contact diminishes prejudice, with a special focus on such mediators as increasing knowledge about the outgroup, reducing anxiety, and encouraging perspective-taking and empathy. Other possible mediators, such as changed behavior, reappraising the ingroup, and perceiving new intergroup norms, are also considered. This chapter will also discuss recent work on so-called "moderated mediation." In particular, we will consider how the salience of group membership moderates such mediating effects as anxiety reduction.

Another question involves whether intergroup contact can be effective in reducing all aspects of prejudice. In Chapter 7, we examine further variability in contact's effects in relation to various components of prejudice. In so doing, we will demonstrate how earlier controversies over contact effects can be reconciled by distinguishing between affective and cognitive dimensions of prejudice. We summarize a vast array of findings indicating that affective dimensions of prejudice (e.g., liking, emotions) are more strongly predicted by intergroup contact than cognitive dimensions (e.g., beliefs, stereotypes). This difference is important, because affect tends to predict later behavior toward outgroups better than stereotypes (Stangor, Sullivan, & Ford, 1991; Talaska, Fiske, & Chaiken, 2008). In addition, the chapter encourages us to look beyond prejudice reduction as an outcome of contact, to consider other important consequences of intergroup contact, such as greater trust of the outgroup.

Chapter 8 centers on the role of the most powerful form of contact – cross-group friendship. It extends our focus on affective processes by highlighting the special roles that the closeness and intimacy of cross-group friendships play in promoting positive contact effects. Recent studies have uncovered markedly stronger intergroup contact effects when the contact involves close friendships across group boundaries. The chapter will present both meta-analytic findings and examples from other research studies that show the particular strength of cross-group friendships – even when it is only an ingroup friend who has the outgroup friendship (indirect or extended contact).

Chapter 9 examines the extent to which contact yields similar or different effects for members of majority groups and minority groups. Several theorists have suggested that pre-existing differences in status severely limit the potential for contact to improve intergroup relations, even when there is equal status within the contact situation (e.g., Foster & Finchilescu, 1986; Robinson & Preston, 1976). Using both our meta-analytic findings and other recent studies, we will show that contact effects tend to be significantly stronger for majority status groups than for minority status groups. We also discuss how members of minority and majority groups may have different views of the contact and their intergroup relationships, and we explore different implications of positive intergroup contact for members of these groups.

In Chapter 10, we consider the importance of intergroup contact in predicting individual prejudice when it is placed in a multivariate context involving many other predictors. Using German survey data regarding attitudes toward immigrants, most of the predictors from different social sciences prove predictive. But even in the midst of these many predictors, the experience of contact with their nation's immigrants remains an important and significant positive influence on the immigration attitudes of the German respondents.

Chapter 11 discusses the principal criticisms that have been leveled at intergroup contact theory. Coming primarily from political science and nations that have witnessed intense ethnic conflict, many critics have raised interesting and instructive points that compel us to take a broader perspective in considering the role of intergroup contact in reducing intergroup tensions. The chapter will summarize and critique the key critical arguments.

Of course, not all intergroup contact causes a reduction in prejudice. Chapter 12 explores negative contact that can lead to increased intergroup prejudice, hostility, and conflict. Though far less common than positive contact, negative intergroup encounters do occur. Here we will find that non-voluntary contact that involves heightened threat represents a common prototype of negative intergroup interaction.

Finally, Chapter 13 summarizes what we have learned to date from contact research, looks to the future of research and theory on intergroup contact, and considers the policy implications of this research.

☐ Note

1 Unfortunately, the original study did not separate Jewish friends from the social class data. But the comparable percentages for Jewish friends were considerably smaller. Thus, even in the highly unlikely event that all Jewish friends were recorded as being from a different social class, the difference of the remaining data on close non-Jewish friends from a different social class still approaches significance ($p<.10$).

Does Intergroup Contact Typically Reduce Intergroup Prejudice?

At its most basic level, intergroup contact theory contends that we can reduce prejudice between groups by encouraging interactions between them. Though we explore many caveats and complexities involved in contact effects throughout this book, this basic premise of contact theory is well-supported by an ever-growing research base. Indeed, over the last several decades, literally hundreds of studies have shown that intergroup contact can reduce prejudice (see Pettigrew & Tropp, 2006, for a review).

One especially notable example is the 4-year longitudinal study of contact effects with data from over 2000 undergraduate students at the University of California Los Angeles in the United States (Levin, Van Laar, & Sidanius, 2003; Sidanius et al., 2008; Van Laar, Levin, Sinclair, & Sidanius, 2005). This extensive study shows that meaningful contact between ethnic groups – both reported by students themselves and evidenced through randomly assigned roommates of diverse ethnicities – predicted significant reductions in interethnic prejudice. Binder et al. (2009) observed similar trends in their multi-national, 6-month longitudinal study of secondary school students in Germany, Belgium, and England. These authors demonstrate that greater contact leads to reduced prejudice, and particularly when the contact is close and intimate in nature. Using a sample of young Belgian adults, Dhont, Roets, and Van Hiel (under review-a) replicated once more the ability of contact to reduce prejudice over time.

Nonetheless, considerable debate has persisted in the research literature regarding the extent to which intergroup contact will generally lead to positive intergroup outcomes. Reviews from many researchers offer support for intergroup contact theory, in which they conclude that intergroup contact is typically effective in reducing intergroup prejudice (Cook, 1984; Harrington & Miller, 1992; Jackson, 1993; Patchen, 1999; Pettigrew,

1971, 1986). However, other reviews propose that outcomes of intergroup contact may be more mixed due to a range of complicating factors. For example, Stephan (1987) highlights the potential of intergroup contact to reduce prejudice, while also emphasizing that characteristics of the contact setting, the groups under study, and the individuals involved are all likely to moderate relationships between intergroup contact and prejudice (see also Patchen, 1999; Pettigrew, 1998; Riordan, 1978).

At the same time, other subjective reviews of the research literature have been more critical regarding the potential for intergroup contact to reduce intergroup prejudice. Although many reviews indicate that intergroup contact can potentially improve attitudes between individuals, one common critique is that intergroup contact can do little to reduce prejudice toward entire outgroups (Amir, 1976; Forbes, 1997, 2004; Rothbart & John, 1985). Several theorists have also critiqued the quality and availability of studies in the research literature that can lend support for intergroup contact theory. For example, McClendon (1974) writes that "contact research has been rather unsophisticated and lacking in rigor" (p. 47). So he concludes that reading this contact literature "would not lead (one) to expect a widespread reduction in prejudice" (p. 52). Similarly, from his review of 53 papers on intergroup contact, Ford (1986) asserts that support for intergroup contact theory is at best "premature," because the available research has been "grossly insufficient" (p. 256) in representing how people experience intergroup contact in their daily lives. Concurring with these views, more recent reviews have proposed that "there are roughly equal numbers of studies showing favorable, unfavorable, and no effects of intergroup contact" (Rothbart & John, 1993, p. 43), such that ". . . the initial hopes of contact theorists have failed to materialize" (Hopkins, Reicher, & Levine, 1997, p. 306).

☐ Meta-Analysis of Intergroup Contact Research of the 20th Century

From these varied perspectives, we are left without a clear view of what the research literature tells us regarding the potential for intergroup contact to promote reductions in intergroup prejudice. To our knowledge, no researchers had ever attempted to quantify the overall effects of contact across the full range of studies that constitute the research literature. We therefore sought to do so by conducting a meta-analysis, so that we could begin to draw firmer conclusions regarding the nature and direction of intergroup contact's effects.

To perform a meta-analysis, researchers attempt to find every study conducted on a particular topic. Then, they statistically pool the results to examine the overall patterns of effects and to uncover additional variables that might enhance or inhibit those effects (Johnson & Eagly, 2000; Rosenthal, 1991). For our analysis, we focused on identifying research studies that examine relationships between intergroup contact and prejudice, to assess more conclusively than in past reviews whether intergroup contact is typically associated with reductions in intergroup prejudice.

Inclusion Criteria for Meta-Analysis

We determined whether studies were suitable for inclusion in the meta-analysis using several criteria. First, we considered only those cases where intergroup contact acts as an independent variable for predicting intergroup prejudice. This means that we excluded studies that treated contact as a dependent variable, such as those explaining how or why intergroup contact occurs. Here, eligible studies included both experimental studies that causally examine the effects of intergroup contact on prejudice, and survey studies that examine intergroup contact as a correlate or predictor of prejudice.

Second, to be included, the research had to involve some degree of direct cross-group interaction, such that members of different groups actually met face-to-face at some point. Such direct contact could have been observed directly in the research study (as in experimental studies conducted in a laboratory, or observational studies conducted in field settings), or this contact could have been reported by participants themselves (as is typically the case in survey studies). Correspondingly, this rule led us to omit studies that assessed contact indirectly, such as those where participants were merely given information about an outgroup or where measures of proximity alone were used to infer cross-group interaction, because these measures could not guarantee that members of the different groups actually came into contact with each other.

Third, we only included studies that explicitly involved contact between members of clearly defined groups, to ensure that we would be able to examine *intergroup* outcomes rather than *interpersonal* outcomes. Additionally, we included only studies where outcome measures were assessed on individuals, and where some comparative data were available, so that we could evaluate variability in individuals' prejudice scores in relation to their contact experiences.

Searching for Relevant Studies

We used a wide range of procedures in searching for relevant studies to be included in the meta-analysis. First, we searched databases of the psychological (*PsychLIT* and *PsycINFO*), sociological (*SocAbs* and *SocioFile*), political science (*GOV*), and education (*ERIC*) research literatures, in addition to reviewing abstracts of dissertations (*UMI Dissertation Abstracts*), and works published in general research periodicals (*Current Contents*) through the year 2000. In these searches, we used 54 different search terms that ranged from single words (e.g., "contact," "interracial") to combined terms (e.g., "disabled + contact"). Across the databases, we used these terms to search by "title words," "key words," and "subject," to maximize our chances of finding all relevant work. Following the "descendancy approach" described by Johnson and Eagly (2000), we also checked on later citations of seminal contact studies using the *Social Sciences Citation Index*. To identify additional papers, we also wrote personal letters or e-mails to researchers who had published relevant work, requested materials through electronic networks of psychologists, and scoured reference lists of gathered studies and prior literature reviews of the contact literature.

These efforts uncovered a total of 515 studies, including 713 independent samples, that met our inclusion criteria (see Appendix A for a full listing of studies in this dataset). These studies span from the early 1940s through the year 2000, and altogether they represent responses from slightly more than 250,000 participants from 38 different countries. Most of the studies and samples came from journal articles published during the past three decades (median year of publication = 1986), with slightly more than half of the samples (51%) focusing on racial or ethnic target groups. For these and other variables, two independent coders achieved highly reliable ratings, with kappas above .80 for each variable and a mean kappa of .86 across all coded variables.

Analytic Procedures

In our analysis, we used the Pearson correlation coefficient r as our primary indicator of effect size. Negative values of r indicate that greater levels of intergroup contact are associated with lower levels of prejudice, and larger r values indicate a stronger association between intergroup contact and prejudice. Effect sizes were also weighted by the inverse of their variance, so that more reliable samples would contribute proportionately more to our estimates of mean effects (see Lipsey & Wilson, 2001). This procedure ensures that studies with large numbers of participants are given greater weight.

We also applied two corrections to the data on which our analyses are based. First, we placed ceilings on sample sizes for seven extremely large samples to keep from overweighting their results in the analysis; specifically, we used ceilings of 5000 participants for analyses based on studies,

3000 participants for analyses based on samples, and 2000 participants for analyses based on tests. We also analyzed results both with and without omitting 17 samples that merely reported "non-significant" results, without providing more detailed statistical information, since the inclusion of these cases might lead to the underestimation of effects (Johnson & Eagly, 2000; Rosenthal, 1991).

We also analyzed our data at three distinct levels of analysis. Analyses conducted at the level of *studies* represent the overall effects for all data reported in each paper. Analyses at the level of *samples* represent the overall effects for *each independent sample* reported in each paper. Since studies often include multiple samples, analyzing data at the level of samples offers larger numbers of cases for conducting more detailed comparisons of effects. Analyses conducted at the level of *tests* represent effects for *each individual test* of the relationship between intergroup contact and prejudice. Analyzing data at the test level offers even more cases for detailed comparisons. But because multiple tests from the same sample violate statistical assumptions of independence, we use tests as our unit of analysis when variables can only be measured at that level.

Although most prior meta-analytic studies in social psychology have relied on fixed effects models (see Johnson & Eagly, 2000), we employed a random effects model in our analysis, given the great variability among the contact studies that comprise the relevant research literature. The random effects model assumes that some portion of the differences in effects across cases is essentially random, and therefore comes from sources we cannot readily identify (see Hedges, 1994; Hedges & Olkin, 1985; Lipsey & Wilson, 2001; Mosteller & Colditz, 1996; Raudenbush, 1994; Rosenthal, 1995). As such, a random effects approach is preferable when the cases are quite varied and effects are likely to be determined by multiple factors (see Cook et al., 1992), as we find in the intergroup contact literature. Random effects models are relatively conservative in reporting tests of statistical significance, and another advantage of this approach is that it allows findings to be generalized to other studies beyond those included in our analysis.

General Research Findings

Overall, results from the meta-analysis show that greater levels of intergroup contact are typically associated with lower levels of intergroup prejudice. Indeed, 94% of the studies revealed an inverse relationship between intergroup contact and prejudice. Hence, to simplify the presentation of results, in this and subsequent chapters, mean effects will be shown as correlations in absolute values, with larger values representing

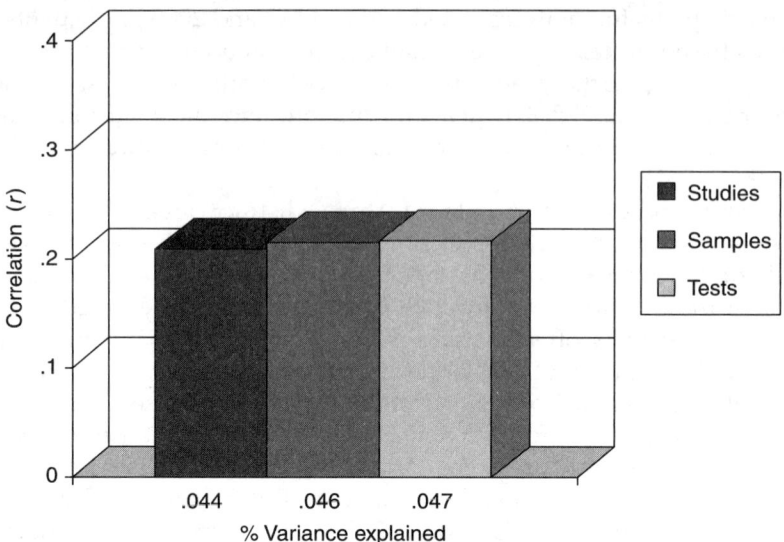

FIGURE 2.1 Mean contact–prejudice effects for studies, samples, and tests.

stronger relationships between intergroup contact and reduced intergroup prejudice.

Figure 2.1 presents estimates of mean effects for studies, samples, and tests. Analyses conducted with and without data corrections showed virtually identical mean estimates of contact–prejudice correlations for studies, samples, and tests. Across all three levels of analysis, we find that greater levels of intergroup contact are associated with lower levels of intergroup prejudice, and the magnitude of the effect corresponds to an r value of approximately –.21, which is significant at the .0001 level of confidence. Hence, we observe a relatively modest yet meaningful relationship between intergroup contact and prejudice that remains consistent across the three levels of analysis. Although the consistency of the contact–prejudice relation is compelling, we must nonetheless consider whether our interpretation of this overall effect could be undermined by biases associated with sampling procedures and participant selection.

Addressing Potential Bias in Sampling Procedures

One major potential threat to our interpretation of the results concerns whether we might have identified only a select subsample of contact studies for inclusion in our analysis (see Rosenthal, 1991). For example, it could be that we were not able to locate all contact studies in the research literature, and it is only those we found that tend to show a significant relationship between intergroup contact and prejudice. However, we conducted multiple tests for sampling bias using a range of approaches, and results from these tests indicate that the contact–prejudice association we observe cannot be explained away simply by sampling bias.

First, we conducted a test using Rosenthal's (1991) fail-safe index, to determine the number of additional samples that average no relationship between contact and prejudice that would be necessary to raise the significance level of the contact–prejudice association above the .05 level of confidence. According to this index, more than 1200 additional samples averaging no relationship between contact and prejudice would need to be included to undo the significant mean effect of contact we observe in our analysis. It should be noted that this figure is substantially greater than the 713 samples we uncovered from our extensive 6-year search for tests of contact–prejudice effects.

Other approaches to testing for sampling bias involve conducting correlations between effect sizes and sample sizes and creating a scatter diagram with these two variables. These tests are based on the principle that larger samples provide more reliable results. Thus, a non-significant correlation between effect size and sample size and a symmetrical, funnel-shaped distribution of cases across these two variables suggest that sampling bias is minimal (Light & Pillemer, 1984). Using contact–prejudice effect sizes from the 713 independent samples in our dataset, we find that the relationship between effect size and sample size is not significant ($r = -.02$, $p = .67$). Moreover, as depicted in Figure 2.2, a scatter diagram of the contact–prejudice correlations plotted by sample size shows that the distribution of effects resembles a funnel and is nicely centered around an r value of $-.21$, which corresponds to the overall mean effect size for our full analysis.

Exploring the Potential for Publication Bias

Another major potential threat to our interpretation of these results involves the possibility of a publication bias (Begg, 1994; Rosenthal, 1991). Specifically, contact studies with statistically significant findings may be more likely to be submitted to and published in academic journals, thereby causing published studies to form a biased subset of all contact studies actually conducted. Such publication biases often have been observed in both the social science and medical research literatures (e.g., Coursol & Wagner, 1986; Dickersin, 1997; Dickersin, Min, & Meinert, 1992; Easterbrook, Berlin, Gopalan, & Mathews, 1991; Glass, McCaw, & Smith,

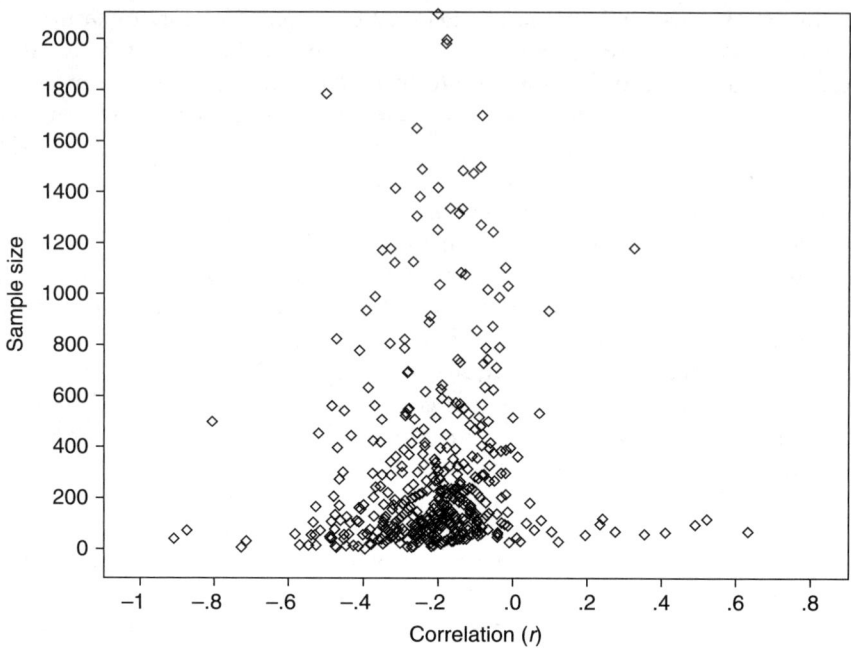

FIGURE 2.2 Scatterplot of contact–prejudice effects. Adapted from Pettigrew and Tropp (2006).

1981; Lipsey & Wilson, 1993; Rotton, Foos, Van Meek, & Levitt, 1995; Shadish, Doherty, & Montgomery, 1989; Sommer, 1987). Consequently, reviews of the contact literature may overestimate its effects to the extent that they rely heavily on published work.

Estimating publication bias can be difficult, yet many approaches have been used to address the issue in recent years. One method, known as the "trim-and-fill" technique developed by Duval and Tweedie (2000a, 2000b), detects the potential for missing studies by adjusting for funnel plot asymmetry. Results using this technique indicate that approximately 72 (10.3%) samples were missing from our meta-analytic database; once these cases are filled in, our mean effect size estimate grows to an r value of –.245 with 95% confidence values of –.231 and –.258, comparing favorably to the mean effects presented in Figure 2.1.

The general linear model approach of Vevea and Hedges (1995) focuses more specifically on the absence of small studies, a relatively conservative method that is noted for having the potential to overestimate publication bias (Sterne & Egger, 2000). An analysis using this method suggests that our meta-analytic database was missing many small studies with small effects, and once accounted for there would no longer be a significant relationship between contact and prejudice. Nonetheless, even with this method, further analysis revealed that for those samples with between-group designs and more rigorous controls the adjusted mean effect size does reach statistical significance at the .05 level of confidence (see Pettigrew & Tropp, 2006).

A more direct approach to testing for publication bias involves comparisons of effect sizes from contact studies that come from published sources (e.g., academic journals and books) and unpublished sources (e.g., doctoral dissertations, master's theses, conference papers, and other unpublished manuscripts). We therefore went to great lengths to gather data from unpublished sources, and altogether we were able to collect 88 unpublished contact studies. As shown in Figure 2.3, contact–prejudice mean effects from unpublished studies are actually slightly *larger* – not smaller – than the effects obtained from published studies, although these means do not significantly differ (mean $r = -.237$ vs. $-.211$, $p = .14$). Thus, across multiple and varied tests, our results suggest that publication bias does not pose a major threat to our interpretation of the effects we have observed, thereby enhancing our confidence that intergroup contact typically is indeed associated with lower levels of intergroup prejudice.

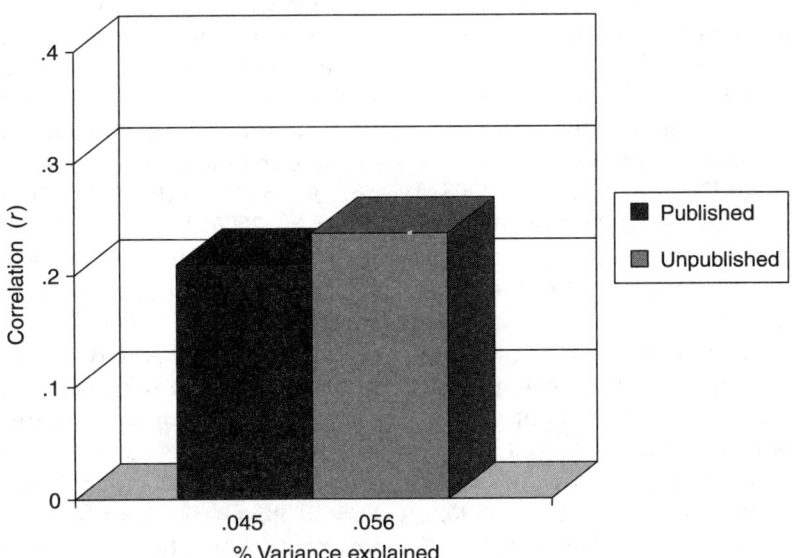

FIGURE 2.3 Mean contact–prejudice effects for published and unpublished studies.

The Role of Participant Choice

Another factor that could influence our interpretation of results concerns the extent to which participants did or did not choose to participate in the contact (see Link & Cullen, 1986; Wilson, 1996). For example, it may be that only tolerant people seek contact with other groups, whereas prejudiced people seek to avoid contact with other groups (see Pettigrew, 1998).

Several methodological approaches have been used to address the issue of selective choice in prior contact research. In part, statistical models of cross-sectional data have compared reciprocal paths to estimate the extent to which contact decreases prejudice, as compared to prejudice decreasing contact. Such models reveal that prejudiced people do avoid intergroup contact (e.g., Binder et al., 2009; Herek & Capitanio, 1996; Pettigrew, 2008), yet the path from contact to reduced prejudice is typically stronger (e.g., Butler & Wilson, 1978; Pettigrew, 1997a; Powers & Ellison, 1995; Van Dick et al., 2004). Analyses of longitudinal data also show that contact can reduce prejudice over time, although these studies also often show that the two causal paths are of approximately equivalent strength (Binder et al., 2009; Eller & Abrams, 2004; Levin et al., 2003; but see Dhont et al., under review-b, who show the greater strength of the contact-to-prejudice path).

In addition, relevant experimental investigations randomly assign participants to have friendly interactions with either a same- or cross-group partner. The random design eliminates the possibility of a selection bias in who does or does not engage in intergroup contact. Experimental studies also reveal that contact can reduce prejudiced attitudes and contribute to many other positive intergroup outcomes (e.g., Page-Gould, Mendoza-Denton, & Tropp, 2008; Wright, Aron, & Brody, 2008; Wright, Aron, & Tropp, 2002; Wright, Brody, & Aron, 2005; Wright & Van der Zande, 1999). Together, these findings offer compelling evidence that intergroup contact holds the potential to reduce prejudice, apart from participant choice.

In the present analysis, we examine this issue meta-analytically by coding samples for the extent to which participants had no choice, some choice, or full choice about whether to engage in the contact. Figure 2.4 presents the results. Overall, the no-choice samples reveal a significantly *larger* mean effect size (mean $r = -.280$) than samples in which participants had some choice (mean $r = -.190$, $Q_B(1) = 20.58$, $p < .0001$) or full choice (mean $r = -.218$, $Q_B(1) = 8.98$, $p < .01$). However, the no-choice studies also tended to be of higher quality, and once we control for four indicators of research quality (see next section) the association between choice and effect size is no longer significant. These analyses suggest that participant choice is unlikely to be a key factor underlying the significant effects we

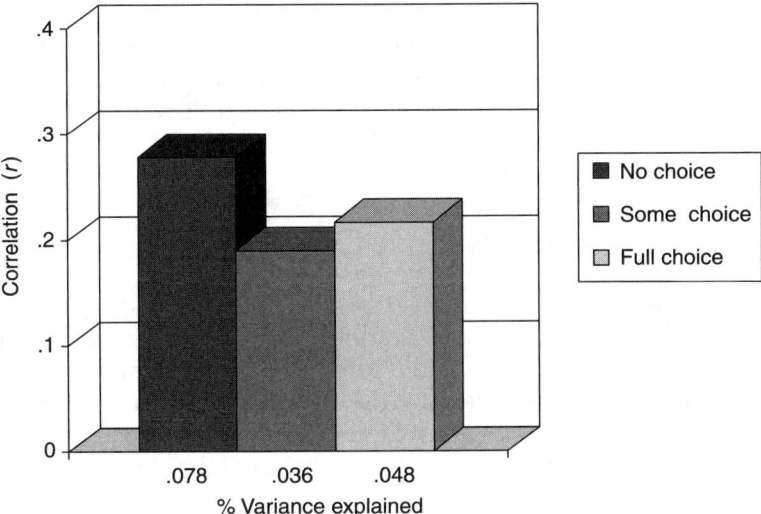

FIGURE 2.4 Mean contact–prejudice effects by level of participant choice.

observe between intergroup contact and prejudice – although we will discuss exceptions to this trend in Chapter 12.

Here, it is important to note that while we find positive contact effects regardless of participant choice, this does not necessarily mean that contact between groups is always easy. Contact can be anxiety-provoking and stressful (Stephan & Stephan, 1985), and people's initial anxieties about contact may motivate attempts to avoid interactions with members of other groups (Plant & Devine, 2003). In Chapter 6, we discuss the role that anxiety plays in intergroup contact effects in much greater depth.

But we raise the issue here to emphasize that, even in circumstances where contact may be challenging or difficult, reduced prejudice and other positive outcomes can still result from such contact. Shook and Fazio (2008) provide a pointed example. They examined the experiences and attitudes of White undergraduate students randomly assigned to have either a White or African-American roommate during their first semester at college. Over the course of the semester, White undergraduates paired with an African-American roommate found their roommate relationships to be less satisfying, less involved, and less comfortable than those paired with a White roommate (see also Towles-Schwen & Fazio, 2006). This finding is hardly surprising given the lack of prior interracial experience that most of these White students had initially. Nevertheless, over time, the White students paired with an African-American roommate showed decreases in automatically activated racial prejudice (see also Dunton &

Fazio, 1997), as well as marginal decreases in intergroup anxiety, relative to White students paired with a White roommate. Together, these findings importantly reveal how even when intergroup contact is not by choice, and may present unique challenges and obstacles, it can still effectively yield reductions in intergroup prejudice.

Methodology and Research Quality

Still, beyond the concerns we have addressed regarding participant choice, we might still be inclined to question our effects from a methodological standpoint. For example, if we believe that a relationship between contact and prejudice truly exists, we should expect the more rigorous research studies to yield particularly strong contact effects. Thus, we examined the magnitudes of the contact–prejudice effects in relation to many methodological indicators of research quality.

First, we coded samples for research design to examine if contact–prejudice effects would vary depending on whether experimental, quasi-experimental, or survey and field methods were used in the research. As shown in Figure 2.5, we typically observe much stronger effects when the research employs experimental procedures (mean $r = -.336$) – which allow for causal tests of the effects of contact on prejudice – as compared to quasi-experimental procedures (mean $r = -.237$) or procedures involving survey and other field methodologies (mean $r = -.204$; $p < .001$).

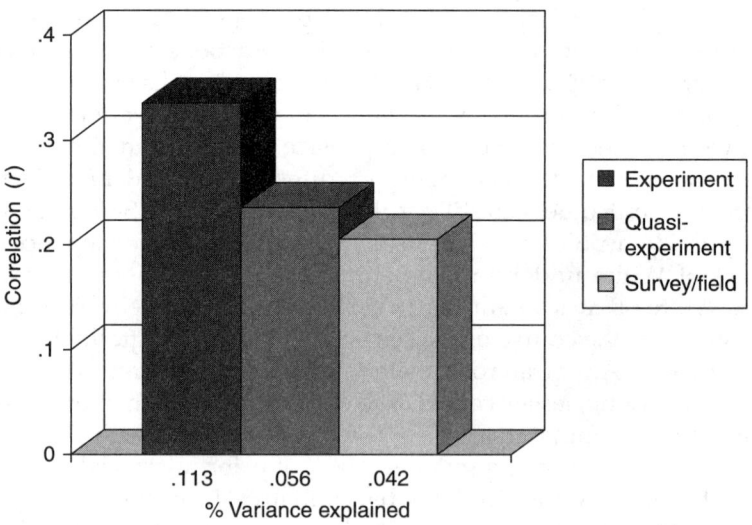

FIGURE 2.5 Mean contact–prejudice effects by research design.

We also examined the kinds of control groups used in statistical comparisons within each sample. While each experiment or quasi-experiment assigned participants to an experimental condition in which they engaged in contact, we found that the control conditions varied considerably in terms of whether participants in those groups had had prior contact with the relevant outgroup. Some control group participants had little prior contact, whereas others had a great deal of prior contact, and this variability makes it difficult to determine whether meaningful contact effects have been achieved through comparisons of the experimental and control conditions. We therefore coded whether the sample had no control group (i.e., within-subject design), a control group with no prior contact, a control group with some prior contact, or a control group with extensive prior contact.

Overall, samples with within-subject designs showed a mean effect size (mean $r = -.221$) that did not significantly differ from that of all between-subject samples combined (mean $r = -.217$; $p = .79$). Yet, as illustrated in Figure 2.6, among those samples with between-subject designs we observe significantly stronger relationships between contact and prejudice as the control group had lower levels of prior contact. In other words, the more appropriate and rigorous the control group, the stronger the contact-reducing–prejudice effect becomes.

In addition, we examined the magnitude of contact–prejudice effects in relation to the reliability of the measures used to assess contact and prejudice. First, we compared effects for samples where contact was assessed

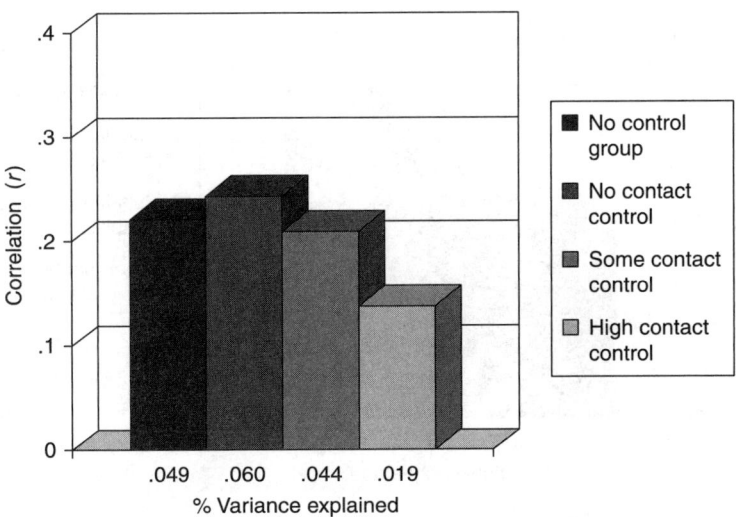

FIGURE 2.6 Mean contact–prejudice effects by type of control group.

using a single-item measure, a multi-item scale with low or unknown reliability, a multi-item scale with high reliability, or an experimental manipulation. Figure 2.7 reveals stronger relationships between contact and prejudice when contact is assessed using more reliable indicators (highly reliable scales and experimental manipulations) than when contact is assessed using single-item or multi-item measures low in reliability.

We also compared effects for samples where prejudice was assessed using a single-item scale, a multi-item scale with low or unknown reliability, a multi-item scale with high reliability, or another highly reliable measure (observer ratings with high inter-rater reliability). Similar to the previous finding, Figure 2.8 shows that stronger relationships between contact and prejudice emerge when prejudice is assessed with more reliable measures.

To demonstrate further the combined importance of these methodological predictors, we formed a subset of 77 samples that boasted highly reliable measures of contact and prejudice, as well as control groups with limited contact. The mean contact–prejudice correlation for this rigorous subset (mean $r = -.323$) was substantially greater than that of the remaining, less rigorous samples (mean $r = -.202$; $p < .0001$). Thus, across multiple indicators of reliability and research quality we consistently find that the more rigorous the measures and research procedures, the more clearly we observe that greater levels of intergroup contact are associated with lower levels of prejudice.

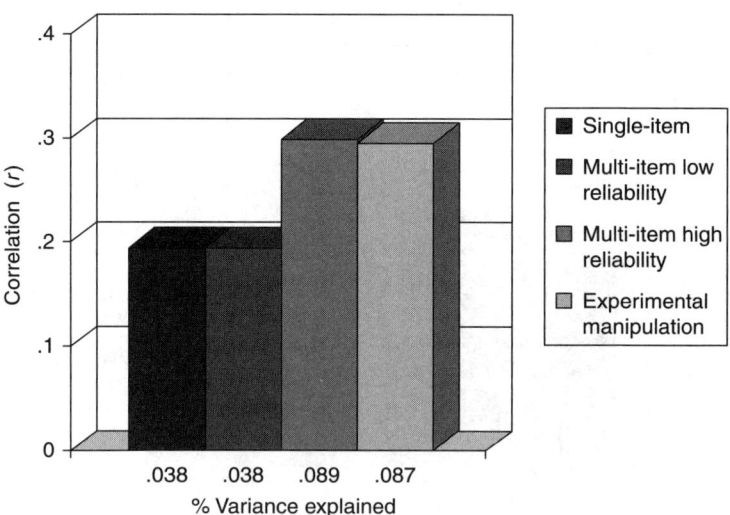

FIGURE 2.7 Mean contact–prejudice effects by reliability of contact measure.

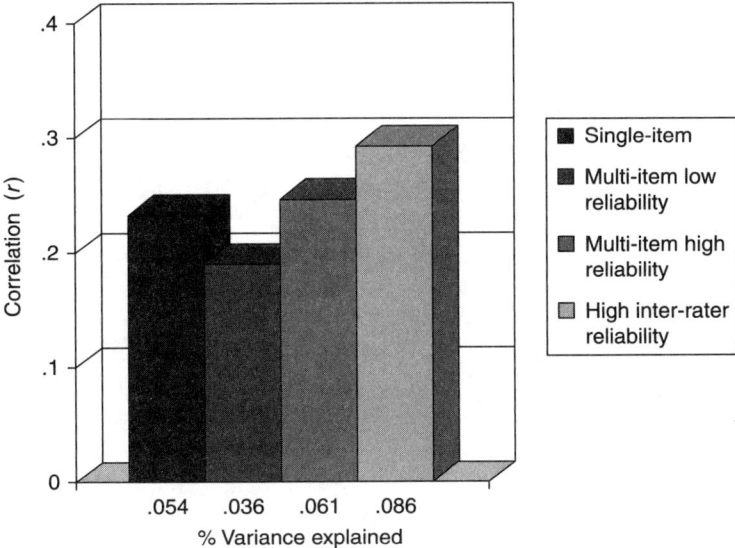

FIGURE 2.8 Mean contact–prejudice effects by reliability of prejudice measure.

☐ Conclusion

Together, our research findings and those of others (e.g., Binder et al., 2009; Shook & Fazio, 2008; Sidanius, Levin, Van Laar, & Sears, 2008; Van Laar et al., 2005) lend considerable support for the basic notion that contact between groups can be effective in reducing prejudice. Our meta-analytic results further show that this overall effect of contact cannot be explained away by publication biases, participant selection, or sampling biases, and that studies conducted with greater research rigor produce even stronger effects.

Still, greater examination is needed to ensure that the effects of contact on prejudice are truly *intergroup* in nature – that is, to show that contact is changing attitudes toward outgroups in general, and not merely changing attitudes toward the individual outgroup members with whom we come into contact. We explore these issues in the next chapter, where we discuss the role of generalization in intergroup contact effects.

Do Intergroup Contact Effects Generalize?

Both the practical and theoretical importance of intergroup contact rests heavily upon how well contact's effects *generalize* to the whole outgroup, to other situations, and even to other outgroups who are not involved in the contact. If the effects of positive intergroup contact do not generalize beyond the contact situation itself and the immediate participants in the contact, the societal value of such interaction would obviously be of minor significance.

There are two basic processes that can inhibit the generalization of positive contact effects. The first involves psychological factors associated with categorization. "Yes, I liked those people," goes the refrain, "but they are certainly different from the rest of their group." Allport (1954) called this "re-fencing"; we exclude the outgroup members we like in the contact situation and categorically separate them from our negative views of the outgroup as a whole. Personality factors are often involved in this process. For example, individuals who score highly on authoritarianism measures are more likely to use this re-fencing technique to safeguard their intergroup prejudices from being altered (Adorno, Frenkel-Brunswik, Levinson, & Sanford, 1950).

Another process by which intergroup contact effects can fail to generalize further than the immediate situation involves social norms. Norms that oppose changes in attitudes brought by the contact can be so strong that people think and behave in conflicting ways across different social contexts without even being aware of the inconsistency. Prior to the Civil Rights Movement of the 1960s, for instance, Black and White coal miners in West Virginia routinely worked together effectively underground. But when they emerged from the mines, they went their separate ways to segregated housing without questioning the inconsistency of their norm-enforced behavior below and above ground (Minard, 1952).

Likewise, at an Indiana steel mill in the 1950s, Blacks and Whites were members of the same racially desegregated union and worked well together (Reitzes, 1953). Only 12% of the White workers reported low acceptance of African Americans on the job. And those most involved in the union were the most responsive to the union's pro-desegregation norms. But these same White workers also lived in segregated, all-White neighborhoods and many belonged to pro-segregation neighborhood groups. Indeed, 84% of those who accepted Blacks at work were highly resistant to Blacks living in their neighborhoods. And, once again, those most involved with their neighborhoods were the most resistant.

In each of these cases, the workers simply followed the norms of the pre-Civil Rights era. In the mines and the union, equal racial contact was the norm, while racial segregation was the largely unchallenged normative expectation in housing. Thus, segregationist norms severely limited the generalization of contact's effects across these situations. Similarly, Blacks and Whites in the American South and South Africa as well as Catholics and Protestants in Northern Ireland have had centuries of contact, but these regions traditionally had stern segregationist policies that severely restrained the typically positive intergroup contact effects we discussed in Chapter 2.

We therefore must check carefully to see if the positive contact effects uncovered by our meta-analysis typically generalize beyond the contact itself. Examples of generalization can take many forms. These include whether intergroup contact yields positive effects consistently across different levels of analysis, situations, and even to outgroups not involved in the contact. We first test these forms of generalization using our meta-analytic data.

☐ Generalization to the Entire Outgroup – The Primary Transfer of Contact Effects

The first form we examine involves generalization *across different levels of analysis* – the primary transfer of contact effects. This refers to the extent to which positive effects resulting from contact experience with one or more outgroup members can generalize into more positive attitudes toward the entire outgroup. It is possible that the significant contact–prejudice association we observed in the full analysis reflects only those studies that assess prejudice toward the individual outgroup members with whom contact occurred, rather than extending beyond the contact situation to affect attitudes toward the outgroup as a whole. Critics of contact theory have often raised this important concern. Such critical perspectives claim that contact may well be effective in improving attitudes between individuals, but it is unlikely to be effective in improving attitudes between groups (see Amir, 1976; Rothbart & John, 1985).

One common critique is that re-fencing and other cognitive barriers almost totally impede the generalization of intergroup contact's positive effects to the entire outgroup. Notice, however, that such critiques focus heavily on cognitive concerns and tend to ignore affective processes, an issue we explore in depth in Chapter 7. This line of reasoning is summarized by Rothbart and John (1993; p. 43): "... [D]o the favorable judgments toward the category members generalize back to the category as a whole? The answer to this question is a strong 'rarely,' as it is clear that the bulk of the research shows little or no generalization." If Rothbart and John were right, contact theory would be of limited value as a strategy for improving intergroup attitudes and relations.

We therefore sought to determine the extent to which contact studies in the research literature have actually investigated this form of generalization, and the kinds of contact effects such investigations typically reveal (see Figure 3.1). As an initial step, we coded each of the 1351 tests in our meta-analysis to see whether their outcome measures assessed (1) prejudice toward the individual outgroup members with whom the contact occurred in the contact situation, or (2) prejudice toward the outgroup as a whole. Overall, we found that only 152 tests in our analysis involve cases where prejudice was assessed in reference to just those outgroup

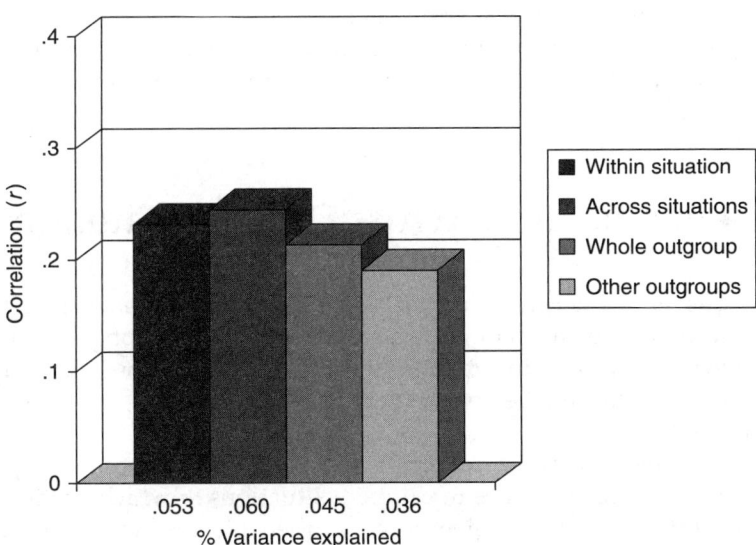

FIGURE 3.1 Mean contact–prejudice effects by type of generalization.

members who participated in the contact situation. By contrast, the great majority of tests in our analysis (1164) were those in which prejudice was assessed in reference to the outgroup as a whole. Apparently, Rothbart, John, and other prior reviewers of this literature were unaware of these hundreds of tests when they wrote that contact research rarely reveals any generalization on the group level.

When comparing the magnitudes of effects for these different types of outcomes, we find that the mean effects of contact do not significantly differ for tests that assess prejudice toward the outgroup as a whole (mean $r = -.21$) and those that assess prejudice toward individual outgroup members within the contact situation (mean $r = -.23$; $p = .33$). Together, these results strongly suggest that positive effects of contact with individual outgroup members do in fact typically generalize to more positive attitudes to the outgroup as a whole.

This meta-analytic finding has theoretical as well as practical importance. On a theoretical level, the *salient categorization model* of intergroup contact holds that generalization to the entire outgroup occurs best when the group memberships are salient in the contact situation (Brown & Hewstone, 2005; Hewstone & Brown, 1986). We shall discuss this and other models in detail in Chapter 5. But at this point we can assert that considerable evidence supports the importance of salient categorization. For example, contact effects tend to be strongest when the participants are viewed as typical group members (Brown, Vivian, & Hewstone, 1999; Johnston & Hewstone, 1992; Voci & Hewstone, 2003; Weber & Crocker, 1983; Wilder, 1984) and when participants are highly aware of their group membership during contact (Brown et al., 2001). On a practical level, our findings suggest that this type of generalization is common, and that most intergroup contact situations involve considerable salience and awareness of group membership.

☐ Generalization Across Different Situations

Do the effects of intergroup contact generalize *across situations* as well? Questions about this form of generalization stem from a long tradition in social psychology pointing to the importance of situations for shaping people's attitudes and behavior (Lewin, 1951; Milgram, 1974; Ross & Nisbett, 1991).

Only 17 tests in our analysis examined contact effects where prejudice is assessed in direct reference to different situations in which participants might encounter outgroup members – at their place of work, at school, and in their neighborhood. Figure 3.1 shows the mean effect for these cases in relation to the mean effects discussed above. The mean contact–

prejudice effect for these tests (mean $r = -.24$) is comparable to the mean effect for prejudice toward individual outgroup members within the contact situation (mean $r = -.23$; $p = .79$). This result provides more evidence that the changes in attitudes resulting from contact are not limited to the situation in which the contact occurred. Striking differences in intergroup norms can deter this process, as we saw in the coal mine and steel plant examples. But typically, the positive effects of contact can generalize beyond the original contact situation to affect people's attitudes toward outgroup members in diverse situations.

One of the most thorough tests of intergroup contact theory specifically tested for situational generalization (Cook, 1984). A leading contact theorist and researcher, Stuart Cook designed a laboratory experiment to test directly his version of contact theory. In two studies, he recruited highly prejudiced White female college students in the American South to participate in 40 separate experimental sessions. Cook's experimental situation ensured equality of status in the situation with an interdependent, cooperative task requiring the White participant to team with a Black student (a confederate of the experimenter) in a friendly, non-threatening situation likely to develop cross-racial friendship.

Cook's initial findings were positive in both studies; as is typically the case, the interracial contact reduced racial prejudice. Then he tested several months later for situational generalization of these contact effects in a non-laboratory setting far removed from the original experimental situation. On a majority of the prejudice measures, the experimental groups of his two studies again showed significantly less prejudice than the control groups who had not experienced the experimental contact. Situational generalization had occurred and lasted over time.

☐ Generalization to Other Outgroups – The Secondary Transfer Effect

Yet another form of generalization involves whether contact with individual members of one outgroup might spill over into more positive attitudes toward other outgroups not involved in the contact. We label this phenomenon *the secondary transfer effect* (Pettigrew, 2009), since it follows after the primary transfer effect from contact participants to their entire outgroup.

It may seem at first an unlikely stretch of the power of contact to achieve such distal change. But if this secondary transfer effect were to occur, it obviously greatly enhances the potential of intergroup contact to change attitudes. Given both its problematic status and its possible theoretical and policy importance, we explore this third type of generalization in considerable depth.

Several processes could underlie this extended form of generalization. First, in line with the concept of *deprovincialization* (Pettigrew, 1997a, 1998), our intergroup attitudes may shift not only as a function of direct contact with an outgroup, but because such contact encourages us to reappraise our own group. To the extent that this process occurs, it should lead us to become less provincial in how we relate to other groups more generally. As such, it refers to the possibility that intergroup contact broadens our experience; we learn that there are other cultural standards and ways in which groups cope with the world besides those of our ingroup with which we are familiar. This does not mean we necessarily disparage our ingroup. But as Brewer (2008) has described, such a deprovincialization process involves greater complexity in how we view our group in relation to others.

Second, social psychology has long known that prejudices of many kinds typically intercorrelate highly and positively (e.g., Adorno et al., 1950; Allport, 1954; Cunningham, Nezlek, & Banaji, 2004; Zick et al., 2008). Hence, an individual who is prejudiced against one outgroup is very likely to be prejudiced against an array of other outgroups. To the extent that various prejudices are linked together, then the decline of one group-based prejudice may help to diminish related prejudices.

Thus, we extend our analysis of generalization to include tests of secondary transfer effects that focus on reduced prejudice toward outgroups beyond those with whom the contact occurred. Altogether, we identified 18 tests of generalization to other outgroups, excluding tests provided by Pettigrew (1997a) that will be discussed later in this chapter. These 18 tests yield a significant mean contact–prejudice effect size of $r = -.19$ ($p < .001$). Moreover, as Figure 3.1 shows, this mean effect for generalization to other groups not involved in the contact does not differ significantly from the mean effect for attitudes toward individual outgroup members in the contact situation (mean $r = -.23$; $p = .41$).

A series of studies lend support for this secondary transfer effect. Recall the investigation of Holocaust rescuers described in Chapter 1 (Oliner & Oliner, 1988). Those brave Europeans who saved Jews during World War II had had more contact as children with people of different social classes who were not Jews. Consider also a study by Weigert (1976) of Black American soldiers stationed in Germany. Those who had more contact with White American soldiers also tended to believe they were less discriminated against by Germans than other Black American soldiers. Thus, greater contact with White Americans related to a more favorable judgment of Germans who were not involved in the initial contact. But there is a problem of interpretation here. This result may have occurred simply because those Black soldiers who had more contact with White soldiers also had more contact with Germans as well. Solid evidence for the secondary transfer effect requires control of any direct contact with the second outgroup.

Speaking to this issue is a study by Clement, Gardner, and Smythe (1977). These authors studied the effects of an excursion to Quebec City on the intergroup stereotypes of 379 English-speaking Canadian eighth-grade students. The children were tested before and after the trip and their data compared with a control group of children who did not take the trip. As expected, those who had maximum contact with Quebec residents evinced significantly more positive views of French-speaking Canadians. But, interestingly, they also revealed significantly more positive views of the European French with whom they had not had contact. In this case, it is highly unlikely that the children had had direct contact with French people from France.

This extension from French-speaking Canadians to French-speaking Europeans constitutes at best a minimal extension. So we turn to a more unusual study by Caditz (1975). She tested 204 Americans who were members of a liberal political organization in Los Angeles. She found that those who were also members of groups that were highly diverse either religiously or ethnically were significantly more likely than the other liberal respondents to support a variety of racial policy issues, such as racially integrated schools, housing, and jobs.

The Caditz study is provocative, yet lacking adequate controls it is open to rival interpretations. We therefore turn to surveys of large probability national samples for more evidence. Wilson (1996) conducted a secondary analysis of the 1990 General Social Survey and its probability subsample of adult non-Jewish and non-Hispanic White Americans. He found that those respondents who reported contact with African Americans in multiple institutions revealed fewer stereotypes about and less social distance from Blacks. And those who engaged in contact with Blacks also revealed similar positive effects in relation to three other minorities – Jewish Americans, Latino Americans, and Asian Americans.

But could these studies' apparent secondary transfer effects merely reflect the general tendency for tolerant people to have more contact with all types of outgroups? As we repeat throughout this volume, many studies have shown this reverse causal effect whereby prejudiced individuals tend to avoid outgroup contact (Binder et al., 2009; Butler & Wilson, 1978; Levin et al., 2003; Pettigrew, 1997a, 2009; Powers & Ellison, 1995; Sidanius et al., 2008; Van Dick et al., 2004). Obviously, the contact–prejudice relationship is complex and bidirectional in nature. But to disentangle possible interpretations, we must focus on this problem: Does the secondary transfer effect largely reflect the bidirectional phenomenon whereby more tolerant people engage in more intergroup contact *and* harbor less prejudice against a variety of outgroups?

Cross-Sectional Evidence

To examine this issue, we first try the rough test of controlling for key demographic variables to limit the bidirectional bias possibility. Two probability surveys have conducted such tests. An initial test analyzed the self-reports of 3800 respondents surveyed in 1988 from seven national probability samples in France, Great Britain, The Netherlands, and then-West Germany (Pettigrew, 1997a). The analysis showed that having immigrant friends related to significantly higher favorability ratings ($p < .001$) for a wide range of outgroups – even those barely present in the nation (e.g., Turks in France or West Indians in Germany). The possibility that these Europeans had had prior contact with these outgroups is remote. Interestingly, results also revealed that secondary transfer effects were strongest for other immigrant groups (Black Africans: $r = .18$; Southeast Asians: $r = .18$; Indians: $r = .18$; North Africans: $r = .17$; Turks: $r = .16$; West Indians: $r = .15$) and weakest for three non-immigrant groups (Jews: $r = .12$; Southern Europeans: $r = .10$; Northern Europeans: $r = .07$). And these results emerged even with the application of seven pertinent controls – political conservatism, group relative deprivation, political interest, national pride, urbanism, education, and age.

Extending this work, Ha (2008) employed two national samples of American adults and found that those with multi-racial friends reported more positive attitudes toward immigrants. Their attitudes toward immigration policy, however, only partly changed. Those with diverse friends tended to oppose strict qualifications for the legal status of immigrants, but they did not necessarily support a more liberal policy that would allow more immigrants to enter the United States. Importantly, these findings held up even after controlling for 13 additional variables: education, age, race, gender, income, religion, political interest, political party, political conservatism, national pride, life satisfaction, generalized trust, and the experience of unemployment. With their extensive use of controls across a wide range of groups, these European and American samples cast initial doubt on the possibility that secondary transfer effects are exclusively due to tolerant people seeking out more contact.

Many survey studies have yielded similar findings from other parts of the world, with the particular advantage of showing that changed attitudes toward the contacted outgroup mediates the secondary transfer effects. The Oxford University team under Miles Hewstone's direction has conducted several of the most thorough studies of contact's secondary transfer effect (see Hewstone et al., 2008; Tausch et al., 2010).

With data from Cyprus, Northern Ireland, and the United States, they have demonstrated the effect across a wide variety of contexts. In their first study, cross-sectional probability samples of Greek and Turkish Cypriots revealed that contact with each other generalized to improved attitudes concerning the national populations of Greece and Turkey. This effect was significantly mediated by contact reducing their prejudice against the Cypriot outgroups. Catholic and Protestant residents of six towns in Northern Ireland comprised the second study in another cross-sectional design. Again cross-group contact reduced their sectarian prejudices, and this reduction significantly mediated a reduction in their attitudes toward racial minorities.

A third investigation took place in Texas with White American respondents. Using a cross-sectional design but controlling for both social desirability and prior contact with the second outgroup, they once again uncovered the secondary transfer effect and demonstrated mediation of the effect by reduced prejudice toward the contacted outgroup. Specifically, those respondents who had Latino friends reported more positive views of Latinos in general, and they also had more positive views of Vietnamese and East Indian immigrants. Along with showing the effect across multiple contexts, these researchers importantly highlight the mediating role of changed attitudes toward the contacted outgroup in the secondary transfer process.

Longitudinal Evidence

These repeated replications of the secondary transfer effect and demonstrations of mediation are highly compelling. Nonetheless, we must acknowledge that these analyses are still based on cross-sectional data and that causal effects in the secondary transfer process cannot be verified. But several longitudinal studies address this point and provide stronger evidence for the secondary transfer effect.

For example, Eller and Abrams (2004) tested for the secondary transfer effect with longitudinal field data. They found that members of their English college student sample who had had positive contact and friendship with the French 6 months later not only had more favorable general evaluations of the French but also of Algerians. This confirmation of the secondary transfer effect was largely mediated through warm, affective ties with the French. But again we must be careful how we interpret these findings. When the English students visited France and met French people, they may have also met Algerians.

A separate study conducted by the Oxford group addressed this limitation by randomly sampling Catholics and Protestants in Belfast, Northern Ireland, with a longitudinal design that consisted of two surveys 1 year apart (see Hewstone et al., 2008; Tausch et al., 2010). This test incorporated three vital controls: the respondents' prior racial contacts, and their sectarian and racial attitudes at Time 1. Again secondary transfer effects appeared. Significantly mediated by a reduction in their sectarian prejudices, neighborhood inter-religious contact diminished their racial prejudices as well.

Perhaps, the strongest confirmation of the secondary transfer effect comes from one of the most extensive and detailed studies of intergroup contact. As mentioned earlier, this impressive research employed five data collection points over a 4-year period with more than 2000 undergraduate students at the University of California Los Angeles (UCLA) (Levin et al., 2003; Sidanius et al., 2008; Sidanius, Van Laar, Levin, & Sinclair, 2004; Van Laar et al., 2005; Van Laar, Levin, & Sidanius, 2008). This extensive longitudinal design allowed a direct test of the causal link between contact and diminished prejudice. The study also boasted an experimental design using randomly assigned roommates of diverse ethnicities. And while most contact studies check on the process for only two groups, this work looked at four groups – Latino, African, Asian, and European Americans. Further, the UCLA investigation tested affective, cognitive, and behavioral dependent variables. In short, this work provides a model for future research because it tests for cumulative effects with longitudinal data for multiple groups within a particular institutional setting.

These investigators found significant reciprocal contact effects across the years: Interethnic friendships reduced prejudice, while initial ingroup bias and intergroup anxiety led to fewer intergroup friends. And unlike previous cross-sectional studies, this longitudinal study found these two effects to be of roughly equal magnitude. A more recent longitudinal study of European school students confirms this finding of roughly equivalent effects (Binder et al., 2009). However, as previously noted, a recent Belgian study of close cross-group friendships found that contact-to-diminished-prejudice was the stronger path (Dhont et al., under review-b).

The UCLA investigators also found substantial secondary transfer effects. Randomly assigned roommates from different ethnicities typically decreased their outgroup prejudices even for outgroups not involved in their roommate relationship. In particular, students who had either Black or Latino-American roommates displayed less prejudice toward both of these groups. Van Laar and colleagues (2005) believe that this reflects the fact that these two groups have the lowest status of the four groups studied. That is, although coming from diverse subcultures, the Black and Latino students shared experiences of discrimination on the UCLA campus and in society generally. Such salient commonality may well enhance the spread of effects across these two groups.

But there was one pointed exception. Students who had an Asian-American roommate developed less prejudice against Asian Americans, but they actually *increased* their negative attitudes toward other outgroups. The investigators surmise that this occurred from peer socialization (Van Laar et al., 2005, p. 340). That is, Asian-American students as a group proved to be the most prejudiced against other groups, and they may have influenced the intergroup attitudes of their White roommates. The importance of this exception for our analysis is that the secondary transfer effect has its limits. We will now explore these limits with new tests.

Possible Moderating Features of the Secondary Transfer Effect

While these cumulating results support the existence of a secondary transfer effect, another issue must be examined in detail. As noted in the European studies (Pettigrew, 1997a), and possibly relevant to the UCLA study (Sidanius et al., 2008), a stimulus generalization gradient may be operating. The secondary transfer effect appears to be stronger for groups that are similar to or overlapping with those with whom the respondents have had contact and weaker for outgroups who are dissimilar from the contacted outgroups. But "similarity" is a difficult concept to define. Among other definitions, it may reflect the perceived stereotypes of the groups, perceived similarities in the groups' experiences, or a person's prior association of the groups based on their own personal experience.

We explore these possibilities in further tests of the secondary transfer effect with three German national probability phone surveys as well as a panel study at three time points. These surveys were conducted as part of the large, 10-year project on prejudice headed by Wilhelm Heitmeyer (2002, 2003, 2005) and employed throughout the volume (see Pettigrew, 2009, for a more extensive analysis of these data). These surveys of German citizens without migratory backgrounds included a three-item measure of positive contact with foreign residents as well as scales of prejudice against five diverse outgroups: resident foreigners, Muslims, Jews, the homeless, and gay men and lesbians (see Appendix B).

Table 3.1 provides the zero-order correlations between positive contact with resident foreigners and prejudice scores in relation to various outgroups. Several trends emerge. First, the results from the two independent probability samples interviewed 2 years apart are remarkably similar and stable. Second, the application of three socio-demographic controls – age, education, and sex – does not diminish the correlations appreciably.

Finally, possible secondary transfer effects emerge in varying strength across the outgroups. Interestingly, they are weak or inconsistent for attitudes against Jews but are strongest for Muslims. Stimulus generalization appears to be operating in this process. We have seen repeatedly that the secondary transfer effect is generally strongest for outgroups that are more closely related to the outgroup with whom the contact occurred

TABLE 3.1 Correlations between Positive Contact with Foreign Residents and Prejudice toward Various Groups

Prejudice Target	Original Correlations		With Control Variables	
	2002	2004	2002	2004
Resident foreigners	−.41**	−.41**	−.36**	−.36**
Muslims	−[a]	−.38**	−[a]	−.34**
Jews	−.15**	−.10**	−.11**	−.06*
Homeless	−.23**	−.22**	−.21**	−.20**
Homosexuals	−.23**	−.22**	−.20**	−.20**

Note: Control variables include age, education, and sex.
[a] These items were not asked in the 2002 survey.
* $p < .05$; ** $p < .01$.

(e.g., attitude change toward French Europeans after contact with French-speaking Canadians; see Clement et al., 1977). In the German context, there is likely to be considerable overlap between Germans' views of Muslims as a group and resident foreigners, a category heavily represented by Turkish immigrants (Pettigrew, Wagner, & Christ, 2007b). By contrast, such a high degree of correspondence does not exist between resident foreigners and Jews.

Falling in between these two extremes are the results in relation to the homeless and gays and lesbians. These effects reflect those observed in the UCLA study for Latinos and African Americans, such that groups with comparable levels of stigmatization are likely to yield similar secondary transfer effects. Thus, our subsequent analysis of secondary transfer effects focuses on the relationships between contact with resident foreigners and prejudice toward the homeless and homosexuals. These two groups show consistent and comparable secondary transfer effects and have limited overlap with the contact group – resident foreigners.

The evidence we have discussed so far strongly suggests that two causal processes are operating, reflecting the bidirectional phenomenon that repeatedly emerges in intergroup contact research. Thus, there seems to be a secondary transfer effect in which contact with one outgroup improves opinion toward a related outgroup. But there is also a strong selectivity factor in which intolerant people are more likely to avoid outgroup contact and be prejudiced toward outgroups in general. So, we must be careful to control for this selectivity factor. We can anticipate smaller secondary transfer effects than those uncovered previously in survey studies that could not control for this selectivity bias. To test this possibility directly, we need longitudinal data. And, fortunately, we have German longitudinal panel survey data for the years 2002, 2003, and 2004.

Table 3.2 checks to see if the link between the contact with foreigners and either anti-gay or anti-homeless prejudice of the following year were

TABLE 3.2 Sobel Tests of Mediation for Secondary Transfer Effects With and Without Controlling for Prior Prejudice

	Sobel Test	Controlling for Prior Prejudice
2002 Prejudice against foreigners as mediator of:		
Effect of 2002 contact with foreigners on 2003 prejudice against gays	9.65***	4.58***
Effect of 2002 contact with foreigners on 2003 prejudice against homeless	6.67***	2.83**
2003 Prejudice against foreigners as mediator of:		
Effect of 2003 contact with foreigners on 2004 prejudice against gays	9.03***	2.47*
Effect of 2003 contact with foreigners on 2004 prejudice against homeless	8.67***	7.38**

Note: Sample numbers range from 732 to 796.
* $p < .05$; ** $p < .01$; *** $p < .001$.

mediated by the prejudice against foreigners in the year of the contact. In other words, does contact's initial reduction in anti-foreigner prejudice spread over to reductions in anti-gay and anti-homeless prejudice in the next year? In all four tests in the left column of Table 3.2, the Sobel tests show strong mediation effects. And in three of these tests, the direct path from foreigner contact and anti-gay or anti-homeless prejudice a year later is not significant. In short, the link between the contact with foreigners and the reduction of prejudice against the other outgroups is fully mediated by the attitude change that initially occurred toward foreigners. A year later, this shift has "sunk in" and diminished prejudice against two other outgroups that were not involved in the initial intergroup contact.

But these tests do not control for a possible selectivity bias. It is conceivable that those German respondents who reveal tolerance of gays and homeless were already less prejudiced. So the Sobel tests in the right column of Table 3.2 show tests for mediation while controlling for the prior year of either anti-gay or anti-homeless prejudice. In all four instances, the Sobel tests continue to indicate significant mediation by the reduction in anti-foreigner prejudice. As might be expected given the bidirectionality of contact–prejudice associations, controlling for the earlier prejudice typically lowers the Sobel test scores, but in each case they remain solidly significant.

The results in Table 3.2 offer strong support for the existence of secondary transfer effects. But we must be careful in discussing actual causation – one of the most difficult concepts in social science (Pettigrew, 1996). Nonetheless, we find support for assumptions underlying the causal sequence specified by the secondary transfer claims. First, these tests extend over a full year, so we know that assessments for prejudice against gays and the homeless occurred *after* the presumed causal variables (contact and the reduced anti-foreigner prejudice). Second, with the potential for selectivity bias removed, we can also be assured that these data are not distorted by bidirectional effects.

Secondary Transfer Effects for Indirect Contact

Asbrock et al. (under review) extend this analysis further by checking to see if these transfer effects emerge for indirect as well as direct intergroup contact. Using the German 2004 survey, they show that the effects do in fact appear for indirect contact – in which the respondent has an ingroup friend with an outgroup friend. Indeed, in one sense, these effects are even stronger than for direct contact. Asbrock and colleagues demonstrate that the secondary transfer effects for direct contact are largely limited to those outgroups that are similar to the contacted outgroup in stereotypical terms of both warmth and competence – the stereotype content model's two dimensions (Fiske, Cuddy, Glick, & Xu, 2002). But the generalization from indirect contact reveals no such limitations. Based in large part on normative effects, the secondary transfer effects from indirect contact extended to all the outgroups tested. In other words, seeing that your ingroup friend has an outgroup friend can shift the perceived norms about intergroup interaction to outgroups in general.

Processes Underlying Secondary Transfer Effects

In speculating about the fundamental processes underlying secondary transfer effects, we can treat it as a special case of the long-standing socio-psychological concern about how attitudes relate to each other over time. Early work on this issue emphasized cognitive processes with consistency and dissonance explanations. Recent research emphasizes affective processes with evaluative conditioning explanations.

The cognitive approach began with McGuire's (1960a, 1960b) studies on syllogistic attitude change. He demonstrated that shifts in one attitude induced shifts 1 week later on logically connected but unmentioned attitudes. Indeed, numerous investigations have noted a time delay in these transfer effects (e.g., Watts & Holt, 1970). A similar phenomenon has emerged more recently in work on "rebound" effects from attempting to suppress negative stereotypes of an outgroup. Such suppression frequently leads later to greater stereotyping not only against the original outgroup but to other outgroups as well (Gordijn et al., 2004). This suggests that it takes time for the inconsistency "to sink in" before the transfer effect is established.

Consider a probability survey study of Riley and Pettigrew (1976). Among White Texans, they found that the tragic assassination of Dr. Martin Luther King Jr. in 1968 was associated with a shift toward more favorable attitudes concerning both formal and informal interracial contact. But there was initially no change in their attitudes toward intimate contact. Three months later, however, these changes had "sunk in." Now more positive views of intimate contact emerged among those types of people who had earlier shown change only toward formal and informal contact. This study also uncovered a "counter-ceiling" effect in that those types of White Texans who had initially shown the most favorable views about interracial contact became even more favorable than other types following King's murder.

Applied to the German results, we can speculate that the initial reduction in anti-foreigner prejudice proved dissonant with their still largely negative views of the homeless. But, after a time delay, this dissonance in turn led to diminished prejudice against the homeless. We also noted a counter-ceiling effect in the German panel data – with the initially more tolerant showing the largest effects.

More recently, the same basic issue has arisen in specialized areas of social influence and attitude change that also stress cognitive factors. Though primarily focused on contrasting problems, the findings of this work shed light on contact's secondary transfer effect. The extensive work on minority influence offers a pertinent example (Martin & Hewstone, 2008; Wood et al., 1994). Research has repeatedly shown that minority influence is greatest for indirect, rather than direct, measures. That is, the influence of minorities emerges most strongly for issues only indirectly related to the content of their direct appeals.

Martin and Hewstone (2008, p. 293) provide a striking example. They found the indirect effect of a lasting change on attitudes toward abortion after minority advocacy of voluntary euthanasia. Though these two issues may seem distantly related, the link existed in that the subjects perceived them both to be concerned with the control and sanctity of life. Similarly, Alvaro and Crano (1997), in their investigation of minority influence, uncovered a connection between gun control and a ban on gay soldiers. This finding suggests the role of ideology in establishing links between attitudes. In this case, a "macho" ideology in the United States combines anti-gun control views with prejudice against gay men.

As demonstrated in the German data, indirect influence can emerge between two attitude domains that are psychologically, if not logically, related to each other. And the distinctiveness of the minority and its position are important elements in the indirect influence process (Alvaro & Crano, 1997). This appears to be the case for the secondary transfer effect. The novelty and strength of the initial favorable contact with the first outgroup governs, as a major mediator, its potential for transferring to the uninvolved second outgroup.

Likewise, normative pressures are typically involved in the minority influence phenomenon, such that majorities tend to avoid aligning themselves openly with the minority source of influence (Wood et al., 1994). In a somewhat different manner, norms are also involved in secondary transfer contact effects. If, for instance, hostile views against the homeless were especially intense and normative in Germany, we might well not have found positive shifts in attitudes toward resident foreigners to transfer to diminished prejudice against the homeless. In addition, the expansive secondary transfer effects of indirect contact appear to be shaped by normative changes.

Quite different explanations arise from the possibilities for affective, rather than cognitive, transfer effects. Evaluative conditioning entails associatively induced changes in liking (e.g., De Houwer, 2007; De Houwer, Thomas, & Baeyens, 2001; Walther, 2002). Working within this paradigm, Walther (2002) provides strong evidence for a "spreading attitude effect" that closely resembles the secondary transfer effects of intergroup contact. After all, as Chapter 6 will demonstrate, intergroup contact's effects on prejudice are goverened largely by affective processes – often involving lessened anxiety and heightened empathy (Eller & Abrams, 2004; Pettigrew & Tropp, 2008; Tropp & Pettigrew, 2004, 2005a; Van Laar et al., 2008).

Walther demonstrates with five studies that affective value is transferred to human faces that were previously associated with the conditioned stimuli because of prior learning. No conscious awareness of the link is necessary – a sharp departure from the consistency and dissonance explanations. As Walther (2002) correctly notes, "(M)any prejudiced people have never encountered the objects of their antipathy. Instead, attitudes are often based on prior experiences with similar attitudinal objects, on second-hand information, or on mere association" (p. 921).

She further demonstrates that the "spreading attitude effect" is resistant to extinction, strengthened by limiting cognitive resources, and applies to both positive and negative affective transfer. The data presented in this chapter have focused on *positive* secondary transfer effects of contact – where initial reductions in prejudice toward the contacted outgroup spill over to diminished prejudice directed at non-contacted outgroups. But Walther's last point raises the possibility of *negative* secondary transfer effects. To our knowledge, no research has directly investigated the secondary transfer effects of highly negative intergroup contact.

However, we do have evidence that collective threat, rather than intergroup contact, can evoke the spread of prejudice toward a range of groups. Terrorist assaults, for example, lead to heightened collective threat. They can trigger enhanced prejudice against the perpetrators, which then secondarily transfers as greater prejudice against uninvolved minorities.

The devastating terrorist attacks on commuter trains in Madrid in 2004 led to major shifts in Spanish opinion that illustrate this phenomenon. Authoritarianism rose and liberal values receded following the train bombings. Stronger prejudices developed in Spain not only against the target group – Arabs – but also against an entirely uninvolved minority – Jews (Echebarria-Echabe & Fernandez-Guede, 2006).

This transfer of changes from one prejudice to another – either positively from intergroup contact or negatively from collective threat – reflects the close links found between prejudices of varying types (Zick et al., 2008). We need to understand this process more thoroughly, and additional research on the topic will require longitudinal and experimental research as exemplified by the UCLA study. And, in particular, the interesting possibility that intergroup contact's secondary transfer effect may be a special case of Walther's (2002) spreading attitude effect deserves future research attention.

☐ Conclusion

Contrary to the claims of critics, there is strong evidence that intergroup contact effects typically generalize in important ways. Although there are both cognitive and normative barriers to such generalization, this chapter has shown that there is extensive research support for contact effects spreading in three significant directions.

First, the effects extend from more favorable attitudes toward the immediate outgroup members in the contact situation to more favorable attitudes toward the entire outgroup. We have noted how this generalization occurs routinely following positive intergroup contact. And it is this phenomenon that makes intergroup contact both theoretically and practically important.

Even in light of this research evidence, one could argue that such generalization is irrational. After all, the few outgroup members encountered are not likely to be a representative sample of the entire outgroup. Granted, our minds do employ cognitive structures that seek to organize information and are often resistant to change (see Hamilton, 1981). But we can also think about how, prior to contact, our knowledge base regarding outgroup members is likely to be limited through little exposure or only indirect experience with them. As such, contact with outgroup members can actually provide us with opportunities to gain information about outgroup members, as well as enhancing our motivation to attend to this information (see McClelland & Linnander, 2006). Thus, just as we "jump to conclusions" when we base initial judgments about groups on stereotypes or limited information, we similarly reach different conclusions about an entire group on the basis of meeting and liking just a few members of the group.

Second, intergroup contact effects also tend to generalize across situations. This phenomenon is also crucial. It would be highly restrictive were our changed attitudes limited just to the specific situation in which the contact occurred. Although this phenomenon has not received the research attention it deserves, our meta-analytic results together with the impressive findings of Cook provide solid support for the widespread existence of situational generalization of intergroup contact effects.

It is the third type of generalization that is the most novel theoretically and upon which most of our chapter has focused – the generalization of contact effects to reduced prejudice against *uninvolved* outgroups. We label this phenomenon "the secondary transfer effect."

After reviewing numerous studies and analyzing German probability survey data, we conclude that the secondary transfer effect exists for both direct and indirect contact. Stimulus generalization gradients appear to be operating both for similarity in the warmth and competence stereotypes and the degree of stigma of the outgroup targets. Thus, we noted that the effect is strongest when there exists cultural similarity or even overlap between the involved and uninvolved outgroups – such as French Canadians to French Europeans (Clement et al., 1977) or resident foreigners to all Muslims in the German samples (Pettigrew, 2009). And the UCLA study's converging secondary transfer effects for Latinos and African Americans, and those we uncovered for attitudes toward the homeless and homosexuals, suggest that the degree of stigma also enhances the effect.

But the most solid evidence for the secondary transfer effect is provided by the strongest data available in the intergroup contact research literature – the longitudinal, experimental roommate data of the UCLA study. Even here the effect was not found for all groups; students with Asian-American roommates became more, not less, prejudiced against other minorities.

Still, there is often a problem concerning the possibility of prior contact with the second outgroup. We have noted that some of the research reviewed here supports the existence of contact's secondary transfer effect only if we assume that there has been no such prior contact (e.g., Eller & Abrams, 2004). But other studies essentially negate this possible source of error (Clement et al., 1977; Pettigrew, 1997a). Most convincing on this point are the two Oxford studies that directly controlled for prior contact with the second outgroup and still obtained strong secondary transfer effects (see Hewstone et al., 2008). Following this lead, future research in this area should always check on this possibility.

Another possible source of error involves social desirability concerns. Perhaps many respondents in these surveys about prejudice just provide a tolerant reply toward a great variety of outgroups simply because it is seen as socially appropriate, normative behavior. Fortunately, the Oxford team's study conducted in the state of Texas explicitly controlled for this possibility using an abbreviated Crowne–Marlowe scale of social desirability (Crowne & Marlowe, 1960) and still obtained the effect.[1]

In the following chapter we continue this inquiry into the generalizability of intergroup contact effects by checking to see how universal the phenomenon is. Does contact between groups operate in similar ways in different areas of the world, with a variety of target groups and settings, and among participants of different ages?

☐ Note

1 One can question the validity of self-reports of intergroup contact. But Dhont, Roets, and Van Hiel (under review-a) found that their self-report measure of contact correlated highly with observer ratings ($r = +.71$).

Are the Effects of Intergroup Contact Universal?

In the previous chapter, we examined whether the positive effects of intergroup contact can generalize across different levels of analysis and diverse situations as well as extend to groups not directly involved in the contact. A closely related question concerns whether the intergroup contact effects we observe can be reasonably applied to contexts beyond those that have been intensively studied.

Given the existing research literature, there are several reasons why we might be inclined to question the reach of intergroup contact's effects. More than 70% of the studies included in our meta-analytic dataset were conducted in the United States. Many of these investigations involved contact between Black and White Americans, reflecting a general bias often noted in intergroup relations research (see Oliver & Wong, 2003). Moreover, a third of the meta-analytic studies examined the effects of contact in educational settings, and more than a third were conducted using convenience samples of college students (see Paluck & Green, 2009; Sears, 1986). Thus, one might question whether the typical effect of intergroup contact would largely be limited to interracial encounters that take place in American educational institutions.

To seek an answer to this limiting possibility, this chapter compares contact's effects on prejudice across a broad range of contexts. Here we assess the extent to which positive effects of contact are generally observed across different areas of the world, target groups, and settings, as well as among participants of different age groups.

☐ Intergroup Contact Effects Across Different Areas of the World

First, we explore whether contact–prejudice effects vary systematically across different geographical areas in which the research was conducted. While 72% of our samples are from the United States, less than 8% of the samples are from Africa, Asia, and Latin America combined. Although a fine-grained analysis by geographical area would be desirable, this distribution of cases limited the granularity with which we could examine this issue meta-analytically. Consequently, we clustered contact effects into six geographical areas: the United States (501 samples), Europe (80 samples), Canada (21 samples), Australia and New Zealand (16 samples), Israel (24 samples), and Africa, Asia, and Latin America (54 samples).

Figure 4.1 shows mean contact–prejudice correlations for the six areas. Initial analysis reveals that the mean effects for these six geographical areas do not significantly differ from each other ($p = .87$). Similarly, a more focused comparison finds no significant difference in mean contact–prejudice effects for samples gathered in the United States (mean $r = -.215$) and those gathered in other countries (mean $r = -.217$; $p = .90$). Note in particular that only two regions yield mean effects lower than that of the United States. Thus, our findings suggest that the potential for contact to reduce prejudice is not

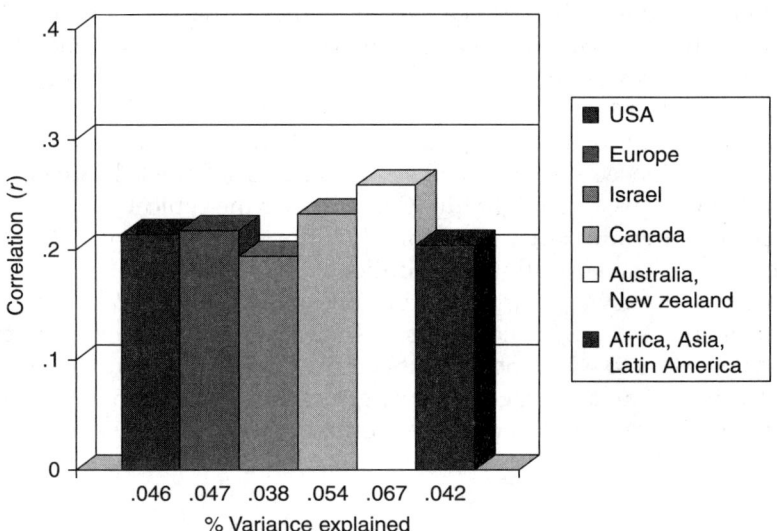

FIGURE 4.1 Mean contact–prejudice effects by geographical area.

limited to any single geographical area. Indeed, significant positive effects of intergroup contact have been found in many parts of the world, including among Chinese and Malay students in Malaysia (Rabushka, 1970), Israeli and Palestinian adolescents in the Middle East (Maoz, 2000), Hindu and Muslim adults in Bangladesh (Islam & Hewstone, 1993), and in other such conflict areas as Northern Ireland (Hewstone et al., 2006) and South Africa (Dixon et al., 2010a; Luiz & Krige, 1985).

☐ Intergroup Contact Effects Across Different Target Groups

Figure 4.2 provides the mean contact–prejudice effects across various target groups. The most commonly studied targets are racial and ethnic groups (362 samples). Together, these samples yield a mean r of −.214, matching the mean contact–prejudice effect for our full analysis. More broadly, we consistently observe significant associations between contact and prejudice, although the magnitudes of the associations vary somewhat in relation to different targets.

Similar mean contact effects emerge when the targets involve people with physical or mental disabilities (mean $r = -.243$ and $-.207$, respectively). For example, Clunies-Ross and O'Meara (1989) evaluated a program designed to improve attitudes toward peers with disabilities among

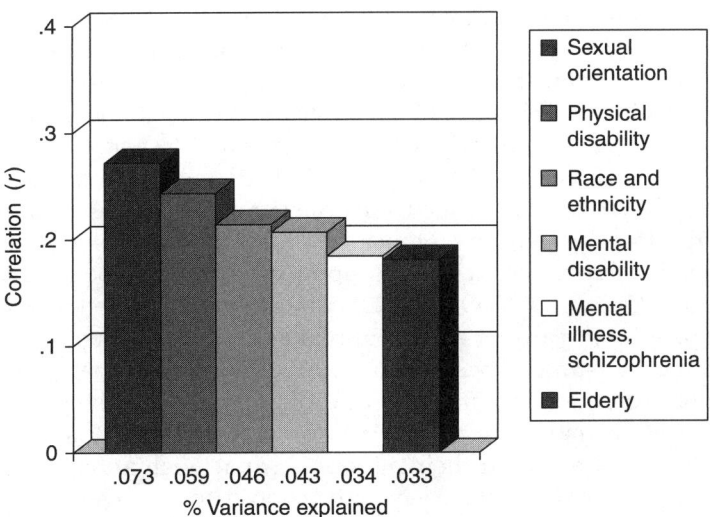

FIGURE 4.2 Mean contact–prejudice effects by type of target group.

Australian fourth-graders. Half of the fourth-grade children were randomly assigned to participate in the program and take part in recreational activities with intellectually disabled children of similar age (program group), while the other half did not (control group). Compared to children in the control group and their own pretest scores, children who participated in the program showed improved attitudes toward peers with disabilities, and these more positive attitudes were maintained over 3 months following the program. Parallel results have been obtained in other studies of children's attitudes toward people with disabilities, ranging from primary school children in Zambia (Ronning & Nabuzoka, 1993) and in the UK (Maras & Brown, 1996) and older children who worked with mentally disabled peers in cooperative groups (Ballard, Corman, Gottleib, & Kaufman, 1977) or as tutors (Fenrick & Petersen, 1984).

Yet the most striking finding is that the strongest mean contact effect emerged for samples where the target groups were gay men and lesbians (mean $r = -.271$). Indeed, this mean effect was significantly larger than that for the other samples combined (mean $r = -.211$; $p < .05$). Gregory Herek and colleagues (e.g., Herek, 1988; 2002; Herek & Capitanio, 1996; Herek & Gonzalez-Rivera, 2006) have conducted numerous surveys of attitudes toward sexual minorities and have consistently uncovered relatively large effects of contact. For instance, in a two-wave longitudinal telephone survey of a probability sample of English-speaking heterosexual Americans, Herek and Capitanio (1996) found a correlation of +.38 between contact with and positive attitudes toward gay men. A cross-wave analysis of the two surveys 1 year apart further replicated the reciprocal relationship between contact and attitudes: contact led to more positive attitudes, and positive attitudes led to more contact.

We can hypothesize why the mean effect for contact with gays is so large relative to other contact effects, although we know of no research that has directly examined this issue. One possibility is that, of all the target groups represented in our meta-analytic dataset, gays and lesbians comprise the primary group for which the defining, stigmatizing characteristics of the group may be concealed. As such, they can generally choose to whom they wish to disclose their group membership, as well as the point in the intergroup relationship at which their group membership will be revealed (see Herek, 2003; Quinn, 2006). On the one hand, we might expect that gay and straight people typically, or at least initially, encounter each other in situations where the straight person does not know the gay person's sexual orientation. Alternatively, in the context of ongoing friendships or family relations, people may have close relationships with individuals who only recognize or identify with their minority sexual orientation later in life. Either way, the gay person may only choose to disclose their sexual orientation to their straight friend or family member once they feel sufficient trust and comfort in the intergroup relationship (see Herek, 2003, for an extended discussion). In turn, the straight friend or family member, who already feels close to the gay person and invested in their relationship, may feel more conflicted about having anti-gay prejudices and potentially be more motivated to curb any prior prejudice they may have harbored against gay people in general. Longitudinal research is needed to test more directly these and other possible explanations for the unusually strong contact effects in the context of gay–straight relations.

By contrast, substantially weaker mean effects were obtained for samples where the target groups involve mentally ill or elderly populations (mean $r = -.184$ and $-.181$, respectively). Together, the mean contact effects for these two target groups were significantly smaller than those for all the other samples combined (mean $r = -.221$; $p < .05$). At least two types of explanations – one involving the research base, and the other concerning the prevailing stereotypes of the two groups – may help to account for these weaker effects.

The research explanation pertains to the types of studies from which these results derive. Investigations of attitudes toward mental illness often sample hospital staff, nurses, or other health practitioners who work with the mentally ill in institutional contexts (e.g., Weller & Grunes, 1988) or arrange for participants to visit mentally ill patients who are in institutional residence. Such contact encounters may be less than ideal, as research participants could become acquainted with individuals who suffer from severe mental illness or who experience diminished levels of psychological functioning. Yet even in such contexts some highly positive effects of contact can be observed. For example, Holzberg and Gewitz (1963) had 59 college students engage mental patients and discuss with professionals the patients' problems. This year-long program led to major positive changes in attitudes toward mental illness in comparison to a comparable control group of students ($r = -.53$).

Similarly, one type of contact study that involved the elderly as the target group has children, adolescents, or college students visit a care facility for the aged. For young children, this procedure can prove threatening and actually increase prejudice. Seefeldt (1987) had preschoolers visit infirm elders in a nursing home once a week for a year. Compared to a control group, these children developed more *negative* attitudes toward the elderly ($r = +.35$) as well as to their own aging. Other studies with preschoolers, however, have shown markedly positive effects of regular contact when the elderly are seen in a variety of roles and in non-threatening situations (e.g., Caspi, 1984; Dellman-Jenkins, Lambert, & Fruit, 1991).

The most incisive research on contact between the young and old has been conducted by Jake Harwood, Miles Hewstone, and their colleagues (e.g., Harwood, Hewstone, Paolini, & Voci, 2005; Harwood, Raman, & Hewstone, 2006; Tam et al., 2006). They found that children who had close relationships with their grandparents demonstrated less implicit and explicit ageism. Specifically, the *quantity* of contact with grandparents and other old people predicted children's implicit age attitudes. But it was the *quality* of the contact that was associated with lower explicit prejudice toward the elderly. Interestingly, self-disclosure and grandparents talking about their pasts also enhanced contact's positive effects.

We can also interpret Figure 4.2's trends for the mentally ill and the elderly in terms of the prevailing stereotypes held about the two groups. As we shall discuss in detail in Chapter 6, interactional anxiety is a critically important variable in intergroup contact. Considerable research has emphasized how uncertainty provokes feelings of anxiety in intergroup encounters (e.g., Stephan, Stephan, & Gudykunst, 1999). The theme of uncertainty has commonly been expressed as a concern in contact with the mentally ill, as they are often stereotyped as dangerous and unpredictable in their behavior (Corrigan, Watson, & Ottati, 2003; Penn et al., 1994). Especially under seemingly dangerous or threatening circumstances, uncertainties associated with predicting others' attitudes and behaviors can be highly anxiety-provoking (Gudykunst, 1985; Stephan et al., 1999). In turn, this anxiety may encourage an avoidance of contact with the mentally ill (Corrigan et al., 2003) or inhibit the potentially positive effects of such contact that does occur (Pettigrew & Tropp, 2008).

A rather different stereotype helps to interpret the somewhat weak trends that we observe for contact with the elderly. Although the elderly and the mentally ill are both prone to be negatively perceived as having some degree of impaired ability (Cuddy, Norton, & Fiske, 2005; Hummert, 1990), the aged are more often viewed as vulnerable rather than as dangerous and threatening (Hummert, 1990). Indeed, older people tend to be regarded with warmth and are more likely to elicit feelings of pity from others rather than fear (see Cuddy et al., 2005; Fiske et al., 2002). Thus, contact effects could be weaker in relation to the elderly simply because initial attitudes toward them typically involve feelings of warmth. In other words, there may be a ceiling effect that makes it more difficult for contact to enhance attitudes that are already largely positive. Again, further research is needed to explore this and other possible explanations.

☐ Intergroup Contact Effects Across Different Settings

Next, we consider the immediate setting in which the contact occurs. Employing our meta-analytic data once again, Figure 4.3 depicts the mean

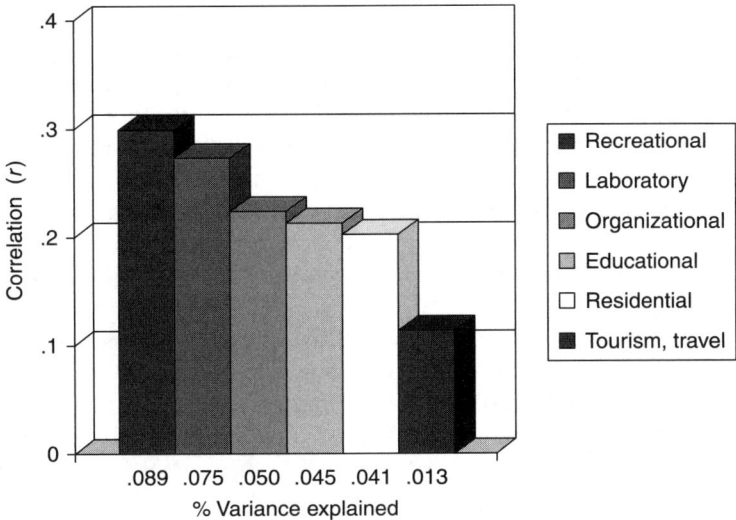

FIGURE 4.3 Mean contact–prejudice effects by type of contact setting.

contact–prejudice correlations for samples gathered from a wide variety of contact settings. The most extensively studied contact settings (i.e., organizational, educational and residential) consistently show significant mean contact–prejudice effects (mean r ranging from −.202 to −.224; $p < .001$). Note that such settings typically provide long-term contact that enables cross-group friendship to develop – which, as Chapter 8 will demonstrate, is the strongest type of contact. Similar to our earlier test of generalization across situations described in Chapter 3, these results indicate that positive effects of contact may be achieved across a wide range of institutional settings.

Additionally, we find that even stronger effects emerge for contact that occurs in recreational and laboratory settings, which together provide a mean contact–prejudice correlation of −.287 ($p < .001$). This mean effect is significantly larger than that of all other contact settings combined (mean $r = -.211$; $p < .01$).

These results are hardly surprising. Laboratory studies are controlled situations where optimal conditions are carefully fashioned by the experimenters. Similarly, recreational settings often provide opportunities for engaging in enjoyable and cooperative activities – an especially powerful type of contact that often meets all of Allport's optimal conditions. Athletic teams furnish a prime example (Patchen, 1982, 1999). In striving to win, teams comprised of different groups need each other and must work together toward a goal that the groups share – the cooperative interdependence emphasized by both Allport (1954) and Sherif (1966).

Conversely, passive contact between groups appears to be of little value. We observe the weakest mean effect for contact occurring in tourist and travel settings (mean $r = -.113$), although even this effect of minimal contact is statistically significant at the .05 level of confidence. Nonetheless, the mean contact effect for tourism and travel is a substantially smaller effect than that of all other settings combined (mean $r = -.217; p < .01$). This result, too, is not surprising. Much travel involves touring to see new places rather than opportunities to meet people at anything other than quite superficial levels. "It's Thursday," goes the touring refrain, "so it must be Paris!"

Highlighting this disparity in contact experiences are results from two studies, both conducted in regions of intense conflict. On the heels of the 1979 Peace Treaty between Israel and Egypt, Amir and Ben-Ari (1985) studied Israelis' intergroup attitudes toward Egyptians before and after a brief tourist visit to Egypt. Even this quite superficial form of contact yielded an inverse contact–prejudice association ($r = -.09$), although it is one of the weaker effects in our meta-analytic study. By contrast, with ethnic tensions running high during the early 1990s, Islam and Hewstone's (1993) study of Hindus and Muslims in Bangladesh showed a far larger contact–prejudice association ($r = -.49$), most likely due to their careful measurement of "high quality" contact between the groups – that is, contact rated as intimate, friendly, and cooperative.

Substantial travel, such as long-term study abroad programs, can have more striking positive effects than those illustrated in Figure 4.3. For example, a survey of 223 Qatari students enrolled in American universities (Kamal & Maruyama, 1990) revealed that those who had greater contact with Americans were more likely to have positive attitudes toward Americans in general and to believe that Americans had more positive attitudes toward Arabs (see also Ibrahim, 1970).

But even with such encouraging examples, the study-abroad results remain mixed. In part, these mixed findings may be due to the varying quality of studies on foreign exchange among the 13 tourism and travel samples in our meta-analytic dataset. For instance, even investigations that were carefully constructed with a control group may suffer from relying on retrospective data, where participants report on their attitudes toward the host country only after they have returned to their homeland (e.g., Carlson & Widaman, 1988).

Another obvious reason for the great range of findings in the realm of foreign study is that the actual experiences of those who study abroad also vary greatly. A particularly insightful study in this area examined such differential experiences through the lens of intergroup contact theory (Stangor, Jonas, Stroebe, & Hewstone, 1996). These researchers intensively studied American college students before and twice after their 1 year of study in either Germany or the UK. The overall result was a change toward somewhat *more negative* attitudes toward the host country, although their mean attitude ratings remained quite high. As such, the reduction in positive evaluations resulted largely from a ceiling artifact – that is, these self-selected American students expressed such extremely positive, perhaps even unrealistic, attitudes prior to starting their study abroad that there was little opportunity for the attitudes to become yet more positive.

Nevertheless, even in this context Stangor et al. (1996) observed that contact once again acted to reduce prejudice. Those American students who reported having spent the most time with either Germans or British reported more favorable intergroup attitudes than other students. And those who upon departure reported having developed close German or British friends had more positive stereotypes of their hosts as well as greater perceptions of variability among people from the host country.

Overall, the findings summarized in Figure 4.3 indicate that the effects of contact are largely consistent and significant across a wide array of social settings. At the same time, our results do reveal variability in contact effects across settings that suggest the role of additional moderating forces. As we will discuss in Chapter 8, recent research on intergroup contact reveals that close, cross-group friendships are especially likely to yield positive contact effects (see also Brown & Hewstone, 2005; Pettigrew, 1997a). However, opportunities for close contact can vary widely across contexts, and limited contact opportunities and experiences will curb its ability to promote positive changes in intergroup attitudes (see Pettigrew, Wagner, Christ, & Stellmacher, 2007c).

☐ Intergroup Contact Effects Across Different Age Groups

We must also consider whether contact effects might vary among participants from different age groups. In the context of racial and ethnic relations, children become aware of group differences from very young ages (Aboud, 1988; Goodman, 1952; Hirschfeld, 1996; Porter, 1971), and their developing views of different racial and ethnic groups can be affected and shaped by others with whom they come into contact (see Aboud, Mendelson, & Purdy, 2003; Ellison & Powers, 1994; Killen, Crystal, & Ruck, 2007a). Children's attitudes toward other racial and ethnic groups tend to grow more positive into middle childhood (Bigler & Liben, 1993; Katz & Zalk, 1978), as they become more able to take others' perspectives and to recognize both similarities and differences among people within groups and across group boundaries (Doyle & Aboud, 1995). At the same time, intergroup attitudes can become harder to change as children grow older (see Aboud & Levy, 2000; Banks, 1995; Killen et al., 2007b).

We therefore examined whether relationships between intergroup contact and prejudice varied across different age groups (Figure 4.4). Specifically, we coded the samples in our meta-analysis to discern whether the participants were children (12 years or younger, $n = 82$), adolescents (13–17 years, $n = 114$), college students (18–21 years, $n = 262$), or adults (older than 21 years, $n = 238$). Contact–prejudice effects for samples of children (mean $r = -.239$), adolescents (mean $r = -.208$), and college students (mean $r = -.231$) did not significantly differ from each other. At the same time, effects for child samples are marginally stronger ($p < .06$) and for college samples significantly stronger ($p < .05$) than those obtained for the adult samples (mean $r = -.197$). The tendency for college student samples to yield stronger mean effects than adults is consistent with Sears' (1986) contention that college students' attitudes are typically more flexible and open to change than those of older adults.

Additionally, while generally effective across age groups, the somewhat stronger mean effect among children suggests that contact may be especially influential at younger ages. For the young, intergroup contact can serve as a formative experience for framing and developing intergroup attitudes. Consistent with this view, several studies indicate that intergroup contact during one's youth can predict reduced levels of prejudice later in life, although such studies often must rely on retrospective reports of childhood contact. For example, Wood and Sonleitner (1996)

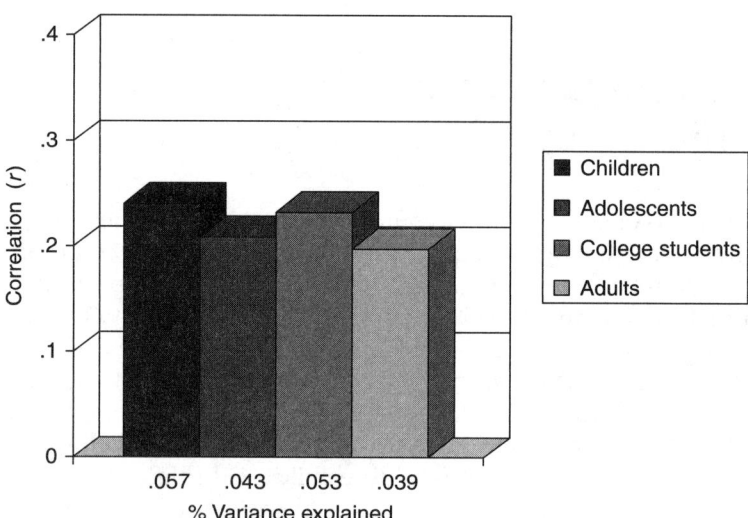

FIGURE 4.4 Mean contact–prejudice effects by participant age group.

analyzed data from face-to-face interviews with 292 White American adults. During the interviews, respondents were asked to report on the degree of contact with Blacks they experienced as children (i.e., in their schools, neighborhoods, churches, and community organizations), as well as to respond to a measure of anti-Black prejudice. The researchers showed that greater reports of childhood contact predicted lower anti-Black prejudice reported as adults. Similarly, with samples of White, Black, and Latino respondents, Emerson, Kimbro, and Yancey (2002) found that those previously exposed to racially diverse schools and neighborhoods were more likely to report racially diverse friendship networks and social ties in their adult lives. And Crain and Weisman (1972) have shown that adult African Americans who reported having played with Whites as children were less anti-White, even though they had typically experienced racially segregated neighborhoods and elementary schools.

These findings highlight both the importance of early contact experiences and the influence of social environments in which young people are likely to experience contact. In particular, researchers have emphasized the critical role that school environments can play in shaping intergroup attitudes and reducing prejudice (e.g., Damico, Bell-Nathaniel, & Green, 1981; Khmelkov & Hallinan, 1999; Patchen, 1982; Schofield, 1978). While many social factors influence children's development (Malecki & Demaray, 2002), children spend significant portions of their lives in school over periods of many years, affording them with experiences that contribute to their understanding of social norms and an emerging sense of themselves in relation to others (Hiner, 1990). We therefore sought to conduct more fine-grained analyses of our meta-analytic data involving children and adolescents in school settings.

We began by selecting the 198 samples that examine contact–prejudice relationships among children and adolescents. Approximately half of the samples ($n = 97$; 49%) involved contact between youth from different racial and ethnic groups. Of the remaining 101 samples, 24 involved contact between youth and the elderly, 43 involved contact between youth with and without physical disabilities, and 29 involved contact between youth with and without mental disabilities or mental illness. An initial comparison revealed that the mean effect for youth samples involving racial and ethnic contact (mean $r = -.228$) is virtually equal to the mean effect for youth samples involving contact with other target groups (mean $r = -.219$; $p > .10$).

Additionally, most of the child and adolescent samples examined contact effects in school settings (57%). We therefore tested whether the effects of contact are generally consistent for samples from schools and in other intergroup contexts. Results show that mean contact–prejudice relationships did not significantly differ among the 113 samples gathered in school settings (mean $r = -.231$) and the 85 remaining samples gathered in residential, recreational, or other settings (mean $r = -.214$; $p > .50$). We also find similar results for samples of children and adolescents in schools, whether they involve racial and ethnic contact ($n = 57$, mean $r = -.231$) or contact in relation to the other target groups ($n = 56$, mean $r = -.235$; $p > .90$). Thus, rather than being limited to any single context, the positive effects of contact among children and adolescents appear to be comparable for many kinds of groups and across a range of settings in which youth from different groups come into contact with each other.

☐ Conclusion

Contact research has not, of course, studied the phenomenon in every nation, nor has it examined effects for all possible target groups, settings, and populations. But our meta-analytic review incorporates data gathered in 38 different nations, with tests pertaining to a great variety of groups and settings and with participants of different ages. Taken together, our meta-analytic findings provide compelling evidence that intergroup contact is universally useful in reducing prejudice across a great range of intergroup situations. There is, as to be expected, variability in the magnitude of contact–prejudice associations across contexts, but the fundamental relationships between contact and prejudice remain strikingly consistent – the more the intergroup contact, the greater the reduction of intergroup prejudice.

When Does Intergroup Contact Reduce Prejudice?

Thus far, our meta-analytic findings suggest that intergroup contact typically promotes reductions in intergroup prejudice among people of many different ages and groups and across a wide range of settings and contexts. But we may still wonder whether there are certain strategies we can use to maximize the extent to which contact between groups will lead to reduced prejudice.

☐ Allport's Optimal Conditions

The most influential statement on this issue was expressed more than a half-century ago by Gordon Allport. As mentioned in Chapter 1, Allport (1954) proposed that intergroup contact will lead to reduced prejudice if the contact situation embodies four conditions: (1) equal status between the groups; (2) common goals; (3) cooperation between groups; and (4) institutional support for the contact. Studies conducted since Allport's time generally lend support for the importance of these four key conditions, as we shall see in the sections that follow.

Equal Status in the Situation

"Equal status" can often be difficult to define, and researchers have used the term in varied ways (Riordan, 1978). What is critical from Allport's perspective is that, regardless of inequities that might exist in the broader society, the groups are granted equal status *within* the contact situation

(Cohen, 1982; Riordan & Ruggiero, 1980; Robinson & Preston, 1976). For example, equal status might be established in the contact situation through giving members of each group equal opportunities to participate in activities, offer opinions, make decisions, and receive access to available resources. As a consequence, both groups have the opportunity, ability, and power to shape the rules of the interaction.

Some writers have also emphasized that the groups should be of equal status *coming into* the contact situation (Brewer & Kramer, 1985; Foster & Finchilescu, 1986). But numerous studies demonstrate that, even when groups initially differ in status, establishing equal status within the contact situation can help to reduce prejudice, as has been found in racially integrated school environments (e.g., Patchen, 1982; Schofield & Eurich-Fulcer, 2001). We shall return to this issue in Chapter 9.

Common Goals

Effective contact also needs to involve compatible goals between groups, where there is a joint effort and commitment to achieving the goals that the groups share. When members of different groups have common goals, they tend to act in more friendly ways and become more inclined to support each other (Johnson & Johnson, 1984; Johnson, Johnson, & Maruyama, 1983). Athletic teams offer a prime example of how common goals can reduce prejudice and promote more positive relations between groups (Chu & Griffey, 1985; Kearney, 2007). Teams that include members of different groups must find a way to work together and rely on each other in order to be successful and achieve their shared goals.

Intergroup Cooperation

Attainment of common goals is closely linked to Allport's third condition, as attempts to work toward common goals should occur under cooperative rather than competitive circumstances. In their classic summer camp research, Sherif et al. (1961) demonstrated this principle by first having groups of campers compete against each other, which provoked conflict and feelings of hostility toward the other group. The researchers then created a series of situations in which the groups were required to work cooperatively toward shared goals that would benefit both groups (e.g., fixing the common water supply and helping to start a truck on the way to a joint picnic). Such interdependent, cooperative activities led to reduced conflict and hostility between the groups, and these improvements in turn allowed positive relations and friendships to develop across group boundaries.

More evidence regarding the benefits of intergroup cooperation comes from cooperative learning programs that aim to enhance students' learning and social experiences in schools (see Aronson & Gonzalez, 1988; Brewer & Miller, 1984; Johnson et al., 1983; Schofield, 1989; Slavin, 1983). A well-known example is the "Jigsaw Classroom" approach developed by Aronson and colleagues (Aronson et al., 1978; Aronson & Gonzalez, 1988; Aronson & Patnoe, 1997). In such classrooms, the teacher separates a lesson plan into smaller pieces and assigns diverse groups of students into "mastery" groups, where their task is to learn their portion of the lesson well enough to be able to teach it to other children in the class. The teacher then reorganizes the class into "Jigsaw" groups, which include one representative from each of the "mastery" groups. Each student therefore has the responsibility of teaching other students in their "Jigsaw" group the piece of the lesson they mastered. By having each student make a unique contribution to the success of the group, diverse groups of students must work both cooperatively and interdependently to master all the course material.

Using this method, Aronson and his colleagues have found that, compared to children in more traditional classes, children in Jigsaw classes develop more positive attitudes toward each other across racial boundaries. Moreover, positive results of this method have been found for children around the globe, including those in Australia (Walker & Crogan, 1998) and Japan (Araragi, 1983), as well as in the United States (Aronson & Gonzalez, 1988).

Institutional Support

As a fourth condition, Allport proposed that positive effects of intergroup contact would be maximized when the equal-status, cooperative nature of the contact takes place with support from institutional authorities. Such authorities establish norms of acceptance and guidelines for how members of different groups should interact with each other (Yarrow, Campbell, & Yarrow, 1958). A great deal of evidence concerning the effects of institutional support comes from studies of interracial contact in schools. For example, children from different racial groups tend to get along better and seek out more interactions with each other when school principals and administrators appear to value positive intergroup relations (e.g., Longshore & Wellisch, 1981; Wellisch, Marcus, MacQueen, & Duck, 1976). Similarly, when they perceive teachers to be in favor of interracial contact, White children develop more positive interracial attitudes and may become less likely to avoid contact with their Black classmates (Patchen, 1982). Parallel evidence for the importance of institutional support comes from studies of contact in the military (Landis, Hope, & Day, 1984), organizational settings (e.g., Kalev, Dobbin, & Kelly, 2006; Morrison & Herlihy, 1992), and religious communities (e.g., Parker, 1968).

Earlier Williams (1947) and later many others have suggested additional facilitating factors. Some of these restate Allport's conditions. For example, Sherif's emphasis upon "group interdependence" essentially combines Allport's focus on common goals without intergroup competition. In particular, writers have often stressed the importance of the potential for the contact situation to foster intergroup acquaintances and friendships (Amir, 1976; Cook, 1984; Pettigrew, 1997a, 1998). We shall examine this important condition at length in Chapter 8.

But the four core conditions described here form the basis of Allport's fundamental contribution to intergroup contact theory. Although they are not directly listed in *The Nature of Prejudice* (Allport, 1954), the book's contentions on contact were later distilled by Pettigrew (1971) in consultation with Allport. Although the four conditions can be described separately, it is important to note that Allport conceived of these conditions as interrelated factors in reducing prejudice. Indeed, establishing equal status between groups will likely require the support of institutional authorities. Encouraging groups to work toward common goals should also involve some degree of cooperative interdependence (see Walker & Crogan, 1998). Thus, we examine Allport's conditions both jointly and independently in predicting contact's ability to reduce prejudice.

☐ Testing the Effects of Allport's Conditions for Optimal Intergroup Contact

Given the central role that Allport's conditions have played in the development of intergroup contact theory and research, we sought to evaluate their effectiveness using our meta-analytic dataset. As a first step, we attempted to rate each study for the presence of each of Allport's conditions in the contact situation. However, these efforts were undermined by two troublesome features of the existing contact research literature.

First, upon initial review of the papers, we realized that most contact studies included in the meta-analysis provided virtually no detailed information about the conditions under which the contact occurred. Researchers typically provided basic information about how contact was measured and the samples that participated in the contact, but only a small subset of studies described any explicit norms, standards, or guidelines that were established for the contact.

Second, among those studies that did provide more detailed information, Allport's conditions were often blended together in terms of how they were implemented in the research studies. Rather than being intended as tests of intergroup contact theory per se, many such cases came from other disciplines and involved evaluations of programs designed to improve relations between groups. Such studies understandably incorporated multiple positive factors to maximize the program's success. For instance, Friedman (1975) describes a program in which sixth-grade children with and without physical disabilities interacted over a 4-month period by visiting each others' schools on an alternating basis. They worked together cooperatively and interdependently on shared projects covering a range of topics (e.g., nutrition, ecology), to which all children could contribute their skills. The groups also developed their projects with the direct supervision of teachers, who had received training prior to the implementation of the program. Clearly, a variety of strategies were used to establish an atmosphere in which all children felt welcome, supported, and able to contribute through cooperative, joint efforts. But how can one delineate between Allport's specific criteria in such a study?

Global Test of Allport's Conditions

We therefore began our analysis by rating samples using a more global indicator: whether the contact situation was explicitly structured to approximate all or most of Allport's optimal conditions. Here, we did not require that the contact situation specifically address each of Allport's conditions. Rather, we rated samples as to whether explicit efforts were made to structure the contact situation in line with Allport's contentions, with the goal of maximizing positive outcomes from the contact. This global rating actually offers a more direct test of intergroup contact theory than our original approach, since Allport held that his four conditions should be integrated and implemented together, rather than being treated as entirely independent factors.

With this coded variable, we then compared the magnitude of the contact–prejudice association for those samples where the contact either was or was not explicitly designed to meet Allport's conditions. As shown in Figure 5.1, the mean association between contact and reduced prejudice is much stronger for the 134 samples where the contact situation is explicitly structured in line with Allport's conditions (mean $r = -.287$) as compared to the mean effect for the remaining 562 samples (mean $r = -.204$; $p < .001$). In terms of variance explained, the effects of structured contact are almost twice that of the remaining samples (.082 vs. .042).

We must recognize that this comparison is between samples where we have information indicating that the contact was explicitly structured to meet Allport's conditions and those for which no such information was

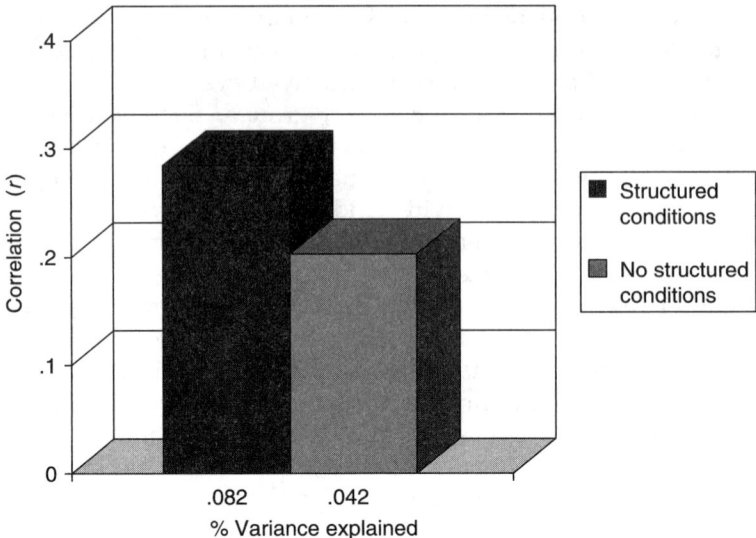

FIGURE 5.1 Mean contact–prejudice effects by conditions of contact situation.

available. Although our ideal comparison would have been between cases with and without Allport's conditions, our meta-analytic data do not allow such a comparison. It is therefore likely that some of the remaining samples could have involved contact that approximated Allport's conditions. If so, the differences between samples with and without Allport's optimal conditions could be even larger. Nonetheless, these data strongly suggest that when we have direct evidence that contact situations are structured in accordance with Allport's conditions, the contact is especially likely to yield noteworthy reductions in prejudice.

Additionally, it is possible that rather than being due to Allport's conditions, the enhanced contact effect could be accounted for by methodological features of the 134 samples included in this subset. We checked on this possibility by conducting a regression analysis using our global indicator of Allport's conditions and our strongest methodological moderators (i.e., design of the study, reliability of the contact and prejudice measures, the adequacy of the control group) as predictors for the contact–prejudice effect sizes. Preliminary correlations revealed that samples with structured programs did in fact tend to employ more rigorous research designs ($r = .570$; $p < .001$), more reliable indicators of contact and prejudice ($r = .390$ and $.102$, respectively; $p < .01$), and more adequate control groups for comparison ($r = .095$; $p < .05$). Also, as shown in Table 5.1, results from the regression analysis show that ratings of reliability for the contact and

TABLE 5.1 Summary of Inverse Variance Weighted Regression Model Predicting Contact–Prejudice Effect Sizes by Samples

Predictor Variables	B	SE	β	z	p
Type of study	.001	.017	.002	.035	.972
IV quality	−.088	.018	−.206	−4.775	.000
DV quality	−.031	.014	−.084	−2.231	.026
Type of control	.034	.010	.121	3.303	.001
Structured program	−.053	.024	−.099	−2.219	.027
R^2			.10***		
Q_{Model}			77.29***		
k			696		

Source: Adapted from Pettigrew and Tropp (2006).

Note: B = raw regression coefficient; SE = standard error for the regression coefficient; β = standardized regression coefficient; z = z-test for the regression coefficient; p = probability of z-test; R^2 = proportion of variance accounted for; Q_{Model} = test of whether the regression model explains a significant portion of variability across effect sizes (see Wilson, 2002); k = number of samples included in the analysis. This analysis was conducted using Fisher's z-transformed r values. The random effects variance component for this analysis (based on Fisher's z-transformed r values) was .020.
* $p < .05$; ** $p < .01$; *** $p < .001$.

prejudice measures and the adequacy of control groups all contribute significantly to predicting stronger contact–prejudice effects. Still, even after controlling for these important methodological variables, our global indicator of Allport's conditions remains a significant predictor of stronger contact–prejudice effects.

Taken together, these findings offer some important insights regarding the global role of Allport's conditions in reducing prejudice through intergroup contact. Consistent with much of the intergroup contact literature (see Allport, 1954; Pettigrew, 1998), we observe a markedly higher mean effect size for those samples that experienced carefully structured contact situations designed to meet Allport's optimal conditions. Moreover, a multivariate model showed that structured contact predicted stronger contact–prejudice effects beyond that explained by multiple indices of research rigor. Thus, our results demonstrate that establishing Allport's optimal conditions in the contact situation typically enhances the positive effects of intergroup contact.

Yet our findings also suggest that Allport's conditions are not *essential* for intergroup contact to achieve positive outcomes. Indeed, we consistently observe significant relationships between contact and prejudice, even among those samples where we do not have direct evidence indicating whether Allport's conditions were met or not.

In concert with other recent empirical advances, these findings suggest that a basic process underlying contact's ability to reduce prejudice involves the tendency for familiarity to breed liking. Emphasized by Homans (1950) and demonstrated experimentally by Zajonc (1968), this phenomenon leads to the prediction that intergroup contact will induce liking under a wide range of conditions. Research consistently finds evidence for the relationship between exposure and liking with a range of targets (e.g., Bornstein, 1989; Harmon-Jones & Allen, 2001; Lee, 2001) and across varied research settings (e.g., Moreland & Zajonc, 1977; Zajonc & Rajecki, 1969). Moreover, research has demonstrated that the increases in liking that derive from exposure can generalize to greater liking for related, yet unknown, targets (Rhodes, Halberstadt, & Brajkovich, 2001) – comparable to the generalization of contact's effects to unknown outgroup members discussed in Chapter 3. Further research by Zebrowitz, White, and Wieneke (2008) supports our supposition that the mere exposure effect underlies intergroup contact's effects. They found that exposure just to other-race faces increases the liking for strangers of that race.

These mere exposure findings may also help to explain why Allport's optimal conditions appear not to be essential for the positive effects of contact to emerge. While 94% of the 713 samples in our analysis showed an inverse relationship between intergroup contact and prejudice, only 19% of the samples involved contact situations structured in line with Allport's conditions. Two cases from our meta-analytic dataset are particularly illustrative here. Van Dyk (1990) found that rural Afrikaans-speaking White housewives who had had close contact with their African domestic workers showed more favorable attitudes towards Africans in general. Conducted during the tense final days of South Africa's *apartheid* policy, this highly constrained contact situation clearly violates Allport's key conditions. Recall also from the previous chapter that Crain and Weisman (1972) found that adult African Americans who reported having played with Whites as children were less anti-White, although they had typically experienced racially segregated neighborhoods and elementary schools. Like these examples, many other studies in our meta-analytic dataset conspicuously lack Allport's key conditions for positive contact outcomes and yet report at least some reduction in prejudice. We therefore should think of Allport's conditions as *facilitating* rather than necessary for producing positive outcomes from intergroup contact.

Let us underline the theoretical importance of this distinction between facilitating and necessary conditions. One of the most serious weaknesses of earlier forms of contact theory was that as the long laundry list of necessary conditions accumulated, the theory set the bar too high and was in danger of becoming meaningless (Pettigrew, 1986). Virtually no real-life situations could meet all the conditions that were being specified as required for contact to yield positive effects. As facilitating moderators, however, these factors help to specify further when we can expect varying effects from intergroup contact.

Individual Tests of Allport's Conditions

In light of this global finding, we then conducted more fine-grained ratings and analyses of Allport's conditions using the 134 samples with structured contact. Although contact conditions were often implemented together in these cases, we used "yes" or "no" ratings to discern whether each program clearly and explicitly (1) established equal status between groups within the contact situation, (2) focused participants on common goals, (3) emphasized a cooperative environment, and (4) demonstrated institutional support for the contact. Ratings of these variables by two independent judges were reliable, yielding kappa coefficients between .76 and .97, with a median kappa coefficient of .84.

We soon noticed that all these cases were rated as having institutional support – an unsurprising finding that was virtually assured by the implementation of structured programs designed to promote Allport's conditions. Given the lack of variability on this rated variable, we then compared mean effects between samples that were rated as with or without each of the three remaining conditions (i.e., equal status, common goals, and cooperation). These tests showed no significant differences in mean contact–prejudice effects for samples rated with and without equal status, common goals, or cooperation. However, additional analyses indicated that ratings of equal status, common goals, and cooperation were highly correlated with each other (r ranging from .51 to .63; $p < .001$), with 72% of samples in this subset rated as having at least three of Allport's four optimal conditions. We therefore conducted additional regression analyses in which we examined equal status, common goals, and cooperation as predictors for the contact–prejudice effect sizes. The models revealed no significant effects for these three conditions either when entered simultaneously as predictors (β ranging from .02 to .18; $p > .15$) or when entered separately alongside our methodological moderators (β ranging from .05 to .06; $p > .50$).

Given that none of these three conditions emerged as a significant, independent predictor, we tested whether institutional support might play a special role in predicting contact–prejudice effects. For this analysis, samples rated as having only institutional support ($k = 31$) were compared with samples rated as having two or more of Allport's conditions ($k = 103$), as well as with the remaining samples in our analysis ($k = 564$). Results showed that the mean effect for samples with only institutional support (mean $r = -.286$) did not significantly differ from the mean effect for samples with two or more of Allport's conditions (mean $r = -.290$; $p = .93$), while both of these groups showed significantly stronger effects than the remaining samples in our analysis (mean $r = -.204$; $p < .05$ and $p < .001$, respectively).

Although the present analysis necessarily offers a relatively crude test, its findings suggest that institutional support may be an especially important condition for facilitating positive contact effects. At the same time, it is important to note that our ratings of institutional support were made in the context of structured programs designed to approximate optimal conditions for positive intergroup contact. Hence, while institutional support appears to play a critical role, this condition should not be conceived of or implemented in isolation. Institutional support for contact under conditions of competition or unequal status can easily enhance animosity between groups, thereby diminishing the potential for achieving positive outcomes from contact (see Sherif, 1966). Thus, consistent with Allport's original contentions, we believe that optimal conditions for contact are still best conceptualized as functioning together to facilitate positive intergroup outcomes, rather than being regarded as entirely separate factors.

Our conceptualization of contact conditions complements earlier work by Green, Adams, and Turner (1988), who developed a multi-dimensional scale to assess perceptions of racial climate in school settings. With data from 3300 American middle-school students and a final pool of 43 items, these authors identified four factors – equal status, interdependence, institutional norms, and acquaintance potential – corresponding directly to the writings of earlier contact theorists such as Allport (1954) and Cook (1984). Moreover, while their scale includes four dimensions that can be distinguished empirically, substantially stronger estimates of internal consistency were obtained when all four factors were combined into one overall scale, thereby leading these authors to conclude that "at a higher level of abstraction the items reflected the same construct" (p. 248).

Nonetheless, there is research evidence that supports the utility of maintaining distinctions among the four conditions in our efforts to predict intergroup outcomes. For example, Molina and Wittig (2006) gathered data from four large samples of American middle- and high-school students, using an adapted version of Green et al.'s (1988) racial climate scale. These authors found moderate, positive correlations among the four subscales, with equal status and institutional support showing the strongest associations with each other. Additionally, when entered simultaneously as predictors, acquaintance potential emerged as the strongest predictor of affective prejudice, whereas interdependence emerged as the strongest predictor of feeling like a common ingroup.

Koschate and Van Dick (under review) also recommend that Allport's conditions be regarded as relatively separate factors. They propose that cooperation be conceived of as a mediator of the effects of contact conditions on prejudice, rather than as one of those optimal conditions. The authors test these proposals with a sample of workers who constituted 48 different working groups within a large German company. They found that the four contact conditions were only weakly related to each other, and that interdependence and equal status were especially likely to predict lower levels of prejudice.

However, Koschate and Van Dick also found that authority support predicted cooperation but not intergroup bias. This unusual result may reflect two factors. First, authority support was measured by asking the authorities themselves, so a self-serving bias may well have introduced measurement error. Second, authority support is most important in conflicted societal contexts such as South Africa, Northern Ireland, and the southern United States. In these settings, prejudice and discrimination can be the traditional and expected norm unless there is direct authority support to counter it.

Taken together, these differences in effects of Allport's conditions suggest that more attention should be granted to the contexts in which the conditions are implemented, and to the particular outcomes that we seek to alter as a result of their implementation. For example, it is understandable that greater degrees of interdependence would predict stronger feelings of common identity in schools (Molina & Wittig, 2006), or less bias in the context of workgroups where members cooperate on joint projects (Koschate & Van Dick, under review), whereas acquaintance potential would more likely predict how one feels about relating to members of other groups (Molina & Wittig, 2006). Future research on potential differences in the effects of Allport's conditions should be careful to examine the correspondence between each condition and the desired outcomes in question.

More broadly, our meta-analytic findings also suggest a new orientation for how we conceptualize conditions for intergroup contact. Ever since Allport's time, explorations of contact conditions have focused principally on the role of positive factors, claiming these to be essential for achieving reductions in prejudice. Indeed, Allport (1954) himself believed that prejudice naturally occurs between groups and that contact holds the potential either to reduce or to exacerbate this prejudice. Hence, he sought to specify the *positive* moderating factors that would maximize the potential for contact to reduce prejudice and promote other positive intergroup outcomes. Instead, our meta-analytic results compel us to reverse this approach. We start with the prediction that, all things being equal, intergroup contact will generally diminish prejudice. From this point, shifts in the direction and magnitude of the contact–prejudice association will depend on the presence or absence of a range of positive and negative moderating factors.

By reframing contact theory in this way, we do not intend to imply that contact between groups will invariably produce reductions in intergroup prejudice. A range of negative factors might understandably inhibit contact's ability to improve relations between groups, such as ongoing violence, threats of terror, or competition over limited resources (see Amir, 1969; Corkalo et al., 2004; McCauley, Worchel, Moghaddam, & Lee, 2004). Yet even in such extreme cases, positive contact between groups may often help to reduce the likelihood of further intergroup violence and promote more positive and cooperative intergroup relations (see Hewstone et al., 2008, for an extended discussion). Thus, rather than maintaining its predominant focus on positive factors, we believe that more research attention must also be granted to *negative* factors that can deter the emergence of positive contact effects – the focus of Chapter 12.

☐ Objective Conditions versus Subjective Responses to Contact

In addition, we propose that future research move beyond the theory's traditional focus on *objective features* of the contact situation and further consider people's *subjective responses* to contact situations. Thus far, our research suggests that the objective establishment of Allport's conditions is not essential to promote positive intergroup relations. But what may be crucial for improved intergroup relations is the extent to which people *perceive* those conditions to be valued and internalized by the outgroup members with whom they interact.

Emerging intergroup research has begun to focus on the concerns and expectations that group members bring to cross-group interactions (Devine & Vasquez, 1998; Shelton, Richeson, & Vorauer, 2006; Tropp, 2006; Vorauer, 2006). Much of this work notes that people's concerns about being rejected by outgroup members contribute to their avoidance of contact and undermine their interest in future contact (e.g., Plant & Devine, 2003; Shelton & Richeson, 2005; Tropp & Bianchi, 2006), along with provoking more hostile responses when contact occurs (Butz & Plant, 2006). However, little of this work has examined the degree to which these concerns predict intergroup outcomes relative to Allport's conditions for optimal contact. Such research is crucial, because even when attempts are made to create optimal conditions within the contact situation, subjective perceptions of contact conditions can still vary widely among members of different groups and be guided by their pre-existing views of the intergroup relationship (see Cohen, 1982; Robinson & Preston, 1976).

Molina and Wittig (2006; see also Molina, Wittig & Giang, 2004) provide a noteworthy research example that links subjective perceptions to the role of Allport's conditions. They examined the extent to which both perceptions of contact conditions (e.g., equal status, interdependence, institutional support) and perceived openness to cross-race interactions among fellow students (e.g., acquaintance potential; see Cook, 1984; Cook & Sellitz, 1955) predicted their own prejudice toward and interest in contact with other racial groups. Across four studies with diverse samples of middle- and high-school students, Molina and Wittig found that perceived openness predicted significant reductions in students' own prejudiced attitudes and their greater willingness to engage in future contact. Thus, rather than reducing prejudice simply through objective conditions of the contact situation, prejudice may be reduced to the extent that we can alleviate group members' concerns and enhance their subjective feelings of acceptance within the contact situation.

☐ The Role of Group Membership Salience in Intergroup Contact

Focusing on people's subjective responses may be a particularly effective strategy for encouraging people to engage in contact and for enhancing their contact experiences. However, the ability for positive shifts in attitudes from such contact to generalize to the outgroup as a whole still depends in part on the degree to which group membership is salient during those intergroup encounters.

As mentioned in our earlier discussion of generalization in Chapter 3, intergroup researchers have long debated the role of group membership salience in promoting positive outcomes of intergroup contact. On the one hand, Brewer and Miller (1984; see also Miller, 2002) note that an emphasis on group differences, particularly at the early stages of intergroup contact, can lead to greater tension and perceptions of conflict between groups. They therefore recommend that the salience of group membership be reduced through processes of *decategorization*. Decategorization strategies seek to differentiate among outgroup members to induce greater perceptions of variability in the outgroup (Harrington & Miller, 1992), and to personalize outgroup members through directing attention to their individual characteristics (Fiske & Neuberg, 1999) and the sharing of personally relevant information (Miller, 2002). By reducing group membership salience through processes of decategorization, people can begin to move beyond perceiving outgroup members merely on the basis of group membership, and this change should minimize tension and conflict during intergroup contact (Bettencourt, Brewer, Rogers-Croak, & Miller, 1992; Miller, Brewer, & Edwards, 1985).

On the other hand, Hewstone and Brown (1986; see also Brown & Hewstone, 2005) have argued that broader shifts in intergroup attitudes will only result when positive contact experiences with an outgroup member are recognized as *intergroup* in nature. Thus, they support a model of *categorization*, whereby group membership salience is enhanced and maintained during intergroup contact. Due to the enhanced salience of group membership, positive effects of contact with individual outgroup members will therefore be more likely to generalize to the outgroup as a whole. Providing considerable support for this perspective, these and other authors have shown greater generalization of positive intergroup attitudes when group membership salience is heightened during contact (e.g., Brown et al., 1999; Brown, Eller, Leeds, & Stace, 2007; Van Oudenhoven, Groenewoud, & Hewstone, 1996; Voci & Hewstone, 2003).

Recognizing merits associated with both of these approaches, Pettigrew (1986, 1998) proposed that they be viewed from a sequential perspective. During the initial stages of contact, diminished salience of group membership might help to reduce intergroup tension and facilitate group members' efforts to get to know one another. Then, once contact is established and relationships have begun to develop across group lines, salience of group membership should be reintroduced so that positive shifts in attitudes resulting from the contact can generalize to the intergroup level. Importantly, the sequential perspective benefits from its integration of theoretical principles associated with social categorization (e.g., Brown & Hewstone, 2005; Brown & Turner, 1981; Miller, 2002), and its attention to group members' subjective experiences as intergroup relationships continue to evolve (e.g., Devine & Vasquez, 1998; Tropp, 2006).

In time, a process of *recategorization* may also emerge, whereby members of initially distinct groups come to recognize their shared membership in a *superordinate* category that includes both groups (Gaertner & Dovidio, 2000). Gaertner, Dovidio, and their colleagues have conducted numerous studies in laboratory and field settings showing the benefits of recategorization for improving intergroup attitudes (e.g., Gaertner & Dovidio, 2000; Gaertner, Dovidio, & Bachman, 1996; Gaertner et al., 1994; Gaertner, Mann, Murrell, & Dovidio, 1989). When recategorization occurs, attitudes toward former outgroup members become more positive due to the same categorization processes that govern other forms of ingroup bias. Depending on the relative salience of subgroup and superordinate categories, however, categorization at the superordinate level can be difficult to maintain, or may not always be successfully achieved when groups come into contact (Hornsey & Hogg, 2000; Dovidio, Gaertner, & Saguy, 2009).

Indeed, people often maintain their original ingroup identity together with a superordinate identity. This *dual identity* is possible because the two identities usually operate at different levels. One can be a French Canadian or Scots American without any conflict between the two identities; indeed, in societies that readily accept such dual identities this category becomes a recognized subgroup of its own. However, Gaertner and Dovidio (2000, p. 50) point out that dual identities risk "a double-edged sword." While they can further intergroup harmony, dual identities can also intensify the salience of separate subgroup identities in times of intergroup conflict – as violent outbursts in Northern Ireland and the former Yugoslavia demonstrate.

The salience of group memberships may be introduced into the contact situation in a variety of ways. For example, experimental studies have induced group membership salience by manipulating the perceived typicality of group members (Brown et al., 1999, Study 1; Ensari & Miller, 2002, Study 1; Wilder, 1984) or simply by reminding people about group membership prior to an interaction (Ensari & Miller, Study 2; Hornsey & Hogg, 2000; Van Oudenhoven et al., 1996). Other studies have assessed salience using more subjective approaches, such as by asking about people's awareness of group membership in intergroup contexts (e.g., Mendoza-Denton, Page-Gould, & Pietrzak, 2006; Pinel, 2002), how much they perceive the outgroup members with whom they interact to be typical of their groups (e.g., Islam & Hewstone, 1993), or about how often references to group membership are made when interacting with outgroup members (e.g., Brown et al., 1999, Study 2; Brown et al., 2001).

It is conceivable that varying conceptions of group membership salience would evoke different responses depending on the stage and nature of the intergroup contact in which it is introduced. Referring back to the sequential model, emphasizing group differences early in the intergroup relationship may be especially threatening (e.g., Islam & Hewstone, 1993), whereas discussing group differences once some degree of rapport and trust has been established might help to build cross-group intimacy and understanding (see Nagda, 2006; Tropp, 2008).

Moreover, larger contextual variables may also influence how we interpret and respond to group membership salience in intergroup settings. For example, we may not want to be perceived on the basis of our group membership if we expect to be rejected or treated differently (Frey & Tropp, 2006). But we may wish to have our group membership recognized if we feel it is being subsumed within a broader social category (e.g., Crisp, Stone, & Hall, 2006; Hornsey & Hogg, 2000), or acknowledged if our group's experiences tend to be disregarded or overlooked (e.g., Eggins, Haslam, & Reynolds, 2002; Tropp & Bianchi, 2007). Thus, this body of work suggests that group membership salience is important for generalizing positive outcomes from intergroup contact, yet close attention must be paid to how it is established and subjectively experienced by group members in the intergroup context (Tropp & Bianchi, 2007).

☐ Conclusion

In sum, theory and research have identified several features of the contact situation that promote further reductions in intergroup prejudice. In line with Allport's (1954) contentions, our meta-analytic work shows that conditions such as equal status between groups, common goals, cooperation, and institutional support can enhance contact's ability to reduce prejudice. However, rather than regarding these as essential conditions, they are best described as facilitating conditions that encourage positive contact effects. Moreover, other research has emphasized the important role that salience plays in encouraging positive changes in attitudes to transcend the contact situation and reduce prejudice toward outgroups in general. We strongly support these lines of work. But we also encourage researchers to explore further potential differences in contact effects depending on whether these factors are assessed as objective features of contact situations or as people's subjective responses to those situations.

CHAPTER 6

How Does Intergroup Contact Reduce Prejudice?

Let's continue to explore the subjective responses to contact in the context of meeting different groups for the first time. Suppose your entire childhood took place in a constrained, homogeneous environment, one that lacked any degree of diversity, and your friends, neighbors, and school classmates were all of your own nationality, religion, race, and social class. *yep.* Now imagine how you would feel when you later meet people who are very different – people who contrast sharply with those whom you have known all your life.

The chances are you would feel rather anxious and uncomfortable at first. You would realize that you knew virtually nothing, apart from a few gross group stereotypes, about these different human beings. Nor would you know how they think and feel about the world. Will they accept or reject you? Will they think you are prejudiced against them and their group? And what do they typically think of your ingroup? If they are speaking in a language you do not know, are they talking about you? If you are unfamiliar with their customs, how should you act? Understandably, you might well become anxious and behave with caution.

These are precisely the variables – intergroup knowledge, anxiety, and empathy – that social psychologists have studied intensively to learn just *how* intergroup contact leads to the positive outcomes described in the previous chapters. The straightforward idea is that successful intergroup contact will provide you with useful knowledge about the outgroup, reduce your anxiety in intergroup encounters, and help you to take the perspective of outgroup members and empathize with their concerns. Such changes, it is hypothesized, will in turn reduce prejudice and enhance the potential for meaningful, trusting cross-group relationships.

In other words, these processes will act as *mediators* of the positive relationship between intergroup contact and prejudice reduction. Figure 6.1 illustrates this general process of mediation. Here, intergroup contact relates negatively with the prejudice outcome (Path C), while it relates positively with the proposed mediating variable (Path A). Like intergroup contact, the mediator also relates negatively to prejudice (Path B). To the extent that this variable significantly predicts prejudice (Path B), at the same time as it diminishes the strength of the direct relationship between intergroup contact and prejudice (Path C), it acts as a mediator for the contact–prejudice association. In short, the mediator, through its association with both contact and prejudice, and its ability to account for a significant portion of the contact–prejudice association, helps to explain *how* intergroup contact contributes to reducing prejudice.

To learn just how much the three mediators of interest – knowledge, anxiety, and empathy – contribute to explaining how contact generally reduces prejudice, we need first to estimate Paths A, B, and C for each proposed mediator. Given that different studies in the research literature have examined different variables as potential mediators for the contact–prejudice association, this requires that we (1) identify research studies that test for mediation with at least one of these three variables and (2) obtain coefficients to estimate the strength of the three paths for each mediator examined.

To do this, we began by extending our database using the same meta-analytic procedures described in Chapter 2. Fortunately, given the enormous research attention that intergroup contact has received in recent years, we were able to gather sufficient numbers of studies to conduct these mediational analyses (Pettigrew & Tropp, 2008). Our search of the research literature through June 2005 uncovered 11 studies

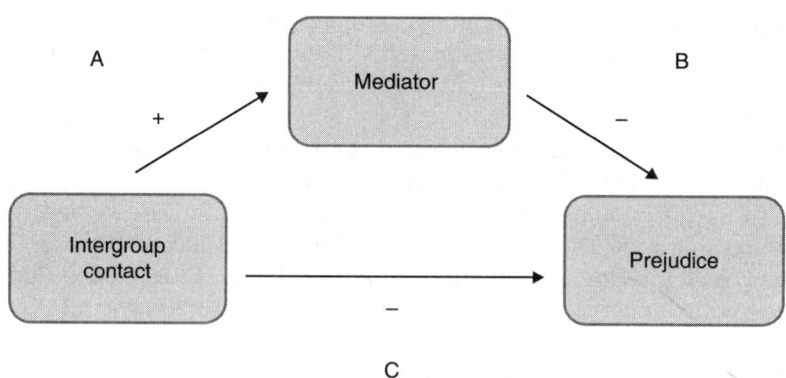

FIGURE 6.1 An illustration of mediation.

with 17 independent samples and 2543 participants that tested knowledge as a mediating process. We also found 45 studies with 60 independent samples and 13,343 participants that tested anxiety reduction as a mediating process. Additionally, we identified nine studies with 14 independent samples and 2362 participants that tested either perspective-taking (cognitive empathy) or feelings of empathy (emotional empathy) as a mediator (see Davis, 1983). Because of their scarcity in the research literature and the fact that these components of empathy are often linked (see Duan & Hill, 1996), we combined these studies to test empathy as a mediating process. In total, then, we uncovered 54 relevant studies with 91 independent samples. Note that the number of participants involved with each potential mediator is far greater than that required to detect mediational effects (Fritz & MacKinnon, 2007).

The next step is to take these mean correlations and, by using three saturated structural equation models (i.e., in which all three paths are specified), obtain the relevant coefficients. This step is necessary to determine the Path B coefficients (mediator-to-prejudice path) while holding constant the Path C coefficients (i.e., contact-to-prejudice path; see Premack & Hunter, 1988; Shadish, 1996). We followed this procedure using random effects models to estimate the coefficients (see Pettigrew & Tropp, 2008, for further details). In the sections that follow, we expand on the conceptual background and analysis regarding each of the tested mediators.

☐ Enhanced General Knowledge of the Outgroup as Mediator

The original idea of early theorists was that intergroup contact facilitated learning about the outgroup, and this new knowledge in turn was assumed to reduce prejudice (see Allport, 1954). This emphasis was in keeping with popular thinking in the United States at the middle of the 20th century. As Chapter 1 described, the Human Relations Movement following World War II advocated formal settings of intergroup contact – such as "Brotherhood Dinners" each February during Black History Month (Pettigrew, 2004a). Recall that the explicit idea of these gatherings was that this kind of interaction would allow the different groups to learn about each other and see how similar they really were. And this process would, it was hoped, lead to greater intergroup acceptance.

Note that this approach focused on general transmission of information as a means of reducing prejudice, while virtually denying actual group differences. But we earlier noted that these well-meaning efforts avoided exploration of such controversial issues as integrated schools and affirmative action. Not surprisingly, Brotherhood Dinners and similar endeavors proved of modest value in improving the nation's intergroup problems. Nonetheless, the Movement directly influenced American social psychology, and, throughout much of the late 20th century, contact research followed Allport's (1954) emphasis on general knowledge as a key mediator.

But was this assumption right? Is enhanced knowledge of the outgroup a valuable result of intergroup contact that promotes prejudice reduction? We know from other research that ignorance contributes to intergroup prejudice, and that corrective information can be useful in improving intergroup attitudes (Stephan & Stephan, 1984). Here, we examine whether enhanced knowledge about the outgroup, in and of itself, is an important mediator of contact's effects.

Figure 6.2 provides an initial answer.[1] Averaging the results of the 17 independent samples that tested knowledge, we find that contact does indeed enhance knowledge about the outgroup (Path A, +.22). But enhanced knowledge has at best only a minor effect in diminishing prejudice (Path B, –.08). Given the large number of participants included in this meta-analytic test, these coefficients are statistically significant at the .0001 level of confidence. But the mediation of contact effects by knowledge appears to be modest. Note that the contact-to-prejudice coefficient in Figure 6.2 is only reduced from .30 to .28. Clearly, intergroup contact typically enhances such knowledge, but the problem is that increased knowledge seems to have at best only a limited effect on prejudice reduction.

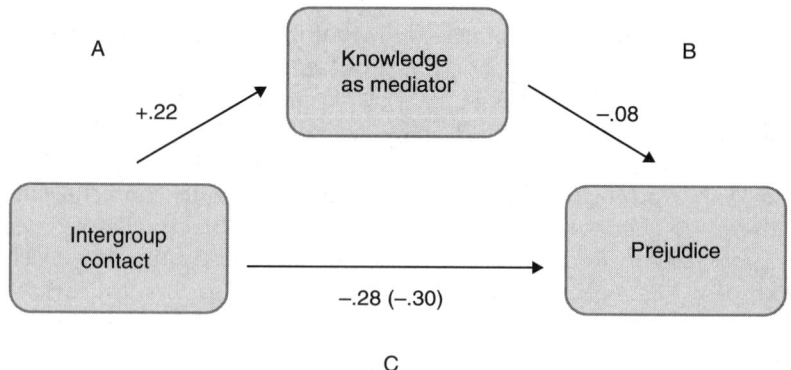

FIGURE 6.2 Enhanced knowledge as mediator of contact–prejudice association.

Reduced Anxiety as Mediator

More recently, researchers have been testing other potential mediators of the contact–prejudice association. Stephan and Stephan (1985), in a much cited paper, drew attention to the critical role of threat in intergroup contact and the corresponding arousal of anxiety. Research inspired by their work has shown repeatedly that intergroup contact typically reduces intergroup threat and anxiety (Blascovich et al., 2001; Page-Gould et al., 2008; Paolini, Hewstone, Cairns, & Voci, 2004; Pettigrew, 1998; Stephan et al., 1999, 2002; Voci & Hewstone, 2003).

Consider the findings of a seminal experiment by Blascovich and his colleagues on the Santa Barbara campus of the University of California (Blascovich et al., 2001). These authors showed in a laboratory setting that interaction with physically stigmatized partners caused threat and anxiety responses measured in three different ways – physiologically, behaviorally, and subjectively. Moreover, in a separate study, they found that Whites who have had prior interracial contact revealed significantly lower levels of physiological stress and self-reported anxiety when interacting with an African American than Whites without such prior contact experiences.

Similarly, using cortisol reactivity as a physiological indicator of stress, Page-Gould et al. (2008) experimentally demonstrated significant attenuation in stress responses over the course of repeated contact meetings between White and Latino undergraduates. By the third contact meeting, the anxious responses of participants randomly assigned to interact with a cross-group partner were comparable to those of participants assigned to interact with a same-group partner. Moreover, those paired with a cross-group partner generally reported *lower* levels of anxiety in subsequent daily diaries than those who were assigned to a same-group partner.

But how important is this anxiety phenomenon as a mediator for contact effects? From our meta-analysis of studies that investigated this issue, we obtain the coefficients shown in Figure 6.3. Unlike the paths for knowledge depicted in Figure 6.2, the coefficients for both Path A and Path B are substantial. And Path B remains strong even after Path C is entered into the model; indeed, the direct contact-to-prejudice path represented by Path C is weakened by the inclusion of Path B. Together, these results suggest that intergroup contact contributes to reducing anxiety, and, in turn, the diminished anxiety predicts lower levels of prejudice. By these estimates, mediation through anxiety reduction appears to account for almost a third of contact's effects on prejudice.

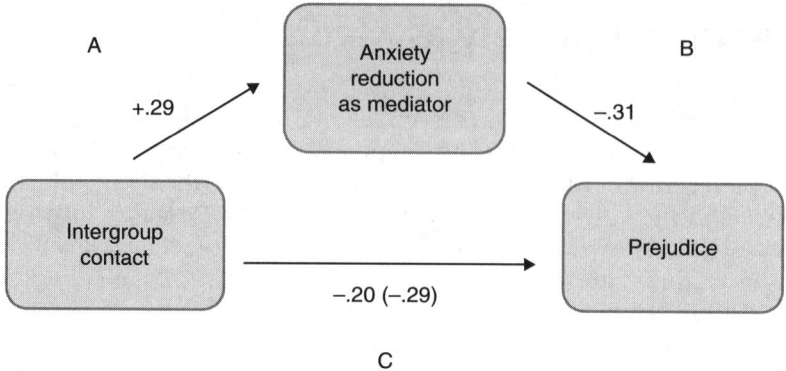

FIGURE 6.3 Anxiety reduction as mediator of contact–prejudice association.

☐ Empathy as Mediator

Social psychology's interest in empathy has been renewed by a series of impressive studies by Batson and his colleagues at the University of Kansas (e.g., Batson, Ahmad, & Stocks, 2004; Batson, Lishner, Cook, & Sawyer, 2005). In one set of studies, Batson et al. (1997b) induced empathy for targets from stigmatized groups (e.g., a young woman with AIDS, a homeless man) and found that it improved participants' attitudes toward their entire groups. In a more extreme test of this phenomenon, these authors induced empathy toward a member of a highly stigmatized group especially likely to provoke hostility (i.e., convicted murderers) and still showed the effect. Only a slight difference emerged between the high empathy and low empathy controls when they were tested immediately following the experiment. But after 1–2 weeks a larger and statistically significant difference emerged, such that participants who had empathized with a single murderer held more positive attitudes toward murderers as a group.

Inspired by this work, research has examined empathy as a possible mediator of the association between intergroup contact and prejudice. Intergroup contact, and especially that involving close, cross-group friendship, may enable one to take the perspective of outgroup members and empathize with their concerns. This new perspective could in turn contribute to improved intergroup attitudes, thereby acting as a mediator in contact's reduction of prejudice.

Consistent with this view, survey research by Turner, Hewstone, and Voci (2007) reveals that self-disclosure during contact predicts less anti-Asian prejudice among White British high-school students through increasing empathy toward Asians. Experimental research by Vescio, Sechrist, and Paolucci (2003) demonstrates how inducing people to engage in perspective-taking can promote more favorable racial attitudes. Similarly, Galinsky and Moskowitz (2010) show experimentally that perspective-taking can decrease both conscious and non-conscious outgroup stereotyping as well as increase the overlap between representations of the self and the outgroup (in this case, the elderly). Further, using Tajfel's (1970) famous minimal group paradigm, they demonstrate that perspective-taking reduced ingroup bias by enhancing the evaluation of the outgroup. Another study revealed that perspective-taking increased the willingness of majority members to join in collective action against hate crimes directed at both homosexuals and Blacks (Mallett, Huntsinger, Sinclair, & Swim, 2008a).

These research results mesh well with closely related research. For instance, McFarland (2010), using both student and adult samples, found that empathy correlates negatively with prejudice, even after controlling for the strong correlations of prejudice with social dominance and authoritarianism. Additionally, Hodson (2008) showed among Whites high in social dominance that enhanced empathy mediated the relationship between greater contact with Blacks and lower intergroup prejudice. And Dhont and colleagues (under review-b) found that close cross-racial friendships altered how their young adult participants thought about racial groups in general. They demonstrated that contact lessened essentialist views of the outgroup, or beliefs that outgroup members are fundamentally alike with shared inherent traits. Such thinking is closely related to prejudice and the very opposite of empathy.

These numerous examples illustrate the broader trend that we observed in our meta-analytic test of empathy as a mediator. As shown in Figure 6.4, empathy importantly mediates the contact–prejudice association. Comparing favorably to the mediational role of anxiety reduction, the data suggest that roughly 30% of the contact–prejudice association is mediated through empathy.

From the results shown in Figures 6.2–6.4, we can employ the Sobel test to gauge the magnitude and statistical significance of the three mediational processes under consideration (Preacher & Hayes, 2004; Preacher & Leonardelli, 2006; Sobel, 1982). All three mediators reveal significant mediation. Although the mediation effect for knowledge – about 5% – is constrained by the small mean negative correlation between knowledge and prejudice, the Sobel test for mediation is significant ($Z = -3.87$, $p < .001$). Much stronger effects emerge from Sobel tests for anxiety reduction (31%, $Z = -26.55$, $p < .0001$) and empathy (30%, $Z = -12.43$, $p < .0001$) as mediators of the contact–prejudice association.

To check on these results further, we repeated the entire analysis using only homogeneous sets of samples. We determined homogeneous samples

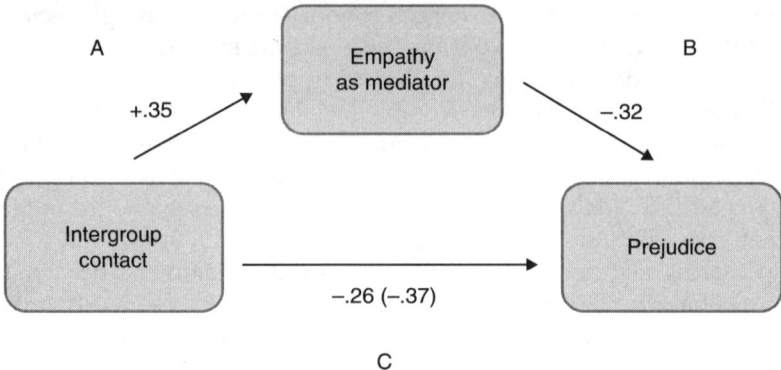

FIGURE 6.4 Empathy as mediator of contact–prejudice association.

by using Johnson's (1993) DSTAT program. One by one, we removed the most extreme outliers until homogeneity was obtained in each of our nine subsets of samples (see Hedges & Olkin, 1985).[2] These additional analyses are useful because they focus only on subsets of samples whose mean effects show no more variation around the mean than would be expected from sampling error alone. As such, this approach eliminates the need for the random effects model and addresses the issue of outliers by removing them.

Using this approach, our initial findings are confirmed. Sobel tests for each of the three mediators remain significant even with the reduced numbers of samples necessary to achieve homogeneity: knowledge ($Z = -3.64, p < .001$), anxiety reduction ($Z = -13.44, p < .0001$), and empathy ($Z = -9.87, p < .0001$). All three continue to explain part of the contact-to-reduced-prejudice effect, although empathy and anxiety reduction remain far more important than knowledge.

☐ Examining Relationships among Mediators

Nonetheless, the data we have presented thus far are slightly deceptive in that they do not indicate how these mediational processes act together. Some of the studies tested two of the mediators, but only one tested all three. This issue is important to consider because the three mediating variables are themselves intercorrelated. In those few studies where two or three of the mediators are used with the same samples, anxiety correlates negatively with both knowledge ($r = -.24; k = 7, N = 1367$) and empathy ($r = -.32; k = 8, N = 1636$). Knowledge and empathy, however, are not related ($r = +.05, k = 2, N = 704$).

We have only nine samples with which to test a saturated path model that employs both anxiety and empathy as mediators for the contact–prejudice relationship. Figure 6.5 presents the results, with all paths represented as standardized betas and statistically significant at the $p < .001$ level of confidence. Note that while anxiety and empathy are significantly and negatively related, the two variables independently and significantly contribute to mediating the contact–prejudice association.

These mediators may function sequentially, in line with our discussions of sequential processes from Chapter 5. Anxiety reduction may well be most crucial during the initial stages of intergroup contact (Blascovich et al., 2001; Page-Gould et al., 2008), thereby making decategorization a particularly useful strategy when groups first come together (Brewer & Miller, 1984). By contrast, enhanced empathy may become more important with continued contact and lowered anxiety, as group members begin to disclose more to each other and share experiences and perspectives (Turner et al., 2007). At this point, reintroducing the group categorization may be especially critical for ensuring that positive outcomes of these individual contacts translate into a greater ability to empathize and improve intergroup attitudes. Indeed, important findings by Voci and Hewstone (2003; see also Harwood et al., 2005) show that contact is generally effective in reducing intergroup anxiety, but particularly when group categorizations are highly salient.

There may even be a more rigid causal sequence operating whereby initial anxiety must first be reduced through intergroup contact before

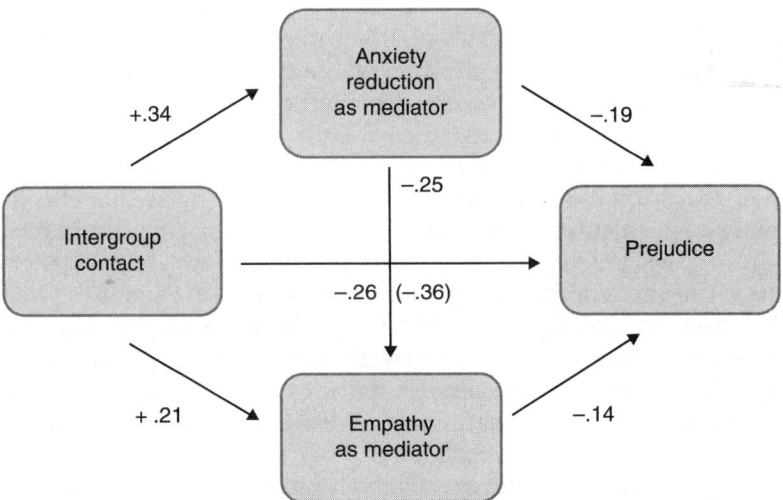

FIGURE 6.5 Saturated path model including anxiety reduction and empathy as mediators of the contact–prejudice association.

increased empathy can effectively develop and contribute to prejudice reduction. This possibility is supported by prior work showing that anxiety in intergroup settings can induce greater reliance on stereotypes and contribute to less favorable impressions of outgroup members (e.g., Wilder, 1993; Wilder & Shapiro, 1989). Such a causal sequence could be tested using a longitudinal survey approach (Binder et al., 2009; Sidanius et al., 2008) as well as experimentally (e.g., Blascovich et al., 2001; Page-Gould et al., 2008). More longitudinal and experimental work is needed to understand how these processes of anxiety reduction and empathy function in concert.

☐ Potential Limitations of This Analysis

Several potential limitations of this analysis must be considered before we discuss the broader implications of the results. First, we have used a relatively new form of analysis – assembling data from multiple meta-analyses to develop structural equation models to determine mediation effects. While acknowledging its usefulness, Shadish (1996) emphasizes two potential problems with this method. First, difficulties can arise when different subsets of studies are used to estimate coefficients within the same test for mediation. We avoided this problem by employing only the same sets of independent samples for all three paths of each mediational test. At the same time, we do use somewhat different, though overlapping, sets of samples for the three separate mediational tests. Thus, differences in magnitudes of effects found between the three mediators could in small part reflect the somewhat diverse subsets of samples in each mediation analysis.

A second issue involves the homogeneity of effects. Shadish (1996) notes that it is optimal if one can achieve homogeneity of effects across samples – that is, if the estimated correlations are similar across samples testing each mediational path. As is typical of most meta-analytic datasets, none of the original subsets of cases revealed homogeneous effects. We therefore also calculated the mediational paths for only homogeneous subsets of cases. We saw that this procedure yields very similar patterns of results. By far, general knowledge about the outgroup remains the weakest of the three mediators tested. While the homogeneity tests eliminate problems with outliers, they necessarily involve fewer samples as well as slightly different sets of samples within the same mediational analysis. Nonetheless, the comparability of the results provides additional confidence for our basic findings.

Still, a third issue concerns the relatively small number of samples available in the literature with which to conduct these analyses. We are confident that these studies and samples comprise the great majority of relevant cases through June 2005. Note also that the number of participants involved with each potential mediator is far greater than that required to detect such mediational effects (Fritz & MacKinnon, 2007). Nonetheless, to maximize our inclusion of cases, we assiduously collected relevant unpublished research, following the procedures outlined in Chapter 2. Altogether, 5 of the 17 knowledge samples, 14 of the 60 anxiety reduction samples, and 10 of the 14 empathy samples were unpublished at the time of our analysis.

The inclusion of these unpublished cases provides us with the opportunity to test for publication biases in our data – always a threat to meta-analytic and qualitative reviews alike, as discussed previously in Chapter 2. Specifically, we tested whether publication status moderates the mediation paths between contact and prejudice, contact and each mediator, and between each mediator and prejudice. Significantly larger coefficients for the published samples would indicate publication bias.

Comparisons between published and unpublished samples for the six paths involving knowledge and empathy showed no significant effects ($p > .10$). In the case of anxiety, only one path was moderated by publication status – the contact-to-anxiety relationship – but in the opposite direction from what publication bias would predict. Specifically, the contact-to-anxiety association was significantly stronger ($p = .05$) among the 13 *unpublished* samples (mean $r = -.36$) than among the 47 published samples (mean $r = -.28$). However, the anxiety-to-prejudice association did not significantly differ depending on whether the samples were published (mean $r = +.38$) or unpublished (mean $r = +.41$). Given the typical concern that estimates of mean effects would be greater for published than for unpublished studies (see Coursol & Wagner, 1986; Dickersin, 1997), these results suggest that a strong publication bias is not operating among contact studies examining the mediational processes of knowledge, anxiety reduction, and empathy.[3]

A further concern is that we cannot directly infer causal influences from these findings. We know that bidirectional paths exist in the complex relationship between contact and prejudice that we have not considered here. As we have often noted, research shows that prejudice can restrict intergroup contact at the same time as contact reduces prejudice. Still, the path from contact to prejudice is typically either stronger than or equal to the path from prejudice to contact (see Binder et al., 2009; Butler & Wilson, 1978; Dhont et al., under review-b; Irish, 1952; Pettigrew, 1997a; Powers & Ellison, 1995; Sherif, 1966; Van Dick et al., 2004; Van Laar et al., 2008; Wilson, 1996).

A final limitation is that there are many more mediators and moderators that exist in the complex relationship between intergroup contact and prejudice beyond just the three tested in this research (see Brown & Hewstone, 2005; Stephan, 1987). Although the mediators under test – especially anxiety reduction and empathy – proved important, there remains considerable unexplained variance in the contact-to-prejudice relationship. To predict more of the remaining variance, other mediators must be considered.

☐ Further Mediators of Intergroup Contact

In addition to the focus on affective processes discussed above (and discussed further in Chapters 7 and 8), we propose four additional directions that researchers should pursue to identify additional mediators of the contact–prejudice association. These include: (1) learning about the outgroup's culture, (2) changing intergroup behavior, (3) restructuring the intergroup relationship, and (4) perceiving shifts in intergroup norms (see Blanchard, Lilly, & Vaughn, 1991; De Tezanos-Pinto, Brown, & Bratt, 2010; Frey & Tropp, 2006; Pettigrew, 1998).

Learning About the Outgroup's Culture

We have just noted that general knowledge per se gained from interaction with an outgroup is not a major mediator of contact's influence on prejudice. But the studies used in this test varied greatly in how they defined "knowledge" in relation to the contact that took place. For instance, one study examined general knowledge about mental illness (Holmes et al., 1999); another tested for general interracial knowledge gleaned from a lecture (Hatanaka, 1982); and a third study assessed general knowledge about AIDS and HIV without direct reference to people living with AIDS (Robbins, Cooper, & Bender, 1992).

The early focus on knowledge (Allport, 1954) reasoned that learning about the outgroup would counter negative stereotypes and thus reduce prejudice. However, there is an array of cognitive mechanisms that cause us to deny or explain away evidence that disconfirms our prejudicial thinking (Pettigrew, 1979; Rothbart & John, 1985). Indeed, information that contradicts our prejudices is often hard to accept.

But there is reason to believe that more direct tests of learning processes are important. There are also different ways in which knowledge and learning can be construed in the context of intergroup relations (see Migacheva, Tropp, & Crocker, in press). A major possibility involves the learning of specifically *cultural* information, beyond mere general information, as a means to improve intergroup attitudes. Stephan and Stephan (1984) studied junior high-school students in New Mexico, and they found that contact allowed Anglo children to learn more about Latino culture. This new cultural understanding, in turn, led to more positive attitudes toward their Latino classmates.

The typically positive results of these techniques show that learning more about the outgroup's culture can improve intergroup attitudes (see Gudykunst, 1986; Kim & Gudykunst, 1988). The most prominent of these methods involves the Culture Assimilator program – an ingenious technique developed by Triandis (1994). A sample item reads:

> Imagine yourself as a factory foreman. You notice that every time you speak to a Hispanic worker, he looks down. Why does he persist in doing this? Is he distracted, fearful, respectful or hostile? Which do you think is the most likely reason?
> (Triandis, 1994, pp. 278–279)

If participants choose distracted, fearful, or hostile, the program tells them their response is incorrect and asks them to choose another possibility. When they select respectful, the program tells them it is correct and provides supporting data. In the validating sample, 85% of Hispanic workers picked this answer compared to only 36% of non-Hispanic foremen. The Culture Assimilator consists of many such episodes between people from different cultures, each involving a critical incident of cultural misunderstanding. The technique has proven effective in various settings for teaching subjective elements of another culture (e.g., Stephan & Stephan, 1984), and trainees become less ethnocentric and biased.

Observe, however, that the Culture Assimilator functions through a *cognitive* process and is not intended to effect direct change on behavioral or affective processes. As Triandis (1994, p. 280) concludes, "Assimilator training increases cognitive complexity. Cognitive complexity makes it possible to consider the subjective culture of the other cultural group as 'valid' and thus lessens prejudice." So as a cognitive process, it neither reduces the preferred social distance from the outgroup nor increases liking for the outgroup. Thus, related research speaks to the value of also focusing on *behavioral* and *affective* processes to improve attitudes through intercultural contact (see Gudykunst, 1986; Spencer-Rodgers & McGovern, 2002).

Research on acculturation and intercultural communication has begun to explore how processes of intercultural communication contribute to attitudes toward people from different cultural groups (see Berry, 2006; Dihn & Bond, 2008). Moreover, Gudykunst and his colleagues have stressed the importance of learning to navigate relationships across cultures, and how gains in competence and communication effectiveness can diminish anxiety about intercultural contact (Gudykunst & Hammer, 1988; Stephan et al., 1999) and enhance positive views and interest in interactions with members of other cultural groups (Lee & Gudykunst, 2001). Similarly, emerging social psychological research indicates that expecting to be able to act effectively in cross-group interactions can reduce our anxieties and inclinations to avoid intergroup contact (Butz & Plant, 2006;

Plant, Butz, & Tartakovsky, 2008). Moreover, multicultural learning from contact in living and adapting to foreign cultures can even facilitate creativity (Maddux & Galinsky, 2009).

Some types of knowledge, however, can have detrimental effects. Learning about how your ingroup has harmed and discriminated against the outgroup can backfire; it can lead to collective guilt, which often results in *increased* prejudice. With two longitudinal studies of non-indigenous (White) Chileans and indigenous Mapuche students, Zagefka, Gonzalez, Brown, and Manzi (under review) found that intergroup contact can enhance self-assessed knowledge for the majority group, which in turn can lead to increased guilt, group salience, intergroup anxiety, and finally prejudice. Such a guilt sequence triggered by greater knowledge could be partly responsible for the restricted effect of knowledge we have found generally. By contrast, the Mapuche respondents, with grievances but no guilt, revealed the usual pattern of more knowledge associated with less anxiety and prejudice. Thus, specific types of knowledge, especially those involving culture, can reduce prejudice; some types, such as historical information about past outgroup mistreatment, may elevate prejudice.

Together, these bodies of research suggest that there is much more to be understood regarding the mediating role of learning about the outgroup in intergroup contact. Intergroup learning may include cognitive, affective, and behavioral processes that involve our understanding of group differences and our perceived ability to navigate cross-group interactions successfully. Thus, rather than focusing merely on gaining general knowledge about outgroup members, future investigations would benefit from a more multifaceted examination of intergroup cultural learning and how it shapes contact's influence on prejudice.

Changing Intergroup Behavior

Conventional wisdom holds that people must be persuaded to engage in new behavior – that attitude change must precede behavioral change. But literally hundreds of social psychological studies have shown the efficacy of precisely the opposite causal sequence: *behavior change is often the precursor of attitude change* (see Olson & Stone, 2005, for a review).

This sequence is important for intergroup contact effects. New situations that involve new norms require us to behave differently and to conform to new expectations. When these expectations include acceptance of outgroup members, this behavior itself can produce attitude change. Several studies show that intergroup situations infused with multiculturalism ideologies can lessen both implicit and explicit forms of intergroup bias (Correll, Park, & Smith, 2008; Richeson & Nussbaum, 2004; Wolsko, Park, Judd, & Wittenbrink, 2000). Moreover, compared to those in racially homogeneous groups, Whites in racially heterogeneous groups have been shown to exchange a broader array of information and engage in more thorough processing of that information, as well as being more open to racially sensitive discussions of group differences (Sommers, 2006; Sommers, Warp, & Mahoney, 2008). These trends demonstrate how, when we are faced with new expectations advocating racial diversity and inclusiveness, our old prejudices may conflict with our new behavior. In turn, we can resolve the cognitive dissonance caused in this new situation by altering our old attitudes (Aronson, 1997). Consequently, optimally structured intergroup contact offers a means of behavior modification, with new behavior leading to changed attitudes.

Here, it is important to note that changes in prejudiced attitudes can result as a by-product of our participation and behavior in intergroup settings. For instance, though students' primary goal in cooperative work groups is to learn the course material, they often show greater cross-racial friendship choices after working in racially diverse groups (Aronson & Bridgeman, 1979; Aronson & Patnoe, 1997; Slavin, 1979). White student athletes who play team sports with higher percentages of Black teammates report more positive attitudes toward Blacks in general and show greater support for granting scholarship preference to qualified racial minority students (Brown et al., 2003). Similar trends have also been observed in the military, where working alongside Blacks leads many Whites to experience positive contact with Blacks during their off-duty hours, which predicts their more positive intergroup attitudes (Butler & Wilson, 1978).

These positive effects of behavior change also benefit from repeated contact. As repetition itself can lead to greater liking (Zajonc, 1968; Zebrowitz et al., 2008), repeated contact experiences are likely to make formerly strange intergroup encounters seem more comfortable and normal. In time, the formerly "new" situation seems normative and "right" – "the way things ought to be." In part, this is due to the fact that with more positive intergroup experiences, the more we become able to envision positive relations with outgroup members rather than automatically anticipating the worst in relations with them (see Frey & Tropp, 2006; Tropp, 2008). Indeed, an intriguing set of studies shows that cross-group interactions are often more positive than we expect them to be (Mallett, Wilson, & Gilbert, 2008b).

Recent research also shows that people's expectations for contact can be enhanced by having them focus on similarities with outgroup members (Mallett et al., 2008b) or by having them focus on one of their cross-group friendships prior to interacting with an unknown outgroup member (Page-Gould, Mendoza-Denton, Alegre, & Siy, 2010). Moreover, repeated contact and reminders of prior positive contact can contribute to our sense of efficacy about being able to navigate cross-group interactions successfully (Butz & Plant, 2006). This enhanced confidence typically predicts greater approach tendencies in contact (see Plant & Devine, 2003). Thus, repeated positive contact experiences should reduce prejudice and improve intergroup relations more broadly through causing shifts in our expectations for and willingness to engage in future contact (Tropp, 2003, 2008).

Perceiving Shifts in Intergroup Norms

Such positive effects of intergroup contact are likely to be enhanced further to the extent that we receive repeated rewards for this new behavior. Here, the norms we perceive either in approval or disapproval of our contact with other groups are likely to be a strong motivating force underlying intergroup attitudes and behavior (Blanchard et al., 1991; Minard, 1952; Pettigrew, 1959, 1991).

Edmonds and Killen (2009) found that Black and White adolescents who perceive that their parents have negative racial attitudes are less likely to experience intimacy in their cross-racial relationships, such as by dating a person from another race or bringing a cross-race friend to their home. Migacheva and Tropp (2008) examined similar relationships among Black and White middle-school students who were asked about their contact experiences and perceived norms of ingroup peers. They found that the relationship between intergroup contact and the desire to make cross-group friends was mediated by perceived ingroup norms. More specifically, greater contact predicted a stronger desire to make cross-group friends among those students who perceived that friends from their own racial group would also wish to have cross-group friends.

Parallel findings have been observed in the case of indirect or extended contact (Wright et al., 2008; Wright, Aron, McLaughlin-Volpe, & Ropp, 1997). When we see members of our own group having contact with outgroup members, it changes our view of what the ingroup norms must be. Even without direct contact experience, this altered perception of ingroup norms can act to diminish one's prejudice against the outgroup (Pettigrew et al., 2007c; Wright et al., 1997) and enhance one's expectations for future contact (Gómez, Tropp, & Fernandez, in press). Turner, Hewstone, Voci, and Vonofakou (2008) examined perceived ingroup and outgroup norms as potential mediators between indirect contact and intergroup attitudes among White British undergraduates toward the Indian-British. They found that both perceived ingroup norms and outgroup norms significantly mediate the relationship between indirect contact and intergroup attitudes, beyond what can be predicted by the mediating role of intergroup anxiety.

We know that vicarious contact of various types, even from television viewing, can erode prejudice and ease the anxiety that often accompanies interracial contact (e.g., Fujioka, 1999; Gómez & Huici, 2008; Graves, 1999; Herek & Capitanio, 1997; Mazziotta, Mummendey, Wright, & Jung, 2010; Schiappa, Gregg, & Hewes, 2005, 2006). Part of this process involves the perception of norm changes and part is mediated by a positive change in meta-stereotypes – what you believe the outgroup thinks of your ingroup (Gómez & Huici, 2008; Vorauer, Main, & O'Connell, 1998).

Comparable findings have been obtained by De Tezanos-Pinto and colleagues (2010) in their study of Norwegian adolescent attitudes toward Turkish, Pakistani, and Indian immigrants. These investigators showed direct contact to be mediated by the reduction of anxiety, but indirect contact to be mediated by both anxiety reduction and by changes in the perception of ingroup norms. Thus, emerging studies have begun to reveal that norms often play an important mediational role in both direct and indirect forms of contact, and future work must enhance our understanding of precisely how they operate.

Restructuring the Intergroup Relationship

A fourth mediating process of positive contact effects involves restructuring how we view the intergroup relationship. This may involve a variety of aspects, including how we appraise the ingroup in relation to other groups (Pettigrew, 1997a), how much overlap we see between our own group and other groups (Aron & McLaughlin-Volpe, 2001; Wright et al., 2008), and how much we recognize our own groups and other groups as part of broader, shared superordinate categories (Gaertner & Dovidio, 2000).

While they suggest somewhat different approaches, what these aspects share is the view that positive intergroup relations can be achieved when people shift their understanding of relationships between the ingroup and the outgroup (see Frey & Tropp, 2006, for an extended discussion). We begin to see that ingroup norms and customs are not the only ways to manage the social world, a perspective that makes us less provincial in how we relate to other groups in general (Pettigrew, 1997a). Our perceptions of our own group memberships broaden and become more complex (Brewer, 2008; Gaertner & Dovidio, 2000). In turn, these trends can lead us to regard diversity and contact with outgroups as more valuable and important (see Adesokan, Van Dick, Ullrich, & Tropp, in press; Tropp & Bianchi, 2006; Van Dick et al., 2004), and we feel more compelled to treat members of other groups as we would treat members of our own group (Aron et al., 2004). Such processes also allow us to discern differences among people in the outgroup. Now we can recognize that outgroup members possess the same variability among themselves as we long knew was true of our own group (Islam & Hewstone, 1993; Oaker & Brown, 1986; Paolini et al., 2004).

A substantial part of this restructuring process often involves having less contact with the ingroup as a result of interacting more with the outgroup. Wilder and Thompson (1980) found that ingroup contact influenced bias toward an outgroup. They covaried contact both with the ingroup and the outgroup in an experiment using student participants. While it had no impact on ingroup ratings, less ingroup contact itself led to less bias toward the outgroup. This experimental finding was replicated with longitudinal survey data among a racially diverse sample of college students in the large UCLA study described earlier (Levin et al., 2003; Sidanius et al., 2008).

This phenomenon also underlines the important point that attitudes toward ingroups and outgroups do not constitute a zero-sum relationship. That is, thinking better of an outgroup does not require disparagement of your own group. Often we can continue to think highly of our own groups while coming to like and appreciate other groups (Duckitt, Callaghan, & Wagner, 2005). And, under some conditions to be discussed in Chapter 11, the reverse can even develop – that is, we can also come to think less of both our ingroup and the outgroup (Putnam, 2007). This demonstrated process reverses the widely believed thesis advanced by Sumner (1906) and described in Chapter 1. Recall that he held that almost all groups are culturally ethnocentric, and this ingroup aggrandizement virtually guarantees rejection of outgroups and enhanced intergroup conflict. Repeated research in different social science disciplines using a variety of methods has led to the rejection of this thesis (Brewer, 1999; Brewer & Campbell, 1976; Pettigrew, 2004b; Putnam, 2007).

☐ Conclusion

Overall, using both meta-analyses and structural equation models, our analyses demonstrate the power of two major mediators of the intergroup contact effect on prejudice. Anxiety reduction is crucially important and may well be the central initiator to the entire process. Once our anxiety is reduced and we grow comfortable in the intergroup situation, we can begin to relate effectively to members of other groups. Empathy processes appear equally important, such that prejudice lessens as we become more able to sense how outgroup members view and feel about the world. Indeed, in his famous 1963 address on race relations, President John Kennedy alluded to this process when he challenged White Americans to "walk in the shoes" of African Americans.

While anxiety reduction and empathy help to explain intergroup contact effects, the original idea of general knowledge about the outgroup as a mediator proves to be of only minor significance. However, it seems likely that richer and more direct cultural conceptualizations of knowledge could bear stronger mediation effects in future research. Yet even these three mediators explain only part of the contact process. Like most phenomena, the more we learn about intergroup contact, the more complex it becomes, and more research is needed to understand other processes in operation. We suggest four broad possibilities, including learning about the outgroup's culture, changing intergroup behavior, perceiving shifts in intergroup norms, and restructuring the intergroup relationship.

☐ Notes

1 The contact-to-prejudice relationships in these analyses are considerably larger than the $r = -.21$ mean effect that we observed in our larger meta-analysis of intergroup contact effects described in Chapter 2. This difference in magnitude reflects the fact that half of these mediational studies were conducted after 2000 and were not included in our earlier work. Our previous analysis found that the mean effect size between contact and prejudice rose with every decade after 1970 – largely a function of more rigorous research methods used in recent intergroup contact research (see Pettigrew & Tropp, 2006). And this trend continued for the studies conducted after 2000.
2 The homogeneity of each subset of effect sizes was tested with the homogeneity statistic Q that has an approximate chi-square distribution with $k-1$ degrees of freedom, where k is the number of effect sizes (Hedges & Olkin, 1985). When Q is no longer significant ($p > .05$), the null hypothesis of homogeneity cannot be rejected.
3 This conclusion is strengthened further by the fact that with six comparisons for publication bias (two mediational paths for each of the three mediators) there is a 26% chance that one of the comparisons would be expected to be significant at the .05 level by chance alone.

CHAPTER 7

Does Intergroup Contact Reduce All Aspects of Prejudice?

In addition to exploring the paths by which contact reduces prejudice, we must also consider the kinds of "prejudice" we seek to reduce through intergroup contact. Specifically, when we bring groups together, what are we hoping to accomplish? Are we seeking to change what people *think* about other groups, how they and their groups *feel* toward other groups, or how they *believe* outgroups should be treated? Defining our goals for outcomes of intergroup contact is of crucial importance, yet this issue is often overlooked.

Social psychological research indicates many ways in which attitudes may be defined, and it is commonly understood to be a multifaceted concept. Attitudes possess cognitive (e.g., thoughts and perceptions), affective (e.g., feelings and evaluations), and sometimes even behavioral components (e.g., intended actions; see Breckler & Wiggins, 1989; Eagly & Chaiken, 1993; Ostrom, 1969; Zanna & Rempel, 1988). In the context of prejudiced attitudes, researchers have similarly distinguished between *cognitive dimensions*, which comprise one's perceptions, stereotypes, and judgments about a group (Ashmore & Del Boca, 1981; Katz & Hass, 1988; Ostrom, Skowronski, & Nowak, 1994), and *affective dimensions*, which involve one's feelings and emotional responses to a group (Esses, Haddock, & Zanna, 1993; Smith, 1993; Stangor et al., 1991; Wagner & Christ, 2007).

Surprisingly, most of the intergroup contact literature has neither acknowledged nor delineated between these quite different types of outcomes in its quest to identify contact effects. Instead, as Chapter 1 mentioned, debates have waged for decades regarding whether intergroup contact can lead to meaningful reductions in prejudice (e.g., Ford, 1986; Jackson, 1993; Pettigrew, 1971; Riordan, 1978; Rothbart & John, 1985).

We suspect that much of the divergence in these perspectives stems from an overemphasis on the general question of *whether* intergroup contact reduces prejudice. We therefore explore how different dimensions of prejudice bear different relationships to intergroup contact (see Brigham, 1993, for a related argument). More specifically, we contend that different branches of the contact literature have focused on different dimensions of intergroup relationships, and in line with the discussion of mediation in Chapter 6, we propose that affective dimensions are especially critical for understanding the links between intergroup contact and prejudice. Here we review the research literature that supports this prediction.

☐ Cognitive Processes and the Potential for Reducing Prejudice

Reflecting a general emphasis on cognition in psychology, cognitively oriented research on intergroup processes flourished throughout the 1970s. This era of work emphasized the role of categorization in stereotyping (Hamilton, 1981; Hamilton, Stroessner, & Driscoll, 1994) and the cognitive functions that underlie social perception and intergroup bias (Rothbart & Lewis, 1994). The newly emerging cognitive emphasis marked a notable shift from an earlier focus on motivation and affect (see Pettigrew, 1997b, 2004a, for extended discussions).

Due to rigid cognitive processes associated with stereotyping and categorization, researchers began to question whether positive contact experiences with individual outgroup members would generalize to more positive views of the entire outgroup (Rothbart & John, 1985; Wilder, 1986). As mentioned in Chapter 3, Rothbart and John (1985) were prominent in advancing this perspective. They proposed that generalization is largely governed by cognitive processes that negotiate relationships between stereotypical characteristics of a group and characteristics of those individuals who belong to the group (see also Rothbart, 1996; Rothbart & John, 1993). A basic premise of the argument is that, when viewing individuals as potential group representatives, people grant more weight to outgroup individuals who confirm the group stereotype and less weight to those who disconfirm the group stereotype (but see Rojahn & Pettigrew, 1992). Thus, when people are asked to make judgments about that group, individuals who possess characteristics that are consistent with the group stereotype are more likely to come to mind as group "representatives" than those who do not possess those characteristics (see Rothbart, Sriram, & Davis-Stitt, 1996).

In turn, such theorizing about processes of perception and categorization led many social psychologists to question whether positive contact experiences with an individual group member would in fact contribute to more positive views toward the outgroup as a whole (Rothbart & John, 1985, 1993; Wilder, 1986). According to this line of reasoning, as we receive individuating information that disconfirms the group stereotype, we may become *more* likely to see outgroup members in a positive light, but we may also become *less* likely to see them as typical representatives of their group. Obviously, this process would severely limit the potential for any positive changes at the individual level to generalize to positive changes in views of the whole outgroup. Thus, while intergroup contact may lead group members to view each other in a positive light, it is conceivable that such personalized contact experiences may also limit the potential for generalization (Rothbart, 1996; Rothbart & John, 1985; Wilder, 1984). This perspective underscores the importance of group membership salience in intergroup contact (see Brown & Hewstone, 2005; Brown et al., 1999), which we raised earlier in Chapter 3.

☐ Affective Processes and Prejudice Reduction

In contrast to this focus on cognitive processes, research on affective processes in intergroup relationships has tended to be far more optimistic regarding the potential for positive contact experiences to generalize. Since the 1980s, social psychologists have broadened the scope of theory and research on prejudice and intergroup relations to grant increased, if belated, attention to the roles of affect and motivation (see Mackie & Hamilton, 1993; Mackie & Smith, 1998; Pettigrew, 1997b, 2004a). Two seminal volumes on stereotypes, both edited by David Hamilton, highlight the overdue correction. In *Cognitive Processes in Stereotyping and Intergroup Behavior* (Hamilton, 1981), affect received brief mention and mood and emotion are not even in the index. A dozen years later, *Affect, Cognition, and Stereotyping* (Mackie & Hamilton, 1993) centers on the role of affect. In this volume, Eliot Smith (1993) even defined prejudice as "a social emotion experienced with respect to one's social identity as a group member, with an outgroup as a target" (p. 304). And a spate of empirical work using a variety of methods supported the critical importance of affect for prejudice (Dijker, 1987; Edwards & von Hippel, 1995; Esses et al., 1993; Pettigrew, 1997a, 1997b; Stangor et al., 2001; Wagner, Christ, & Pettigrew, 2008).

Corresponding to this dramatic shift, much of the recent contact literature emphasizes the importance of affective processes in intergroup relationships, both in terms of the bonds we establish with outgroup members through contact and the intergroup outcomes that can result from such contact (see Pettigrew, 1998). To date, much of this work has explored the functions of *affective ties* with outgroup members, such as feelings of comfort and liking that develop through close, cross-group relationships (e.g., Herek & Capitanio, 1996; Levin et al., 2003; McLaughlin-Volpe, Aron, Wright, & Reis, 2000; Paolini et al., 2004; Pettigrew, 1997b). We will elaborate on the role of close, cross-group friendships in Chapter 8, but findings from this body of research typically find that close relationships with outgroup members help to establish affective ties with the outgroup, which in turn encourage the generalization of positive feelings toward the outgroup as whole.

☐ Differentiating between Affective and Cognitive Outcomes of Contact

We emphasize here how these varying emphases on affective and cognitive processes suggest contrasting views regarding the potential for positive contact outcomes to generalize. Researchers who focus on *affective* dimensions propose that affective ties to outgroup members can promote positive feelings toward the entire outgroup. By contrast, researchers who focus on *cognitive* dimensions suggest that the inertial nature of stereotyping and categorization renders the generalization of positive contact outcomes extremely difficult. Viewing these traditions together (Mackie & Smith, 1998), we believe that a straightforward reconciliation and integration of these traditions is possible, depending on the dimensions on which we focus. Rather than pursuing the general question of *whether* positive outcomes of contact will or will not generalize, we investigate the *kinds* of contact outcomes that may be more or less likely to generalize. And based on the prior work we have reviewed, we propose that affective outcomes of intergroup contact are more likely to generalize than cognitive outcomes (see Tropp & Pettigrew, 2005a).

By emphasizing this distinction, we do not wish to imply that cognition and affect are entirely independent (see Eagly & Chaiken, 1993). Much recent work has explored the complex bidirectional interplay between cognitive and affective processes (see Mackie & Hamilton, 1993). Rather, we raise the distinction because we believe that it highlights different ways in which we can conceive of intergroup relationships and respond to outgroup members as the targets of our attitudes. In focusing on cognitive dimensions, such as making judgments and stating beliefs, we assume the role of relatively detached observers as we evaluate outgroup targets.

By contrast, when focusing on affective dimensions, we shift the bases of our attitudes such that they become more relational in nature, reflecting our feelings toward outgroup members in the context of our relationships and experiences with them (see Esses & Dovidio, 2002; Zajonc, 1980; Zanna & Rempel, 1988, for related arguments). Thus, because affective ties with outgroup members are established through intergroup contact – and particularly ties that involve close, cross-group relationships – it is likely that such contact would predict greater shifts on affective dimensions of prejudice than on cognitive dimensions of prejudice.

In line with this view, Wolsko, Park, Judd, and Bachelor (2003) demonstrate that contact can promote positive changes on some aspects of prejudice but not on others. In their study, participants interacted with an outgroup member and indicated both their evaluations of outgroup members in general and the extent to which they believed stereotypical characteristics applied to the outgroup as a whole. These authors showed that contact with a single outgroup member significantly enhanced participants' evaluations of outgroup members, yet did relatively little to affect the extent to which they applied stereotypes to the outgroup as a whole.

Similarly, Miller, Smith, and Mackie (2004) examined emotions and stereotypes as possible mediators of intergroup contact's effects on prejudice. Their first study revealed that intergroup contact was more strongly associated with prejudice as measured using feeling thermometer scores ($r = -.22$, $p < .001$) than when prejudice was measured with racial beliefs using modern racism scores ($r = -.04$, ns). Moreover, across two studies, they found that emotions were more likely mediators of contact's effects on both of these prejudice measures than were stereotypes. Together, these programs of research hint at the possibility that affective and cognitive dimensions of prejudice would tend to show different relationships with intergroup contact.

☐ Testing Affective and Cognitive Outcomes of Contact

We therefore conducted a more formal investigation of these issues using our meta-analytic data, by comparing the magnitudes of contact–prejudice effects across several distinct categories of prejudice measures (Tropp & Pettigrew, 2005a). Specifically, we coded each test to determine whether the outcome represented one of four broad types of prejudice measures, based on converging descriptions from the research literature (see Crites, Fabrigar, & Petty, 1994; Dovidio, Brigham, Johnson, & Gaertner, 1996; Dovidio, Esses, Beach, & Gaertner, 2002a; Esses et al., 1993). Two types of measures assess affective dimensions of prejudice (emotions, favorability) and two others focus on cognitive dimensions of prejudice (stereotypes, beliefs).

We conducted these ratings at the test level of analysis, because the studies and samples often included multiple prejudice measures. Measures coded as *emotions* (5.0%) involved felt or anticipated emotions in intergroup contexts (e.g., comfort, sympathy). Measures of *favorability* (12.5%) included general ratings of positivity toward outgroup members, along with ratings of intergroup liking. Measures coded as *beliefs* (38.3%) asked participants to report the degree to which they endorse certain beliefs about the values of a specified outgroup, and their judgments about the lives and experiences of that group in society. Measures coded as *stereotypes* (15.2%) assess the degree to which people hold certain attributes to be associated with an outgroup, including those that ask people to rate outgroup traits in a semantic-differential format (Osgood, Suci, & Tannenbaum, 1957). Prejudice measures not covered by any of these categories (29.0%) were classified as *other*.

As a first step in our analysis, we calculated the proportion of tests corresponding to each type of prejudice measure, so that we could examine trends in contact research over time. Figure 7.1 shows that belief measures have been by far the most commonly used to assess prejudice in contact research. At the same time, the use of stereotype measures peaked during the 1970s and remained strong through the 1980s, while the use of emotion measures waned. But since the 1990s, we observe a resurgence of affect measures.

We then compared mean effects across different types of prejudice measures and found significant variability in contact–prejudice effects depending on how prejudice is assessed. Figure 7.2 shows the mean contact–prejudice effects by type of prejudice measure, and specifically for those that focus on generalization to the outgroup as a whole. Measures

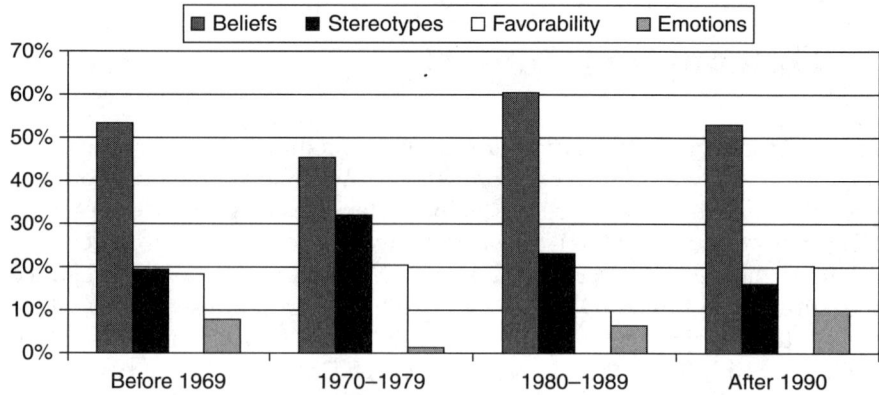

FIGURE 7.1 Proportions of tests recorded for different prejudice outcomes.

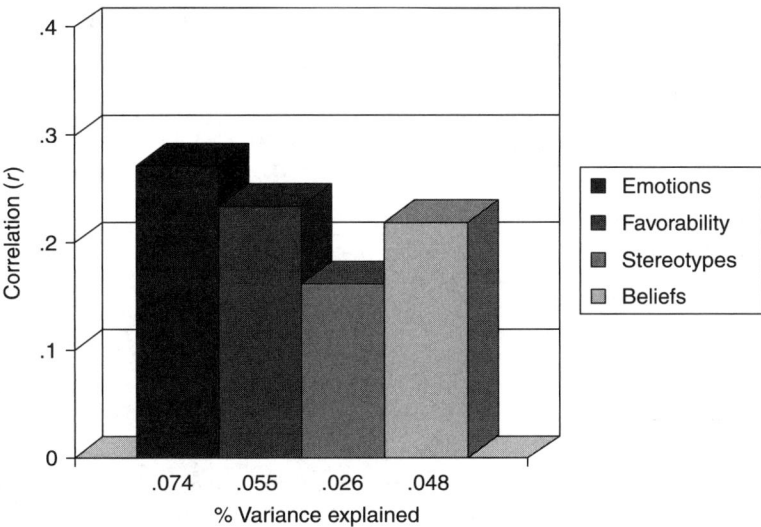

FIGURE 7.2 Mean contact–prejudice effects by type of prejudice measure.

of emotion (mean $r = -.272$) and favorability (mean $r = -.235$) yield especially strong effects, and their mean effects do not differ significantly from each other. Effects obtained with emotion measures were significantly stronger than those obtained for measures of stereotypes (mean $r = -.161$) and beliefs (mean $r = -.219$). In addition, the effects for favorability measures were significantly stronger than those obtained for stereotype measures.

As a next step, we used regression analysis to test whether differences between prejudice measures could uniquely predict contact–prejudice effects, beyond what can be accounted for by the reliability of the contact and prejudice measures. For this analysis, we created four dummy-coded variables based on ratings of type of prejudice measure. "Dummy variables" are simply dichotomous measures; either a given test has an emotional measure of prejudice (score = 1) or it does not (score = 0). This procedure allowed us to predict contact–prejudice effects based on whether the tests did or did not include measures of emotion, favorability, stereotypes, and beliefs.

We also dummy-coded variables that assess the reliability of the contact and prejudice measures (low vs. high) and generalization to the outgroup as a whole (yes vs. no), and entered these variables simultaneously as predictors for the contact–prejudice effect sizes (see Table 7.1). As noted in Chapter 2, the results show that the reliability of the contact and prejudice measures contributes significantly to predicting contact–prejudice effects

TABLE 7.1 Summary of Inverse Variance Weighted Regression Model Predicting Contact–Prejudice Effects

Predictor Variables	B	SE	β	z
Reliability of contact measure	−.068	.013	−.143	−5.25***
Reliability of prejudice measure	−.043	.012	−.101	−3.68***
Generalization	.022	.016	.036	1.35
Emotions	−.075	.026	−.081	−2.88**
Favorability	−.050	.018	−.078	−2.63**
Stereotypes	.029	.018	.049	1.63
Beliefs	−.019	.014	−.044	−1.38
R^2			.06***	
Q_{Model}			78.94***	
k			1361	

Source: Adapted from Tropp and Pettigrew (2005a).

Note: B = raw regression coefficient; SE = standard error for the regression coefficient; β = standardized regression coefficient; z = z-test for the regression coefficient; p = probability of z-test; R^2 = proportion of variance accounted for; Q_{Model} = test of whether the regression model explains a significant portion of variability across effect sizes (see Wilson, 2002); k = number of tests included in the analysis. These analyses were conducted using Fisher's z-transformed r values. The random effects variance component for this analysis (based on Fisher's z-transformed r values) was .030.
* $p < .05$; ** $p < .01$; *** $p < .001$.

(β = −.143 and −.101, respectively; $p < .001$), with stronger effects observed when more reliable measures are used in the research studies. Moreover, we find that the emotion and favorability measures of prejudice uniquely and significantly predict stronger contact–prejudice effects (β = −.081 and −.078, respectively; $p < .01$), beyond what can be predicted by indices of measure reliability. At the same time, neither the generalization variable (β = .036) nor the stereotypes and beliefs categories of measures (β = .049 and −.044, respectively) yield significant effects.

Taken together, these findings further support our contention that contact–prejudice effects notably vary depending on the ways in which prejudice is assessed. Affective measures of prejudice tend to show stronger relationships with intergroup contact than such cognitive measures as stereotypes. Moreover, these patterns of effects are consistent even when only those tests involving generalization are examined and when the measures' reliabilities are controlled. Nevertheless, while more modest in magnitude, significant mean contact–prejudice effects were still observed when only stereotype measures were used. Although past research might lead us to expect that such cognitive effects would be unlikely (see Rothbart & John, 1985), it appears that the non-significant trends often observed in individual studies of stereotypes manage to reach significance when pooled together with meta-analytic techniques.

Overall, these patterns of findings support our prediction that affective outcomes of intergroup contact are more likely to generalize than cognitive outcomes. Still, although the results are informative, there are some limitations on the conclusions we can draw from these meta-analytic comparisons. Indeed, skeptics often criticize meta-analytic techniques for conducting comparisons across studies where variables, samples, and testing procedures are not uniform (see Rosenthal, 1991). Meta-analysis also confines us to those variables measured in the original research and those that meta-analysts can later rate reliably.

To address these limitations, we conducted an additional survey study to complement our meta-analytic investigation (see Tropp & Pettigrew, 2005a, Study 2). In this study, we asked a single sample of undergraduate participants to complete a range of measures assessing intergroup contact and varying dimensions of prejudice. Included among these measures were multiple measures of affective dimensions of prejudice (emotions, favorability, and liking) and cognitive dimensions of prejudice (stereotypes, beliefs, and judgments). Thus, using the same measures and procedures across all participants, this study allowed us to test whether contact-prejudice effects vary significantly across different types of prejudice measures.

Moreover, this survey study allowed an assessment of participants' contact experiences in a variety of ways as we examined variability in contact-prejudice effects. Specifically, we assessed contact in terms of numbers of cross-group acquaintances and friends, since research suggests that high quality contact in the form of cross-group friendships is especially critical for promoting reductions in prejudice. The next chapter will provide an extended discussion of this phenomenon.

Altogether, 126 White undergraduates completed a survey concerning their experiences with and attitudes toward African Americans in a private laboratory setting. As noted above, participants reported both the number of Black people they know at least as acquaintances, as well as the number of Black people they would consider to be friends. Participants also responded to a range of affective and cognitive measures to reflect the main categories of prejudice measures identified in our meta-analysis and in prior research (Dovidio et al., 2002a; Esses et al., 1993).

To assess affective dimensions of prejudice, we included separate measures of emotions, favorability, and liking. *Emotions* were assessed by asking participants to report the extent to which they would expect to feel different emotional states when interacting with a Black person (Stephan & Stephan, 1985). These item responses loaded onto two separate and highly reliable factors: one for *positive emotions* (e.g., confident, accepted, secure; $\alpha = .91$) and one for *negative emotions* (e.g., suspicious, awkward, nervous; $\alpha = .84$). *Favorability* was assessed by asking participants how warm or cold and how positively or negatively they felt toward Black people (McLaughlin-Volpe et al., 2000; α = .94). *Liking* was assessed by asking participants to indicate how much they anticipated liking and enjoying interactions with Black people (Tropp, 2003; α = .85).

To assess cognitive dimensions of prejudice, we included independent measures of stereotypes, beliefs, and judgments. *Stereotypes* were assessed using a semantic-differential scale (e.g., smart–dumb), where participants indicated how they view Black people in response to different word pairs (Osgood et al., 1957; α = .89). *Beliefs* were assessed using a composite measure including items from Brigham's (1993) Attitudes toward Blacks Scale, the Modern Racism Scale (McConahay, Hardee, & Batts, 1981), and Kinder and Sanders' (1996) Racial Resentment Scale (α = .87). *Judgments* about Black people's lives and experiences were measured using Katz and Hass' (1988) *Pro-Black and Anti-Black Racial Attitudes* scales (α = .84 and .76, respectively).

First, we examined intercorrelations among the many prejudice measures. Nearly all the prejudice measures correlated significantly with each other at least at the .05 level of significance. Nonetheless, there was considerable variability in the magnitudes of the correlations, with absolute values ranging from .18 to .67. In addition, three associations between prejudice measures were not statistically significant: positive emotions did not correlate significantly with intergroup beliefs or with pro-Black and anti-Black racial attitudes (r ranging between –.15 and .11, ns).

Next, we entered the prejudice measures into a principal-axis exploratory factor analysis with oblique rotation, to examine how they cluster together. Two clear factors accounted for 54% of the variance in participants' scores, with each prejudice measure loading above .40 on only one of the two factors. A first factor included primarily *affective* measures of prejudice, with strong loadings for positive emotions, negative emotions, favorability, and anticipated liking. A second factor included *cognitive* measures of prejudice, with strong loadings for stereotypes, beliefs, and pro- and anti-Black racial attitudes. These two factors were only moderately correlated (r = +.40, p < .001).

We then conducted a confirmatory analysis for this factor structure, using maximum likelihood estimation. The fit indices consistently indicated a good model fit (CFI = .985, IFI = .985). Moreover, this two-factor model fit the data significantly better than a one-factor model in which all the prejudice indicators contribute to a single latent factor without a cognitive–affective distinction (CFI = .976, IFI = .976, X^2_{diff} (1) = 28.28, p < .01). Together with prior research (e.g., Esses et al., 1993; Stangor et al., 1991), these results suggest that measures of prejudice tend to emphasize either *affective* dimensions such as emotions and feelings about the outgroup, or *cognitive* dimensions such as perceptions and beliefs about the outgroup.

Using these factors in a structural model, we then examined relationships between the contact measures and our latent factors of affective and cognitive prejudice (see Figure 7.3). In the model, the number of outgroup acquaintances and the number of outgroup friends are entered simultaneously as predictors for the latent factors of affective prejudice and cognitive prejudice, while also represented as being correlated with each other. The number of outgroup acquaintances contributed little to predicting either type of prejudice ($z = .28$ and $.56$, respectively; $p > .50$), independent of its relationship to the number of outgroup friends. However, the number of outgroup friends significantly predicted the latent factor of affective prejudice ($z = -2.40$, $p < .02$), but it did not predict the latent factor of cognitive prejudice ($z = -.05, p > .90$). In short, intergroup contact in the form of cross-group friendship showed more consistent relationships with prejudice measures assessing affective dimensions of prejudice than those assessing cognitive dimensions of prejudice.

These survey results nicely correspond with those from our meta-analysis, suggesting that affective dimensions are especially critical for illuminating the relationships between intergroup contact and prejudice. Moreover, in light of these findings, we can revisit contributions from varying traditions of contact research that have often arrived at conflicting conclusions regarding contact's effects. On the one hand, cognitively oriented theorists may well be correct to highlight cognitive barriers that can limit contact effects; yet by neglecting affective factors these theorists have overlooked the many positive, generalizable affective outcomes that can be achieved through intergroup contact. On the other hand, affectively oriented theorists may be correct in contending that contact can promote

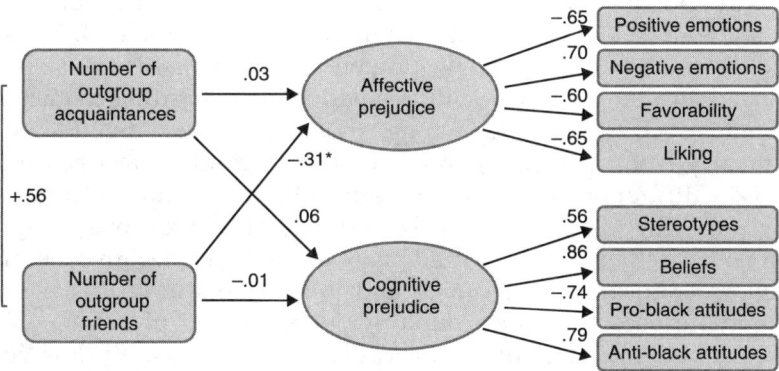

FIGURE 7.3 Path model showing relationships between contact measures and latent prejudice factors.

meaningful changes in how people feel toward other groups, but at the same time they may risk being too enthusiastic regarding the potential for contact to reduce prejudice in all its forms. Thus, from these studies, we learn that measures assessing different dimensions of prejudice should not be used interchangeably, and that affective processes play a special role in defining contact–prejudice relationships.

More broadly, these patterns of findings suggest that we may adopt different orientations in responding to outgroup members, depending on whether we are focused on affective or cognitive dimensions of the intergroup relationship. When we focus on cognitive dimensions, we may act as relatively detached observers and regard outgroup members as targets of our perceptions, beliefs, and judgments. But when we focus on affective dimensions, we may be more inclined to respond to outgroup members in terms of the emotions and feelings that are relevant to our relationships with them (see Esses & Dovidio, 2002; Zanna & Rempel, 1988, for related arguments). Consistent with this view, strategies that emphasize affective dimensions, such as asking people to imagine how outgroup members feel, have been particularly effective in reducing intergroup prejudice (Batson et al., 1997a; Finlay & Stephan, 2000), and in predicting intergroup behavior (Dovidio et al., 2002a; Esses & Dovidio, 2002; Stangor et al., 1991; Talaska et al., 2008). Thus, highlighting distinctions between affective and cognitive dimensions of intergroup relationships helps us to recognize the different orientations we use in relations with outgroup members, along with clarifying why affective dimensions are especially likely to render positive outcomes from intergroup contact.

Considering these trends, we might initially be tempted to conclude that intergroup contact should generally do little to promote positive changes on cognitive dimensions of prejudice. However, it is possible that intergroup contact may lead to other subtle cognitive changes that have been less widely studied. For example, Crystal, Killen, and Ruck (2008), working with 685 American children in public school grades 4, 7, and 10, found that contact related to how judgments of race-based exclusion were evaluated. In all three grades, children with more intergroup contact rated on average such exclusion as "wrong" more than those with little contact.

Similarly, Vollhardt (2010) shows that intergroup contact can reduce negative attributional biases regarding the outgroup. In line with Pettigrew's (1979) discussion of the ultimate attribution bias, Vollhardt examined whether people would tend to attribute negative outgroup behaviors to dispositional causes and positive outgroup behaviors to situational causes. Vollhardt found evidence for this phenomenon, but also observed that this attributional bias was significantly less strong among people who had experienced contact (i.e., by hosting a foreign exchange student) than a comparable sample of people who were willing but yet to be hosts.

Additionally, it is conceivable that more pronounced contact–prejudice relationships might be observed for cognitive dimensions depending on the kinds of contact experiences involved. For example, interacting with multiple and varied outgroup members may afford the kinds of contact experiences that would relate to shifts on cognitive dimensions of prejudice, such as decreased endorsement of outgroup stereotypes (see Wilder, 1986). At the same time, people must also have sufficient motivation to attend to information about outgroup targets in order to reduce their reliance on stereotypes (Moreno & Bodenhausen, 1999; Operario & Fiske, 2001). Thus, contact may be more likely to reduce stereotyping to the extent that it involves both substantial numbers of and meaningful relationships with a variety of outgroup members (see Van Dick et al., 2004, for a related perspective).

☐ Looking Beyond Affective and Cognitive Outcomes of Contact

Findings from our studies, coupled with those of other researchers (e.g., Miller et al., 2004; Wolsko et al., 2003), converge to demonstrate the differential effects that intergroup contact is likely to have on affective and cognitive dimensions of prejudice. This finding provides important theoretical clarification for the extant research literature while also highlighting that varied prejudice measures should not be interpreted equally nor used interchangeably. Still, the dichotomy between affective and cognitive dimensions of prejudice identified thus far leads us to question whether other types of contact outcomes should also be considered. In particular, three additional types of contact outcomes appear worthy of greater research attention, although as yet they remain relatively understudied in the broader contact literature.

Relationships between Intergroup Contact and Implicit Prejudice

Rather than emphasizing distinctions between affective and cognitive dimensions, a great deal of contemporary research has focused on distinguishing between implicit and explicit forms of prejudice (Dovidio et al., 1997; Greenwald, McGee, & Schwartz, 1998; McConnell & Leibold, 2001). This work has shown important ways in which implicit and explicit biases manifest themselves differently in the context of cross-group interactions. Thus, Dovidio, Kawakami, and Gaertner (2002b) conducted a study in which White participants completed both implicit and explicit measures of racial attitudes and then participated in an interaction with either a White or Black partner from which their verbal and non-verbal behaviors were coded. These authors found that, among participants paired with a Black partner, self-reported explicit racial attitudes more strongly predicted their verbal behavior and the extent to which they believed they exhibited friendly behavior during the contact. By contrast, participants' implicit racial attitudes more strongly predicted their non-verbal behavior and the extent to which their partners and uninvolved observers perceived friendliness in the participants' behavior.

Such findings have inspired a new generation of research focusing on relationships between intergroup contact and implicit forms of prejudice. Survey studies have uncovered significant associations between greater levels of contact and lower levels of implicit prejudice in studies of White Americans toward Black Americans (Aberson & Haag, 2007; Aberson, Shoemaker, & Tomolillo, 2004), British attitudes toward South Asians (Turner et al., 2007), Catholics' and Protestants' attitudes toward each other in Northern Ireland (Tam et al., 2008), Lebanese Muslims' attitudes toward Christians (Henry & Hardin, 2006), Latino Americans' attitudes toward White Americans (Aberson, Porter, & Gaffney, 2008), heterosexuals' attitudes toward gays and lesbians (Dasgupta & Rivera, 2008), and the non-disabled's attitudes toward the disabled (Pruett & Chan, 2006).

Especially impressive is a recent study by Akinola and Mendes (2008), who experimentally tested whether intergroup contact can cause reductions in implicit prejudice. After an initial assessment of implicit prejudice, White participants were randomly paired with either a same-race or a cross-race (African-American) confederate for a series of interactions, after each of which their implicit attitudes were again assessed. These authors observed significant reductions in Whites' implicit prejudice over the course of these interactions, suggesting the important role that intergroup contact may play in promoting the malleability of implicit attitudes (see also Dasgupta & Rivera, 2008).

Relationships between Intergroup Contact and Policy Attitudes

Other researchers have looked beyond the goal of improving attitudes between groups, calling for a greater focus on policy-relevant outcomes of contact. Often coupled with this focus is a lingering doubt that people's reported attitudes will necessarily translate into support for structural changes that can eradicate existing inequalities between groups that differ in power or status (e.g., Dixon, Durrheim, & Tredoux, 2005, 2007; Jackman, 2005; Jackman & Crane, 1986; Reicher, 2007). Reflecting on findings from early contact studies of Whites' attitudes toward Black Americans, Jackman and Crane (1986) ask, "Do the positive effects observed for the more personal, affectively loaded measures also hold for more political orientations toward Blacks?" (p. 463). In their own research, they found that contact readily predicted Whites' emotional acceptance of Black people, but they claimed that it was far less effective in supporting policies to assist Black people in such domains as employment, education, and housing. However, this claim, as we shall discuss in Chapter 11, was based on a limited analysis of their survey data.

This focus on policy implications and outcomes has been slow to develop in the contact literature, and we are not suggesting that contact will override all other material and psychological concerns involved in relations between groups. Nonetheless, we wish to highlight findings from several research studies that do suggest encouraging trends regarding the potential for contact to positively impact policy attitudes in a range of intergroup contexts. Chapter 11 will supply additional research evidence on this key point.

For example, in the context of Black–White relations in the United States, Jeffries and Ransford (1969) assessed middle-class Whites' reactions to the Watts Riot[1] as a function of their prior contact with Blacks (i.e., in their neighborhoods, at work, in organizations, and in other contexts). Those who had prior contact with Blacks tended to report less fear about being attacked by Black people and to believe that smaller proportions of the Black population participated in the violence. Additionally, these respondents were asked what steps should be taken to prevent future riots, and their open-ended responses were classified either as punitive policies (e.g., stricter penalties in court, racial segregation, and the use of massive force by law enforcement) or as ameliorative policies (e.g., greater opportunities for Blacks in employment and education, racial integration, police reform). Compared to other Whites, Whites who had prior contact with Blacks were significantly less likely to suggest punitive policies (18% vs. 48%) and substantially more likely to suggest more supportive, ameliorative policies to prevent future riots (68% vs. 28%).

Joseph, Weatherall, and Stringer (1997) found contact differences in intergroup attribution biases in samples of Catholic and Protestant Northern Irish students. In segregated school settings, each group gave more negative explanations for outgroup unemployment and more favorable explanations for ingroup unemployment. However, this biased group attribution effect (see Pettigrew, 1979) was less pronounced in an integrated college sample. As mentioned earlier, this subtle finding has been replicated in Germany (Vollhardt, 2010).

Dixon et al. (2010b) conducted a national survey of racial attitudes and policy support among White South Africans. Generally, the results show that high quality intergroup contact predicts greater support for a range of race-targeted policies, including both *compensatory policies* that support Blacks yet do not directly disadvantage Whites, and *preferential policies* that more directly challenge Whites' privilege. Moreover, these positive effects of contact remain significant even after accounting for Whites' prejudices and perceptions of threat and injustice regarding their relative status.

Positive contact effects have also been observed in predicting employment attitudes in reference to other stigmatized groups. For instance, Gerbert, Sumser, and Maguire (1991) conducted telephone interviews with a random sample of 2000 adults in the United States to examine public attitudes toward people living with AIDS. Relative to those who did not know someone with AIDS, respondents who reported they knew someone with AIDS were more likely to support the rights of people living with AIDS to continue working in a wide variety of occupations (e.g., surgeon, dentist, police officer, cook).

In another compelling study, Levy, Jessop, Rimmerman, and Levy (1993) recruited over 300 "Fortune 500" executives responsible for hiring decisions to complete surveys concerning their prior experiences with and attitudes toward people with severe disabilities. Their study showed that executives who had prior experience working with disabled people were not only more likely to have more positive attitudes toward the disabled, but were also more likely to believe in the employability of people with severe disabilities.

Although still removed from actual implementation, we can see how such findings serve as building blocks to make the transition from studying positive feelings about other groups to support for policies designed to improve their life circumstances and opportunities for advancement. As such, they bring us several steps closer to understanding the role that intergroup contact may play in influencing policy-related outcomes involving institutional change.

Relationships between Intergroup Contact and Subsequent Intergroup Behavior

Nonetheless, prior research also emphasizes the lack of connection that often occurs between people's attitudes and subsequent behaviors (Ajzen & Fishbein, 1980), an issue that is especially important to consider in the context of intergroup relations (Dovidio et al., 2002a; Talaska et al., 2008). Thus, a third set of contact outcomes in need of greater exploration are those that pertain to actual intergroup behavior following the contact.

Although several studies include direct observations of behavior, such as varying degrees of voluntary segregation or integration across groups (e.g., Clack, Dixon, & Tredoux, 2005; Schofield & Sagar, 1977), or patterns of cross-group helping (e.g., Dovidio & Gaertner, 1981; Saucier, Miller, & Doucet, 2005), they typically lack precise measures of individuals' prior contact as predictors for engagement in these behaviors. By contrast, few studies have demonstrated the ways in which intergroup contact can either inhibit negative intergroup behaviors or promote more positive intergroup behaviors (see McCauley, Plummer, Moskalenko, & Mordkoff, 2001; Schofield, 1995), although some select examples do exist.

Johnson and Johnson (1981) randomly assigned disabled and non-disabled third-grade students to work either in cooperative learning groups or independently on identical assignments for 25 minutes on each of 16 days of instruction. In addition to having the students complete sociometric measures of friends, the authors coded students' behaviors both during the work sessions and during periods of free play outside of the instructional context. Compared with those who worked independently, students in the cooperative learning condition evinced significantly more cross-group friend nominations and more actual cross-group interactions – both during instruction and free play.

Similarly, Rooney-Rebeck and Jason (1986) studied the effects of mixed-ethnic cooperative peer tutoring groups on interethnic relations among Black, Latino, and White children in the first and third grades. Like Johnson and Johnson (1981), their measures included sociometric nominations of cross-group friendships as well as direct observations of children's interactions during playtime. These were assessed both before and after children worked closely together in an 8-week peer tutoring program, thereby following a within-group research design. While positive effects of the learning groups were limited for third-graders, results for first-graders showed greater cross-group friendship nominations and increases in observed cross-ethnic interactions during playtime following participation in the peer tutoring program. Findings from these and related studies suggest that positive contact experiences may not only facilitate close ties across group boundaries (see Chapter 8), but more broadly they may reinforce people's willingness to engage in future contact that can serve to facilitate future cross-group interaction.

☐ Conclusion

In sum, beyond exploring the general question of whether contact reduces prejudice, research findings suggest varying effects of contact depending on the kinds of outcomes we examine. In particular, a substantial body of work now suggests that affective outcomes – emotions, feelings, and liking – are more likely to be positively influenced by intergroup contact than cognitively oriented outcomes – stereotypes and beliefs. These results coincide with our discussion of mediators in Chapter 6, in that they both indicate the central importance of affective processes in intergroup contact effects. In addition, new research indicates that contact can have significant effects on implicit attitudes and such far-reaching outcomes as policy attitudes and behaviors.

More work is needed to understand the processes that underlie shifts in these alternate outcomes, so that we can develop a more integrated view regarding the effects of intergroup contact. But what findings from these varied branches of research share is the recognition that high quality contact – such as close, cross-group friendships – is especially likely to promote positive outcomes of contact. We therefore turn to a discussion of cross-group friendships in Chapter 8.

☐ Note

1 The Watts Riot grew from growing racial tensions with the police. The rioting lasted for 5 days in Los Angeles in August 1965, and was the largest and most violent riot in Los Angeles' history.

Does Cross-Group Friendship Play a Special Role in Reducing Prejudice?

We now know that affective dimensions are crucial for identifying the forms of prejudice that are especially likely to be reduced through intergroup contact. But might affect also play a role in defining the kinds of contact that would be most likely to reduce prejudice? What does it mean when we say we feel "close" to members of other groups, and how do these feelings of closeness affect our intergroup prejudices?

Such questions have led researchers to develop programmatic studies and theoretical extensions of contact theory to consider why and how cross-group friendships predict reduced prejudice and other intergroup improvements. Recall from Chapter 1 the dramatic role of friendships in the heroic saving of Jews from the Holocaust (Oliner & Oliner, 1988). And in Chapter 3, we learned how close affective ties generated by cross-group friendships can lead to greater liking for and identification with outgroup members. These changes in turn can feed into more positive feelings toward the outgroup as a whole.

Pettigrew (1997a) analyzed cross-sectional survey responses from seven European samples, in which respondents were asked to state whether they had any friends of a different culture, nationality, race, ethnicity, or social class, as well as to complete several measures of intergroup prejudice. Having cross-group friendships was consistently and significantly associated with lower intergroup prejudice, particularly for such affective prejudice measures as feelings of sympathy and admiration for the outgroup. By contrast, less intimate contact with outgroup members, such as coworkers or neighbors, yielded far smaller effects (see also Hamberger & Hewstone, 1997).

In a related vein, Wright, Aron, and their colleagues (Wright et al., 2000, 2002, 2005; Wright & Van der Zande, 1999) propose that greater closeness to individual outgroup members corresponds with lower prejudice toward the whole outgroup through the mechanism of including the outgroup in the self. By having a friend in another group, these authors state, we begin to grant that outgroup friend (and other members of that friend's group) the same kinds of psychological benefits we normally reserve for ourselves and members of our own group. For example, cross-group friendships may compel us to make more positive attributions for outgroup members' intentions and behaviors (Joseph et al., 1997; Vollhardt, 2010; Wright et al., 2002), and to express enhanced concern for the outgroup's welfare (Aron & McLaughlin-Volpe, 2001).

In an early test of these ideas, McLaughlin-Volpe and her co-authors (2000) asked participants to report how many interactions they had had with outgroup members (quantity of contact), and how close they felt to the outgroup member with whom they had the closest relationship (quality of contact), along with reporting their feelings toward outgroup members in general. Greater numbers of cross-group interactions were associated with more positive feelings toward outgroup members, but only among those who reported having close cross-group relationships.

Armed with these results, we used our original meta-analytic dataset to test whether cross-group friendships typically show stronger effects than other forms of contact. For this analysis, we examined effects at the test level, and compared mean contact–prejudice effects for those tests that either did or did not include cross-group friendship as a measure of intergroup contact. Figure 8.1 summarizes the results from this analysis. Overall, the 154 tests that included cross-group friendship as a contact measure provide a significantly stronger mean effect (mean $r = -.246$) than the 1211 contact tests that did not include a cross-group friendship measure (mean $r = -.212$; $p < .05$).

Although this finding is encouraging, some researchers express concern that any positive effects of cross-group friendship may be limited to the outgroup members with whom one has such friendships. This returns us to the issue of generalization discussed in Chapter 3. Jackman and Crane (1986) go so far as to assert that "having one or two black friends gives [people] a license to think what [they] please about the group as a whole" (p. 462). We therefore investigated this issue to the extent possible using our meta-analytic data.

First, we tallied the number of friendship tests that examined prejudice outcomes in relation to individual outgroup members within the contact situation, and those that examined prejudice outcomes in relation to the outgroup as a whole. Of the 154 tests that assess friendship, only a handful ($k = 5$, < 4%) focus on prejudice outcomes toward individual group members, whereas most ($k = 134$, 87%) assess prejudice outcomes toward the outgroup as a whole.[1] Although it is less than ideal to conduct statistical comparisons when groups include such small numbers of

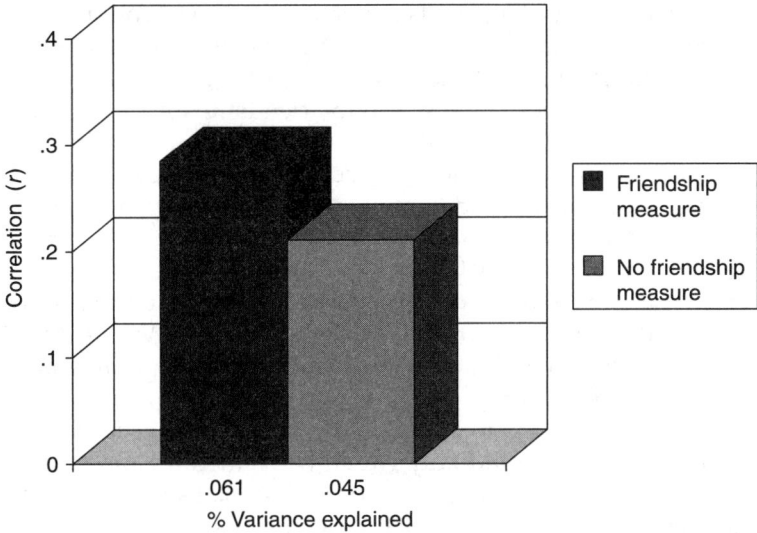

FIGURE 8.1 Mean contact–prejudice effects by presence of cross-group friendship measure.

cases, we proceeded to do so in order to address directly the concern raised by Jackman and Crane (1986). Our decision to do so was also informed by the knowledge that the five tests examining prejudice toward individual outgroup members are extremely diverse. They originate from studies conducted by four different authors across different decades and countries (Bullock, 1978; Maras & Brown, 1996; Webster, 1961; Yinon, 1975). Comparing these groups of cases revealed that friendship effects do tend to be especially strong when prejudice is assessed toward individual outgroup members in the contact situation (mean $r = -.296$). This mean effect is not significantly greater than that for cases where prejudice is assessed toward the entire outgroup (mean $r = -.237$; $p = .20$), although this may well be due to the tiny size of the first comparison group.

Taken together with other recent findings, there is now a growing consensus that while intergroup contact typically reduces prejudice, it is most effective for reducing prejudice when it consists of close, high quality intergroup relationships such as those afforded by cross-group friendships. This work largely supports Pettigrew's (1998) proposition that *friendship potential* is an important enhancing condition for intergroup contact effects. Pettigrew defines friendship potential as the ability of the contact situation to provide people with the opportunities to become friends. Friendship potential is typified by extensive and repeated contact across a range of social contexts, which over time would encourage greater degrees of shared experience, self-disclosure, and other kinds of friendship-building processes (see also Cook, 1984).

Thus far, most studies of cross-group friendships have been correlational in nature (e.g., Aberson et al., 2004; Herek & Capitanio, 1996; Paolini et al., 2004; Pettigrew, 1997a) and longitudinal studies are rare (e.g., Binder et al., 2009; Dhont et al., under review-b; Eller & Abrams, 2003; Eller, Abrams, & Gómez, under review; Sidanius et al., 2008). To better account for potential causal relationships, researchers have therefore begun to conduct experimental studies of the effects of cross-group friendship.

Pioneering this research, Wright and his colleagues (Wright et al., 2000, 2002; Wright & Van der Zande, 1999) describe an experimental study using University of California students that offers initial evidence for the causal effects of cross-group friendship on prejudice reduction. White female participants were randomly paired with either a same-race partner (White) or a cross-race partner (Latina or Asian) for a series of four testing sessions over 8 weeks, during which they engaged in a series of friendship-building activities. Participants' feelings of closeness to their partner were assessed following each testing session. After the final session, participants completed measures of intergroup outcomes, ostensibly as part of a separate study. Data from the White participants showed that both women paired with a same-race and cross-race partner developed strong feelings of closeness to their partners over the testing sessions. Compared to participants paired with a same-race partner, however, those who were paired with a cross-race partner tended to report lower intergroup anxiety by the end of the study. Moreover, using a subtle "budget-cutting task" as an indicator of intergroup attitudes (see Haddock, Zanna, & Esses, 1993), Wright and his colleagues found that relative to participants with a same-race partner the White participants paired with a cross-race partner were less likely to cut university funding for ethnic minority organizations supporting the partner's ethnic group.

Building upon this work, Page-Gould et al. (2008) experimentally tested the effects of cross-group friendship among both ethnic minority and majority participants (Latino and White), who were paired with either a same-group or cross-group partner for three friendship meetings. Prior to the meetings, the researchers measured participants' initial intergroup prejudice using the Implicit Associations Test (IAT; see Lane, Banaji, Nosek, & Greenwald, 2007; Rudman, Greenwald, Mellott, & Schwartz, 1999) and their sensitivity to being rejected on the basis of ethnic group membership (see Mendoza-Denton et al., 2002). A physiological indicator of stress (cortisol reactivity) was also included to assess anxious responses during the friendship meetings. Among participants highly sensitive to group-based rejection, those paired with a cross-group partner peaked in cortisol reactivity following the first friendship meeting, indicating greater anxious responding, but their stress responses attenuated considerably by the third friendship meeting. Now they showed comparable levels of anxiety to participants less sensitive to group-based rejection and to participants who were paired with a same-group partner.

In addition, using diary procedures, participants reported how often they initiated cross-group interactions in their daily lives for 10 days following the three friendship meetings. Particularly among those initially high in prejudice, participants were more likely to initiate cross-group interactions after making a cross-group friend than after making a same-group friend. Thus, the results extend the work of Wright and colleagues to suggest that, even among people who may initially be the most concerned or uncomfortable about intergroup interactions, developing a cross-group friendship can lower intergroup anxiety and encourage a greater willingness to engage in further intergroup contact. Together with the research cited previously, these studies offer compelling evidence that cross-group friendships are especially effective in reducing prejudice and promoting a host of positive intergroup outcomes.

☐ Processes in Cross-Group Friendship

But is it really closeness in cross-group friendship that is producing these effects? Only limited research has begun to identify the processes that explain why cross-group friendships are uniquely effective for yielding reduced prejudice. Research by McLaughlin-Volpe and colleagues (2000) suggests that closeness moderates the relationship between quantity of contact and prejudice, such that greater quantity of contact only meaningfully reduces prejudice when people report feeling close to the outgroup members with whom they had contact.

Other studies demonstrate the mediational role that anxiety reduction plays in the relationship between cross-group friendship and prejudice reduction, complementing the trends reported in Chapter 6. Paolini et al. (2004) used structural equation models to analyze surveys of cross-community relations in Northern Ireland. They found that increases in the number of cross-group friends lessen the anticipated feelings of anxiety about future intergroup encounters, and this process in turn predicts diminished intergroup prejudice. In their UCLA longitudinal study of students' contact experiences, Levin et al. (2003) similarly reveal that greater numbers of cross-group friendships during the college years predict both significant reductions in intergroup anxiety and intergroup prejudice by the end of college.

Researchers have also sought to move beyond studies of psychological processes to understand how behavior in cross-group friendships may contribute further to positive intergroup changes. Friendship research from the literature on interpersonal relations highlights certain behaviors, such as shared activities and self-disclosure, that influence the development of intimacy with a close other (Fehr, 2004; Reis & Shaver, 1988).

Recent findings from the intergroup literature are now revealing similar trends in the context of cross-group friendship (see Ensari & Miller, 2002; Tam et al., 2006; Turner et al., 2007). For example, Turner et al. (2007) find self-disclosure to be an especially powerful mediator – even more powerful than anxiety reduction – in accounting for the relationship between cross-group friendship and improved intergroup attitudes. Coupled with the mediation findings described in Chapter 6, it seems likely that anxiety reduction plays a critical role in prejudice reduction at the early stages of contact, whereas over time and in joint activities self-disclosure plays a greater role later as more intimate cross-group relationships begin to form.

☐ Indirect Effects of Cross-Group Friendship

Cross-group friendship effects also spread widely. As noted briefly in Chapter 6, having an ingroup friend who has an outgroup friend tends to improve attitudes toward the outgroup (Wright et al., 1997, 2008). This process replicates "the friend-of-my-friend-is-my-friend" phenomenon from balance theory (see Heider, 1958). At least in the short term, this indirect effect does not typically produce outgroup attitudes that equal the attitude strength gained by direct contact. But over longer time periods the new attitudes from indirect contact appear to gain strength (Christ et al., in press). Such indirect contact also yields secondary transfer effects and is especially important for those who live in segregated areas and lack cross-group friends (Christ et al., in press; Eller et al., under review).

☐ Measurement of Cross-Group Friendship

Surveying the burgeoning literature on cross-group friendship reveals great diversity in how this concept has been assessed. To date, most studies of cross-group friendship have asked participants to report how many outgroup friends they have (e.g., Hamberger & Hewstone, 1997; Paolini et al., 2004; Pettigrew, 1997a; Simon, 1995; Spangenberg & Nel, 1983). Other studies inquire about one's friendship network, such as asking respondents to report the racial composition of their circle of friends (e.g., Emerson et al., 2002) or the percentage of their friends who are outgroup members (e.g., Stearns, Buchmann, & Bonneau, 2009; Tropp, 2003). Additional studies operationalize friendship in terms of closeness, such as how close one feels to outgroup members with whom they are closest (e.g., McLaughlin-Volpe et al., 2000), or to indicate the group membership of their closest friends (e.g., Johnson & Marini, 1998; Webster, 1961). Still other approaches assess the amount of time one spends with outgroup friends, such as how often one has contact with outgroup friends (e.g., Van Dick et al., 2004) or the frequency with which one engages in friendly interactions with outgroup members (e.g., Patchen, Davidson, Hofmann, & Brown, 1977).

Yet little is known regarding whether these various approaches to assessing cross-group friendship *typically* produce different relationships between cross-group friendship and prejudice reduction. Spearheaded by Kristin Davies, we therefore have extended our earlier meta-analytic work to determine whether the relationships between friendship contact and intergroup attitudes vary depending on the precise ways in which friendship is conceptualized and assessed (see Davies et al., in press). We extracted studies assessing cross-group friendship from our larger meta-analysis and conducted new searches of the research literature to identify additional studies examining the effects of cross-group friendship through August 2009. These procedures allowed us to pool together findings from a total of 208 samples (including 501 individual tests) testing the effects of friendship contact. This number is more than three times that of friendship samples available from our original meta-analytic investigation (61 samples and 154 tests) – an indication of the growing interest in this research area since the turn of the century.

We first examine the mean effect of friendship contact in this combined dataset and compare it to the mean effect of friendship contact observed in our smaller, original subset of samples. At both the sample and test levels, mean effect sizes for friendship contact in the combined dataset (mean $r = -.236$ for samples and tests without data corrections, $-.240$ for samples, and $-.239$ for tests with data corrections) were comparable to those reported in our original meta-analytic dataset (mean $r = -.246$ at the test level).

Further analysis of the friendship contact dataset reveals similar trends to those reported in previous chapters in relation to our larger meta-analytic dataset of general contact effects. For example, we typically find stronger associations between more reliable measures of both friendship contact (mean $r = -.307$) and prejudice (mean $r = -.280$) than those among less reliable measures (mean $r = -.223$ and $-.206$, respectively). We also observe stronger effects of friendship contact when outcome measures assess affective dimensions of intergroup attitudes (mean $r = -.263$) rather than cognitive dimensions (mean $r = -.177$) (see Davies et al., in press).

Of particular relevance to the present discussion, however, is whether the variability in the assessment of friendship contact produces meaningful differences in its relationship to intergroup attitudes. We therefore compared mean effects for samples that employ the six most common categories of friendship indicators in the research literature: (1) the number of reported cross-group friendships; (2) the percentage of outgroup members in one's friendship network; (3) the reported feelings of closeness to the outgroup friend; (4) the reported inclusion of the outgroup friend in the self; (5) the degree of self-disclosure to outgroup friend(s); and (6) the amount of time spent with outgroup friend(s). Figure 8.2 provides the mean effects for these various types of friendship indicators.

Significant relationships between cross-group friendship and intergroup attitudes were obtained for samples employing each of the six categories of friendship contact. Nonetheless, those samples that assess friendship in terms of time spent or self-disclosure with outgroup friends yield significantly larger effects than samples relying on other friendship indicators. Specifically, tests measuring time spent and self-disclosure with outgroup friends together yield a significantly stronger association to decreased prejudice (mean $r = -.267$) than measures assessing the number of outgroup friends, the proportion of outgroup members in friendship network, and the closeness and inclusion of other in self combined (mean $r = -.218$; $p < .01$). At the same time, there are no significant differences in mean effects between samples that assessed friendship contact in terms of time spent or self-disclosure with outgroup friends.

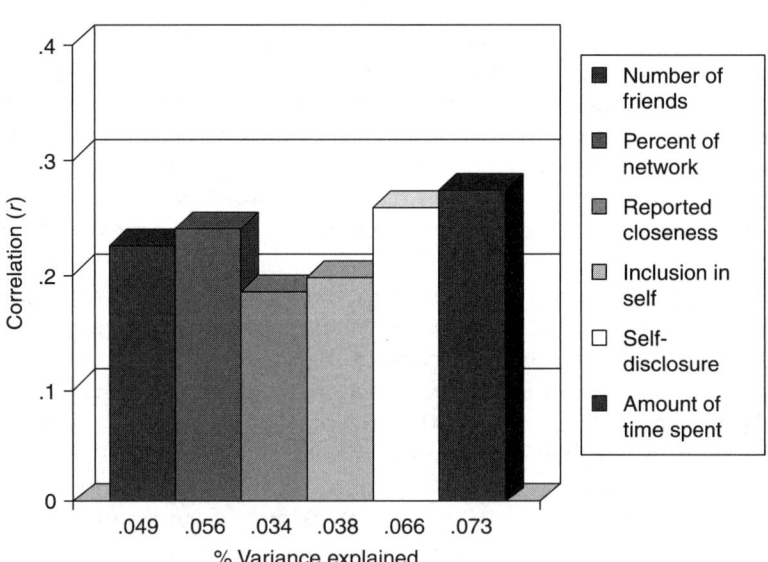

FIGURE 8.2 Mean contact–prejudice effects by type of friendship indicator.

The special importance of the time spent measure may well reflect less time spent with ingroup members – which we noted earlier is also a correlate of lowered prejudice (Wilder & Thompson, 1980).

These findings both complement and challenge recent theorizing regarding the special role of friendship contact in promoting positive contact effects. In one respect, the fact that all six categories of friendship indicators yield significant effects underscores the importance of interpersonal processes (Aron & McLaughlin-Volpe, 2001), such as the development of trust and comfort (Tropp, 2008), that occur as meaningful cross-group relationships develop and progress over time (Pettigrew, 1998). But in another respect, time spent and self-disclosure with outgroup friends not only yield the strongest effects, but they are the most *behaviorally oriented* indicators of the different modes of friendship contact employed in the research literature. It is also interesting to note that the two most subjective indicators of cross-group friendship depicted in Figure 8.2 – reported closeness and inclusion of outgroup member in self – tend to reveal weaker effects than these behaviorally oriented measures. Thus, a greater focus on observable friendship behavior may be necessary to understand the contours and effects of friendship contact, rather than relying only on more subjective assessments of the closeness of those friendships.

Alternatively, it could be that through their focus on behavior, indicators of self-disclosure and time spent together imply some level of mutual participation between the person studied and the outgroup friend. Perhaps, then, these indicators implicate the actual involvement of both parties to a greater extent than the indicators that focus more on the subjective responses of any single individual engaging with an outgroup friend. This interpretation coincides with the important distinction drawn by Aboud et al. (2003) between friendships reported by individual children versus *mutual friendships*, where pairs of children rate each other as best friends. Their study reveals that while cross-race friendships tend to be less numerous than same-race friendships, children rate their same- and cross-race mutual friendships similarly on such dimensions as emotional security, reliability, receiving help, and satisfaction. These results coupled with our own meta-analytic findings suggest that greater attention to the dynamics, behaviors, and content of cross-group friendships are crucial issues to explore in future research.

☐ Potential Biases in Reports of Cross-Group Friendship

A greater focus on relational dynamics must also address the concerns of some researchers who contend that people inflate reports of the number and intimacy of their cross-group friendships in an effort to appear tolerant of other groups (see Bonilla-Silva, 2003; Jackman & Crane, 1986). Indeed, subjective reports of friendship may not be as representative of their quality as reports of actual involvement in friendship behaviors. Smith (2002) has noted that people often estimate greater numbers of cross-group friendships when asked directly about them ("How many White friends do you have?"), as compared to when they are first asked to list the names of friends and then later to identify their group membership ("Of the friends you mentioned, how many are White?").

Experimental studies where cross-group friendships are initiated in the laboratory (e.g., Page-Gould et al., 2008; Wright et al., 2002, 2005) now provide causal evidence for the positive effects of cross-group friendship and eliminate the need to rely solely on participants' subjective self-reports. But to address this methodological issue, we conducted a separate analysis for the 203 samples in which participants reported on their cross-group friendships to determine whether different modes of friendship assessment predict different magnitudes of friendship effects (see Figure 8.3). We did in fact find a greater mean effect for the 180 samples where participants were asked directly to report their cross-group friendships (mean $r = -.247$) as compared to that for the 23 samples where participants first reported their friendships and later described the group membership of those friends (mean $r = -.158; p < .01$).

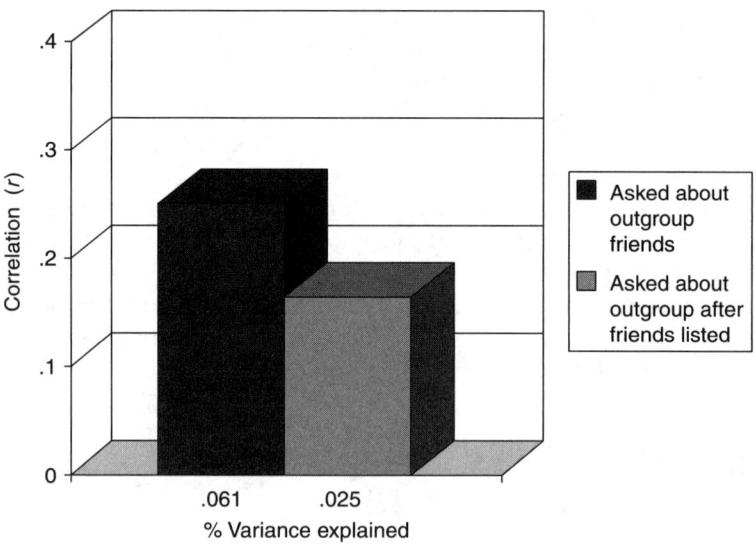

FIGURE 8.3 Mean contact–prejudice effects by mode of friendship assessment.

These findings are consistent with Smith's (2002) analysis and with the view that people may be inclined to inflate their reports of cross-group friendship (e.g., Jackman & Crane, 1986). And they are also consistent with other work indicating that cross-race friendships tend to be less common (e.g., Clark & Ayers, 1992; Hallinan & Teixeira, 1987; Shrum, Cheek, & Hunter, 1988) and sometimes less intimate (Aboud et al., 2003) than same-race friendships. But as we have seen from a broad range of experimental and survey studies (see Davies et al., in press; Pettigrew & Tropp, 2000), even if they may be less common and intimate than same-group friendships, cross-group friendships still typically yield strong and positive intergroup effects.

Moreover, there are at least two ways in which the apparent inflation of cross-group friendships can be interpreted. It could represent individuals' concerns associated with appearing prejudiced (Plant & Devine, 1998) or their tendencies to deny any prejudices they may have (Gaertner & Dovidio, 2000). But, alternatively, it could be that by asking people to report on their cross-group friendships, they become focused on those friendships where group membership is salient, thereby enhancing the connection between those friendships and their reported intergroup attitudes (see Brown & Hewstone, 2005). That is, we should observe more positive intergroup outcomes growing from cross-group friendships to the extent that an outgroup friend's group membership is cognitively accessible.

An exciting new line of research by Page-Gould et al. (2010) provides some evidence in support of this second view. In one study, they recruited White participants who reported having both cross-group and same-group friends of comparable closeness (i.e., 6 or 7 on a 7-point scale), based upon responses to a pretest questionnaire. During a subsequent experimental session, the participants were asked to describe their friendships and provide the names of same-group and cross-group friends. To manipulate the cognitive accessibility of cross-group friendship, participants were randomly assigned to describe either their cross-race friend (high accessibility) or same-race friend (low accessibility). They then completed a reaction time task to assess self–outgroup associations (see Aron & McLaughlin-Volpe, 2001; Wright et al., 2002), and they read a vignette in which they imagined themselves interacting with an unknown outgroup member. Then the subjects rated how much they would enjoy this imagined interaction. Participants in the high accessibility condition revealed stronger self–outgroup associations on the reaction time task; and they also reported more positive expectations for interacting with the unknown outgroup member.

Taking this research a step further, Page-Gould and her colleagues tested whether similar effects would emerge in the context of a real, novel cross-group interaction. Using the same recruitment procedures, participants were randomly assigned to describe a cross-group or same-group friend when they arrived at the experimental session. After the reaction time task, they were introduced to an unknown outgroup member for an unstructured interaction. Both before and after the interaction, saliva samples were collected from participants to assess their hormonal stress responses as well as their ability to recover from stress responses. Findings once again showed that participants who described a cross-group friend (the high accessibility condition) had stronger self–outgroup associations than those who described a same-group friend (the low accessibility condition). In addition, stronger self–outgroup associations mediated the effect of the accessibility manipulation on greater hormonal balance during the novel cross-group interaction. In line with prior work on salience in intergroup contact (Brown et al., 1999; Brown & Hewstone, 2005; Voci & Hewstone, 2003), such findings led the authors to conclude that intergroup benefits of cross-group friendship are likely to depend on how accessible cross-group friendships are when responding to unknown outgroup members.

☐ Obstacles Associated with Cross-Group Friendships

While these and other studies clearly point to the benefits that may be gained from cross-group friendship, there are two interrelated types of formidable obstacles and challenges that exist to their formation. To start with, in order to have cross-group friends, there obviously must exist opportunities to make cross-group friends (see Cook, 1962; Pettigrew, 1998; Wagner et al., 2006).

Even when there are ample contact opportunities, severe norms against cross-group interaction and friendship may exist. South Africa's *apartheid* and the American South's racial segregation offer salient examples of the first type of barrier. A central challenge involves residential segregation, which feeds into segregation in schooling and in other areas of social life (see Massey & Denton, 1993; Orfield & Lee, 2006; Pettigrew, 1971, 2007c; Schofield, 1995). Studies in American schools suggest that children and adolescents are much more likely to choose same-race friends than cross-race friends (e.g., DuBois & Hirsch, 1990; Hallinan & Teixeira, 1987). However, with greater representation of students from other races in their schools, they become more likely to report having cross-race friendships (e.g., Hallinan & Smith, 1985; Joyner & Kao, 2000; Khmelkov & Hallinan, 1999) – particularly when class sizes are small enough to encourage cross-group interaction (Hallinan & Teixeira, 1987). A recent study of White undergraduates also shows that those who have at least one roommate of a different race are likely to develop more diverse friendship networks during their first year in college (Stearns et al., 2009).

Nonetheless, there is also evidence to suggest that cross-group friendships can be more difficult to sustain over time. Cross-group friendships typically decrease during the transition from childhood to adolescence (Asher, Singleton, & Taylor, 1982; DuBois & Hirsch, 1990; Epstein, 1986); thus, the tendency for children to have more same-race than cross-race friends increases as they grow older (Aboud et al., 2003). These phenomena reflect the second class of barriers to cross-group friendship – societal and situational norms against intergroup interaction and friendship.

Recent work also suggests that varying conceptions of cross-group friendships may also inhibit the ability for them to develop and be maintained. West and colleagues (2009a) examined how perceptions of commonality (i.e., that members of different racial groups are all part of one group) predicted the development of cross-group friendships among college roommates. Among those randomly assigned to a cross-race roommate, initially high perceptions of commonality predicted greater feelings of friendship toward their cross-race roommate. However, those who initially perceived low commonality, or who were paired with a roommate who perceived low commonality, showed decreased feelings of friendship toward their roommate over time.

Thus, akin to what we proposed in Chapter 5, more research is needed to understand not only how negative factors curb the positive effects of contact, but also how they inhibit the creation and positive potential of cross-group friendships. One particularly relevant feature of cross-group friendship involves normative influences from trusted others, and the extent to which we perceive them to approve or disapprove of our developing friendships across group boundaries. Developmental research shows that parents are important sources of information who can either discourage or encourage children's willingness to engage in contact and develop cross-group relationships (Aboud, 2005; Edmonds & Killen, 2009).

Children are also highly motivated to conform to the expectations and standards of ingroup peers, and this can make them reluctant to pursue cross-group friendships (Aboud & Sankar, 2007; Fishbein, 1996). Furthermore, as children make the transition from childhood into adolescence, social norms and group identities are likely to assume even greater levels of importance in how they respond to intergroup encounters (see Horn, 2003; Killen et al., 2007a; Turiel, 1983). These tendencies complement what we observe in studies of adults, which show how people rely on trusted ingroup members as sources of information about other groups (e.g., Hogg & Reid, 1996; Sechrist & Stangor, 2001; Stangor et al., 1991). It may well be for these reasons that cross-group ties are more vulnerable and harder to maintain than same-group ties (Reagans, 1998), and why people may re-segregate voluntarily even when there are opportunities for intergroup contact (Rogers, Hennigan, Bowman & Miller, 1984; Schofield, 1979; Tatum, 1997).

Although these social pressures and challenges are considerable, we can also envision how – by reversing the processes – we can enhance the potential for cross-group friendship. Returning to themes discussed in Chapter 5, situational features such as institutional support, cooperation, common goals, and equal status can facilitate positive contact experiences, and in turn promote the development of cross-group friendships. Indeed, studies have shown that when students from different racial backgrounds participate cooperatively in shared school activities, they become more likely to choose each other as best friends (Hallinan & Teixeira, 1987; Patchen, 1982). Additionally, when children from different ethnolinguistic groups are educated in classes where their languages have equal status sanctioned by the school, they can become more likely to choose children from the other group as friends (Aboud & Sankar, 2007; Wright & Tropp, 2005). And these positive effects can be cumulative over time, such that students who have greater proportions of cross-race friends during their high-school years have a greater tendency to form cross-group friendships in college (e.g., Stearns et al., 2009).

Similarly, strategies that focus on shifting social norms so that ingroup members appear more supportive of positive intergroup relations can also facilitate cross-group friendship development (see De Tezanos-Pinto et al., 2010; Frey & Tropp, 2006; Mallett, Wagner, & Harrison, in press; Migacheva & Tropp, 2008). A prime example is provided by Mallett and Wilson (2010). These authors had White participants watch either a videotaped interaction of two White students, or one White student and one Black student. In both cases, students depicted in the video reported that they became friends even though they initially had low expectations about the friendship. In addition, some participants were asked to relate the interaction to their own experiences by writing either about a time when an interaction went better than expected or when it went just as expected. Following these procedures, participants interacted with an unknown Black partner; then they were contacted a week later to discern whether they had formed any new friendships. The authors found that participants who wrote about a prior experience that exceeded their expectations not only had a more positive interaction with their Black partner, but they also reported forming significantly more cross-race friendships during the week following the study.

☐ **Conclusion**

Emerging intergroup research highlights the importance of cross-group friendship in reducing prejudice and promoting positive intergroup effects. Although there has been great variability in how cross-group friendship has been operationalized in the research literature, studies reveal that cross-group friendships typically yield large reductions in prejudice. This effect is particularly strong when the assessment is based on behavioral measures. And cross-group friendship often triggers indirect contact effects through which ingroup friends of those with cross-group friends also become more tolerant.

Many obstacles still exist in the development of cross-group friendships, including patterns of intergroup segregation and strong social norms against associating with outgroups. However, by reversing these trends through establishing more optimal conditions for contact and providing norms that support and encourage ties across groups, we can enhance the positive potential afforded by cross-group friendships.

☐ Note

1 Of the remaining 15 friendship tests, only one tested generalization in different situations. The rest came from Pettigrew (1997a) and tested secondary transfer effects as discussed in detail in Chapter 3.

CHAPTER 9

Does Group Status Moderate Contact Effects?

In the preceding chapters, we have shown that intergroup contact can promote reductions in intergroup prejudice. And this is particularly the case when the contact situation is explicitly structured to enhance positive intergroup outcomes (see Allport, 1954; Pettigrew, 1998).

Still, despite the wealth of research on intergroup contact, researchers have only begun to consider the distinct ways in which group status might moderate contact effects. This inattention is surprising given the differing histories and experiences of minority and majority status groups. As with many areas of research, prior contact studies have tended to assume that the same basic psychological processes underlie contact effects for members of different groups (see Hunt, Jackson, Powell, & Steelman, 2000). Thus, the research literature has until recently neglected the perspectives of minority status groups (Ellison & Powers, 1994; Shelton, 2000).

However, emerging work has begun to stress the importance of examining contact effects for people on both sides of the intergroup relationship (Sigelman & Welch, 1993; Tropp, 2006), along with suggesting that members of minority and majority status groups often have different challenges with which they must contend as they approach cross-group interactions (e.g., Devine & Vasquez, 1998; Hyers & Swim, 1998). For example, members of majority status groups typically experience concerns about being perceived as prejudiced by those lower in status, while members of minority status groups experience concerns about becoming targets of prejudice from those higher in status (see Plant, 2004; Plant & Devine, 2003; Shelton, 2003; Stephan & Stephan, 1985; Vorauer, Main, & O'Connell, 1998).

These perspectives offer important advances for understanding how minority and majority group members might approach and experience cross-group interactions. Nonetheless, relatively little is known regarding whether group differences in status moderate the extent to which intergroup contact can promote positive intergroup attitudes among members of minority and majority status groups.

Both theory and research now suggest that group differences in status may compel members of minority and majority status groups to differ in how they conceive of their intergroup relationships and define relations between their groups (see Blumer, 1958; Bobo, 1999; Sidanius & Pratto, 1999). For instance, relative to members of minority status groups, members of majority status groups are generally less inclined to reflect on their group's privileged status (Leach, Snider, & Iyer, 2002), or to think of themselves in terms of their group membership (Pinel, 1999), unless there are demands to do so in the immediate social context (McGuire, McGuire, Child, & Fujioka, 1978).

By contrast, members of minority status groups tend to be well aware of their group's devalued status (Jones et al., 1984). They recognize that they are likely to be perceived and evaluated in terms of their devalued group membership (Goffman, 1963). They live with the constant threat of becoming targets of prejudice and discrimination (Crocker, Major, & Steele, 1998), as well as receiving inferior treatment due to their group's devalued status (see Swim et al., 2003; Swim, Hyers, Cohen, & Ferguson, 2001). Correspondingly, compared to majority group members, they may be less satisfied with efforts to achieve intergroup equality (Eibach & Ehrlinger, 2006) and may be less inclined to perceive equal status during contact (Riordan, 1978; Robinson & Preston, 1976).

We must consider the implications of these contrasting orientations for achieving positive outcomes from intergroup contact among members of minority and majority status groups. For example, repeated recognition of their group's devalued status may negatively affect minority group members' feelings about the intergroup relationship, while this issue may be considered less relevant to the intergroup relationship among majority group members. Thus, even when contact is used to improve relations between groups, long-standing histories of devaluation could well inhibit the degree to which intergroup contact can promote positive intergroup attitudes among members of minority status groups, relative to the effects among members of majority status groups (see also Ellison & Powers, 1994).

☐ Meta-Analytic and Survey Tests of Group Status Effects

Again using our meta-analytic data, we examined whether relationships between intergroup contact and prejudice typically differ among members of minority and majority status groups (see Tropp & Pettigrew, 2005b). Specifically, we coded each sample as to whether participants in the contact situation belonged to a devalued, lower status group (i.e., minority status), or a dominant, higher status group (i.e., majority status). These codings were conducted at the level of samples, since many studies included separate samples of both minority and majority status participants. Additionally, a coding of "both minority and majority" was used for samples that combined responses from members of both status groups. Two independent judges achieved a kappa of .94 for the group status ratings, and discrepancies between the judges were resolved through further discussion.

As a first step in our analysis, we tallied the number of samples that examined relationships between intergroup contact and prejudice among members of minority and majority status groups. Of the 698 samples included in this analysis, only 142 samples (20.3%) examined contact outcomes among members of minority status groups, while 505 samples (72.4%) examined contact outcomes among members of majority status groups. The remaining 51 samples (7.3%) assessed contact outcomes for both status groups. A chi-square analysis indicates significant differences in distributions of these samples ($X^2(2) = 495.94, p < .001$) with the proportion of minority samples being substantially lower, and majority samples substantially higher, than what would be expected by chance. This comparison reveals the relative scarcity of contact research from the perspectives of minority status groups (see Devine & Vasquez, 1998; Shelton, 2000).

As described in Chapter 3, approximately half of our samples (52%) involve contact between racial and ethnic groups, while the remaining samples involve groups that vary in terms of age, sexual orientation, disability, or mental illness. We therefore analyzed effects for the racial and ethnic samples both combined with and separate from the rest of the samples, to check for consistency in patterns of effects across intergroup contexts.

First, we compared mean contact–prejudice effects for all minority and majority samples, and separately for those minority and majority samples involving racial and ethnic contact. As shown in Figure 9.1, significant contact–prejudice effects were observed in all cases, but the magnitudes of the effects differ significantly across our minority and majority samples. Contact–prejudice associations were generally weaker among the minority samples (mean $r = -.18$) than among all majority samples (mean $r = -.23$; $p < .001$). Moreover, these patterns were consistent regardless of whether all samples, or only those involving racial and ethnic contact, were included in the analysis.

Next, we conducted regressions to test whether differences in group status could significantly and uniquely predict contact–prejudice effects,

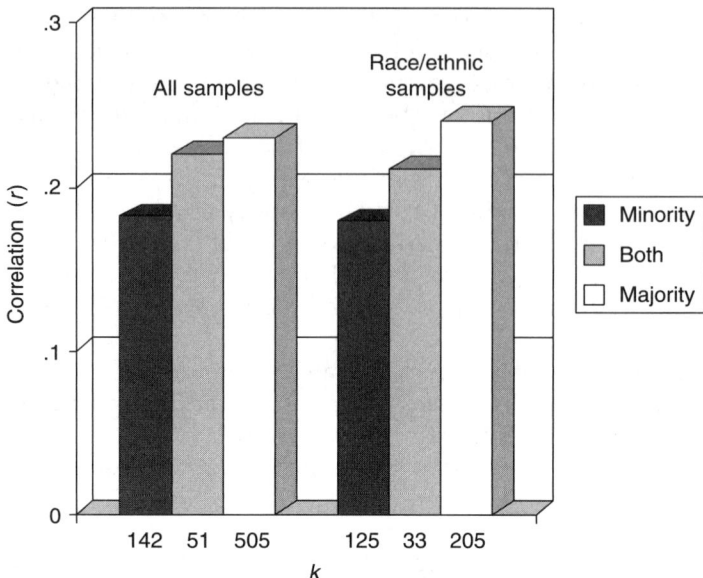

FIGURE 9.1 Mean contact–prejudice effects by group status.

beyond what can be accounted for by our many coded methodological moderators (e.g., design of study, reliability of contact, and prejudice measures) and by participant choice to engage in the contact. Table 9.1 shows that the minority–majority status distinction significantly predicts contact–prejudice effects, beyond what can be predicted by the methodological variables. Moreover, we find that the minority–majority status distinction emerges as a significant predictor both when all samples are included in the analysis and when the racial and ethnic samples are analyzed separately.

Intrigued by these results, we wanted to see whether we could replicate these findings in a single study. As we noted earlier in Chapter 7, meta-analyses are often criticized for testing comparisons across studies with different variables, samples, and procedures – the so-called apples-and-oranges problem (Rosenthal, 1991). Additionally, given the meta-analytic nature of our data, we were not able to specify the processes by which group devaluation would contribute to weaker contact–prejudice effects among members of minority status groups (see Sigelman & Welch, 1993).

Consequently, we conducted a secondary analysis of data from the *Taking America's Pulse* survey (National Conference for Community and Justice, 2000), which includes responses from 995 White Americans and 709 Black Americans as part of a nationally representative sample of adults in the United States (see Tropp, 2007). Respondents indicated whether

TABLE 9.1 Summary of Inverse Variance Weighted Regression Model Using Group Status as Predictor for Contact–Prejudice Effect Sizes

Predictor Variables	All Samples		Racial/Ethnic Samples	
	β	z	β	z
Type of study	.01	.12	.10	1.59
Type of contact measure	−.06	−1.19	−.04	−.58
Reliability of contact measure	−.23	−5.30***	−.23	−4.16***
Reliability of prejudice measure	−.09	−2.29*	−.13	−2.43*
Sample size	−.02	−.55	−.00	−.03
Participant choice	−.01	−.22	.02	.33
Minority–majority status	−.10	−2.81**	−.15	−2.97**
R^2		.09***		.11***
Q_{Model}		68.29***		43.32***
k		698		363

Source: Adapted from Tropp and Pettigrew (2005b).

Note: β = standardized regression coefficient; z = z-test for the regression coefficient; p = probability of z-test; R^2 = proportion of variance accounted for; Q_{Model} = test of whether the regression model explains a significant portion of variability across effect sizes (see Wilson, 2002); k = number of samples included in the analysis. These analyses were conducted using Fisher's z-transformed r values. Random effects variance components (based on Fisher's z-transformed r values) ranged between .019 and .020.
* $p < .05$; ** $p < .01$; *** $p < .001$.

they do or do not currently have contact with the racial outgroup (in a "yes" or "no" format), and they reported their feelings of closeness toward outgroup members in general, on a scale ranging from 1 (very far) to 5 (very close). Replicating our meta-analytic findings, results showed that the relationship between contact and intergroup closeness was significantly weaker among Black respondents ($r = .078$, $p < .05$) than among White respondents ($r = .223$, $p < .001$). Moreover, these patterns persist even after controlling for a range of demographic indicators (age, gender, geographic region, level of education, family income, political ideology, and religiosity).

Some researchers have proposed that contact effects may be weaker among members of racial minority groups because of differential frequencies of contact. That is, minorities are more likely to come into contact with the racial majority group compared to the frequency with which racial majority group members have contact with the racial minority group (see Butler & Wilson, 1978; Forman & Rodriguez, 2003; Sigelman & Welch, 1993). However, additional analyses of the American survey data revealed that Black and White respondents in this sample did not meaningfully differ in the extent to which they reported having current interracial contact ($X^2(1) = 2.01$, $p = .16$) or in their overall reports of interracial closeness (means = 3.68 and 3.63, respectively; $t(1,654) = 1.24$, $p = .21$).

Although these particular samples of Black and White Americans reported similar degrees of current interracial contact, other work suggests that Blacks typically do experience more interracial contact than Whites due to their smaller numerical representation (see Blau & Schwartz, 1997). As such, it is possible that the similar reports of contact among Black and White respondents may actually reflect a tendency for Whites to inflate numbers of their interracial relationships and to exaggerate the closeness of those relationships, as suggested by Bonilla-Silva (2003).

☐ Minority–Majority Relations and the Roles of Prejudice and Discrimination

We further sought to test whether the patterns of intergroup contact effects might correspond with other potential points of divergence between members of minority and majority status groups, in line with recent theorizing about minority–majority relations (see Bobo & Fox, 2003, for an extended discussion). Specifically, we tested whether a factor such as perceived racial discrimination might curb contact–prejudice associations among minority group members (i.e., Black Americans), but not among majority group members (i.e., White Americans). In the survey, respondents reported the extent to which they perceive discrimination against their racial group in society, with reverse-coded responses ranging from 1 (not at all) to 4 (a great deal).

Several studies show that Black and White Americans sharply differ in their views of interracial relations (Eibach & Ehrlinger, 2006; Gallup Organization, 2001; Kluegel & Bobo, 2001), with most Black Americans perceiving substantial discrimination against their group (Sigelman & Welch, 2001). Indeed, racial discrimination continues to play a significant role in the lives of Black Americans (see Feagin, 1991; Pettigrew, 2007c). And this persistent recognition of discrimination is likely to influence how members of racial minority groups feel toward relations with the racial majority group (see Tropp, 2003). Consistent with this view, other work suggests that perceptions of discrimination often contribute to predicting racial minority group members' interracial attitudes, while such perceptions are generally unrelated to interracial attitudes among members of the racial majority group (see Alexander, Brewer, & Livingston 2005; Monteith & Spicer, 2000).

Correspondingly, in further analysis of these national survey data, we found that Black respondents perceived greater racial discrimination against their own group ($M = 3.43$) than did White respondents ($M = 2.37$; $t(1691) = 24.89$, $p < .001$). Additionally, greater perceptions of racial discrimination significantly related to less interracial closeness among Black respondents ($r = -.116$, $p < .01$) while no significant relationship between perceived discrimination and interracial closeness emerged among White respondents ($r = .031$, $p > .30$).

More importantly, however, we found that perceptions of racial discrimination moderated the effects of contact in different ways for Black and White respondents. Among those Black and White respondents who perceived no, little, or only some discrimination against their racial group, interracial contact consistently predicted greater intergroup closeness (t's ranging from 3.54 to 4.60, $p < .01$). However, among those who perceived a great deal of discrimination against their racial group, contact still predicted greater interracial closeness for White respondents ($t = 2.62$, $p = .01$) but not for Black respondents ($t = .84$, $p = .40$). Additionally, it is important to note that more than half of the Black respondents in this sample ($n = 396$, 56%) reported a great deal of discrimination against their racial group. This result reveals the special importance of perceived discrimination as a negative force in the interracial relationship from their perspective. Perceived threat may well be involved for those African-American respondents who believe that considerable racial discrimination continues to exist in the United States. We will see in Chapter 12 that threat is typically involved when intergroup contact fails to reduce prejudice. Thus, although positive outcomes can often be achieved through interracial contact (Allport, 1954; Pettigrew & Tropp, 2006), positive contact effects may be diluted to the extent that members of minority status groups perceive considerable discrimination against their groups (see also Tropp, 2006).

Related findings have been observed in other empirical studies that examine how minority group members feel about intergroup contact in relation to the prejudice and discrimination they perceive. Tropp (2003) experimentally tested how ethnic minority participants (Asian Americans and Latinos) would respond to an ostensible expression of prejudice from an ethnic majority (White) confederate partner. Participants were randomly assigned to overhear one of two scripted dialogues between their partner and the experimenter, in which the partner did or did not make a seemingly prejudiced comment in relation to the participant's ethnic group (i.e., preferring not to be matched with a member of this group). Following these procedures, participants completed questionnaires including measures of hostility and anxiety, chronic perceptions of discrimination, and feelings about interacting with the White confederate partner and with Whites in general.

Participants exposed to the prejudiced comment reported greater hostility and anxiety, and less positive feelings about interacting with both their partner and with Whites in general, as compared to those not exposed to the prejudiced comment. Moreover, correlations revealed that chronic perceptions of discrimination predicted stronger feelings of hostility and anxiety, and less positive feelings about interacting with their White partner, even after controlling for exposure to prejudice within the experimental setting. These findings indicate that exposure to even a single instance of prejudice from the racial outgroup can have profound, negative effects on racial minority group members' feelings about intergroup contact, which may be exacerbated further by ongoing perceptions of racial prejudice and discrimination.

Similarly, Shelton and Richeson (2006) studied relationships between Black participants' attitudes toward and feelings about contact with Whites, and how these relationships might relate to perceiving a White interaction partner to be prejudiced. Several weeks after completing an initial attitude survey, Black participants were invited to come to the laboratory to interact with a White partner. Afterward, they reported how they felt during the interaction, and the extent to which they thought their White partner was prejudiced. Results showed that the more negative Black participants' initial racial attitudes were, the more they perceived their White partner to be prejudiced, the less they reported liking their White partner, and the less they enjoyed the interaction. Additionally, perceived prejudice mediated the relationship between participants' racial attitudes and enjoyment of the interaction. That is, participants' negative attitudes toward White people predicted less enjoyment of the interaction to the extent that they perceived their White partner to be prejudiced.

These various findings suggest that positive contact outcomes for members of minority status groups may be greatly inhibited by perceptions of prejudice and discrimination. Indeed, with good reason, minority group members' responses to contact with the majority are likely to be tainted by histories of and experiences with prejudice and discrimination. Such prior intergroup experiences obviously can fuel negative expectations for future contact and poison the intergroup relationship with continued suspicion and distrust.

☐ Minority–Majority Effects and Optimal Conditions for Contact

Relating these findings to the broader framework of intergroup contact theory (Allport, 1954; Brown & Hewstone, 2005; Pettigrew, 1998), we must therefore question whether establishing Allport's optimal conditions within the contact situation can sufficiently alleviate these negative forces. Indeed, as noted in Chapter 5, several researchers have noted that conditions of equal status may be defined and interpreted in various ways (e.g., Foster &

Finchilescu, 1986; Riordan, 1978). Moreover, members of different status groups may not always agree about the extent to which equal status has been achieved within the contact situation (Robinson & Preston, 1976). Thus, even when objective attempts are made to establish such conditions as equal status, group members' subjective responses to intergroup contact may still vary depending on the perceptions and experiences that inform their understanding of the intergroup relationship (see Cohen, 1982; Livingston, Brewer, & Alexander, 2004). As such, implementing optimal conditions within the contact situation may not necessarily be enough to ensure positive contact outcomes among members of both minority and majority status groups. Put simply, optimal conditions for majority participants in intergroup contact are not necessarily optimal for minority participants.

We return to our meta-analytic data to pursue a preliminary test of these ideas (see Tropp & Pettigrew, 2005b). Specifically, we sought to examine whether samples from minority and majority status groups would still show different patterns of contact–prejudice relationships even in those cases where the contact situation was purposely designed to maximize positive intergroup outcomes. We examined this issue by testing whether our global indicator of Allport's conditions would predict stronger contact–prejudice effects for both the minority and majority samples, beyond what could be accounted for by our coded methodological variables. Specifically, we conducted regression analyses for our minority and majority samples in which we simultaneously included our global indicator of Allport's conditions and our coded methodological variables as predictors for the contact–prejudice effect sizes (see Table 9.2). Again, we conducted these analyses both for all samples combined and separately for those samples that just involve racial and ethnic contact.

Overall, our results indicate that Allport's optimal conditions predict significantly stronger contact–prejudice effects for the majority samples, while they do not contribute significantly to predicting contact–prejudice effects for the minority samples. Moreover, we observe similar patterns of results whether we look at all samples combined (z's from -2.12 to -1.09) or only those samples involving racial and ethnic groups (z's from -2.67 to -1.40).

In part, the lack of statistical significance in the minority context reflects the relatively small number of studies included in this comparison. Nonetheless, given the difference in magnitude of the effects in the minority and majority contexts, these patterns suggest that members of minority and majority status groups may still show different responses to intergroup contact, even when the contact situation is explicitly structured to maximize positive intergroup outcomes. Specifically, it may be that establishing Allport's conditions within the contact situation typically enhances the positive effects of contact among members of majority status groups, while these conditions may often not enhance the positive effects of contact among

TABLE 9.2 Summary of Inverse Variance Weighted Regression Model Testing Contact Conditions as Moderator for Effect Sizes

	All Samples				Racial/Ethnic Samples			
	Minority		Majority		Minority		Majority	
Predictor Variables	β	z	β	z	β	z	β	z
Type of study	.01	.10	−.01	−.16	.04	.35	.19	2.00*
Type of contact measure	−.00	−.03	−.02	−.36	−.00	−.00	.03	.31
Reliability of contact measure	−.23	−2.71**	−.20	−3.87***	−.24	−2.68**	−.20	−2.64**
Reliability of prejudice measure	−.21	−2.54*	−.05	−1.13	−.21	−2.38**	−.12	−1.64
Sample size	−.06	−.75	−.03	−.68	−.08	−.92	.00	.06
Participant choice	−.05	−.65	−.04	−.76	−.09	−1.01	.00	.04
Contact conditions	−.10	−1.09	−.12	−2.12*	−.13	−1.40	−.22	−2.67**
R^2		.14**		.08***		.15**		.09**
Q_{Model}		22.39**		44.48***		22.68**		21.17***
k		142		505		125		205

Source: Adapted from Tropp and Pettigrew (2005b).

Note: β = standardized regression coefficient; z = z-test for the regression coefficient; R^2 = proportion of variance accounted for; Q_{Model} = test of whether the regression model explains a significant portion of variability across effect sizes (see Wilson, 2002); k = number of samples included in the analysis. Analyses were conducted using Fisher's z-transformed r values. Random effects variance components (based on Fisher's z-transformed r values) ranged between .016 and .021.

* $p < .05$; ** $p < .01$; *** $p < .001$.

members of minority status groups. For example, a situation that is perceived as welcoming by a majority group may be perceived by the minority group as demeaning or patronizing. Related work also suggests that minorities are more likely than majorities to prefer inclusive representations of intergroup relations that preserve subgroup identities rather than those that appear to be more assimilationist in nature (see Dovidio, Gaertner, & Kafati, 2000).

As suggested previously, we believe that these findings grow from more general differences in perspective regarding the nature of relationships between the groups (see Bobo, 1999; Livingston et al., 2004). Members of minority status groups are more likely to perceive prejudice and discrimination as integral to the intergroup relationship, while these are less prominent features of the intergroup relationship in the minds of majority group members. As such, the effects of positive conditions within the intergroup context may be diluted for members of minority status groups, as their feelings about relations with the majority group are shaped by long-standing histories of devaluation.

Taken together, these findings compel us to question traditional intergroup contact theory as a general conceptualization of what occurs when members of different groups interact. Rather, in our efforts to understand the effects of contact, we must recognize that group members have perceptions and experiences that they bring to the contact, which may in turn influence their responses to cross-group interactions (Devine & Vasquez, 1998; Plant & Devine, 2003; Tropp, 2003).

Moreover, our research suggests that establishing optimal conditions within the intergroup context may not always be enough to promote positive intergroup relations among members of both minority and majority status groups. Even when objective attempts are made to create optimal conditions, subjective responses to contact may still be guided by long-standing views of the intergroup relationship, which often involve histories of prejudice and disadvantage (Cohen, 1982; Robinson & Preston, 1976; Tropp, 2006). Thus, we must enhance our understanding of how different histories can lead members of different status groups to show varying responses to intergroup contact, and to recognize the important role that prejudice and discrimination can play in shaping minority group members' attitudes toward intergroup relationships.

☐ Positive Potential of Cross-Group Friendship in Minority–Majority Relations

Still, recent work demonstrates the potential for intergroup contact to yield positive outcomes among both minorities and majorities when the contact takes the form of cross-group friendships. Indeed, several studies now suggest that friendship contact can promote comparably positive outcomes among members of minority and majority groups. Recall the study by Page-Gould et al. (2008) reported in Chapter 8, which showed that experimentally manipulated friendships significantly reduced anxiety and encouraged the initiation of cross-group interactions. Moreover, these authors found similar patterns of results among both their Latino and White participants. Similarly, Levin et al.'s (2003) longitudinal UCLA study showed that greater numbers of cross-group friendships predicted less ingroup bias among students from both ethnic minority and ethnic majority groups.

In South Africa, Tredoux and Finchilescu (2010) found for both Black and White university students that greater amounts of cross-racial friendship were inversely associated with negative meta-stereotypes – stereotypes that one believes outgroup members hold to be true of your ingroup (Vorauer, 2006; Vorauer et al., 1998; see also Frey & Tropp, 2006). This finding is of both practical and theoretical importance for members of both minority and majority groups. Cross-group friendship should help to ameliorate some of the principal reasons why intergroup contact is avoided – minority group members' fear than the majority will discriminate against them and majority group members' fear that they will be perceived as prejudiced.

In three separate experiments with various racial groups, Finchilescu (2010) demonstrated that such negative meta-stereotypes are even more important than prejudice in heightening anxiety about cross-racial interaction. Consistent with these results, Crisp and Abrams (2008) show how intergroup contact can reduce "stereotype threat" – the process by which meta-stereotypes can impede performance of many kinds (Steele, 1997). Stereotype threat is triggered by the perception that others view you and your group as deficient in a given domain. People often have negative expectations regarding how they will be viewed by outgroup members (Krueger, 1996; Vorauer et al., 1998). These negative expectations can hinder the potential for intergroup contact to promote positive relations between groups (Frey & Tropp, 2006; Shelton et al., 2006; Vorauer, 2006). Weakening negative meta-stereotypes should, therefore, have markedly positive consequences for both performance and further cross-group interaction.

Further analysis of the national survey data reported by Tropp (2007) also shows that interracial friendship can render perceptions of racial discrimination less important for predicting Black Americans' racial attitudes toward Whites. In addition to the general contact measure, the survey asked participants who reported contact whether they had a White friend. Even after controlling for demographic variables, Black participants who reported having a White friend reported significantly greater closeness to Whites overall than those who did not report a White friend. Moreover, perceptions of discrimination did not significantly predict interracial closeness among Black respondents who reported interracial friendships. But perceived discrimination did significantly predict interracial closeness among those who reported no interracial friendships. Thus, while discrimination exists as a prominent feature of the interracial relationship, friendships across racial boundaries diminish the extent to which Black Americans rely on perceptions of discrimination to form their intergroup attitudes.

☐ Conclusion

This chapter highlights the role of group status in interpreting intergroup contact effects. At a basic level, the recent work reviewed compels us to recognize that contact can often produce different outcomes for members of minority and majority status groups, and this well-established fact has important implications for the strategies we use to improve relations between groups. Beyond the traditional focus on objective conditions of contact, we urge that greater attention be given to subjective responses to contact among minority and majority groups as shaped by the histories and experiences that group members bring to the contact situation.

Moreover, emerging work shows that there can be varied implications of intergroup contact – both positive and negative – depending on the nature and goals of the contact, and the status relations of the groups involved. We discuss these issues further in Chapter 11, and we are certain that future research will continue to elucidate the conditions that give rise to different contact outcomes.

Intergroup Contact as One of Many Predictors of Prejudice

Although our central focus is on the effects of intergroup contact, our book would be incomplete if we did not acknowledge the many other variables that relate to prejudice. In his classic volume, *The Nature of Prejudice*, Gordon Allport made it clear that there existed no "simple and sovereign" theory of prejudice. He writes:

> There is no master key. Rather, what we have at our disposal is a ring of keys, each of which opens one gate of understanding. . . . We may lay down a general law applying to all social phenomena that *multiple causation* is invariably at work and nowhere is the law more clearly applicable than to prejudice.
> (Allport, 1954: pp. 208, 218; italics in the original)

Throughout the previous chapters, we have seen that intergroup contact typically diminishes prejudices of many types. But we must ask whether intergroup contact still relates significantly to prejudice once the many other strong predictors of prejudice are entered into the analysis. To answer this question, this chapter places contact's effects in a more realistic context of other prejudice predictors. Specifically, we examine the extent to which intergroup contact predicts reduced intergroup prejudice when other major predictors are also taken into account.

☐ Eight Classes of Predictors of Prejudice

In broad strokes, we can delineate eight classes of prejudice predictors that have consistently proven important in the extensive research literature concerning prejudices across many nations and groups. These predictors involve all the social sciences and range across all levels of analysis, from the widest macro-level of society to the narrowest micro-level of individual concerns and personality characteristics:

(1) *Social context predictors* comprise the broad social milieu captured by such variables as the prevailing norms of prejudice and population ratios of the ingroup and outgroup.
(2) *Socio-location predictors* include demographic variables that indicate one's position in society, such as age, sex, and education level.
(3) *Economic predictors* focus largely on indicators of income, wealth, and perceived economic deprivation.
(4) *Political predictors* entail both the right–left political dimension as well as a person's sense of political efficacy or powerlessness.
(5) *Personality predictors* include such well-researched syndromes as authoritarianism and social dominance orientation.
(6) *Identity predictors* concern an individual's group identifications – how strongly people think of themselves in national, ethnic, and other group terms.
(7) *Threat predictors* capture how threatening the outgroup is perceived to be to one's self and to one's group.
(8) *Experiential predictors* primarily involve people's experiences with both positive and negative intergroup contact.

Fortunately, the two German national probability surveys conducted in 2002 and 2004 that were analyzed earlier (see Heitmeyer, 2002, 2003, 2005) set out to measure each of these eight classes of variables that predict attitudes toward immigrants (see Appendix B). Their data allow us to determine how well indicators of contact relate to prejudice in the full context of these other major predictors of prejudice. Consider in detail each of these types of predictors.

Social Context Predictors

These predictors gauge the social context within which respondents live. The German surveys provide two examples – *the prejudice norm and the population ratio of immigrants* (Pettigrew, Wagner, & Christ, 2007b). Each of these variables was measured at the district level. In Germany, a district is a state-organizational unit that usually comprises a big city or a number of smaller cities, towns, or rural areas. District populations vary widely – between 36,000 and 3,400,000 inhabitants. For each district, the norm for anti-immigrant prejudice was calculated by averaging the responses of interviewees in that district to this question: *Which opinion do your friends or acquaintances have – mostly pro-immigrants, mostly against the immigrants, equally many support as reject?* Census data provided the population ratio of foreigners in each district.

We know from previous research that these two indicators relate to prejudices in general and anti-immigrant prejudice in particular. For instance, anti-Black and pro-segregationist norms in the southern United States shaped the racial views of White Southerners for years (Pettigrew, 1959, 1961). In Chapter 3, we also saw examples of how both pro-segregationist as well as pro-integrationist norms led to inconsistent behavior among steelworkers and coalminers (Minard, 1952; Reitzes, 1953). And using a normative index for cities and towns in Alberta, Canada, Mulder and Krahn (2005) found that norms significantly related to their respondents' support for ethnic diversity.

The role of population ratios in predicting prejudice is also important but more complex. As we shall learn in Chapter 12, two countervailing processes are in operation. A high proportion of the outgroup can potentially create threat that in turn leads to heightened prejudice. But the presence of numerous outgroup members simultaneously maximizes opportunities for intergroup contact, and we know that when contact occurs it can lead to diminished prejudice. A host of moderators determine which of the two conflicting effects of the outgroup percentage is dominant.

Not surprisingly, then, research on prejudice that employs proportion indices or population ratios has found varied patterns of results, ranging from greater prejudice (Dixon, 2006; Pettigrew & Cramer, 1959; Taylor, 1998), to no significant effects (Citrin, Green, Muste, & Wong, 1997; Kessler & Freeman, 2005; Pantoja, 2006; Pew Research Center, 2006), to greater intergroup acceptance (Dixon, 2006; Fetzer, 2000b; Hayes & Dowds, 2006; Hood & Morris, 2000; Kalin, 1996; Stein, Post, & Rinden, 2000; Taylor, 1998). But one caveat must be made. The apparent effects of population proportions may reflect, at least in small part, a self-selection bias (Dustmann & Preston, 2001). That is, more tolerant individuals may be more willing to move to areas with large numbers of outgroup members, while more prejudiced people may take care to avoid such areas.

Socio-Location Predictors: Age, Gender, and Education

Where people are located in society, as indexed by *age, gender, and education*, also shapes their prejudices. Education is especially important as it constitutes a more reliable indicator of social class than such other variables as income and occupational prestige – although we will consider economic predictors in the next general category.

Age

Older people tend to be more prejudiced than the young on most, but not all, types of prejudice. Having lived longer in the society, they are likely to be more enmeshed in their national cultures and traditions; they can recall their society "in the good old days" before the newcomers arrived. Hence, we might well expect that age would relate positively with anti-immigration views, and that is generally the case in both Europe and North America.

Repeatedly, European studies have found stronger anti-immigrant attitudes among the elderly (Fetzer, 2000a, 2000b; Kessler & Freeman, 2005; Mayda, 2006). In their analyses of 15 European Union countries, Jackson, Brown, Brown & Marks (2001) found a zero-order correlation of +.13 between age and the extreme response of wanting "to send immigrants back." But these investigators also uncovered a reversal in Great Britain, where younger Britons more often chose this response. And Hayes and Dowds (2006) report no age differences in immigration attitudes in Northern Ireland.

Age has also been repeatedly found to be a positive correlate of anti-immigration opinion in North American research. In an 11-variable model, Mulder and Krahn (2005) found age to be a major predictor of Canadians' attitudes toward immigration. As elsewhere, older Canadians were significantly more opposed to immigration than were younger Canadians. With a national sample, Palmer (1996) reported a more complex pattern. Older Canadians favored low levels of immigration, but younger Canadians were more opposed to non-White immigration.

Fetzer (2000b) found that Americans 60 years of age or older were significantly more anti-immigrant and anti-immigration than were others. With two American surveys, Ha (2008) noted that age was significantly and positively related to attitudes against both immigrants and immigration. And older Californians voted more frequently than younger voters for the anti-immigrant Proposition 187 in 1994 (Hood & Morris, 2000). Other American studies report that older Americans are somewhat, though not significantly, more negative toward immigration (e.g., Burns & Gimpel, 2000; Citrin et al., 1997; Pantoja, 2006; Stein et al., 2000).

Gender

Gender is one of the weakest predictors of prejudice generally. For some outgroups, men are somewhat more prejudiced; for others, women are somewhat more prejudiced. Not surprisingly, then, research on immigration attitudes has rarely found gender to be important. In Europe, Fetzer (2000b) found no significant gender differences in anti-immigration attitudes in either France or Germany, nor did Hayes and Dowds (2006) in

Northern Ireland. In their test of 15 European Union countries, Jackson and colleagues (2001) found women to be more negative toward immigration in just three countries, and there was no overall gender effect for the complete dataset. For the full European Union, Kessler and Freeman (2005) obtained mixed results. There were no appreciable gender differences on whether there were "too many" immigrants in the country, but men were significantly more likely to believe that their nation should "not accept" immigrants.

Blake (2003) and Mulder and Krahn (2005) failed to unearth significant gender differences in Canada using their immigration measures, but Palmer (1996) found Canadian females to be more resistant to immigration. American data are similar. Espenshade and Hempstead (1996) uncovered no gender differences concerning their respondents' desired level of immigration. Likewise, Citrin et al. (1997) failed to obtain any significant gender differences on the desired level of immigration or on delaying benefits to immigrants. Changing results across time were discovered by Burns and Gimpel (2000). In the 1992 American National Election Study, females voiced significantly more often a desire to "decrease immigration a lot." Four years later, in the 1996 election study, females advocated an increase in immigration significantly more than did men. Ha (2008) obtained a racial difference: White American males were significantly more prejudiced against immigrants, while there were no gender differences among Black Americans.

Education

Better-educated people are generally more tolerant toward a range of outgroups, and attitudes toward immigrants are no exception. Studies in both Europe and North America have also found educated respondents to be more accepting of both immigrants and immigration (Fetzer, 2000a; Hayes & Dowd, 2006; Kessler & Freeman, 2005; Mayda, 2006). Mulder and Krahn (2005) found education to be the most important of 11 predictors of support for immigration in Canada. Both Blake (2003) and Palmer (1996), who analyzed national probability sample surveys, also determined education to be a major predictor of positive Canadian attitudes toward immigration.

Similar results are routinely uncovered in American studies (e.g., Burns & Gimpel, 2000; Fetzer, 2000a; Ha, 2008). Fetzer (2000b) found education to be a major negative predictor of both anti-immigrant and anti-immigration views. For Citrin and colleagues (1997), education proved to be the most important predictor of immigration attitudes in their 20-variable regression. Well-educated Californians voted against the anti-immigrant Proposition 187 more often than did others (Hood

& Morris, 2000). Likewise, the Pew Research Center (2006) found well-educated respondents to be more resistant to extreme anti-immigration policies such as requiring new identification cards, restricting social services for illegal immigrants, and amending the American Constitution to bar citizenship to the children of illegal immigrants.

But can we accept these consistent results at face value? Jackman (1973) thinks not. She questions the lower scores of the well-educated on various measures of authoritarianism and prejudice. Jackman holds that the greater cognitive sophistication of the educated puts in doubt their responses to such scales. The well-educated, she believes, are more likely to perceive the prejudice measure's purpose and respond with more socially acceptable answers. However, later research, using both survey and experimental data from Western Europe, casts serious doubt on Jackman's contentions (Pettigrew et al., 2007a; Wagner & Zick, 1995). In general, more educated people are less influenced by their ingroup's prejudices and parochialisms.

Economic Predictors

Perhaps the most popular explanations for intergroup bias and such exclusionary policies as opposition to immigration involve economic factors. It is commonly assumed that the economically vulnerable – the unemployed and the poorest citizens – will be the most likely to resist the advancement of other groups. While not entirely wrong, extensive research reveals that the role of economic factors is considerably more complex. The German surveys lack straightforward measures of unemployment, but three measures that tap economic deprivation offer correlates in both the 2002 and the 2004 samples. These relationships, however, are relatively modest in predictive value compared to many other predictors.

Anti-immigrant prejudice is strongest among those who *cannot afford many things that they would like to have*, who think *the current German economic situation is poor*, and who think *foreigners are doing economically better than Germans* (see Appendix B). This third measure, *group relative deprivation*, has often been found to correlate positively with a wide array of prejudice measures (Pettigrew et al., 2007a; Walker & Pettigrew, 1984; Walker & Smith, 2002). All three measures suggest that subjective judgments of economic deprivation are more important correlates of anti-immigrant opinions than are such objective measures as unemployment.

Although these results run counter to much popular discourse about resistance to immigration, they are consistent with other research. Fetzer (2000a) failed to find any significant relationships between unemployment and immigration opinions in France, Germany or the United States. Kessler and Freeman (2005) also failed to find unemployment links with overall anti-immigration sentiment in the European Union. Other survey research did not find unemployment to be a predictor of immigration opinions in the United States (Citrin et al., 1997; Ha, 2008). And neither poor nor unemployed Californians voted more than others for the anti-immigrant Proposition 187 (Hood & Morris, 2000).

But Canadian research offers an exception. Palmer (1996) reported that unemployment status and the unemployment rate were significant predictors of his respondents' desires for minimal immigration. Although he showed that concerns about culture and crime are also important, Palmer concluded that unemployment concerns were central among many types of Canadians.

But these gross unemployment results cannot tell the full story. With their European Union data, Kessler and Freeman (2005) discovered that an interaction term for unemployment with the area's foreign population was highly related with the views that there were "too many" immigrants and that immigrants should not be allowed to take jobs. This suggests that it is not unemployment per se that evokes opposition to immigration, but the fears it provokes when there are many immigrants in the immediate locality. This possibility is supported by further findings. An index that taps how survey respondents believe that immigration will impact jobs is highly correlated with American opinions about immigration (Citrin et al., 1997). And detailed socio-psychological research in Canada shows that the belief in zero-sum resources – that what the immigrants get economically will necessarily come out of the dominant group's pocket – is central to such fears (Esses, Dovidio, Jackson, & Armstrong, 2001; Jackson & Esses, 2000).

Income and personal financial predictors provide modest results at best. In Canada, neither Blake (2003) nor Mulder and Krahn (2005) uncovered significant relationships between personal finances and opinions concerning immigration. Other studies show only small effects (Burns & Gimpel, 2000; Ha, 2008; Hayes & Dowds, 2006; Hood & Morris, 2000; Pantoja, 2006). For instance, in a national survey, 31% of economically secure Americans thought that Hispanic immigrants significantly increased crime, compared to 43% of less secure Americans (Pew Research Center, 2006).

Similar to the German results, two studies using diverse measures uncovered significant positive associations between pessimism about the American economy and anti-immigration opinions (Burns & Gimpel, 2000; Espenshade & Hempstead, 1996).

We concur with Citrin and his colleagues (1997) that for anti-immigration prejudice there is only a "restricted role of economic motives rooted in one's personal circumstances" (p. 875). Our only caveat is that subjective economic deprivation indicators, such as group relative deprivation, have some predictive power and are involved in the perception of collective threat.

Political Predictors

Two favorite variables of political scientists, *political conservatism* and *political inefficacy*, contribute substantially to the prediction of anti-immigration attitudes. Political conservatives are usually more prejudiced than others for a wide range of target groups, and once again attitudes toward immigrants are no exception.

Previous research on both sides of the Atlantic has shown that respondents with conservative ideologies are typically more opposed to immigrants and immigration. Conservatives in the European Union believe significantly more often than others that there are too many immigrants in their countries and that no further immigrants should be accepted (Kessler & Freeman, 2005).

Using Canadian university students, Beaton and colleagues (Beaton, Francine, Clayton, & Perrino, 2003) showed that conservative values relate to anti-immigration opinions directly ($r = +.43$) as well as indirectly by enhancing both traditional ($r = +.28$) and newer forms of racism ($r = +.41$). Using a sample of American university students, Short (2004) found political conservatism to be a major predictor of their negative attitudes toward immigrants. Similarly, three surveys found political conservatives to be more anti-immigration in American probability samples (Burns & Gimpel, 2000; Citrin et al., 1997; Ha, 2008). Political conservatives also act on their beliefs in the voting booth; they were strong supporters of the anti-immigrant Proposition 187 vote in California (Hood & Morris, 2000).

American opposition to immigration also relates to a general isolationist perspective on many international issues (Espenshade & Hempstead, 1996). Finally, in a 2006 Pew Survey, 83% of conservative Republicans would deny basic social services to illegal immigrants and 52% would bar citizenship to their children (Pew Research Center, 2006).

But much of this effect can be attributed to threat. Respondents on the political right report considerably more personal and collective threat from immigrants, and this enhanced sense of menace accounts in large part for their greater prejudice against immigrants (Pettigrew et al., 2007a).

Political inefficacy and political interest generally have not been studied together with prejudice as thoroughly as the right–left dimension. The German surveys measure it with a three-item scale provided in Appendix B. With such items as *"Political engagement makes no sense for me,"* the scale taps a sense of alienation and powerlessness specifically involving the political system. It is frequently used in political science to predict nonvoting (Prewitt, 1968; Southwell & Everest, 1998), but it also correlates positively with prejudice (Pettigrew & Meertens, 1995; Pettigrew, 2000). It proved to be a significant correlate of anti-foreigner bias in the German surveys, and the reverse phenomenon of political trust is associated with pro-immigration attitudes (Blake, 2003; Ha, 2008).

Personality Predictors

Authoritarianism and *social dominance orientation* (SDO) are the two primary personality predictors of most types of prejudices. As listed in Appendix B, the 2002 and 2004 German national surveys measured these much-studied major predictors of prejudice with three items each. One of the authoritarian items reads: *Two of the most important characteristics should be obedience and respect for one's superiors*. A sample SDO item reads: *Groups at the bottom of our society should stay there*.

For more than half a century authoritarianism has predicted most prejudices, with a vast array of diverse item sets translated into numerous languages from the original Berkeley measures (Adorno et al., 1950) and the more recent right-wing authoritarianism (RWA) measures offered by Altemeyer (1981, 1988, 1996). For example, in the 2002 probability sample of German citizens used in this chapter, authoritarianism correlates positively and significantly with all five of the prejudices tested: prejudice against homosexuals ($r = +.31$), Jews ($r = +.26$), resident foreigners ($r = +.54$), the homeless ($r = +.35$), and even new residents of all types to the respondents' areas ($r = +.36$).

Considerable research in recent years has shown SDO to relate in varying degrees to both authoritarianism and prejudice (Sidanius & Pratto, 1999). In their review of RWA–SDO correlations, Roccato and Ricolfi (2005, Study 1) found that only 1 of 51 independent samples obtained a negative relationship between the two measures. The weighted mean correlation was $r = +.33$, and, as Duckitt (2001) noted, the largest correlations occur in nations characterized by strong ideological contrasts. This association is hardly surprising given the orientation of both variables to power – one individually focused, the other group focused.

Yet, despite their positive association, RWA and SDO typically both contribute positively to the prediction of prejudice. Indeed, McFarland (2010) refers to the two measures as "the lethal union" in that they typically prove to be among the major predictors of individual prejudice in large regression analyses. And, as expected, they are among the most important predictors of attitudes toward immigrants in both German surveys. Authoritarianism taps conformity to authority and tradition, while SDO emphasizes group hierarchy and dominance.

Canadian experiments shed further light on why SDO proves to be so central in understanding anti-immigration attitudes (Jackson & Esses, 2000). Because participants who score high on SDO are concerned with group power, they view immigrants to "their" country not so much as a personal threat but as a collective threat to the societal and cultural dominance of the native population. The experiments demonstrated that high-SDO participants were far less willing than others to grant empowerment to immigrants in such forms as helping them to adjust to Canadian life and to overcome the barriers they face in Canadian society. Moreover, this unwillingness to help by those with a socially dominant orientation was largely explained by their firm belief in the zero-sum nature of societal resources. They tend to believe that if the immigrants get more, then they and other Canadians will get less.

Identity Predictors

In studying prejudice, many social psychologists favor measures of social identity. The German surveys measured *German identity* with two items – *how proud are you to be German* and *how much do you feel like a German?* (see Appendix B). The 2002 survey also asked the same questions about *European identity*. Both the 2002 and 2004 data reveal German identity to relate positively and significantly with anti-foreigner attitudes. But the two identities – German and European – have contrasting relationships with anti-immigrant prejudice: while German identity correlated with *anti*-foreigner views, the superordinate European identity correlated with *pro*-foreigner views. This difference emerges despite the fact that the two identities are not rivals; people can easily think of themselves as German *and* European, for the two identities operate at different levels. Indeed, the two identities correlate positively ($r = +.42$), and yet they relate differently to immigration attitudes (Pettigrew, 2007a, 2007b).

Two earlier studies have shown that European identity relates to more positive opinions about immigration (Kessler & Freeman, 2005; Luedtke, 2005). In addition, the finding that German identity relates positively to anti-immigration views replicates previous work. In Europe, national identity and national pride typically relate positively with anti-immigration views (Luedtke, 2005; Jackson et al., 2001). Indeed, Luedtke (2005) maintains that strong national identities are primarily responsible for the European Union's difficulties in gaining central control over immigration policy for the entire union.

Only in Belgium is there a more complex situation, reflecting its deep ethnic divide (Maddens, Billiet, & Beerten, 2000). In Dutch-speaking Flanders, strong Flemish identification links with anti-foreigner attitudes, while Belgian identification links with greater acceptance of resident foreigners. However, in French-speaking Wallonia, just the opposite applies: strong Wallonian identity and weak Belgian identity relate to less anti-foreigner sentiment.

Three American survey studies support the dominant trend. In a Texas survey, a strong American identity significantly predicted that the respondent wished to restrict the number of immigrants allowed into the United States (Stein et al., 2000). Using probability data from various national surveys, Mayda (2006) and Ha (2008) both have shown that national pride correlates significantly with anti-immigration opinions.

Threat Predictors

Much popular discussion about resistance to immigration in both Europe and North America centers on the notion of threat. Immigration is said to threaten jobs, culture, and the traditional way of life. Research on both continents lends support to such contentions.

Inspired by the work of Stephan and Stephan (1985), the threat scales shown in Appendix B and used in the 2004 survey tap two types of threat. Four items each tap threats from immigration in four domains that can be felt personally and/or collectively for the German people. *Individual Threat* is determined by whether respondents feel that "Foreigners living here threaten *my* personal freedom and rights; . . . *my* personal economic situation; . . . *my* personal way of life; and . . . *my* personal security." *Collective Threat* is assessed by whether respondents believe that "Foreigners living here threaten *our* freedom and rights; . . . *our* prosperity; . . . *our* culture; and . . . *our* security." Chapter 12 will examine these same variables in more detail.

Note that the term *foreigners* in these items refers only to foreigners who are living in Germany. From the German perspective, Turkish migrant workers constitute the prototype of foreigners residing in the nation. In 2003, 8.9% (7.34 million) of Germany residents were officially recognized as foreigners; those of Turkish descent constituted the largest foreign group (1.88 million). Pretests revealed that about half of German respondents think of a person of Turkish origin when asked about a resident foreigner in Germany.

Jackson and his coworkers (Jackson et al., 2001) noted in 14 out of 15 European nations that threat from immigrant "encroachment" correlated significantly and positively with the extreme response of wanting to send all immigrants back to their home countries. Much like the items in the collective threat scale of the 2004 survey in Appendix B, "encroachment" in this study included insecurity fears and threats to their way of life.

A German study observed that both realistic and symbolic threat correlated with negative contact, as it does in our results ($r = +.29$ with personal threat and $r = +.22$ with collective threat). This work also discovered strong relationships between "cultural discordance" and threat. Thus, the culturally more similar Italian immigrants are seen as far less threatening than Turkish immigrants (Rohmann, Florack, & Piontkowski, 2006).

The dependent variable in our analysis differs between the two national surveys – as indicated in Appendix B. In 2002, a six-item scale ($\alpha = .84$) measured prejudice against resident foreigners with such blatant items as:

"Foreigners have jobs that we Germans should have." But in 2004, only two of the original six items were available ($r = +.59$): "There are too many foreigners living in Germany" and "When jobs become scarce, foreigners who live in Germany should return to their home country."

Experiential Predictors

The final class of predictors introduces the experience that the respondent has had, both positive and negative, in direct contact with immigrants. We know from the previous chapters that intergroup contact is a major experiential predictor of prejudice. In the present analysis, *negative contact* is measured by a single question: *How often has a foreigner pestered you? Positive contact* was tapped by a three-item index ($\alpha = .75$): *How often has a foreigner helped you? How often do you have interesting conversations with a foreigner? How many of your friends and close acquaintances are foreigners?*

European studies have also revealed the importance of direct contact in shaping attitudes toward immigrants. In their Northern Ireland research, Hayes and Dowds (2006) concluded that friendship across sectarian lines was the most important correlate of attitudes toward immigrants. They found that even having friends from another nation significantly related to greater acceptance of immigrants – another instance of the secondary transfer effect discussed in Chapter 3. Fetzer (2000b) found that personal contact was significantly related to pro-immigration opinions, but he also noted that proximity measures had little effect – a common finding because proximity does not guarantee actual face-to-face contact, much less the possibility of friendship (Festinger & Kelley, 1951).

Studies in receiving countries further corroborate the importance of contact with immigrants. Fetzer (2000b) noted that personal contact in the United States related to reduced anti-immigrant attitudes. In New Zealand, contact with immigrants proved to be the central predictor in Ward and Masgoret's (2006) model of attitudes toward immigrants. Generalization of intergroup contact with non-immigrant groups can also influence immigration attitudes. Hence, Americans who have cross-racial friends who are not immigrants are significantly more accepting of immigrants – the secondary transfer effect once more (Ha, 2008). In short, intergroup contact has largely positive effects in the immigration domain, as we have noted in many other domains throughout this volume.

Indeed, there is ample research to suggest that greater levels of contact with outgroup members can predict greater decreases in intergroup prejudice (see Eller & Abrams, 2004; Levin et al., 2003; Paolini et al., 2004; Van Laar et al., 2008). Nonetheless, changes in intergroup attitudes do not depend solely on degrees of contact with the outgroup, but also on degrees of contact with members of one's ingroup. Recall from Chapter 6 that

Wilder and Thompson (1980) found that, independent of contact with the outgroup, participants who experienced less contact with members of their own group showed less intergroup bias. Thus, intergroup bias lessens as intergroup contact increases and as ingroup contact decreases. Although both of these factors are clearly operating in prejudice reduction, like other predictors of prejudice, neither can claim to be the single key to understanding prejudice.

☐ Testing the Predictors of Anti-Immigrant Prejudice in Germany

For our German results, we utilize the two surveys conducted in 2002 and 2004 by the 10-year project on prejudice headed by Wilhelm Heitmeyer (2002, 2003, 2005). The respondents were all 16 years of age or older. Our analyses treat the responses of only those respondents who had no migration background (2722 respondents in 2002 and 1314 in 2004). These well-conducted phone surveys of large probability samples of German citizens provide all the highly relevant predictors of prejudice that we have just discussed.

Figure 10.1 presents the results of the 2002 regression predicting anti-foreigner prejudice. The threat scales were not included in the 2002 survey. Without them, all the variables tested, except gender and education, attain statistical significance ($t > 1.96$, $p < .05$). Note especially that both negative

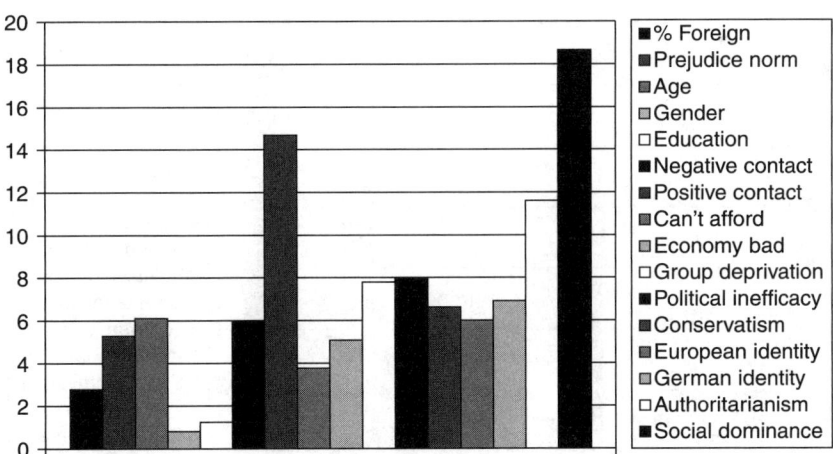

FIGURE 10.1 Correlates of anti-foreigner prejudice 2002 German survey (in t scores).

and positive contact remain critical predictors of prejudice even in this 16-variable regression. Positive contact in particular is critical and rivals in importance the two personality predictors – authoritarianism and social dominance orientation. There is, of course, considerable multicollinearity in these results – that is, many of the predictors are accounting for the same variance in the prejudice-dependent variable. Hence, a leaner model with just four predictors – *positive contact, prejudice norm, authoritarianism, and SDO* – can account for 51% of the prejudice variance compared with 59% for the entire 16-variable regression.

Figure 10.2 repeats the test using the results of the 2004 German national survey. Now we have measures for both personal and collective threat, but we no longer possess measures for the prejudice norm and European identity predictors. Here we see the great importance of collective threat. Many Germans resent the resident foreigners in their midst, because these newcomers are viewed as threatening not so much their personal lives but the security and way of life of German society itself. Personal threat is far less involved. In fact, collective threat mediates most of the association between personal threat and anti-immigrant prejudice (Sobel test: $z = 11.96, p < .0001$). In other words, personal threat appears to be important in increasing anti-immigration views largely through heightening the sense of collective threat.

But note that, even with the addition of these threat variables, positive contact remains a major and highly significant predictor of anti-foreigner prejudice. By contrast, negative contact, because it strongly relates to the threat indices, no longer significantly relates to prejudice.

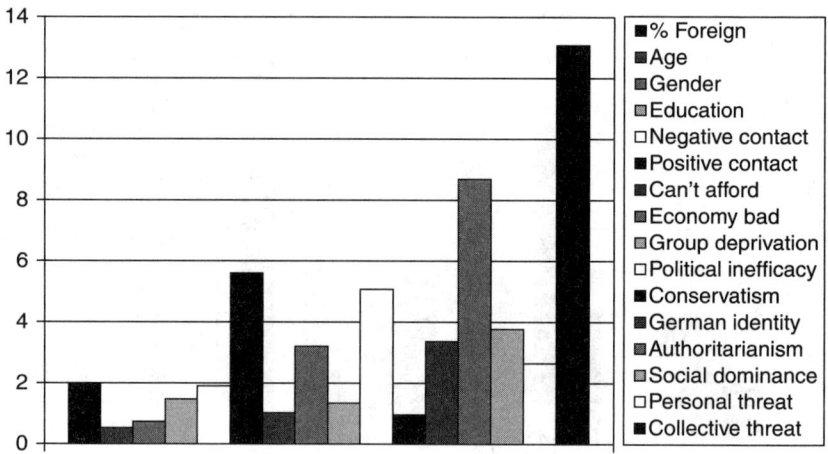

FIGURE 10.2 Correlates of anti-foreigner prejudice 2004 German survey (in *t* scores).

And just three key predictors with the 2004 sample – positive contact, along with collective threat and authoritarianism – account for 54% of the prejudice variance compared with 58% for the entire 16-variable regression.

☐ Conclusion

Our analyses, supported by research literature from four social science disciplines, highlight the importance of an array of predictors of attitudes toward immigration and immigrants. Each of the disciplines supplies important predictors from their varying perspectives. From sociology, *normative context, population ratios, age,* and *education* are all important. From economics, several forms of *perceived economic deprivation* predict anti-immigration views. From political science, *conservatism* and a sense of *political inefficacy* link with opposition to immigration. And from social psychology, *intergroup contact, national identity, authoritarianism, social dominance orientation*, and *perceived threat* all predict at the individual level of analysis.

Two trends are conspicuous. First, the consistency of these findings across such a wide range of factors, as evidenced by the diversity of the cited research, is remarkable. We have noted the same predictors in studies of both sending and receiving countries with contrasting national immigration histories and policies. We found the same predictors in work guided by different theories from four social science disciplines, using dissimilar datasets, methodologies, sets of control variables, and types of target groups and respondents.

Within the context of industrial nations, immigration appears to evoke opposition from similar segments of the native population. Why is this? We offer two explanations. Prejudice against immigrants is highly correlated with other forms of prejudice, and thus it shares with prejudice many common features found in prejudice research throughout the world. In addition, immigration can threaten native populations in similar ways across industrial nations. Economic and political threats are aroused, but considerable research points to the special significance of cultural threats experienced as collective rather than directly individual in nature.

Second, intergroup contact, especially positive contact, is a centrally important predictor of prejudice in general and prejudice against immigrants in particular. We have noted this relationship throughout this volume, but now we see that it holds even when tested together with a great array of other prejudice predictors. Of course, we know from earlier discussions that this strong link between contact and prejudice is bidirectional. Prejudice limits intergroup contact and contact reduces prejudice. But the finding that intergroup contact remains a major predictor of prejudice even after such variables as SDO and authoritarianism – strong correlates of prejudice – are controlled offers strong evidence that the prejudice-reducing power of contact remains even after other prejudice predictors are considered.

Criticisms of Intergroup Contact Theory

Informed criticism is an important feature of science. Together with empirical falsifications of a theory's predictions, logical critiques of existing theories are an invaluable means of advancing both the social and physical sciences. And, like all important theories, intergroup contact has received its share of critical attention. In this chapter, we will consider criticisms of intergroup contact theory carefully in order to detect weaknesses of the theory and to learn where theoretical extensions and further research could advance our understanding of the effects of intergroup contact.

☐ Uninformed Criticism

Uninformed criticism, by contrast, is of little value. In part, it may indicate that some contact researchers have failed to communicate adequately and accurately the theory's basic assumptions and predictions. But contact theory has often been attacked broadly by those who appear not to have read the contact research literature. Based, perhaps, on simply the theory's title, these critics see its ideas as being naïvely simple. They mistakenly believe that contact theory proposes that virtually all intergroup contact invariably leads to strong positive outcomes irrespective of the conditions and settings of the contact. Ray (1983, p. 3), for example, writes: "The American version of the contact hypothesis as it is usually applied to race relations is that the more you get to know blacks, the better you will like them." Similarly, McGarty and de la Haye (1997, p. 155) presume that the theory holds that intergroup contact "... will of itself produce better relations" between groups. We have seen throughout this volume that

161

these overly simplified views of contact theory are mistaken; these critics appear to ignore the many complexities of the phenomenon that we have discussed, and Chapter 12 will discuss the predictors of intergroup contact that fail to reduce prejudice.

Others, too, have criticized intergroup contact theory apparently without regard for its supporting evidence. "Sometimes," write McGarry and O'Leary (1995, p. 210), "good fences make good neighbors." But when would this be true? Consider the repeated failures of "fences" from the Great Wall of China and Hadrian's Wall on Scotland's southern border to the modern examples of the Berlin Wall, the Green Line of Cyprus, Israel's new West Bank Wall, and America's disputed wall along its long border with Mexico. "Good neighbors" hardly resulted from any of these prominent experiments with "good fences."

More generally, McGarry and O'Leary (1995) contend that intergroup contact does not typically reduce prejudice. They focus their analysis on the tragic "Troubles" between Catholics and Protestants in their native Northern Ireland. They emphasize that contact can, under the hostile normative conditions that have long characterized their homeland, actually confirm and enhance rather than allay prejudice. But, extensions of contact theory, with their focus on intergroup anxiety and threat, amply allow for this possibility in such historically violent and divided societies as Northern Ireland.

Thus, our broader concern is that these critics appear to ignore the subtleties of contact theory and its supportive research. Instead, they stress how those Northern Irish who lived in urban neighborhoods predominantly occupied by members of the other religious community were among the most seriously victimized – often forced to move out under threats of violence. But this process was not principally a process of neighbors evicting their neighbors. Rather, it was violent, extremist groups from both religious communities that orchestrated most of the removal (Darby, 1986). One suspects that these groups were motivated largely by a desire to form tightly segregated communities, so that neighborhood contact would not undermine the intense sectarian bigotry upon which their movements depend.

Such hostile activities of extremist organizations hardly constitute a refutation of contact theory. Abundant studies by social psychologists in *Northern Ireland itself* repeatedly find that Catholic–Protestant contact typically lessens prejudice to the same or even greater degree as intergroup contact in other parts of the globe (e.g., Hewstone et al., 2005, 2006; McClenahan, Cairns, Dunn, & Morgan, 1996; Niens, Cairns, & Hewstone, 2002; Paolini et al., 2004; Tam, 2006; Tam et al., 2008; Tausch et al., 2007a, 2007b). In addition, this work has also demonstrated the beneficial effect of *indirect* (or "extended") contact. Thus, even those Northern Irish respondents who know that a friend in their religious community has a friend in the other religious community reveal less sectarian bigotry (Christ et al., in press; Paolini et al., 2004).

Further research in conflict-ridden Northern Ireland has shown that intergroup contact not only reduces prejudice, but can even engender trust and forgiveness. Having friends in the other religious community relates to greater *forgiveness* even among Catholics and Protestants who have suffered personally from violence during the "Troubles" (Hewstone et al., 2006, p. 113). Remarkable as this finding is, it has been matched by research on an aggressor group in another region torn by intergroup violence – Bosnia and Herzegovina. Cehajic and Brown (2010) found that Serbian adolescents who had contact with Bosnian Muslims were significantly more willing to acknowledge that their ingroup was largely responsible for the atrocities committed during the 1992–1995 war in the former Yugoslavia. This interethnic contact effect was mediated by increases in perspective-taking and decreases in perceived ingroup victimhood.

These striking results are consistent with studies that demonstrate how positive contact acts to diminish both individual and collective threat (see Chapter 12, Figure 12.3). Thus, contrary to McGarry and O'Leary's unsupported speculations, intergroup contact theory has received some of its strongest empirical support in research conducted in Northern Ireland and such other regions with elevated intergroup violence as Bosnia and Herzegovina.

☐ Five Types of Informed Criticism

We can learn, however, from informed criticism that responds more directly to the extensive contact literature we have discussed in the previous chapters. Five diverse types of informed criticism have been advanced: (1) the claim that societal diversity reduces trust; (2) the problem of achieving intergroup contact; (3) the assertion that intergroup contact does not influence attitudes toward social change and policies; (4) the contention that intergroup contact retards social change; and (5) the assertion that shifts in attitudes at the micro level (i.e., intergroup prejudice) have little to do with macro-level phenomena (i.e., intergroup conflict and collective violence). Interestingly, all these critiques acknowledge that intergroup contact typically reduces the prejudice of individuals. But each then proceeds to raise questions and delimit the basic finding described in Chapter 2. Taken together, these critiques argue that contact theory is not relevant for intergroup trust, does not address how to achieve optimal intergroup contact, does not influence attitudes toward social policy, diminishes minority group efforts for social change, and has little to do with group-level intergroup conflict and violence. Let us discuss each of these important points in detail.

Societal Diversity Reduces Trust

The most publicized disparagement of intergroup contact theory is that advanced by the political scientist Robert Putnam (2007). Focusing on the concept of "social capital" and its relation to ethnic diversity, he analyzed an American national survey together with community-level surveys from 41 non-random American areas of widely varying sizes. Social capital is primarily measured by the trust that respondents report in their ingroup and outgroup neighbors. Putnam reports that at both the aggregate and individual levels of analysis ethnic diversity is negatively associated with community trust. From these results, Putnam concludes that diversity has a dual negative effect: it reduces both ingroup and outgroup solidarity. Low trust with high diversity, he claims, is also associated with lower confidence in local government, leaders, and news media, reduced political efficacy, less voting, fewer contributions to charity, less reported happiness, more television viewing, and fewer friends and confidants. Thus, Putnam argues that Americans in ethnically heterogeneous areas "hunker down" and participate less in civil society. Intergroup contact, it is contended, is too weak in diverse communities to build trust and other forms of social capital.

Publicizing his thesis widely, Putnam's contentions gained immediate media attention. A Google search uncovers such headlines as "diversity is our destruction," "Harvard study says diversity is bad for you," and "diversity harms human relations." A *Wall Street Journal* columnist cheerfully pronounced "the death of diversity" (Henninger, 2007).

Such headlines tell considerably more about intergroup tensions and the media in the United States than they do about Putnam's research. Indeed, Putnam modified his contentions in several important ways – all of which the media ignored. For example, he noted that the problems with diversity that he identified held only for the short term. In the long run, Putnam (2007, p. 137) writes, ". . . successful immigrant societies have overcome such fragmentation by creating new, cross-cutting forms of social solidarity and more encompassing identities." Such disclaimers were lost in translation once the mass media seized upon the research – a not uncommon event when social science findings are sensationalized.

But what about the specific nature of this highly publicized research? The media apparently neither understood nor cared about details associated with its methodology. But as Dawkins (2008) and others point out, there are important technical issues raised by the study,[1] two of which are directly relevant to contact theory. Gross aggregation across ethnic groups

Criticisms of Intergroup Contact Theory   165

and imprecise measurement of "diversity" raise special concerns. For example, collapsing across ethnic groups to report effects at the societal level may hide substantial differences in social capital variables between groups, especially given ethnic disparities and the typically larger levels of distrust among minority groups (see Tropp, 2008).

But the biggest problem is simply that Putnam does not include either intergroup contact or segregation indices in his published analyses. Of course, one cannot assume contact from proximity – a fallacy that we have pointedly noted throughout this volume. However, Putnam (R. Putnam, personal communication, August 26, 2009) has kindly supplied us with further information on this critical point. Cross-group friendship and group segregation were measured in his dataset, but they were not included in his regressions. He set the friendship indicator "aside," he wrote us, because it is bidirectional and thus its causal relationship is difficult to interpret with cross-sectional data. He also set the segregation measure "aside" after finding that it (net of diversity) did not influence his main findings.

Putnam advises us that he uncovered only a weak zero-order correlation of +.13 between cross-group friendship and trust toward other groups. This finding stands in sharp contrast to the +.41 correlation found in Northern Ireland between intergroup friendship and outgroup trust (Hewstone et al., 2006, p. 112). It is possible that this difference results from the use of dissimilar measures of trust across academic disciplines. But, if this were the case, Putnam's interpretations of trust in the context of intergroup contact theory require further elaboration.

Putnam also fails to distinguish between "diversity" at the broad community level and at the level of neighborhood segregation – the latter a critical indicator of opportunities for intergroup contact. Also, his cross-sectional data do not allow us to know whether the diverse areas he identified are stable or in the midst of rapid transition, such as when Whites are hastily replacing Blacks (so-called gentrification) or when Blacks are exploding out of the crowded ghetto and swiftly replacing Whites. Both of these rapidly changing situations can erode trust as well as restrict intergroup contact.

With these phenomena far less prevalent in Europe, it is perhaps not surprising that tests in 28 European countries failed to confirm Putnam's thesis that diversity erodes social capital (Gesthuizen, Van der Meer, & Scheepers, 2008). Instead, economic inequality and a national history of continuous democracy were found to be key predictors of the wide differences in social capital between European nations.

Despite these limitations, Putnam (2007, p. 142) asserts:

> For progressives, the contact theory is alluring, but I think it is fair to say that most (but not all) empirical studies have tended instead to support the so-called "conflict theory", which suggests that, for

various reasons – but above all, contention over limited resources – diversity fosters out-group distrust and in-group solidarity. On this theory, the more we are brought into physical proximity with people of another race or ethnic background, the more we stick to "our own" and the less we trust the "other".

In response, given the literature we have reviewed in this volume, we and others (e.g., Hewstone, 2003) think it is definitely *not* fair to say that most of the research supports any such trend. In social psychology, theories of threat and conflict are not viewed as being in opposition to intergroup contact theory, and it is a misreading of both to regard them as rival theories.

Moreover, other investigators of diversity have found results that contrast sharply with those of Putnam. When they enter contact or segregation directly into their analyses, they find that the bleak picture painted by Putnam is dramatically altered. For example, Stolle, Soroka, and Johnson (2008) utilized survey data from both Canada and the United States, and they replicated Putnam's results without considering intergroup contact. But when they examined responses from those individuals who regularly talked to their neighbors, they found that these individuals were far less influenced by the racial and ethnic character of their neighborhood. In short, social ties moderated the negative effects of diversity just as contact theory would predict.

Similarly, Rothwell (2009) studied how residential segregation of minorities, which severely restricts intergroup contact, alters trust in American cities. He analyzed the same data and used the same methods of an earlier study by Alesina and La Ferrara (2002), whose results mirrored those of Putnam's (2007). But Rothwell added a comprehensive measure of neighborhood segregation into his analysis. This one change reversed the findings. Rothwell's (2009, p. 1) results suggest that residential ". . . integration increases trust, and if anything, diversity fosters trust for any given level of segregation." He then replicated this finding using voting behavior, rather than trust, as the dependent variable. Rothwell concludes that earlier analyses suggesting negative effects of diversity had suffered from an "omitted variable bias" by excluding measures of neighborhood segregation.

It should be noted that Rothwell employed a different dataset than Putnam, one that included only respondents residing in American metropolitan areas. Uslaner (in press, 2011), on the other hand, in part used the same dataset as Putnam and obtained results consistent with those of Rothwell. He demonstrates in repeated analyses that it is the residential segregation of groups, not diversity per se, that drives down generalized trust. First, Uslaner estimates a hierarchical model of trust across 30 nations and finds that residential segregation is highly associated with reduced trust. Then he shows that American residents of integrated neighborhoods who have diverse social networks evince greater trust using two different national surveys – including the one used by Putnam (the Social Capital Benchmark Survey). From these results, Uslaner (in press, p. 1) forcefully concludes:

> ... [S]everal people, most notably Robert Putnam, now argue that trust is lower when we are surrounded by people who are different from yourself. This view is mistaken. Diversity (fractionalization) is not the culprit in lower levels of trust. Instead, it is residential segregation which isolates people from those who may be of a different background. Segregation is one of the key reasons why contact with people who are different from ourselves does not lead to greater trust: Such contact may not be so frequent and it is not likely to take place frequently and in an atmosphere of equality, as argued by Allport, Forbes, and Pettigrew.

How can we explain these contrasting results? Some of the differences in findings are almost certainly a function of different measures for the same key concepts – such as "trust" and "segregation." And the neighborhood segregation measures employed by Rothwell and Uslaner are different from those used by Putnam and may more closely tap the probability of intergroup contact in a given area.

In any event, contact theory on the whole cannot be effectively critiqued when measures of contact and group segregation are omitted from the analysis. Moreover, the Rothwell and Uslaner results are consistent with the basic contentions of intergroup contact theory. Diversity can involve both intergroup threat *and* greater contact; the problem lies in understanding how they both function within the same model rather than selecting only one or the other as the key process. In Chapter 12 we offer further support for this position, demonstrating how threat and contact fit neatly into the same predictive model of prejudice.

At this point, accumulating research suggests that Putnam is half right and half wrong. Diversity can indeed decrease trust and other indicators of social capital when there is strict group segregation to prevent intergroup contact. But diversity alone, without restrictive segregation operating, will not decrease trust – thanks to the ameliorative effects of intergroup contact.

Achieving Intergroup Contact: The Leading-the-Horses-to-Water Problem

A second critique concerns how we can encourage groups with histories of conflict to interact with each other. It is hardly surprising that many of the strongest critics of contact theory come from parts of the world – such as Northern Ireland and South Africa – that have experienced long and bitter histories of intergroup strife. They have witnessed first hand the harmful effects of group segregation and negative contact. Understandably, these commentators are skeptical of theories that hold out promise for positive change in intergroup relations. Yet, like inhabitants of rain forests reporting on weather patterns, these critics offer a pessimistic view of intergroup contact theory in part biased by what they observe in their immediate environments.

In particular, Dixon et al. (2005) highlight the obstacle of achieving intergroup contact after centuries of intergroup strife and discrimination – "the leading-the-horses-to-water" problem. This raises an issue that intergroup contact theory was not initially designed to address, but this criticism is important. Achieving effective intergroup contact in the first place is obviously essential, and these critics have themselves initiated the study of this problem with a series of ingenious studies.

They recommend a "reorientation" of the field with more discursive, comparative, and qualitative analyses that would support a richer description of actual intergroup contact and how people commonly view their everyday contact experiences. As Chapter 9 makes clear, we heartily agree with this proposal, and we concur with papers published both before and after their critique that offer similar views regarding necessary extensions of contact research and initial findings on this path (Devine & Vasquez, 1998; Shelton & Richeson, 2005; Swim et al., 2003; Tropp, 2006). However, we view such efforts as useful extensions of present work rather than a complete "reorientation." We would also add to the list the need for longitudinal and multi-level research – points to be discussed in the final chapter.

Three of the critics' own papers offer novel contributions concerning informal racial segregation in the new South Africa. Using photographs taken from a helicopter, Dixon and Durrheim (2003) describe the elaborate patterns of racial positioning and avoidance on Durban's long, lovely, and formerly Whites-only beach. They found that Whites arrived early in the day and often left before many Blacks arrived. When the two races did occupy the large beach together, they typically chose quite separate spaces.

Tredoux and Dixon (2009) describe racial seating patterns at popular bars and nightclubs in Cape Town, and how they slowly change as the night wears on. They also show how the degree of racial contact or segregation recorded depends on the particular scale of analysis used. The researchers used four levels of analysis: the nightclubs, subsectors of the clubs, tables within the subsectors, and interpersonal interactions. The results showed a clear scale pattern – the narrower the level of analysis, the more racial segregation observed. Thus, the nightclub level revealed the most interracial contact while the interaction level showed the least.

In another study of small seminars held at the University of Cape Town, Alexander and Tredoux (2010) show that without intervention by the instructors, voluntary seating was highly segregated by racial group. Initial patterns of seating segregation largely persisted over the semester. This finding suggests that instructors should initially assign seating alphabetically or by some other means that eliminates ethnically segregated seating at the onset before the segregation norm solidifies. Such patterns of initial avoidance are also widespread in other areas with prior histories of intense segregation and discrimination – such as Northern Ireland and the American South. The old norms slowly recede while the new equalitarian norms have yet to develop fully. So, it is hardly surprising that in all three societies reticence and awkwardness characterize intergroup interaction, together with widespread intergroup avoidance. Clearly, the process of achieving intergroup contact deserves increased attention, and intergroup contact theory must be expanded to examine how we can effectively bring past adversaries together.

Some lessons might be gleaned from earlier generations of research that involve direct applications of contact theory. Following legacies of formal racial segregation in the United States, strategies that foster cooperative interdependence, such as the Jigsaw Classroom technique (Aronson & Gonzalez, 1988; Aronson & Patnoe, 1997), have been successful in engaging children from different racial and ethnic backgrounds (Slavin, 1985; Slavin & Cooper, 2000). Children who have had such cooperative intergroup experiences become more inclined to seek out further contact across group boundaries and even develop greater cross-group friendships (Slavin & Cooper, 2000).

A key lesson here is that patterns of segregation are likely to perpetuate further segregation, unless there are interventions in place to curb those tendencies (Orfield & Lee, 2007). Cumulative processes are at work. Segregation makes further segregation more probable, and positive contact leads to further contact.

However, this key issue is obscured by attacks on contact theory and its research with a myriad of additional and dated criticisms.[2] The presumed naïve "utopianism" of the theory requires, in their view, a "reality check" (Dixon et al., 2005, p. 679). Their principal objection involves "the optimal contact strategy" – the focus of earlier work on Allport's (1954) four conditions of optimal contact. Decades ago, this would have been a timely argument, but our meta-analytic findings show that these conditions are facilitating but not necessary (Pettigrew & Tropp, 2000, 2006). As discussed in Chapters 2 and 12, respondents overwhelmingly report positive, not negative, outcomes of intergroup contact even when there is no evidence to suggest that Allport's conditions were met. Thus, contact theory and research have moved beyond the focus that these critics belatedly attack.

Likewise, in urging the use of different methods, their critique objects to work conducted in laboratory settings with its presumed "rarified" and unrealistic conditions. Repeatedly (see also Dixon & Durrheim, 2003), these critics mistakenly assert that research has typically investigated contact under "optimal conditions." Instead, these authors argue that much contact in the "real world" actually leads to negative effects. As we note in Chapter 2, the meta-analysis revealed relatively few laboratory experiments in the contact literature. More than 70% of the contact work conducted in the 20th century and analyzed in Chapter 2 involved questionnaire and survey studies in which respondents reported on their intergroup experiences under a vast array of everyday contact situations – the very types of contact that these critics believe should be studied intensively. Indeed, since the end of *apartheid*, numerous questionnaire and survey studies have been conducted *in South Africa itself* and show that intergroup contact typically corresponds with less prejudice (e.g., Dixon et al., 2010b; Durrheim & Dixon, 2010; Gibson, 2004, 2006; Gibson & Claassen, 2010; Holtman, Louw, Tredoux, & Carney, 2005; Swart, Hewstone, Christ & Voci, 2010; Tredoux & Finchilescu, 2010).

Yet another issue raised by Dixon et al. (2005, p. 697) concerns "the use of shifts in personal prejudice as the primary measure of outcome." It is true that explicit prejudice at the individual level has been the major dependent variable employed in contact research. This is hardly surprising given that the reduction of prejudice was Allport's initial focus. But as we discussed at length in Chapter 7 (see also Tropp & Pettigrew, 2005a), prejudice outcomes have been assessed in many different ways and, increasingly, researchers are employing varied and subtle means of capturing contact's effects.

Recall the earlier discussions of how two studies – one conducted in Northern Ireland, the other in Germany – found contact differences in intergroup attribution biases. Those with intergroup contact evinced less of the ultimate attribution bias (Pettigrew, 1979) in which ingroups are systematically given more positive attributions than outgroups (Joseph et al., 1997; Vollhardt, 2010). Recall also the Crystal et al. (2008) study that revealed how school children with more intergroup contact rated racial exclusion as "wrong" more on average than those with little contact.

Indeed, previous chapters have shown that a great range of effects have been investigated successfully in contact research during the last two decades. For example, researchers have uncovered significant relationships between contact and implicit prejudice in both experimental and field settings, and in relation to groups that differ in race, ethnicity, nationality, sexual orientation, and physical ability (e.g., Aberson et al., 2004, 2008; Akinola & Mendes, 2008; Henry & Hardin, 2006; Pruett & Chan, 2006; Tam et al., 2008; Turner et al., 2007). Additional explicit outcome variables used in psychology and sociology include anxiety, individual threat, collective threat, trust, forgiveness, empathy, perspective-taking, outgroup knowledge, ingroup identification, job attainment and satisfaction, and perceptions of outgroup variability – all of which reveal positive contact effects.

Researchers in social sciences other than social psychology and sociology have also uncovered a variety of contact effects. For instance, in economics, Burns (2007) finds in South Africa that White students from interracial high schools, when compared with White students from all-White high schools, indicate significantly greater trust of Black students. In political science, Mutz (2002) has demonstrated with both national survey data and experiments that contact with those who harbor dissonant political opinions fosters political tolerance. A later study, however, modifies this finding: Popan and his colleagues (2010) find that this contact effect across political lines is limited to occasions where people cede that their opponent's arguments are rational.

Thus, the charge that contact research has featured limited dependent variables is seriously outdated. Work in recent years has greatly expanded our understanding of the intergroup contact process by vastly expanding the range of contact effects studied and including both cognitive and affective domains.

Does Contact Influence Attitudes About Social Policy?

Of special concern to Dixon and his colleagues is their claim that contact fails to improve attitudes about social policy. Here they cite the previously discussed study by Jackman and Crane (1986) that purported to show with an American survey that contact reduced prejudice but "had little effect on Whites' support for political policies designed to redress racial inequalities" (Dixon et al., 2005, p. 697). Actually, this statement is not correct. When one reanalyzes Jackman and Crane's data (1986, Table 1, p. 469), there are statistically significant differences in policy support between those with no African-American acquaintances or friends and those who have them. White Americans with cross-racial ties are more likely to favor greater government intervention to insure both equal housing opportunity ($\chi^2 = 7.73, p < .01$) and equal job opportunity ($\chi^2 = 12.18, p < .001$) than those without these ties.

As Chapter 7 documented, many other studies have also found substantial intergroup contact effects on policy attitudes. Studies in Western Europe and the United States routinely find that contact with immigrants is significantly associated with stronger pro-immigration attitudes and policy preferences (e.g., Fetzer, 2000b; Hayes & Dowds, 2006; Pettigrew et al., 2007a). Consider, too, the findings from survey data on

3800 majority group respondents from seven probability samples in France, Great Britain, The Netherlands, and West Germany (Pettigrew, 1997a, p. 178). Controlling for seven key demographic and attitudinal correlates, those who had immigrant friends were significantly ($p < .0001$) more likely to believe that immigrants' rights should be extended, that all immigrants should be allowed to stay, and that citizenship should be made easier.

Indeed, the critics themselves, together with this book's second author, have obtained some of the strongest evidence yet obtained of intergroup contact shaping policy preferences (Dixon et al., 2010b). As mentioned in Chapter 7, using a random digit dialing telephone survey of South Africans, they found that both the frequency and quality of Whites' interracial contact with Blacks related positively to their support for both compensatory and preferential racial policies that would support Black advancement. For example, agreement with "spending more of your province's education budget on schools in largely black neighborhoods" correlated significantly with both contact quantity (+.13) and quality (+.33). In general, the quality of the interracial contact had greater predictive value than the quantity of such contact, and the less threatening compensatory policies related somewhat more strongly to contact than the preferential policies (see also Durrheim & Dixon, 2010).

To be sure, intergroup contact tends to be associated with somewhat larger effects on prejudice and interactional preferences than on policy preferences. If we reanalyze Jackman and Crane's (1986, table 1, p. 469) data further, we find that the largest effects concern preferences for interracial contact. Those White respondents with African-American acquaintances and friends are far less likely than other Whites to prefer all-White work situations ($\chi^2 = 59.9$, $p < .00001$) and all-White neighborhoods ($\chi^2 = 62.2$, $p < .00001$) and to harbor such anti-Black stereotypes as undependable ($\chi^2 = 16.58$, $p < .0001$) and unintelligent ($\chi^2 = 14.97$, $p < .0005$).

In our view, the limited reading of the evidence in Jackman and Crane's (1986) influential paper has led these and other critics to charge that contact theory is severely restricted in its influence on intergroup relations. We interpret the often-obtained distinction between attitudinal and policy outcomes to be a special case of stimulus generalization: The more closely the outcomes correspond with people's lived experiences, the greater the effect that contact will have on those outcomes. But this does not mean that intergroup contact has no effect on policy support. Contact does typically improve attitudes toward policy changes beneficial for the less-powerful outgroup. And effective intergroup contact is directly relevant for institutional remedies by lessening prejudice and creating meaningful ties across group boundaries, thereby making the needed remedies more politically viable.

Intergroup Contact and the Potential Retardation of Social Change

Stephen Reicher (2007) argues that negative attitudes, even hatred, toward the majority are necessary for a minority group to initiate the protest efforts necessary for social change. To the extent that minority group members engage in contact with the majority, it may soften or improve their views of the majority, as held by intergroup contact theory. This change could potentially diminish minority group members' perceptions of discrimination, and in turn their motivation to mobilize in order to end structural inequality. We shall call this *the Reicher effect*.

In partial support of his view, Reicher points to the frequent need for minority change movements to expel majority members. This was true early in the history of the African National Congress and later in Steve Biko's Black Consciousness Movement in South Africa. It also occurred midway in the history of America's Student Non-Violent Coordinating Committee in the American South of the 1960s (Zinn, 1964).

Reicher also emphasizes the findings of Wright and Taylor (1998, 1999). These Canadian researchers found that even modest token gains for a group suffering from discrimination had the surprising effect of greatly reducing the likelihood of collective action to overcome the general pattern of discrimination. While not directly relevant to intergroup contact, Wright and Taylor's findings point to the fragility of a minority's willingness to organize and initiate collective protest to combat collective injustice. There are multiple barriers to a minority developing the unity and resources required for a successful uprising to end discrimination and inequality. Warm feelings toward the adversary obviously do not facilitate such an effort.

Survey studies show support for the Reicher effect (e.g., Dixon et al., 2010a; Saguy et al., in press; Wright & Lubensky, 2009), although there are exceptions. For example, Poore et al. (2002) found that the more Canadian Inuits experienced intergroup contact outside of their isolated community, the *more* they perceived the systematic discrimination their group faced. Similarly, Tropp (2007) observed a small positive, though not significant, relationship between interracial contact and perceptions of racial discrimination ($r = +.064$) in a national sample of African Americans. At the same time, Rodriguez and Gurin (1990) found that among Mexican Americans, contact with Anglo-Americans was negatively associated with how "illegitimate" they thought discrimination against their group was. And in another investigation, Ellison and Powers (1994) found that African Americans with White friends reported lower estimates of racial discrimination.

Experimental research also generally supports the Reicher effect. Saguy, Tausch, Dovidio, and Pratto (2009) randomly assigned college student participants to groups who possessed either high or low power in the situation. Representatives from the different groups came together to discuss either commonalities they shared or differences between them: the commonalities groups reflected more optimal contact, the differences groups more negative contact. Just as Reicher predicts, discussion of commonalities led the low-power participants to develop heightened and unrealistic expectations for fair treatment by the high-power participants.

Turning to the real life of the truly disadvantaged (Arab citizens of Israel), Saguy and collaborators again replicated the Reicher effect. Arab Israelis who report the most positive contact with Jewish Israelis showed greater perceptions of Jewish Israelis as fair and less support for social change. There is probably some verisimilitude involved here. Those Jewish Israelis who have genuinely positive contact with Arab Israelis are more likely than others of their group in fact to be fairer and more open to equitable intergroup relations. Thus, selection biases may often enhance the Reicher effect.

Wright and Lubensky (2009) present two further relevant studies. First, they surveyed African-American and Latino-American students on a predominantly White university campus. For both minority groups, contact with White students related to lower ingroup identification and this effect in turn related to more positive racial attitudes and less endorsement of collective action. But two additional points are important to note. Intergroup contact was not related to viewing Whites as "oppressors," nor were attitudes toward Whites significantly related to support for collective action. In short, the Reicher effect emerged via a two-step linkage between contact and support for collective action, with ingroup identification serving as a key mediator.

In their second study, Wright and Lubensky (2009) conducted a survey of African-American students at a predominantly Black university. These results replicated the findings of their first study. But this time, boundary permeability – the minority perception that upward mobility is possible – was also measured. This new variable, like ingroup identification, mediated intergroup contact's effects. Contact related positively with the perception of mobility, which in turn related with more favorable attitudes toward Whites and less endorsement of collective action. Once again, however, views about Whites and collective action were not significantly associated.

Additional relevant research comes from South African surveys. With 596 Black African respondents, Dixon and his colleagues (2010a) showed that the quality of intergroup contact was associated with less perception of group-level discrimination. This effect was mediated by both racial attitudes and personal experiences of racial discrimination. Thus, intergroup contact quality – measured by such ratings as how friendly, cooperative, and equal status the contact was (basically tapping

Allport's key dimensions) – related to more positive racial attitudes and fewer reports of personal discrimination. These mediators in turn were associated with a diminished sense of group discrimination. Additionally, this survey did not find the *quantity* of intergroup contact to be significantly related to any of its measures except for contact quality.

With another South African survey, Durrheim and Dixon (2010) uncovered contrasting contact effects for his Black and White respondents. Among White South African respondents, extensive contact with Black South Africans related to both lessened racial stereotyping and enhanced support for major social policies that would be "transformative." This finding replicates the studies discussed previously. However, among Black respondents, contact with Whites had little overall effect on their views of Whites and related to decreased support for transformative policies – once again, the Reicher effect. But Durrheim and Dixon also noted that those Black respondents who reported having contact with high-status Whites revealed a particular *lack* of sympathy for Whites. Gibson and Claassen (2010) uncovered similar survey results with their Black South African subsample. Again, this counter-Reicher effect suggests the operation of additional processes that further minority mobilization.

We offer three responses to this intriguing phenomenon. First, recall in Chapter 9 that the prejudice-reducing effects of cross-group interaction are considerably stronger among advantaged majorities than for the typically disadvantaged minorities. Indeed, the South African surveys suggest that interracial contact can sometimes lead Blacks to hold *greater* prejudice against the majority when status differences between the groups are large. These majority–minority differences mitigate, but do not resolve, Reicher's contentions.

Second, Reicher's analysis focuses exclusively on the need to mobilize the disadvantaged group to achieve social change. This factor is, of course, critically important, but it is not the whole story (Simon & Klandermans, 2001; Walker & Smith, 2002). Successful social change also requires some waning in the power of the advantaged and some recognition by the advantaged of the unfairness and illegitimacy of the hierarchical situation. For example, in American history, every major societal change – from the American Revolution and the abolition of slavery to the Civil Rights Movement of the 1960s – first witnessed this weakening of resolve in the dominant group. Recall from Chapter 6 the research by Robyn Mallett and her colleagues (2008a) that found that increased perspective-taking by the majority – a major effect of intergroup contact – enhances the willingness of majority members to join in collective action against hate crimes committed against African Americans as well as gay men and lesbians. Such weakening of the majority's resolve to maintain discriminatory norms is just as important as furthering the minority's direct actions for social change. Indeed, the two processes are inseparably intertwined. The weakening of majority resolve helps to advance the minority's perceptions not only that the status quo is unjust but also that it can be altered.

Furthermore, one can question Reicher's basic assumption that intense conflict between social groups is always necessary to generate needed social change. Of course, conflict has often preceded widespread societal changes throughout the world, but not always. The non-violent uprising of the 1960s Civil Rights Movement served as an important impetus for racial change in the United States. And not unlike the Eastern European countries that threw off Russian dominance, South Africa dodged the massive violence that many observers had predicted and thought necessary for sweeping change when the racist apartheid system largely imploded. Other societal pressures – such as economic distress and natural disasters – can usher in large-scale societal changes without intense intergroup conflict. Nonetheless, Reicher's argument alerts us to the need for intergroup contact theorists to understand contact effects in a broader net of societal and intergroup processes. Social phenomena and social change in particular are complex processes with multiple and often conflicting effects.

It is also too simple to hold that a strident ingroup identification and rejection of the majority group is required for political mobilization. Studying Turkish immigrants in Germany, Simon and Ruhe (2008) found that dual identity – identifying *both* as a minority group member (Turkish) *and* as a member of the larger society (German) – maximizes politicization. Discussions between minority and majority group members also illuminate crucial differences in perspective that can compel the groups to build alliances toward social change (Nagda, 2006). Thus, under certain circumstances, contact between minorities and majorities may stimulate, rather than retard, mobilization and the desire for social change.

Moreover, minority members can learn from encounters with majority members the full extent of the discrimination their group faces. They learn what majority members possess, their lifestyles and opportunities – many of which are denied them and their group. In short, contact not only can make majority group members aware of the discrimination minorities face, but also can enhance minority group members' awareness of and frustration with the collective discrimination endured by their group, thereby generating feelings of group relative deprivation. Recall findings that suggest that the more contact minorities have outside of their communities, the more they perceive systematic discrimination against their group (Poore et al., 2002).

There is an extensive research literature that shows how group relative deprivation and perceptions of group discrimination can add to the potential for collective action (Dion, 2002; Smith & Pettigrew, 2011; Walker & Smith, 2002; Wright & Tropp, 2002). In the United States in the 1960s, it was the better-educated young African Americans who had had the most interracial contact who led the Civil Rights Movement (Mathews & Prothro, 1966; Pettigrew, 1964; Searles & Williams, 1962). They had the resources, and their interracial contact experiences gave them the necessary knowledge of the White world to lead the protest effort. They also were more likely to know White allies who would join the cause.

Clearly, the relationships between intergroup contact and social change are complex. The impressive studies reviewed above lend considerable support for Reicher's contention that intergroup contact may limit minority resolve for social change (see also Dixon, Tropp, Durrheim, & Tredoux, 2010c). But to date, studies have not sufficiently tested the potential effects of intergroup contact on heightening minority awareness of discrimination and diminishing the resolve of majorities to maintain the status quo.

We posit that at least three additional processes are involved. Indeed, there is supporting research for each of the three, but research has yet to study them concurrently:

(1) *Intergroup contact improves the attitudes of members of the advantaged group toward the disadvantaged and intergroup policies for change.* These effects can weaken their resolve to maintain the discriminatory status quo, and they can even lead members of the advantaged group to join as allies in the collective actions of the disadvantaged.
(2) *Contact also improves the attitudes of the disadvantaged toward the advantaged, and this process can lessen their resolve to mobilize for social change* (the Reicher effect). But since intergroup contact typically has greater effects on majorities than minorities (Tropp & Pettigrew, 2005b; see also Chapter 9), this effect may be less pronounced than the previous process.
(3) *Intergroup contact can also operate to heighten a minority's sense of group relative deprivation.* This occurs because contact provides the opportunity for minorities to learn what the majority possesses that is denied them. Witness the contact experience of America's Civil Rights Movement leadership, the Poore study of Canada's Inuits, and Durrheim and Dixon's finding that South African Blacks' contact with upper-status Whites relates to *less* sympathy for Whites. Intergroup contact also allows the minority to gauge majority weaknesses that can be exploited through minority mobilization. Research that simultaneously studies all three of these complex processes in relation to the Reicher effect is a needed next step.

Dixon and his co-authors (2010a) add an interesting fourth process that is highly relevant to multi-group societies. Contact *between* minorities can help unite them so that they can mount a stronger and combined protest that offers a better chance for success. Yet, as with other forms of contact, building coalitions across racial and ethnic minority groups can involve complex processes due to both positive and negative factors. Minority attempts to work together toward social change may evolve through recognition of shared experiences of oppression, at the same time as they may reveal differences in perspective and uncover potential sources of tension and conflict (see Delgado, 2003; Guinier & Torres, 2002; Wilson, 1999).

In sum, we conclude that the Reicher effect often occurs, but it is an incomplete description of the complex relationship between intergroup contact and efforts for social change. In our view, the distinction made by Wright and Lubensky (2009) between collective action participation and such "prejudice reduction" approaches as intergroup contact is too sharply drawn. As with most social phenomena, the two approaches are intricately linked. Some contact outcomes further mobilization, whereas others counter it. And mobilization itself will in turn influence intergroup contact – increasing it with outgroup allies and decreasing it with outgroup opponents.

Contact Effects at Different Levels of Analysis

A separate and final critique involves distinct levels of analysis. It proposes that micro-level changes (i.e., intergroup prejudice) have little influence on the potential for change at the macro level (i.e., intergroup conflict and collective violence). This is a recurrent debate between largely micro- and meso-level disciplines such as social psychology and largely macro-level disciplines such as political science and economics.[3]

For example, a Canadian political scientist at the University of Toronto, H. D. Forbes, devoted an entire book (1997) and a later book chapter (2004) to this very issue[4] (see also McGarry & O'Leary, 1995). Unlike some critics who are unfamiliar with the extensive relevant literature, Forbes provides an intensely close reading of the theory and research on intergroup contact through 1996. After inspecting "about 250" contact studies in a non-quantitative review, he concludes that intergroup contact at the individual level of interaction typically leads to less prejudice – in agreement with the meta-analytic findings reported in Chapter 2.

But Forbes maintains that there is an important disconnection between the two levels of analysis: Contact correlates negatively with prejudice at the individual level while proxies for contact (i.e., larger proportions of minorities, closer proximity between groups) correlate positively with intergroup conflict at the aggregate level. Discrepancies between levels have often been noted throughout the social sciences. For example, American political science has shown that rich states tend to support Democrats (e.g., California, Connecticut, Massachusetts, and New York) while poor states tend to support Republicans (e.g., Alabama and Mississippi) – yet rich individual voters tend to vote Republican while the poor overwhelmingly vote Democratic (Gelman et al., 2008). Such discontinuities have also been observed between individual and group levels in studies of conflict and competition in social psychology (Wildschut & Insko, 2007). Yet Forbes (1997, p. 113) writes, "[This] . . . is an intellectual puzzle with no obvious solution. . . . How should it be explained?"

First, the puzzling pattern he observes does not always emerge; there are many instances where *smaller* population ratios of minorities are actually associated with increased prejudice against them. For example, the former East Germany has significantly smaller percentages of resident foreigners but consistently more anti-foreigner antipathy than the former West Germany. Restricted intergroup contact in the East, compared to that of the West, explains much of this difference in prejudice (Wagner, Van Dick, Pettigrew, & Christ, 2003). Similarly, Zick (1997) finds that German cities with large immigrant populations tend to evince on average *less* prejudice than other areas of Germany. Kunovich and Hodson (2002) find similar effects for areas within Bosnia and Croatia.

Not surprisingly, different indices of cross-group relations are understandably likely to yield different patterns of results. Proportion ratios and proximity do not in themselves guarantee intergroup contact – a misguided notion that we have discussed throughout this volume. Festinger and Kelley (1951) made it clear more than a half-century ago that proportions and proximity are necessary but not sufficient conditions for social contact. Moreover, in some situations the proxies for contact at the aggregate level actually correlate *negatively*, not positively, with prejudice and conflict – just as contact theory would predict. Indeed, Forbes himself (1997, chapter 3) finds many exceptions to his aggregate finding of assumed contact leading to enhanced prejudice. But examples where proxies for contact correlate positively with prejudice and conflict may well reflect situations in which racial segregation limits intergroup contact while increasing threat – the same issue we encountered in discussing Putnam's claims about diversity. From these observations, we find that there *is* an "obvious solution" to Forbes' apparent puzzle.

Forbes (2004) approaches the problem of the supposed discrepancy between the two levels of analysis by providing an elegant demonstration of how a relationship can present diametrically opposite results at the individual and aggregate levels of analysis – the well-known ecological fallacy previously discussed (Pettigrew, 1996, 2006). Forbes uses this demonstration to set up his explanation for what he believes to be the puzzle of opposite effects. He maintains that at the aggregate level a new element is added – namely, that intergroup contact causes other minority group members who are *not* involved in the contact to become *more* hostile to the outgroup. This assumes that *intra*group dynamics are causal and determining, but these dynamics are not detailed in the theory (Van Houton, 1998). Drawing on Karl Deutsch's (1966) communication model of nationalism, Forbes argues that this increased hostility is a result of trying to prevent the costs to the ingroup of assimilation – such as learning the outgroup's language. One suspects that Forbes' contentions are highly influenced by the special case of the French-speaking *Quebecois* in his native Canada. Yet there is a mismatch between this intra-minority theory and the "puzzle" that is supposedly being addressed. The apparent discrepancies between the micro- and macro-level findings involve primarily data on majority effects, while the theory centers on minority effects.

This reasoning leads Forbes (2004, p. 85) to advocate minimizing ". . . the tensions that contact produces by suppressing its worst manifestations while quietly promoting cultural harmonization or heterogenization." In other words, he sees direct, if discreet, assimilation as the way out of his apparent dilemma – a solution often rejected by minorities.

Two features are critical to Forbes' argument. First, he emphasizes intergroup contact's potential for reducing negative group stereotypes. But we have noted earlier in Chapters 2 and 7 that contact has only moderate success in reducing stereotypes compared to its major effects on affective aspects of prejudice. Yet emotions play no part in Forbes' theory.

Second, he stresses only *cultural* dissimilarities and threat when groups interact. But there are many other types of threat – economic, political, etc. – that can arise when groups meet. And Forbes treats cultures as distinct, rather than fuzzy, categories; but cultures typically possess considerable overlap because they all must address the same problems of human existence (Ross, 1998).

In addition, cultural dissimilarities between groups do not provide an accurate gauge of the potential for intergroup conflict. As Ross (1998, p. 394) points out, bloody conflicts in ". . . Cyprus, Northern Ireland, Rwanda, Sri Lanka, Spain, or the ex-Yugoslavia are better understood in terms of Freud's concept of the narcissism of minor differences" rather than major cultural dissimilarities. And there are numerous examples where cultural conflicts would be predicted but where they have not fully burst forth: the Balts and Russians in the Baltic nations (Draguns, 2004), the Christian Bulgarians' protection of Jewish Bulgarians from the Nazis in World War II, and even in parts of India between Hindus and Muslims and in Northern Ireland between Roman Catholics and Protestants (Levin & Rabrenovic, 2004; Varshney, 2002). Indeed, individual-level affective ties created by prior contact are credited with being an important factor in the avoidance of conflict in these situations. Levin and Rabrenovic (2004) stress the key role in preventing conflict is one of contact theory's facilitating conditions – group interdependence. The economist Ashutosh Varshney (2002) reaches a similar conclusion while ignoring all social psychological materials. He shows that Muslim–Hindu contact and interdependence explain why particular Indian cities have been remarkably free of sectarian violence.

Unfortunately, Forbes does not test his theory. No data are presented in either his book or later chapter that would allow us to evaluate his theory's claims. Forbes thus unfolds for us two interesting issues to consider in further research: (1) the relationship of intergroup contact to prejudice and conflict at both the individual and intergroup levels of analysis; and (2) the reactions of that segment of the minority population that does not have intergroup contact. Indeed, what is needed for evaluating both the Putnam and Forbes critiques is a model that brings contact and conflict into a single framework. This is an issue that has central importance for both contact theory and its application to social policy, and it is to this task that we turn in the next chapter.

☐ Conclusion

Apart from erroneous, dated, or overstated criticisms of intergroup contact theory, five valuable points are raised by its critics: (1) if strict group segregation severely restricts intergroup contact, diversity can reduce such important sources of "social capital" as generalized trust; (2) the problem of establishing intergroup contact; (3) the significance of intergroup contact's influence on attitudes toward social policy; (4) the concern that intergroup contact could retard efforts toward social change; and (5) the complexity of the links between contact's effects on the micro and macro levels of analysis. Our summary responses to each of these points follow:

(1) The Putnam thesis that diversity leads, at least initially, to limited social capital is overstated. Repeated analyses indicate that this result occurs when there is substantial group segregation that effectively retards the development of intergroup contact. But when intergroup contact is not hampered by such barriers as segregation, it can effectively diminish both individual and collective threat as well as prejudice (as we shall see in the following chapter).
(2) The theory's usefulness for social policy is hampered by its inattention to the question of how to get members of different groups to meet in the first place. This weakness is especially glaring in those parts of the world where racial and ethnic conflict has traditionally marked the society for years – such as in Northern Ireland, South Africa, and the American South. The problem is difficult but essential for converting contact theory into effective social policy.

(3) Contrary to earlier claims, numerous investigations reveal that effective intergroup contact positively influences not just prejudice but also attitudes toward social policy and many other important outcomes. The claim that tests of the theory have been limited to prejudice reduction is outdated.

(4) Both the Reicher and Forbes critiques stress that far more attention must be paid to disadvantaged minority reactions to contact with advantaged majorities. They each propose critical and unique responses among minorities: for Reicher, decreased commitment for social change; for Forbes, intragroup conflict. There is growing empirical confirmation of what we have called the Reicher effect: Increased intergroup contact relates to reduced minority focus on protest and mobilization for change. But this is not the only effect of contact that relates to efforts for social change. We cite additional processes that potentially promote change efforts, each of which also has empirical support: Intergroup contact improves the attitudes of majority members toward the minority and can weaken their resolve to maintain the discriminatory status quo, and contact can also heighten a minority's sense of group relative deprivation.

This point of differential minority effects of contact has often been raised in recent years (see Devine & Vasquez, 1998; Shelton, 2000; Tropp, 2006). We noted in Chapters 2 and 9 that minorities evince, on average, smaller reductions in prejudice from intergroup contact than majorities. What may well be an ideal contact situation for maximizing the reduction in the prejudice of majority members can sometimes be perceived as far less than ideal by minority members. Fortunately, there is now a marked increase in research attention to contact effects on minorities.

(5) Although Forbes exaggerates the discrepancies in intergroup contact effects across levels of analysis, he points to an interesting and important phenomenon that often arises. At the individual level, positive intergroup contact effects are routinely found, while at aggregate levels these effects can be muted or even reversed. Our structural equation model in the next chapter resolves this apparent discrepancy across levels. It employs threat and contact as having counterbalancing effects whose ultimate outcome in any given situation is shaped by a range of moderating factors – most importantly, group segregation.

☐ Notes

1 One of the technical problems arises from the fact that Putnam employed an ordinary least-squares regression (OLS) with a four-step, categorical

dependent variable. This procedure risks violating the OLS assumption that the error term is constant across the data; in statistical terms, heteroskedasticity could have influenced the study's significance tests (see Dawkins, 2008).

2 To demonstrate the presumed disconnection between "real life" and contact theory, these critics begin their paper by seriously misreporting a 1-day conference held in December 2002 (not January 2003 as reported) at New College, Oxford University (Dixon et al., 2005, p. 697). This conference was organized and chaired by Professor Miles Hewstone and attended, among others, by the first author of this volume, Bruce Berry (a school master from riot-torn Bradford, England), and a reporter from *The Guardian*. The reporter apparently did not know how to make "a story" out of a sedate academic meeting at Oxford. So he turned to the old journalistic formula of "what do these ivory-tower academics know about real life anyway." He wrote that the Bradford school master had protested that "... all the research in the world is not addressing the situation that some cities find themselves in now." No such statement was made at the conference; nor did the school master question contact theory. Unfortunately, the critics repeated this erroneous newspaper story without checking on its accuracy with their social psychology colleagues who were present.

3 Such claims appear dubious. If our understanding is sufficient, the various levels of analysis should be in concert and not conflict. It is the task of social science to put the levels together in broader and more useful multi-level models (Pettigrew, 1996, 2006). For instance, John Duckitt (2004), in contrasting racial prejudice in his native South Africa with that of his new home in New Zealand, provides a striking example of how such personality variables as authoritarianism can meld with cultural variables for a rounded explanation.

4 Among its idiosyncratic features, *Ethnic Conflict* chides the first author of this volume for not studying intergroup contact in his doctoral thesis at Harvard about authoritarianism more than half a century ago (Forbes, 1997, p. 117).

CHAPTER 12

When Intergroup Contact Fails

Not all intergroup contact reduces prejudice. While we have focused principally on the likely benefits of intergroup contact, some situations in which groups come into contact engender enhanced prejudice. Think of a tense checkpoint on the Palestinian West Bank (Conover, 2006). Neither the Israeli soldiers nor the Palestinian civilians passing through have chosen to be in this situation, and both parties are understandably threatened. The soldiers fear the possibility of a suicide bomber or other attacks upon them. The Palestinians fear humiliation and violence from the gun-toting soldiers. Contrary to the assertions of some critics, no intergroup contact theorist has ever thought that such a stressful contact situation would do anything but exacerbate intergroup conflict. Note the critical elements of the checkpoint situation. Both parties feel highly threatened. And the context starkly violates Allport's facilitating factors – involuntary contact that is at best superficial between tense interactants of unequal status.

Negative intergroup contact itself has received sparse direct research attention. But renewed consideration of this issue recently has shed new light on this important phenomenon (e.g., Christ, Ullrich, & Wagner, 2008). Most social psychological research on negative contact effects has focused on dimensions of intergroup threat, studied intensively since the seminal publication on the subject by Stephan and Stephan (1985). In this chapter, we will examine the roles that threat and other negative factors may play in contact effects.

First, we revisit our meta-analytic dataset to examine in more detail those studies that yielded negative contact effects. Based on our meta-analytic findings reported in Chapter 2, recall that we found that studies showing that contact related to increased prejudice were surprisingly rare – only 4% (an additional 2% found no effect). But now we want to know more about how studies that uncovered negative contact effects differ from the 94% of studies that found positive effects of contact.

Second, using the same national probability sample of Germans employed in Chapter 10 (see Heitmeyer, 2005), we will examine how common individuals' reports of negative intergroup contact are in comparison with their reports of positive contact. We will also explore potential differences between people who often report either negative or positive contact, and whether there are particular situational conditions that most often invoke reports of negative contact.

☐ Negative Intergroup Contact Effects: Examples from the Meta-Analysis

Here we return to our meta-analytic data reported in Chapter 2, to examine how the relatively rare studies that link contact with increased prejudice differ from those that show contact linked to decreased prejudice. A mere 21 (4%) of the 515 studies yield a positive association between contact and prejudice (mean r = +.21). Trimmed of three outliers (14%), this special subset of 18 studies constitutes a homogeneous distribution of effect sizes with a mean r of +.11.

These studies are distinctive in numerous ways. They focus on stereotypes disproportionately (38% vs. 14% of other studies); and recall that stereotype measures generally yield smaller effects than affective dependent measures. Thirty-eight percent involve international contact, compared with only 10% of the other studies. In addition, these exceptional cases were among the least rigorous investigations. They include no experiments, in contrast to 5% of the other studies; 81%, compared with 52% of other studies, measured prejudice with low reliability scales; and 29%, compared with 8% of other studies, had control groups that had already experienced extensive contact with the outgroup.

Consider a prototype of these rare cases in which intergroup contact heightened prejudice. As mentioned in Chapter 4, Seefeldt (1987) had 4- and 5-year-old children visit incapacitated elders in a nursing home once a week for a full year. Using a between-group design with 30 children in each group, Seefeldt (1987) uncovered an overall r of +.36 with various measures of stereotypes. The experimental group of children rated the elderly more "passive," "terrible," and "unfriendly," and they adopted a more negative view of their own aging. Although some of Seefeldt's measures had low reliabilities, the key factor appears to be threat. The elderly in the study were quite impaired and thus likely to have confirmed rather than countered existing stereotypes of the elderly.

Threat is often involved in these "error cases." In another investigation on attitudes toward the elderly, Auerbach and Levenson (1977) investigated the changes among young college students caused by classroom interaction with elderly fellow students. With a measure of prejudice of unstated reliability, these researchers found that the experimental group became considerably more negative to the elderly over the course of a semester ($r = +.52$). These students typically viewed the elderly as unfair competitors and as putting "an inordinate amount of time and energy" on their class work and using their age to usurp the attention of the instructor (Auerbach & Levenson, 1977, p. 365).

A principal differentiation between the two types of studies is the majority or minority status of the respondents ($p < .001$). Remember that we noted in Chapter 9 that minorities typically reveal effects that are smaller than those of majorities. In line with this, we now see that minorities also are more likely to have their intergroup contact actually increase their prejudice. This suggests that minority status in the contact situation may often involve more distinct forms of threat than for majorities – a possibility supported by a growing body of research reviewed in Chapter 9 (see Robinson & Preston, 1976; Tropp, 2007).

The importance of threat in these studies is underlined by research on international contact. For example, Greenland and Brown (1999) studied the effects of contact between Japanese and British nationals in the United Kingdom. They found high levels of intergroup anxiety, especially among the Japanese visitors. And this in turn related positively with enhanced intergroup bias and negative affect. Similarly, studies of the effects of American students studying abroad have sometimes shown increased prejudice toward the host nationals. This result appears to emerge less in culturally similar countries (e.g., the United Kingdom) than in countries where language and cultural differences are greater (e.g., France; see Nash, 1976; Smith, 1955), again suggesting the central role of threat.

☐ Comparing Reports of Negative and Positive Contact: German Survey Evidence

Examining individual cases from the meta-analysis can provide some important insights regarding the nature of negative contact effects. Nonetheless, it remains difficult to interpret clear trends across these cases as they involve different samples of participants and methodological procedures, a concern that besets all meta-analytic reviews (see Rosenthal, 1991).

We are fortunate that Heitmeyer's (2005) prejudice project included a 2004 national probability survey of 1383 Germans that allows us – with the same sample of participants – to compare and examine simultaneously individuals' experiences with negative and positive contact. Using the context of Germans' contact experiences with foreigners, we can address such questions as: How common are reports of negative intergroup contact in comparison with those of positive contact? Who are the people who often report either negative or positive intergroup contact? What are the situational conditions that most often invoke reports of negative contact? And, finally, given the extent of negative intergroup contact, why are outcomes of intergroup contact typically so positive?

Prior to our analyses of these data, we imputed all missing values using the expectation maximization algorithm (Little & Rubin, 1987). Appendix B provides the complete listing of the items used in the analyses. Since the 2004 German survey included emotion items, we measure positive and negative contact here with slightly different and enhanced measures. Four questions of the survey measured positive contact ($\alpha = .79$). Two of these items that we employed earlier tap constructive behaviors in relation to foreigners – having helped the respondents and having had an interesting conversation with them. Two others check on the emotions that respondents may have experienced when in contact with foreigners – cheerful and satisfied.

Items assessing negative contact asked if foreigners had ever pestered the respondents, and whether respondents had experienced such emotions as anger, fear, and irritation during contact with foreigners ($\alpha = .78$). These additional items are added to record the negative affect involved in such contact, because throughout this volume we have shown that affect is a core component of the intergroup contact phenomenon.

Three additional items gauged the nature of the contacts – was it substantial, equal status, and voluntary? These questions essentially measure the respondents' perception of some of Allport's key contact conditions. The scales for individual and collective threat posed by foreigners and prejudice against foreigners are the same as used in Chapter 10.

We must note that there are varying degrees of opportunity for intergroup contact among the sample respondents. One in every six of the survey's respondents neither lives in a neighborhood with foreigners nor works with them (241 of the total sample of 1383). The variable that most strikingly characterizes these more isolated people is age. Older Germans are far less likely to report that they live in diverse neighborhoods ($p < .001$) or work with foreigners ($p < .001$) than younger respondents. There is also a tendency for those scoring high on authoritarianism to avoid living in mixed neighborhoods ($p < .004$) or working with foreigners ($p < .004$).

In the final chapter, we shall discuss further this general tendency for authoritarians to avoid intergroup contact. Nonetheless, these relatively isolated respondents still report considerable contact with foreigners – albeit less than those who live and work with foreigners. Therefore, we retain these sample respondents in the following analyses. With these data, we can now seek initial answers to the critical questions surrounding negative intergroup contact.

☐ How Common are Reports of Negative and Positive Contact?

Our first question concerns the relative degree to which these German respondents report negative and positive contact experiences with foreigners. Figure 12.1 highlights the dramatic differences in the responses to the items that assess negative and positive contact.

In every instance, far fewer German respondents report negative reactions than positive reactions to contact with resident foreigners. Indeed, almost two-thirds of those surveyed report virtually no negative reactions, while half report considerable positive contact with foreigners. Consequently, in the range 4–16, the full negative contact scale's mean ($M = 6.04$, $SD = 2.2$) falls well below that of the positive contact scale

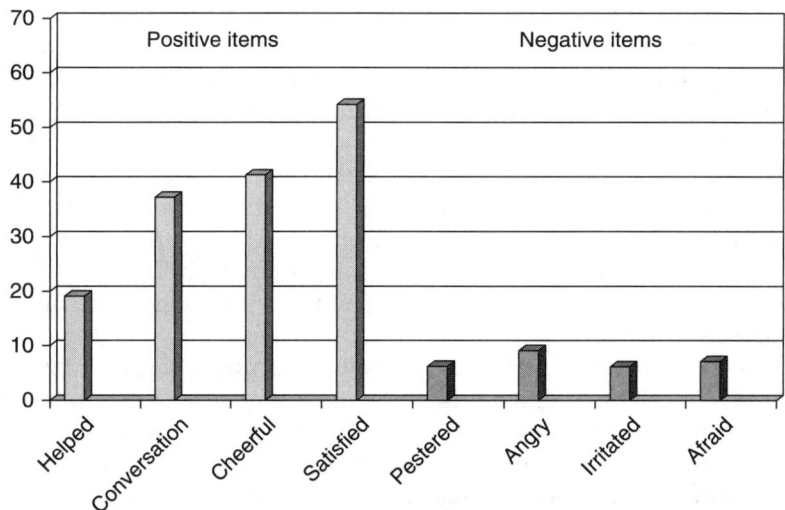

FIGURE 12.1 Reports of positive and negative contact (% saying either often or very often).

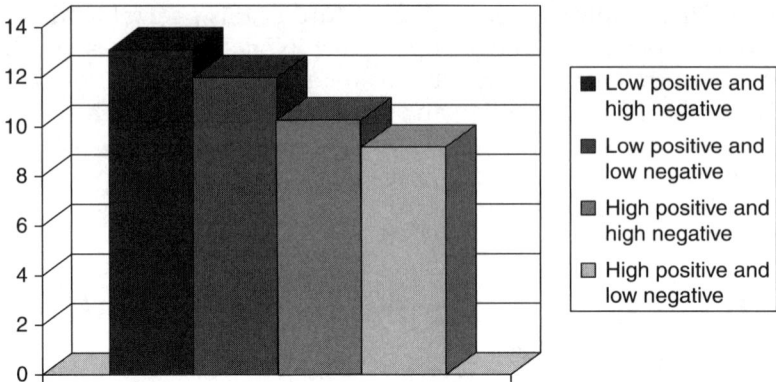

FIGURE 12.2 Prejudice means for positive and negative contact groups.

($M = 9.30$, $SD = 2.6$; $p < .0001$). The two measures have only a modest negative association ($r = -.16$, $p < .001$). Moreover, the positive contact scale predicts the prejudice-against-foreigners scale significantly better than the negative contact scale ($r = -.45$ compared with $+.28$; $p < .001$). Both are important, however, as shown by the fact that the strongest relationship with the prejudice measure is achieved by a predictor comprised of the positive contact scale minus the negative scale ($r = -.49$); this relationship is significantly larger than that of positive contact alone ($p < .04$).

Another way of viewing the results is shown in Figure 12.2. Splitting the two distributions as nearly as possible at their medians, each of the four categories combining positive and negative contact are significantly different in mean prejudice from the other three ($p < .001$). Not surprisingly, those high in positive contact and low in negative contact show the least prejudice. Of particular interest are those respondents who are relatively high in both types of contact. As a group, they are sharply *less* prejudiced than those who score low on both positive and negative contact, and they approach the mean of those who have virtually all positive contact. They are also almost a decade younger on average than the rest of the sample.

We can conclude from this probability sample of Germans that positive reactions to contact with foreigners are far more common than negative reactions. Furthermore, positive contact is more predictive than negative contact of prejudiced attitudes toward foreigners in Germany. And negative intergroup contact relates to raised prejudice largely in the absence of positive contact. This is an important but often ignored point: Positive contact can counter much of the harmful effect of negative contact.

☐ Who Most Often Reports Negative or Positive Contact?

The histogram of Figure 12.3 graphically displays the results of a seven-variable multiple regression of predictors of reports of negative contact. Not surprisingly, age is a major factor; younger Germans are far more likely to report negative intergroup contact. They live and work among foreigners and have far more interaction with them – both negative and positive – than older Germans.

Threat is also strongly involved. As expected, both the individual and collective threat scales significantly relate positively with reports of negative contact. In addition, educated respondents provide somewhat more frequent reports of negative contact – possibly a reflection of social class differences between them and less-educated resident foreigners. The situational variables tapping Allport's ideal conditions will be discussed below.

Compare these results with those shown in Figure 12.4 for positive contact. Again, age predicts more positive contact, such that younger Germans provide more positive reports; and the threat variables are predictive but in the opposite direction. Respondents who describe their intergroup contact as generally positive are not threatened by the foreigners in their midst either individually or collectively. The results further suggest that political ideology and authoritarianism are also important. Those who regard themselves as being on the political left and who score low on authoritarianism are more likely to report positive contact.

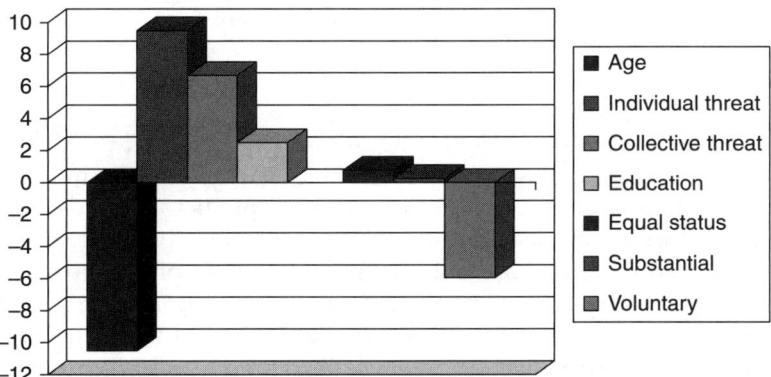

FIGURE 12.3 Predictors of negative contact (in *t* scores, from multiple regression).

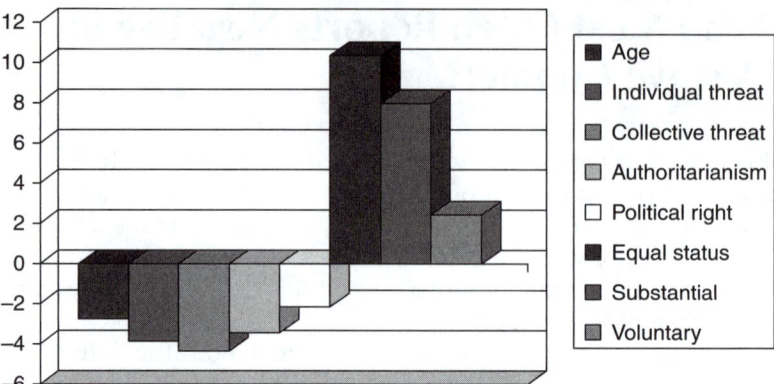

FIGURE 12.4 Predictors of positive contact (in *t* scores, from multiple regression).

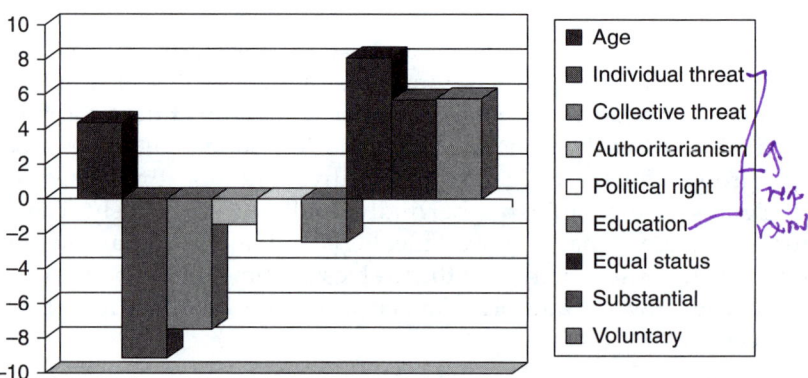

FIGURE 12.5 Predictors of positive minus negative contact (in *t* scores, from multiple regression).

Finally, Figure 12.5 reveals the significant predictors of the difference variable – negative responses to contact subtracted from positive responses. Recall that this variable is a stronger predictor of anti-foreigner prejudice than either negative or positive contact alone. Here the age variable is reversed; it is the older respondents who provide the greater difference between positive and negative contact reactions. The two threat indices are the chief predictors; those who are the most threatened are the most likely to declare more negative reactions in comparison with positive reactions to intergroup contact. Finally, as anticipated, the poorly educated, the political right, and those scoring high on authoritarianism are significantly more liable to score lower on this index.

The consistent importance of threat, both individual and collective, requires further examination. A more fine-grained analysis looks at the individual predictive power of the eight items contained in the two threat scales. Seven of the items are negatively associated with both the positive contact and the positive-minus-negative contact measures. This indicates that those reporting pleasant interactions with foreigners are markedly less threatened than other sample respondents. This lack of individual and collective threat is especially strong in the economic and security domains. By contrast, negative contact reports relate positively with six of the threat items – especially threats to "our freedom and rights," "our security," "my security," and "my lifestyle." Interestingly, the major exception involves any threat to "our culture" – which is apparently of less concern although it was the major focus of the analysis of Forbes discussed in Chapter 11.

In sum, age and both individual and collective threat are major predictors of positive and negative reports of intergroup contact. Young respondents have the greatest contact with foreigners and consequently report the most reactions to intergroup contact – both positive and negative. Many types of threat predict how contacts with foreigners are reported. Those who regard their encounters with foreigners as positive typically are quite unthreatened both individually and collectively by the foreigners residing in Germany. But those reporting negative encounters are highly threatened by foreigners in various domains.

☐ Which Conditions Most Often Invoke Reports of Negative Contact?

Although we learned in Chapter 2 that particular situational conditions are not essential to reducing prejudice, they do importantly influence the process. So we test for the effects of three situational conditions that speak to the *quality* of the contact: Was the respondent voluntarily in the contact situation? Was the contact superficial or was it substantive? And was there equal status between the interactants? Figures 12.2–12.4 provide some answers. In the three regressions, all three qualities are major predictors except for the equal-status and substantial conditions relating to negative contact. When placed in terms of zero-order correlations, voluntary (+.25), substantive (+.29), and equal-status (+.35) conditions all positively relate to positive contact. And they also relate negatively to negative contact – voluntary (–.28), substantive (–.10), and equal status (–.13). Indeed, the three situational conditions also relate to the positive minus negative predictor – voluntary (+.35), substantive (+.27), and equal status (+.32). All nine of these correlations are significant at the .001 level.

When added to the predictors discussed previously, these three qualities of contact significantly add to the total variance explained in all three regressions ($p < .001$). For positive contact, equal status is especially important – as Allport (1954) insisted years ago. The effects for negative contact are less dramatic. While the variance prediction is again significantly increased, only the voluntary status of the contact remains highly and negatively significant. In short, the effects of negative contact are particularly strong for involuntary contact.

The three qualities of contact are also negatively associated with prejudice. The more the contact is reported as voluntary (–.25), intimate (–.24), and equal status (–.27), the less prejudice is reported by the survey respondents. These trends suggest that these contact quality variables may act to moderate the relationships between negative and positive contact with prejudice. Indeed, the association between negative contact and prejudice is significantly moderated by substantive contact ($p < .05$) and equal status ($p < .01$). These findings indicate that the link between negative contact and prejudice is stronger when the contact is superficial and between people of equal status. The most important situational influence for negative contact appears to be whether the respondent had entered the intergroup contact voluntarily. For those who reported that their intergroup contact was involuntary, the correlation between negative contact and prejudice was +.29; but for those for whom it was voluntary, the correlation was significantly lower ($r = +.18, p < .02$).

This close look at negative contact reverses the prior focus on positive contact. Now we know that there are somewhat different patterns of predictors for negative contact. Hopefully, this new information can help us to understand what triggers negative responses to contact (e.g., feeling it is involuntary) as opposed to factors that promote positive responses (e.g., intimacy, equal status).

☐ Why Are Contact Outcomes Typically So Positive?

These findings both raise and answer an important question. Given the existence of negative contact, why do our meta-analytic findings reported in Chapter 2 report such overwhelmingly positive effects of contact in reducing prejudices of many kinds?

In this chapter, we have uncovered several factors that help to explain this apparent puzzle. First, we have seen in a single survey study that German respondents report far more positive than negative intergroup contacts with resident foreigners. These results may seem surprising since negative intergroup encounters are often publicized, while the far more numerous positive encounters go unrecognized or are not viewed as newsworthy. But this finding helps to explain why contact leading to increased prejudice is so relatively rare in the research literature.

Second, we have also noted that the effects of negative intergroup contact are strongly predicted by whether the participant entered the contact voluntarily. When the contact involves voluntary contact, the effects of negative contact are far smaller than when the contact involves involuntary contact. This again suggests the importance of threat. People rarely voluntarily enter threatening situations, but they may often discover threatening new situations they did not choose to enter.

Third, not surprisingly, those who have lots of intergroup contact tend to report both positive and negative contact. Thus, while some might question whether people who have positive contact are inherently different from people who have negative contact, in this sample we observe that people who have contact are likely to report a combination of positive and negative intergroup experiences. These are typically younger respondents who reveal significantly less prejudice than those with neither positive nor negative contact. Thus, negative contact is primarily problematic in the absence of positive contact. Put differently, positive contact appears to counteract the prejudice-inducing effects of negative intergroup encounters. This is an important finding since many respondents in the German survey had both types of encounters with foreigners. This phenomenon limits to some degree the selectivity bias of more tolerant people having positive contact and more prejudiced people having negative contact.

This analysis was carried further by Christ et al. (2008), who analyzed two German probability surveys – one of which we analyzed above. Using slightly different indicators from our analysis, they studied the *strength* of anti-foreigner attitudes. Attitude strength consisted of three key elements: How certain were the respondents of their opinions about foreigners? How much knowledge about foreigners did the respondents believe they possessed? And how important is the topic of foreigners for the respondents? Positive contact related not only to more favorable attitudes toward foreigners but to stronger attitudes on all three of these dimensions. Negative contact also led to stronger attitudes, but not as powerfully as positive contact. And when combined with positive contact, negative contact resulted in less prejudiced attitudes (as in figure 12.2) that were "stable, consequential and difficult to change" (Christ et al., 2008, figure 12).

Given these various phenomena, negative intergroup contact as captured in these German survey data may often not be as crucial as some critics have assumed. But special groups within the society, such as the police, will often have markedly different experiences than the general population. Flemish police in Belgium, for example, report somewhat more negative than positive contact with racial minorities. In addition, negative contact for these police relates to more reported discriminatory behavior ($r = -.24$) than positive contact counteracts such behavior ($r = -.08$) (Dhont, Cornelis, & Van Hiel, 2010). More generally, negative contact involving extreme humiliation, violence, genocide, and the death of family members will also maximize negative contact effects. Individual and collective threat is maximized by such extreme encounters, and the resulting intergroup hatred can last for years. But while such brutal confrontations fill the headlines, most negative intergroup contact around the globe more closely resembles the non-violent types measured by surveys in Europe and the United States.

This critical role of intergroup threat – both individual and collective – is fundamental to the criticisms of contact theory reviewed in the previous chapter and to understanding the results of this chapter concerning both negative and positive contact. Critics typically believe that threat is critical for the development of negative contact but is not involved in positive contact. Yet we have just seen that the *absence* of both individual and collective threat is a major predictor of positive contact as well. Recall, too, that Putnam (2007) views threat and contact as separate processes leading to rival hypotheses. But later studies demonstrate that this is not the case. Indeed, we have seen in Figures 12.3–12.5 that the two are firmly interrelated, and that it is possible and useful to combine threat and contact into a single model.

☐ A Combined Model of Intergroup Contact and Threat

Drawing on work we have done with our German colleagues (Pettigrew, Wagner, & Christ, 2010; Wagner et al., 2006), we offer such a model that combines the two independent variables in question – intergroup contact and threat. This model helps to explain the apparent "puzzle" presented by Forbes (1997, 2004) and discussed in Chapter 11, and it also serves to illustrate our view that intergroup conflict and contact processes should not be regarded as competing theories (e.g., Putnam, 2007).

Much of the debate involves the nature of intergroup "diversity" that exists in a given geographical area. This variable is usually measured as the ratio of the minority group in the area's total population. The question then becomes framed as: Is a large or a small minority population typically related to increased prejudice against them by the majority?

Two interlocking processes underlie the complex relationship between population proportions and prejudice. Typically, larger outgroup population proportions simultaneously increase *both* threat and intergroup contact: the first process increases prejudice, the second decreases it. Using the same extensive survey data from the 2004 probability sample of the adult German population without a migration background, we test to see how these two processes can be effectively combined into one complex model using structural equation analysis.

Putnam (2007) and Forbes (1997, 2004) employ the percentage of the minority as a key proxy for contact at the aggregate level. So our models begin with this variable and take the perspective of the majority. We seek to show how threat and contact jointly operate to produce a range of outcomes. Threat is perceptual (Stephan, Ybarra, & Morrison, 2009); it involves what people *think* is the outgroup proportion, and thus it can be easily manipulated by dramatic events, political leaders, and the mass media. These subjective estimates are often wild exaggerations of the true minority percentage, and many researchers omit this subjective psychological measure in their analyses. Our model includes both the actual percentage of foreign residents and the respondents' subjective estimates of the percentage of foreign residents.

Moreover, the intricate relationship between threat and contact can be substantially altered by numerous moderators. For instance, rigid group segregation can limit contact, while unemployment can amplify threat. Indeed, we posit several such moderators of the effect of the minority percentage upon the majority's prejudice. In particular, the primary means of restricting intergroup contact – segregation – can moderate the process, as the previously described analyses in Chapter 11 by Rothwell and Uslaner demonstrated. Other moderators include: unemployment, a sudden increase in the size of the outgroup; politicians endorsing threatening sentiments; barriers to citizenship and other means for the outgroup to enter the mainstream of national life; and the outgroup's multiple distinguishing characteristics from the indigenous ingroup – race, social class, language, etc. All these internal factors can potentially heighten threat while simultaneously acting to limit positive intergroup contact.

Recall in the previous chapter that Putnam held that diversity itself leads to distrust. Forbes maintained that intergroup contact enhances prejudice at the aggregate level because minorities not involved in the contact become agitated. These claims may be interpreted alternatively as threat effects. Neither critic considers that increased intergroup contact at the aggregate level can also offer a counterbalancing effect of diminished prejudice. Figures 12.6 and 12.7 show these dual effects with structural equation models (SEMs). Note that single variables are shown in rectangles while latent factors comprised of multiple variables are shown in circles. Fit indices for all three models indicate good fits to the data. For clarity, error and disturbance terms are not shown.

Figure 12.6 displays the SEM upon which both Putnam and Forbes concentrate. Note how most of the effect of the area's foreign percentage is mediated through the *perception* of this percentage. In turn, both

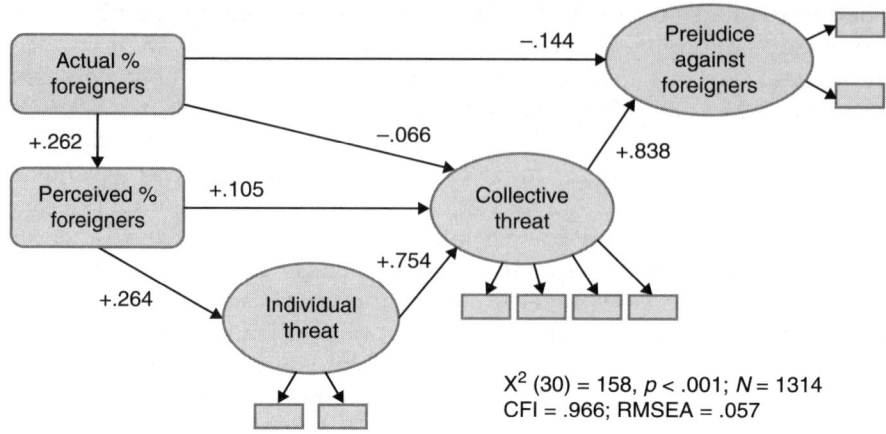

FIGURE 12.6 Population ratio effects mediated by individual and collective threat.

individual and especially collective threat mediate the increase in prejudice against resident foreigners related to the foreign percentage. In viewing SEM diagrams, it is always useful to look carefully for which paths are missing. In Figure 12.6, two paths are not significant and thus not shown. The perceived percentage of foreigners has no direct effect on prejudice; instead, it is fully mediated by the two latent threat variables. Similarly, the effect of individual threat on prejudice is fully mediated by collective threat, consistent with what we have noted concerning the special importance of collective threat. Indeed, the largest path links collective threat with prejudice – a finding completely in line with the meta-analytic results of studies showing the close association of many types of threat with outgroup prejudice (Riek, Mania, & Gaertner, 2006).

Figure 12.7 reveals the other process by which higher ratios of foreigners in a given area of Germany lead to reduced prejudice through positive intergroup contact. Again note the missing path: In this simple model, contact effectively mediates the entire relationship between the foreigner percentage and prejudice.

Finally, Figure 12.8 combines the two processes. With this structural model, we learn that the major means by which positive intergroup contact relates negatively with prejudice is through its association with diminished individual and collective threat – a result consistent with our previous discussion in Chapter 6 of the affective mediators of the contact–prejudice relationship. This finding also indicates that the contact and threat theories are best combined rather than treated as rival theories. Notice also in this final model that the area's percentage of foreigners has

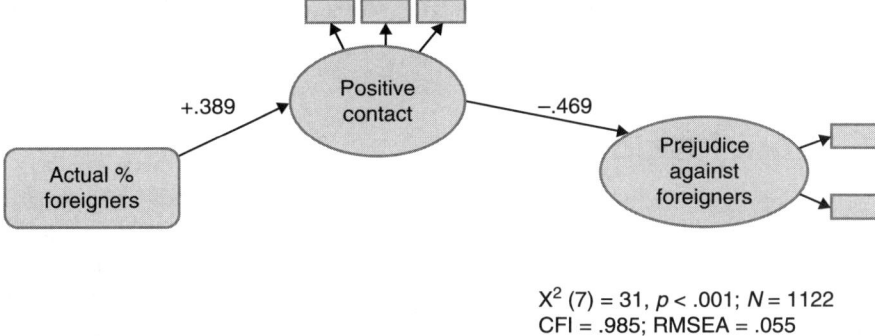

FIGURE 12.7 Population ratio effects mediated by positive contact.

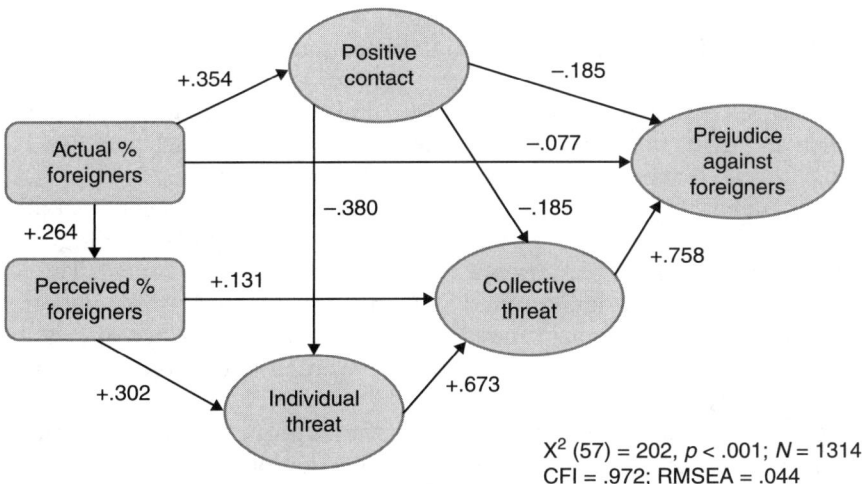

FIGURE 12.8 Complete model with threat and contact as mediators.

no direct links with the threat variables; all its influence is mediated indirectly through its increase of the *perceived* percentage of foreigners – the often overlooked variable. Together these two interrelated processes – threat and contact – explain most of the relationship between the true foreigner percentage and prejudice against resident foreigners; only a small direct coefficient (–.077) remains.

This model is not restricted to the particular measures we used or to this 2004 probability sample of German respondents. In an independent study, Schlueter and Scheepers (2010) essentially and independently replicated the model using different measures and a 2000 Dutch national sample of respondents.

☐ Conclusion

Contact can exacerbate intergroup prejudice and conflict, especially when it involves threat. So we have explored in this chapter the nature of negative contact and how it differs from the more common experience of positive contact.

The operation of negative intergroup contact is more complex than generally recognized. Understandably, minorities tend to report more of it than majorities. Among majorities, it appears to be far less often experienced than positive contact in non-violent situations. When it does occur, negative contact typically involves situations where the participants feel threatened and did not choose to have the contact. These situations often occur in work environments where intergroup competition exists, as well as in situations involving intergroup conflict. Indeed, individual and collective threat are primary correlates of negative contact and can be quite varied – from political to security and even lifestyle.

Much negative contact is reported by people who have a considerable amount of outgroup contact. These respondents are typically young and also report a considerable amount of positive intergroup contact. This is important because, when coupled with positive intergroup encounters, non-violent negative contact may be far less lethal than critics of contact theory have assumed. And, if the contact were entered voluntarily, the effects of negative contact are also muted.

Contrary to the claims of some critics, intergroup contact and intergroup threat are not separate phenomena. As demonstrated in our structural equations model, negative contact is related to greater prejudice, while positive contact is even more closely related to lowered prejudice (see p. 90).

Summing Up and Looking to the Future

Hundreds of research papers and book chapters on intergroup contact have appeared during the last few decades. We have noted how this intense renewed interest in Allport's (1954) "hypothesis" has led to a burgeoning area of the social psychology of intergroup relations. The modest "hypothesis" has now expanded into a developed theory (Brown & Hewstone, 2005; Pettigrew, 1998). In this final chapter, we will review the varied dynamics of intergroup contact theory, offer suggestions for future work to advance our understanding of intergroup contact's complexities, and close by considering the implications of intergroup contact theory for social policy in intergroup relations.

☐ Recapitulation

The Basic Effect

We tested the core of intergroup contact theory in Chapter 2. Our meta-analysis, combining the results of 515 studies conducted during the 20th century, definitively established that prejudice is typically reduced when groups meet. While the mean effect is relatively modest in size ($r = -.21$; Cohen's $d = -.43$), it cannot be explained away by participant selection, publication bias, sampling biases, or poorly conducted research. Indeed, the most rigorous studies tend to provide the largest effects. This phenomenon is repeated again in 21st century research. Recent research is more rigorously executed and typically yields larger contact effects.

Widespread Generalization

Later chapters demonstrated that the positive effects of intergroup contact tend to generalize broadly. Thus, the effects are not confined to just those outgroup members who directly participated in the contact. Chapter 3 showed that contact's effects spread in numerous ways. The initial and primary generalization typically extends from the immediate outgroup members who participate in the contact to the entire outgroup. This primary transfer effect is enhanced when the contact situation makes participants' group identities salient.

Contact's effects also normally extend to situations different from the original contact situation. And they even extend to other outgroups who were not involved in the contact – the secondary transfer effect.

Furthermore, positive contact effects are not limited to particular situations, populations, or nations. Chapter 4 supplied evidence for the apparent universality of the intergroup contact phenomenon across varied settings, age cohorts, and countries throughout the world. We have also noted significant contact effects for groups that differ in race, ethnicity, nationality, sexual orientation, and physical and mental disabilities. Of course, there is considerable variability in these effects but the positive trend is remarkably consistent. The apparent universality of the intergroup contact phenomenon suggests that there is a basic underlying process. We propose that this process involves the fact that familiarity generally leads to liking – the mere exposure effect detailed by Zajonc (1968).

Several chapters cited a further spread of effects, such as the indirect or extended contact effect. Having an ingroup friend who has an outgroup friend tends to improve attitudes toward the outgroup. We noted in Chapter 8 that such indirect effects can yield secondary transfer effects and this is especially important for those who live in segregated areas without outgroup friends. Other vicarious forms of intergroup contact, even through television viewing, also seem generally to result in improved attitudes. Consequently, intergroup contact effects spread broadly through several processes – a vital point for social policy.

Moderators

To learn *when* contact effects will occur and are maximized, we must seek the *moderators* of the contact–prejudice relationship. Allport's (1954) formulation specified four key situational factors for contact to exert its beneficial intergroup effects: equal status in the situation, common goals, intergroup cooperation, and institutional support. Chapter 5, utilizing our meta-analytic results, found these conditions to be important moderators.

They enhance the effect, but they are *not* essential conditions. We stressed that these situational moderators should also be viewed as subjectively perceived, rather than merely objective, features of the situation. In addition, investigators have uncovered many other moderators that influence contact's effects. For two examples, the salience of group membership during contact and the importance that they assign to intergroup contact also act as moderators.

Mediators

To learn *how* contact reduces prejudice, we must uncover the principal *mediators* of contact's effects. Two largely affective mediators have proven to be critically important in explaining how intergroup contact relates to prejudice. Anxiety reduction appears to initiate the process, followed by the emergence of empathy for the outgroup. Gaining general knowledge about the outgroup from contact, long thought to be the foremost mediator, proves less important in Chapter 6's multiple meta-analyses. But these three mediators taken together do not explain all of contact's influence on prejudice. We suggest that additional key mediators will be found in four areas: (1) contact may enhance *cultural* understanding, and (2) it can change intergroup behavior that in turn alters attitudes. Further mediation of the contact–prejudice link can also result from (3) the perception of shifts in intergroup norms, and (4) the general restructuring of intergroup relations.

Intergroup Contact Especially Reduces Affective Forms of Prejudice

There are many forms of intergroup prejudice – ranging from stereotypes to feelings. This raises the question as to whether intergroup contact influences all forms of prejudice. Chapter 7 provided the evidence that it is useful to compare cognitive and affective effects of contact. Our meta-analysis of 20th century research shows that contact is far more likely to influence affective components of prejudice (e.g., emotions, feelings, and liking) than cognitive components (e.g., stereotypes and beliefs). Contact typically does have significant cognitive effects, but they are consistently less substantial than affective changes. This result is consistent with the importance of anxiety reduction and empathy in contact's results. This trend is fortunate, since affective elements of prejudice are typically more closely related to intergroup behavior (Esses et al., 1993; Stangor et al., 1991; Talaska et al., 2008). In addition, we have noted significant relationships between contact and implicit prejudice in both experimental and field settings.

The Special Role of Cross-Group Friendship

Given the particular significance of contact's affective effects, it is not surprising that cross-group friendship ties are especially important. Chapter 8 supplies consistent evidence that underlines the special role of cross-group friendship. Many different measures of friendship yield strong effects, but those assessments that are based on behavioral measures, especially time spent together, tend to yield the largest effects.

The Importance of Differences in Group Status

Intergroup contact theory is often presented as a broad conceptualization of what occurs when members of different groups interact. However, in Chapter 9, we consider how members of minority and majority status groups may perceive, experience, and respond to intergroup contact in quite different ways. Our research reveals that contact effects are typically stronger for majority status groups than for minority status groups. Further research suggests that positive contact effects may be weaker for minority group members to the extent that they perceive discrimination against their groups. At the same time, having positive contact with the majority can also diminish the extent to which minority group members perceive their groups to be discriminated against.

The Predictive Power of Intergroup Contact

As Chapter 2 demonstrated, the bidirectional link between intergroup contact and prejudice is a solid one. But how powerful is contact as a predictor of prejudice when it is located in the context of other, well-established predictors of prejudice? Chapter 10 set out to answer this question using varied research from Western Europe and North America that studied the many correlates of prejudice against immigrants. Even when placed in regressions of prejudice predictors from throughout the social sciences, intergroup contact remains a major correlate. The normative context, population ratios, age, education, perceived economic deprivation, political conservatism and efficacy, national identity, authoritarianism, and social dominance orientation all proved to be significant predictors of prejudice. Nonetheless, intergroup contact remained a major predictor of anti-immigration attitudes on both sides of the Atlantic Ocean, even among this large cluster of relevant variables.

Multiple Outcomes of Intergroup Contact

Diminished prejudice is by no means the only result of intergroup contact. Contrary to the claims of some critics, we have noted throughout the volume an array of other effects of importance to intergroup relations. Thus, we have noted that intergroup contact relates to anxiety, individual threat, collective threat, trust, forgiveness, empathy, perspective-taking, outgroup knowledge, perceived outgroup rationality, ingroup identification, job attainment and satisfaction, attitudes toward social change and policies affecting outgroups, and perceptions of outgroup variability – all of which reveal positive contact effects. Future work is needed to understand the full patterning and the time sequencing of this constellation of strongly interrelated outcomes.

The Principal Criticisms of Intergroup Contact Theory

Apart from erroneous, dated, or overstated criticisms, Chapter 11 discusses five valuable points that have been raised in critiques of intergroup contact theory: (1) if segregation severely restricts intergroup contact, diversity can reduce such important "social capital" as generalized trust; (2) the importance of the leading-the-horses-to-water problem of initially establishing optimal intergroup contact; (3) the significance of intergroup contact's influence on attitudes toward social policy; (4) the critical role of understanding minority perspectives and contact effects on efforts toward social change; (5) the complexity of the links between contact's effects on the micro, meso and macro levels of analysis. These five points suggest future paths for intergroup contact research to pursue – as we discuss in the following section.

Not All Intergroup Contact Has Positive Effects

Chapter 12 discussed negative intergroup interaction – contact that relates to *greater* prejudice and conflict. Chapter 2 showed such instances to be far less frequent than positive contact except in regions of extreme intergroup conflict. Yet negative contact still occurs regularly around the world and makes headlines that positive contact rarely attains. Again analyzing German survey data, we show that such contact typically involves not only both individual and collective threat but is also often involuntary. The full effects of negative contact, however, are blunted by the fact that it is often accompanied by considerable positive contact as well. Both types of encounters are recorded by people who have considerable amounts of diverse contact. Indeed, positive contact can apparently counter many of the harmful effects of negative contact. The intergroup attitudes of those respondents reporting both types of contact approach those of people who report only positive contact. Nonetheless, intergroup threat provides a major barrier to achieving positive contact's beneficial effects.

Suggestions for Future Intergroup Contact Research

The more we learn about a phenomenon, the more we realize what we do not know and must study further. Our various suggestions for further research on intergroup contact advanced throughout the previous chapters fall into five general categories: (1) greater focus on process; (2) further attention to minorities and subjective perceptions in contact; (3) more research on negative intergroup contact; (4) linking the meso level of contact with micro and macro levels of analysis; and (5) enhancing the policy relevance of contact research.

Greater Focus on Process

We have learned much about the intergroup contact process in recent years. Brown and Hewstone (2005) provide an intensive examination of the moderators and mediators of the phenomenon, and Chapters 5 and 6 further explored these process findings. But there is much more to uncover. Undoubtedly more moderators and mediators exist, and Chapter 6 suggested four promising areas in which to search for them. Consider also what we need to understand about several key findings described in this book.

For example, how do the many moderators and mediators relate to each other? Are they sequenced in any discernible pattern? Here we suggested that anxiety reduction may be the initial and vital first mediator in the process. And we further advanced the idea that the group salience models for optimal intergroup contact can also be roughly sequenced: first decategorization, followed by categorization, followed by superordinate identity and the dual identity models.

Similarly, we have noted the many and varied positive outcomes that research has shown for contact between groups. How are they interrelated? We hypothesize that these outcomes form a tightly interrelated cluster that ranges widely from physiological changes to altered perceptions of the prevailing intergroup norms. Such a pattern would throw revealing light upon the contact process itself.

Even more fundamental are the basic psychological processes that apparently make intergroup contact's effects such a universal phenomenon. What are they? We suggested that the mere exposure effect and its reduction of uncertainty leading to liking may be the essential psychological grounding of the contact link to reduced prejudice. If this were so, it would help to explain several points at issue: why affective outcomes of contact are so consistently more pronounced than cognitive outcomes; why cross-group friendship effects are so strong; and why Allport's four key contact variables turn out to be facilitating but not essential for contact's effects to unfold.

Further Attention to Minorities and Subjective Perceptions in Contact

Chapter 9 showed that the great preponderance of contact research has focused on members of majority groups, and critics have rightly pointed to the need for attention to minority effects. Forbes pointed to the need to study those segments of minority populations that do not have intergroup contact, and Reicher emphasized the potential of intergroup contact to dampen minority group members' zeal for social protest.

Recent years have witnessed a growing interest in how minorities react to and view intergroup contact. For instance, studies now show that racial minority and majority students reveal different reactions when race is discussed, especially in terms of their feelings of anxiety (Trawalter & Richeson, 2008) and their interest in further intergroup contact (Tropp & Bianchi, 2007). Such work has been a valuable addition to contact theory, and it introduces two further areas in need of exploration.

As we learn increasingly more about minority reactions to intergroup contact, we now need to integrate these new insights with what we already know about majority reactions. Such integration would provide us with a rounded understanding of the complexities and flow of intergroup interaction. Several scholars have begun such work (e.g., Hebl & Dovidio, 2005; Page-Gould et al., 2008; Richeson & Shelton, 2007; Vorauer, 2006). Research by Page-Gould et al. (2008) reveals that among participants concerned with race-based rejection, interacting with an outgroup partner who has considerable prior contact experience helps to attenuate their anxiety over time. And West and coworkers (2009b) have shown that the anxiety of one partner in intergroup interactions is importantly shaped by the anxiety level of the other partner.

Such work can yield some surprising results. For instance, African Americans may, ironically, prefer to interact with highly prejudiced Whites, at least in initial, short-term interactions. Shelton, Richeson, Salvatore, and Trawalter (2005) had White participants complete the

Implicit Association Test (IAT) as a measure of racial bias and then discuss race relations with either a White or a Black partner. Whites' IAT scores predicted how positively they were perceived by Black (but not White) interaction partners. And this relationship was mediated by Blacks' perceptions of how engaged the White participants were during the interaction. With the more prejudiced Whites "trying harder," they came to be initially preferred by the Black participants.

The second implication of this interactive research is that it is important to know how contact participants subjectively view the situation (see Tropp, 2006). Allport's four moderators are often viewed as strictly situational conditions. But growing from the contentions of earlier writings (e.g., Riordan, 1978; Robinson & Preston, 1976), emerging research on minority reactions makes it clear that we must concentrate more on the subjective perceptions of the contact situation by participants (e.g., Molina et al., 2004; Tropp & Bianchi, 2006). For a case in point, what might be seen as equal-status contact by majority members can often be seen by minority members as contact involving unequal status.

More Research on Negative Intergroup Contact

Cross-group interaction that leads to *increased* prejudice has not been studied extensively and systematically. As Chapter 12 makes clear, intergroup contact holds the potential to increase prejudice and conflict. We saw that both individual and collective threat typically triggered negative effects of contact. We also saw that if such contact were voluntarily entered and if the person also enjoyed considerable positive contact, negative contact's effects are significantly abated. But, given the relative dearth of research in this area, we know little as yet about the underlying processes involved with this dark side of intergroup contact. How do voluntary and positive contacts limit the effects? And how best can threats of all types be alleviated in intergroup contact situations? Future research in this area is a primary need if intergroup contact theory and its applications are to advance.

Linking the Meso Level with Micro and Macro Levels of Analysis

Intergroup contact occurs at the situational, meso level of analysis. But if the theory is to be broadened, grounded, and made more policy relevant, it must be connected with the physiological and personality micro levels as well as the macro-institutional levels of analysis. We have already mentioned instances of initial research that attempt to achieve such links. Recall the studies that have used new indices of anxiety to record contact's effects at the physiological level. We also saw that such personality syndromes as authoritarianism are closely related to who avoids intergroup contact. And we noted in Chapter 4 the sizable differences in contact's effects across such structural domains as recreational, educational, and work institutions.

To link the various levels of analysis, we will need to study intergroup contact in its longitudinal, multi-level social context. But we have seen that the contact research literature suffers from a scarcity of both longitudinal and multi-level studies. Remember that the findings from Chapter 2 revealed that more than 70% of the intergroup contact research of the 20th century involved participants retrospectively reporting prior contact without any information on the longitudinal or situational contexts of this contact. Indeed, our meta-analysis uncovered only two longitudinal studies and no multi-level studies.

Yet such studies are obviously necessary to place the intergroup contact phenomena in their full and evolving social context. Additional longitudinal studies, with statistical modeling procedures borrowed from economics to examine effects over time, can be helpful. And, as described in Chapter 5, Sherif's (1966) brilliant field study, Robbers' Cave, offered an initial quasi-experimental, longitudinal field study with positive results for contact theory. The critical point of Sherif's famous research was that he obtained repeated attitude measures as the contact experiences evolved between his two groups of young boys (Pettigrew, 1991). Had he stopped after the first or second optimal contact events, as many social psychological studies do, Sherif would have failed to have uncovered his dramatic findings.

More recently, an increasing number of longitudinal studies have been published that also support the theory (e.g., Christ et al., in press; Eller et al., under review; Eller & Abrams, 2003, 2004; Levin et al., 2003; Binder et al., 2009). Especially impressive is the longitudinal research conducted at UCLA by Sidanius and his colleagues (Sidanius et al., 2008) – a landmark study that we have cited repeatedly throughout this book. Of particular importance, this study's five data points allowed us to see the evolving pattern of roommate effects over a 4-year period. Longitudinal studies using daily questionnaires have also proven valuable. For example, Trail, Shelton, and West (2009) found that minority students with White roommates reported declining positive emotions when their roommate seldom performed "intimacy-building behaviors."

Another way to look at the evolving development of intergroup contact in its social context is to think of it in terms of a stochastic set of cumulative processes involving a series of selection stages (Pettigrew, 2008). Although best studied with longitudinal data, the point can be illustrated with data from the previously used research survey of Germans conducted in 2004.

Figure 13.1 illustrates one such model that employs three separate processes related to neighborhood contact. The first selection process involves those Germans who live in neighborhoods with resident foreigners – obviously a prerequisite for neighborhood contact. Figure 13.1 shows that this selection removes 25% of the total sample. But the mere presence of foreigners does not guarantee intergroup contact – the second selection process. And, indeed, 25% of the German respondents who live in mixed areas report having no contact whatsoever with resident foreigners. Finally, simple intergroup contact does not ensure that intergroup friendship will develop – a major means, as we saw in Chapter 8, for such contact to diminish prejudice. Interestingly, this last selection process removes only 18% of the German respondents who have neighborhood contact but no foreign friends. This result suggests that once contact is made, friendship typically evolves.

Table 13.1 tests for the predictors of these three selection processes. Education, surprisingly, does not emerge as a significant correlate of any

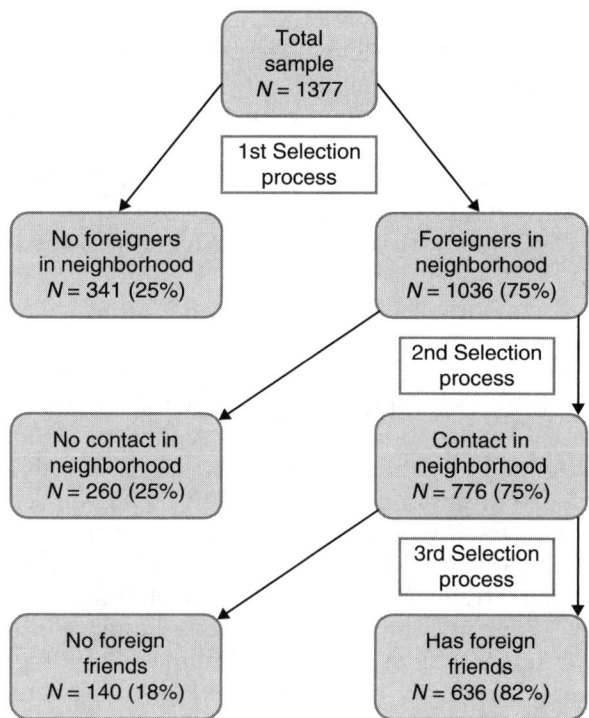

FIGURE 13.1 Three selection processes in contact effects. Adapted from Pettigrew (2008).

of the three selections – but two social location variables are important. Age proves to be significant at two points: Younger respondents are more likely to live in a mixed neighborhood and to make friends with foreigners after neighborhood contact. Gender becomes important in the last two selection stages: Males have more contact with foreign neighbors and make more friends. This finding reflects the fact that foreign men are more likely to learn the German language and culture than women, because they are more often in the labor force.

Two psychological variables are also implicated in these selection processes. Authoritarianism is highly and negatively related to all three processes. Authoritarians are significantly less likely to be living in an area with foreigners, less likely to have contact with them even when they do live in such an area, and less likely to make friends with those foreigners with whom they do have neighborhood contact. In other analyses, intergroup contact has been shown to be a strong, negative mediator of the positive authoritarianism–prejudice relationship (Stellmacher, Pettigrew, Christ, & Wagner, under review). The present data indicate that this mediation consists of authoritarians typically being careful to avoid resident foreigners at multiple levels.

Table 13.1 also reveals the reverse causal sequence in the contact–prejudice link that has so often been found in previous research. Respondents who are highly prejudiced against Muslims are significantly less likely to have contact with their foreign neighbors and significantly less likely to make friends with them even when they do have contact – the second and third selection stages.

Thus, the leading-the-horses-to-water problem is especially severe for authoritarians and the highly prejudiced. Yet, in both this test and in other

TABLE 13.1 Predictors of the Three Selection Processes

Predictor Variables	Are there Foreign Neighbors? 1st Selection Process			Contact with Foreign Neighbors? 2nd Selection Process			Any Foreign Friends? 3rd Selection Process		
	β	t	p	β	t	p	β	t	p
Respondent age	−.111	−4.10	.001	.026	0.83	.406	−.111	−3.22	.001
Respondent gender	.007	0.27	.784	−.087	−2.81	.005	−.072	−2.08	.038
Authoritarianism	−.111	−3.63	.001	−.088	−2.49	.013	−.096	−2.46	.014
Anti-Muslim prejudice	−.038	−1.24	.214	−.084	−2.39	.017	−.208	−5.26	.001
N		1377			1036			776	

Source: Adapted from Pettigrew (2008).

Note: β = standardized regression coefficient; t = student's t-test; p = probability.

studies, those rare authoritarians and bigots who do manage to have close contact with outgroups reveal *greater* reductions in prejudice from intergroup contact than do the less authoritarian and prejudiced respondents (Dhont & Van Hiel, 2009; Hodson, Harry, & Mitchell, 2009). Much of the effect is simply a ceiling effect – that is, those low in authoritarianism and prejudice have far less prejudice to reduce through contact. But there may also be a dissonance effect operating: High authoritarians and the prejudiced may initially have such negative opinions of the outgroup that quality contact may present a sharp contrast. In any event, we have seen that the major problem entails getting authoritarians and the prejudiced into the intergroup contact situations in the first place. Structural societal alterations that require diversity are clearly indicated.

Placing intergroup contact in its micro and macro contexts will also require multi-level analyses (Pettigrew, 2006). In the past, we lacked the statistics and software to exploit multi-level data. Fortunately, we are now blessed with an abundance of appropriate programs. There are at least 16 programs that analyze multi-level data, and HLM, LISREL, Mplus, MLwIN, SAS, SPSS, and SYSTAT are among the most used by social psychologists. With this barrier removed, multi-level analyses that consider the macro level of institutions and societies together with social psychological levels should flourish in the future. And we know from the history of science that once innovative methods open up new empirical observations, theory to explain the findings soon follows.

A principal reason for applying multi-level analyses is to avoid the recurrent problems posed by compositional and ecological fallacies (Pettigrew, 1996, 2006). The compositional fallacy involves drawing conclusions at the macro level of analysis from individual data alone – a problem that all-too-often arises in psychological theorizing. This is a fallacy because organizations and societies are social systems and as such are more than the sum of their individual parts. Macro units have unique properties of their own that the macro-social sciences specialize in studying.

The ecological fallacy involves the exact opposite confusion of levels. Here we draw conclusions about individuals from macro-level data alone – a mistake often seen in statements made about individual voters from aggregate voting results. It is a fallacy because macro units are typically too broad to determine individual-level data, and individuals also have unique properties that cannot be inferred from macro-level data. Working at both levels simultaneously protects against these common fallacies in social science.

To be sure, multi-level approaches are complex, but "the real world" *is* complex. Consequently, multi-level perspectives are arguably closer to the real-life circumstances into which remedial applications must fit. Paradoxically, this complexity can often untangle puzzles that arise at a single level of analysis. Remember how Wagner and his colleagues (2003) were able to explain persistent differences in anti-foreigner prejudice between East and West Germany using individual differences in intergroup contact.

Enhancing the Policy Relevance of Contact Research

Finally, more direct applications to social policy are needed in which intergroup contact is grounded within specific social situations. Just how do you structure optimal contact situations in concrete institutional settings? All the previously discussed future directions would contribute answers to this critical question: specifying the processes of intergroup contact; granting more attention to minority reactions and subjective perceptions of the contact situation; exploring further when intergroup contact leads to negative effects; and placing intergroup contact in its longitudinal, multi-level social context.

Policy-makers need to have concrete recommendations that they can apply directly to the institutional structures they command. Social psychologists in sociology have been keenly aware of this need, but those in psychology have been less directly concerned. Strict attention to institutional and situational norms offers one means of gauging structural effects. Social psychologists in psychology have long recognized the importance of norms – from the early work of Sherif (1936) to the present day – but rarely are norms fully taken into account. And this, unfortunately, has been particularly the case in intergroup contact studies. We have often cited in this book the valuable roommate studies conducted on university campuses, precisely because they are institutionally grounded. The policy implications of these studies for campus administrators are direct and apparent – which brings us to our final discussion.

☐ Implications for Social Policy

Intergroup contact theory, as developed in this book, has two clear and interrelated implications for social policy. The first is obvious. A society's social structure must provide its people with opportunities for extended face-to-face cross-group interaction. We have noted how South Africa's history of apartheid, Northern Ireland's sectarian segregation, and the American South's racial segregation all acted to elevate threat and lessen positive contact. Little wonder, then, that these and other segregated regions conspicuously developed highly conflicted group relations.

All three of these embattled regions are now undergoing social change, with their barriers to intergroup interaction slowly unwinding. Apartheid has ended, but informal racial contact is still tightly circumscribed. A truce holds in Northern Ireland, and small steps toward greater Catholic–Protestant contact are being taken. Legal segregation has been abolished in the South but, as in the other areas, informal racial contact remains restricted and tentative. South Africans, the Northern Irish, and American Southerners of all groups have limited experience in equal-status intergroup contact. Thus, one should expect that an extended period of accommodation is necessary in such regions. Moreover, there has been stout resistance of the privileged amassed against these changes in all three of these areas that further impedes the learning process.

Policy-makers must keep a close eye on four important intergroup indices that gauge the likelihood and extent of intergroup contact. These are measures of (1) intergroup segregation in the labor force, (2) intergroup residential segregation, (3) intergroup educational segregation, and (4) intergroup marriage. Increasing intergroup separation on two or more of these indices often signals future intergroup conflict. Such trends also tend to correspond with increasing group discrimination and a dangerous decline in optimal intergroup contact situations. When groups live largely segregated existences residentially, educationally, and in the work force, optimal contact is severely restricted. Intergroup friendships are limited and intergroup marriages remain rare and stigmatized.

Creating optimal intergroup contact situations in a society requires many of the same remedies needed to deter intergroup discrimination and conflict. This is hardly unexpected for we are dealing with a tightly interwoven system of intergroup relations that involves prejudice, discrimination, separation, and conflict. So the same policies that foster optimal intergroup contact will also serve to decrease discrimination and conflict. Such policies include increasing access for all to citizenship, equal legal rights, and equal opportunities for education, jobs, and housing.

Such policies, of course, are far easier to enumerate than to achieve. A major reason for the difficulty in institutionally establishing these efforts is the threat involved for people, both majorities and minorities, who have long been exposed to traditional norms of segregation and discrimination. Recall the findings of the previous chapter on negative contact. Not only are individual and collective threat key ingredients of such contact, but so is involuntary involvement. Yet for these policies to take hold in societies with long and bitter histories of intergroup separation and conflict, some degree of force and involuntary participation is required. Little wonder, then, that the powerful often strongly resist such needed policies as desegregation and affirmative action.

The second policy implication of our analysis concerns the types of contact to be encouraged. It is not enough for societies simply to provide more opportunities for intergroup contact. The new contact must, to the fullest extent possible, approach the optimal forms described throughout this volume. Allport's original four conditions provide a start, but we must combine them with the additional optimal conditions discussed throughout the book. While formidable to be sure, the achievement of optimal conditions may not be quite as difficult as commonly thought. Once the threat from the initiation of change has subsided, everyday contact appears to be often more optimal than one might expect. Consider the results of our meta-analysis in Chapter 2 and the German survey in Chapter 12. In both datasets, positive contact proves to be far more prevalent than negative contact.

Two Objections

Critics of this social psychological approach raise two problems. First, they might ask, "What about Bosnia? Is it not a disconfirming case for this analysis?" Second, critics often wonder if this view is actually a subtle argument for assimilation, one that simply ignores cultural differences and asks minorities to surrender their distinctiveness in the name of intergroup harmony. We wish to address these objections.

At first glance, Bosnia appears to raise problems for the social psychological perspective on intergroup contact. Whatever else may be said about him, the late Marshall Tito followed an intergroup policy in the former Yugoslavia that resembled the policies outlined here. Of mixed Slovenian and Croatian heritage himself, Tito attempted to increase optimal intergroup contact in housing, jobs, education, sports, and other areas. Indeed, at least in Bosnia's major cities, these policies succeeded in making intergroup housing, education, and even intermarriage more commonplace. Yet, as we know, armed intervention in Bosnia quickly toppled these integrated structures and set the major ethnic groups against each other.

Why? Was it inevitable, as some claim, given the tortured history of the Balkans? Did the conflict expose the failure of Tito's integration policies? We believe the answer is "no" to both questions. There are good reasons to deem that Bosnians, had they been left alone, would not have begun internecine war. Prior to the military incursions, a massive demonstration occurred in Sarajevo involving all three major ethnicities. The demonstrators made it clear that they identified with a superordinate group – they were Bosnians first who intended to live in peace. It appears that had a referendum been held at that point, Bosnians of all stripes would have voted for an independent and ethnically integrated state. But they were never allowed such a vote. Tito's policies had succeeded within their scope, but these new intergroup ties could not withstand Serbian armed intervention and "ethnic cleansing."

Turning to the second criticism, are contact theory's policy implications simply a modern disguise for insistence on minority assimilation? Some legitimate claims have been made concerning risks associated with attempts to unite groups in unequal societies (see Hornsey & Hogg, 2000; Mummendey & Wenzel, 1999). And some supporters of multiculturalism come perilously close to advocating intergroup separation as a means of maintaining cultural purity.

But other multiculturalists understand that their goals and those of providing greater societal access to minorities need not conflict (Pettigrew, 2004c). Some degree of accommodation is, of course, necessary for new groups to thrive, but this process is more complex than critics concede. Integration, after all, is a two-way street; majority cultures also change from intergroup contact (see Berry, 2009). Witness major shifts in European eating habits and the arts as a function of immigration over the past two generations. And the process of expanding integrated opportunities for minorities must entail structural changes in the broadened institutions themselves – schools and the work place – that reflect their culturally diverse participants.

But Contact is Not a Panacea

Let us be clear. We join other specialists in specifically rejecting the notion that intergroup contact is a panacea for intergroup conflict (Hewstone, 2003). But we believe the research described in this volume shows that cross-group contact is *an essential, though not sufficient, component* for lasting remedies to intergroup conflict. Intergroup contact is by no means the only important process in intergroup harmony, but it is an essential one. Ultimately, lasting institutional alterations are necessary, but these macro changes both initiate and are supported by positive intergroup contact. It is a mistake found in many social scientific analyses to consider these two levels as separate and independent, rather than as mutually influencing each other.

Strict segregation between groups, limiting positive intergroup contact, has failed around the globe. From the southern United States and Northern Ireland to India and South Africa, intergroup separation guarantees smoldering resentment and eventual conflict. But with increased intergroup contact in these regions, we are beginning to see the slow winding down of centuries of separation and conflict. Indeed, some of the most dramatic research findings in support of contact theory in this book have come from these changing areas of the world. Thus, active structural remedies to achieve both greater social equality and integration – such as equal access to high-quality education, good jobs, and comfortable housing – are called for in multi-group societies around the world.

APPENDIX A

☐ Bibliography of Research Papers in the Intergroup Contact Meta-Analysis[1]

Abu-Hilal, M. M. (1986). *Foreign students' interaction, satisfaction, and attitudes toward certain aspects of American culture: A case of Arab students in southern CA.* Unpublished doctoral dissertation, University of California, Riverside, California.

Adams, S. E. (1992). *The relationship between social contact and comfort with social interaction among student ethnic groups at Oregon State University.* Unpublished doctoral dissertation, Oregon State University, Corvallis, Oregon.

Aday, R. H., McDuffie, W., & Sims, C. R. (1993). Impact of an intergenerational program on black adolescents' attitudes toward the elderly. *Educational Gerontology, 19,* 663–673.

Aday, R. H., Sims, C. R., & Evans, E. (1991). Youth's attitudes toward the elderly: The impact of intergenerational partners. *Journal of Applied Gerontology, 10,* 372–384.

Alderfer, C. P., Alderfer, C. J., Bell, E. L., & Jones, J. (1992). The race relations competence workshop: Theory and results. *Human Relations, 45,* 1259–1291.

Aljeaid, M. O. (1986). *Perceptions of American college students about Arabs: The role of mass media and personal contact in the formation of stereotypes.* Unpublished doctoral dissertation, Western Michigan University, Kalamazoo, Michigan.

Allport, G. W., & Kramer, B. M. (1946). Some roots of prejudice. *Journal of Psychology, 22,* 9–39.

Alreshoud, A., & Koeske, G. F. (1997). Arab students' attitudes toward and amount of social contact with Americans: A causal process analysis of cross-sectional data. *Journal of Social Psychology, 137,* 235–245.

Altrocchi, J., & Eisdorfer, C. (1961). Changes in attitudes toward mental illness. *Mental Hygiene, 45,* 563–570.

Amir, Y., & Ben-Ari, R. (1985). International tourism, ethnic contact, and attitude change. *Journal of Social Issues, 41,* 105–115.

Amir, Y., & Garti, C. (1977). Situational and personal influence on attitude change following ethnic contact. *International Journal of Intercultural Relations, 1,* 58–75.

Amir, Y., Sharan, S., Bizman, A., Rivner, M., & Ben-Ari, R. (1978). Attitude change in desegregated Israeli high schools. *Journal of Educational Psychology, 70,* 129–136.

Amsel, R., & Fichten, C. S. (1988). Effects of contact on thoughts about interaction with students who have a physical disability. *Journal of Rehabilitation, 54,* 61–65.

Angermeyer, M. C., & Matschinger, H. (1997). Social distance towards the mentally ill: Results of representative surveys in the Federal Republic of Germany. *Psychological Medicine, 27,* 131–141.

Anthony, W. A. (1969). The effects of contact on an individual's attitude toward disabled persons. *Rehabilitation Counseling Bulletin, 12*, 168–171.

Antonak, R. F. (1981). Prediction of attitudes toward disabled persons: A multivariate analysis. *Journal of General Psychology, 104*, 119–123.

Antonak, R. F., Fiedler, C. R., & Mulick, J. A. (1989). Misconceptions relating to mental retardation. *Mental Retardation, 27*, 91–97.

Archie, V. W., & Sherrill, C. (1989). Attitudes toward handicapped peers of mainstreamed and nonmainstreamed children in physical education. *Perceptual and Motor Skills, 69*, 319–322.

Arguc, S. (1995). *Bedrohung und Gewaltbereitschaft türkischer Männer* (Threat and readiness for violence of Turkish men). Unpublished diploma thesis, Marburg, Germany.

Arikan, K., & Uysal, O. (1999). Emotional reactions to the mentally ill are positively influenced by personal acquaintance. *Israel Journal of Psychiatry and Related Sciences, 36*, 100–104.

Arkar, H., & Eker, D. (1992). Influence of having a hospitalized mentally ill member in the family on attitudes toward mental patients in Turkey. *Social Psychiatry and Psychiatric Epidemiology, 27*, 151–155.

Aronson, D. W., & Page, H. A. (1980). Attitude change toward the self and others as a function of helper training and experience. *Journal of Community Psychology, 8*, 75–79.

Auerbach, D. N., & Levenson, R. L. (1977). Second impressions: Attitude change in college students toward the elderly. *The Gerontologist, 17*, 362–366.

Bagget, S. (1981). Attitudinal consequences of older adult volunteers in the public school setting. *Educational Gerontology, 7*, 21–31.

Ballard, M., Corman, L., Gottlieb, J., & Kaufman, M. J. (1977). Improving the social status of mainstreamed retarded children. *Journal of Educational Psychology, 69*, 605–611.

Barnard, W. A., & Benn, M. S. (1987). Belief congruence and prejudice reduction in an interracial contact setting. *Journal of Social Psychology, 128*, 125–134.

Barnea, M., & Amir, Y. (1981). Attitudes and attitude change following intergroup contact of religious and nonreligious students in Israel. *Journal of Social Psychology, 115*, 65–71.

Basu, A. K., & Ames, R. G. (1970). Cross-cultural contact and attitude formation. *Sociology and Social Research, 55*, 5–16.

Beh-Pajooh, A. (1991). The effect of social contact on college students' attitudes toward severely handicapped students and their educational integration. *Journal of Mental Deficiency Research, 35*, 339–352.

Bekker, L. D., & Taylor, C. (1966). Attitudes toward the aged in a multigenerational sample. *Journal of Gerontology, 21*, 115–118.

Belan, I. V. (1996). *Cubans' attitudes toward mental illness: The effects of level of acculturation and contact with a mentally ill family member*. Unpublished doctoral dissertation, California School of Professional Psychology, Fresno, California.

Bell, A. H. (1962). Attitudes of selected rehabilitation workers and other hospital employees toward the physically disabled. *Psychological Reports, 10*, 183–186.

Benedict, A., Shaw, J. S., & Rivlin, L. G. (1988). Attitudes toward the homeless in two New York City metropolitan samples. *Journal of Voluntary Action Research, 17*, 90–98.

Benedict, A., Shaw, J. S., & Rivlin, L. G. (1992). Attitudes toward homeless persons of those attending New York City community board meetings. *Nonprofit and Voluntary Sector Quarterly, 21*, 69–80.

Berg, M., & Wolleat, P. (1973). A comparison of the effects of information and the effects of contact on children's attitudes toward other national groups. *California Journal of Education, 24*, 200–208.

Bergmann, W., & Erb, R. (1997). *Anti-Semitism in Germany* (B. Cooper & A. Brown, Trans.). New Brunswick, New Jersey: Transaction Publishers. (Original work published 1996).

Bicknese, G. (1974). Study Abroad Part I: A comparative test of attitudes and opinions. *Foreign Language Annals, 7*, 325–345.

Biernat, M. (1990). Stereotypes on campus: How contact and liking influence perceptions of group distinctiveness. *Journal of Applied Social Psychology, 20*, 1485–1513.

Biernat, M., & Crandall, C. S. (1994). Stereotyping and contact with social groups: Measurement and conceptual issues. *European Journal of Social Psychology, 24*, 659–677.

Borus, J. F., Fiman, B. G., Stanton, D., & Dowd, A. F. (1973). The racial perceptions inventory. *Archives of General Psychiatry, 29*, 270–275.

Bowman, R. (1979). Public attitudes toward homosexuality in New Zealand. *International Review of Modern Sociology, 9*, 229–238.

Bradnum, M., Nieuwoudt, J., & Tredoux, C. (1993). Contact and the alteration of racial attitudes in South Africa. *South African Journal of Psychology, 23*, 204–211.

Brewer, M. B., & Campbell, D. T. (1976). *Ethnocentrism and intergroup attitudes: East African evidence*. New York: John Wiley & Sons.

Brigham, J. C. (1993). College students' racial attitudes. *Journal of Applied Social Psychology, 23*, 1933–1967.

Brigham, J. C., & Barkowitz, P. (1978). Do "they all look alike?": The effect of race, sex, experience, and attitudes on the ability to recognize faces. *Journal of Applied Social Psychology, 8*, 306–318.

Brigham, J. C., & Malpass, R. S. (1985). The role of experience and contact in the recognition of faces of own- and other-race persons. *Journal of Social Issues, 41*, 139–155. (See also Brigham and Ready, 1985).

Brigham, J. C., & Ready, D. J. (1985). Own-race bias in lineup construction. *Law and Human Behavior, 9*, 417–424. (See also Brigham and Malpass, 1985).

Brink, W., & Harris, L. (1964). *The Negro revolution in America*. New York: Simon & Schuster.

Britt, T. W., Boniecki, K. A., Vescio, T. K., Biernat, M., & Brown, L. M. (1996). Intergroup anxiety: A person × situation approach. *Personality and Social Psychology Bulletin, 22*, 1177–1188.

Brockington, I. F., Hall, P., Levings, J., & Murf, C. (1993). The community's tolerance of the mentally ill. *British Journal of Psychiatry, 162*, 93–99.

Brockman, J., & D'Arcy, C. (1978). Correlates of attitudinal social distance toward the mentally ill: A review and re-survey. *Social Psychiatry, 13*, 69–77.

Brooks, Jr., G. C., Sedlacek, W. E., & Mindus, L. A. (1973). Interracial contact and attitudes among university students. *Journal of Non-White Concerns in Personnel and Guidance, 1*, 102–110.

Brooks, W. D., & Friedrich, G. W. (1970). Police image: An exploratory study. *Journal of Communication, 20*, 370–374.

Brophy, I. N. (1945). The luxury of anti-Negro prejudice. *Public Opinion Quarterly*, 9, 456–466.
Brown, B. S., & Albee, G. W. (1966). The effect of integrated hospital experiences on racial attitudes – a discordant note. *Social Problems*, 13, 324–333.
Brown, R., Condor, S., Mathews, A., Wade, G., & Williams, J. (1986). Explaining intergroup differentiation in an industrial organization. *Journal of Occupational Psychology*, 59, 273–286.
Brown, R., Maras, P., Masser, B., Vivian, J., & Hewstone, M. (2001). Life on the ocean wave: Testing some intergroup hypotheses in a naturalistic setting. *Group Processes and Intergroup Relations*, 4, 81–97.
Brown, R., Vivian, J., & Hewstone, M. (1999). Changing attitudes through intergroup contact: The effects of group membership salience. *European Journal of Social Psychology*, 29, 741–764.
Brown, S. A. (1997). *Intergroup anxiety in Whites: The impact of the motivation to control prejudice and Black ethnic identity*. Unpublished doctoral dissertation, University of Georgia, Athens, Georgia.
Bucich-Naylor, D. A. (1978). *The comparative effectiveness of a direct contact program and a didactic program in effecting changes in attitude of nondisabled children toward disabled children*. Unpublished doctoral dissertation, Hofstra University, Hempstead, New York.
Bullock, C. S. (1976a). *School desegregation, inter-racial contact and prejudice*. Unpublished manuscript, Houston University, Houston, Texas. (See also Bullock, 1976b and Bullock, 1978).
Bullock, C. S. (1976b). Interracial contact and student prejudice: The impact of southern school desegregation. *Youth and Society*, 7, 271–310. (See also Bullock, 1976a and Bullock, 1978).
Bullock, C. S. (1978). Contact theory and racial tolerance among high school students. *School Review*, 86, 187–216. (See also Bullock, 1976a and Bullock, 1976b).
Buono, A. F. (1981). *Prospects for interracial harmony: The impact of desegregated and integrated situations on attitudinal and behavioral receptive outcomes*. Unpublished doctoral dissertation, Boston College, Chestnut Hill, Massachusetts.
Burgin, M., & Walker, I. (2000). *Intergroup contact and prejudice in junior Australian Rules football teams*. Unpublished manuscript, Murdoch University, Perth, Australia.
Butler, J. S., & Wilson, K. L. (1978). The American soldier revisited: Race relations and the military. *Social Science Quarterly*, 59, 451–467.
Caditz, J. (1976). Ethnic identification, interethnic contact, and belief in integration. *Social Forces*, 54, 632–645.
Campbell, E. Q. (1958). Some social psychological correlates of direction in attitude change. *Social Forces*, 36, 335–340.
Canter, F. M., & Shoemaker, R. (1960). The relationship between authoritarian attitudes and attitudes toward mental patients. *Nursing Research*, 9, 39–41.
Carlson, J. S., & Widaman, K. F. (1988). The effects of study abroad during college on attitudes toward other cultures. *International Journal of Intercultural Relations*, 12, 1–17.
Carstensen, L., Mason, S. E., & Caldwell, E. C. (1982). Children's attitudes toward the elderly: An intergenerational technique for change. *Educational Gerontology*, 8, 291–301.

Carter, C. A., & Mitchell, L. E. (1956). Attitudes of Negro pupils toward Whites. *Journal of Human Relations, 4,* 90–99.

Casey, K. (1978). The semantic differential technique in the examination of teacher attitudes to handicapped children. *The Exceptional Child, 25,* 41–52.

Caspi, A. (1984). Contact hypothesis and inter-age attitudes: A field study of cross-age contact. *Social Psychology Quarterly, 47,* 74–80.

Catlin, J. B. (1977). *The impact of interracial living on the racial attitudes and interaction patterns of White college students: Volume I.* Unpublished doctoral dissertation, University of Michigan, Ann Arbor, Michigan.

Chadwick, B. A., Bahr, H. M., & Day, R. C. (1971). Correlates of attitudes favorable to racial discrimination among high school students. *Social Science Quarterly, 51,* 873–888.

Chang, H. (1973). Attitudes of Chinese students in the United States. *Sociology and Social Research, 58,* 66–77.

Chang, S. (1998). A study of the Korean–Black conflict in black neighborhoods. *Korean Journal of Sociology, 32,* 137–177.

Chen, M., Shapira, R., & Housedorf, H. (1970). Interactions with Israelis and changes in attitudes among exchange students in an Israeli university. *Megamot, 17,* 158–165.

Chinsky, J. M., & Rappaport, J. (1970). Attitude change in college students and chronic patients: A dual perspective. *Journal of Consulting and Clinical Psychology, 35,* 388–394.

Chou, K., & Mak, K. (1998). Attitudes to mental patients among Hong Kong Chinese: A trend study over two years. *International Journal of Social Psychiatry, 44,* 215–224.

Cleland, C. C., & Cochran, I. L. (1961). The effect of institutional tours on attitudes of high school seniors. *American Journal of Mental Deficiency, 65,* 473–481.

Clément, R., Gardner, R. C., & Smythe, P. C. (1977). Inter-ethnic contact: Attitudinal consequences. *Canadian Journal of Behavioral Science, 9,* 205–215.

Clore, G. L., Bray, R. M., Itkin, S. M., & Murphy, P. (1978). Interracial attitudes and behavior at a summer camp. *Journal of Personality and Social Psychology, 36,* 107–116.

Clunies-Ross, G., & O'Meara, K. (1989). Changing the attitudes of students toward peers with disabilities. *Australian Psychologist, 24,* 273–284.

Colca, C., Lowen, D., Colca, L. A., & Lord, S. A. (1982). Combating racism in the schools: A group work pilot project. *Social Work in Education, 5,* 5–16.

Cook, J. W., & Wollersheim, J. P. (1976). The effect of labeling of special education students on the perceptions of contact versus noncontact normal peers. *Journal of Special Education, 10,* 187–198.

Cook, S. W. (1969). Motives in a conceptual analysis of attitude-related behavior. In W. J. Arnold & D. Levine (Eds.), *Nebraska symposium on motivation* (pp. 179–197). University of Nebraska: University of Nebraska Press.

Cookston, R. R. (1973). *Effects of a short-term, intensive, interracial living experience on interracial social distance and attitudes toward interracial issues.* Unpublished doctoral dissertation, East Texas State University, Commerce, Texas.

Cotten-Huston, A. L., & Waite, B. M. (2000). Anti-homosexual attitudes in college students: Predictors and classroom interventions. *Journal of Homosexuality, 38,* 117–133.

Couper, D. P., Sheehan, N. W., & Thomas, E. L. (1991). Attitude toward old people: The impact of an intergenerational program. *Educational Gerontology, 17,* 41–53.

Cousens, P., & Crawford, J. (1988). Moving the mentally ill into the community: The problem of acceptance and the effect of contact. *Australian Journal of Social Issues, 23,* 196–207.

Cowen, E. L., Underberg, R. P., & Verrillo, R. T. (1958). The development and testing of an attitude to blindness scale. *Journal of Social Psychology, 48,* 297–304.

Crain, R. L., & Weisman, C. S. (1972). *Discrimination, personality and achievement: A survey of northern Blacks.* New York: Seminar Press.

Creech, S. K. (1977). Changes in attitudes about mental illness among nursing students following a psychiatric affiliation. *Journal of Psychiatric Nursing and Mental Health Services, 15,* 9–14.

Crull, S. R., & Bruton, B. T. (1979). Bogardus social distance in the 1970's. *Sociology and Social Research, 63,* 771–783.

D'Augelli, A. R. (1989). Homophobia in a university community: Views of prospective resident assistants. *Journal of College Student Development, 30,* 546–552.

D'Augelli, A. R., & Rose, M. L. (1990). Homophobia in a university community: Attitudes and experiences of heterosexual freshmen. *Journal of College Student Development, 31,* 484–491.

Davidson, G., Hansford, B., & Moriarty, B. (1983). Interpersonal apprehension and cultural majority–minority communication. *Australian Psychologist, 18,* 97–105.

Dellmann-Jenkins, M., Lambert, D., & Fruit, D. (1986). Old and young together: Effect of an educational program on preschoolers' attitudes toward older people. *Childhood Education, 62,* 206–212.

Dellman-Jenkins, M., Lambert, D., & Fruit, D. (1991). Fostering preschoolers' prosocial behaviors toward the elderly: The effect of an intergenerational program. *Educational Gerontology, 17,* 21–32.

Desforges, D. M., Lord, C. G., Ramsey, S. L., Mason, J. A., Van Leeuwen, M. D., West, S. C., et al. (1991). Effects of structured cooperative contact on changing negative attitudes toward stigmatized social groups. *Journal of Personality and Social Psychology, 60,* 531–544.

Deutsch, M., & Collins, M. E. (1950). Interracial housing III: Influence of integrated, segregated occupancy on racial attitudes measured. *Journal of Housing, 7,* 127–129. (See also Deutsch & Collins, 1951).

Deutsch, M., & Collins, M. E. (1951). *Interracial housing: A psychological evaluation of a social experiment.* New York: Russell & Russell. (See also Deutsch & Collins, 1950).

Deutsche Shell (2000). *Jugend 2000 (Youth 2000).* Opladen, Germany: Leske + Budrich.

Diamond, M. J., & Lobitz, W. C. (1973). When familiarity breeds respect: The effects of an experimental depolarization program on police and student attitudes toward each other. *Journal of Social Issues, 29,* 95–109.

Dijker, A. J. M. (1987). Emotional reactions to ethnic minorities. *European Journal of Social Psychology, 17,* 305–325.

Distefano, M. K., & Pryer, M. W. (1970). Stability of attitudes in psychiatric attendants following training. *Mental Hygiene, 54,* 433–435.

Di Tullio, B. J. (1982). *The effect of employing trainable mentally retarded (TMR) students as workers within the Philadelphia public school system: Attitudes of supervisors and non-handicapped co-workers toward the retarded as a result of contact.* Unpublished doctoral dissertation, Temple University, Philadelphia, Pennsylvania.

Dodson, J. P. (1970). *Participation in a biracial encounter group: Its relation to acceptance of self and others, racial attitudes, and interpersonal orientations.* Unpublished doctoral dissertation, Purdue University, West Lafayette, Indiana.

Doka, K. J. (1986). Adolescent attitudes and beliefs toward aging and the elderly. *International Journal of Aging and Human Development, 22,* 173–187.

Donaldson, J., & Martinson, M. C. (1977). Modifying attitudes toward physically disabled persons. *Exceptional Children, 43,* 337–341.

Dooley, S., & Frankel, B. G. (1990). Improving attitudes toward elderly people: Evaluation of an intervention program for adolescents. *Canadian Journal on Aging, 9,* 400–409.

Drake, J. T. (1957). Some factors influencing students' attitudes toward older people. *Social Forces, 35,* 266–271.

Dubey, S. N. (1979). Positive discrimination policy and ethnocentric attitudes among the scheduled castes. *Public Opinion Quarterly, 43,* 60–67.

Duckitt, J. H. (1984). Attitudes of White South Africans toward homosexuality. *South African Journal of Sociology, 15,* 89–93.

Dunbar, E. (2000). [Knowledge of human rights laws and policies in Spain]. Unpublished raw data.

Eaton, W. O., & Clore, G. L. (1975). Interracial imitation at a summer camp. *Journal of Personality and Social Psychology, 32,* 1099–1105.

Eberhardt, K., & Mayberry, W. (1995). Factors influencing entry-level occupational therapists' attitudes toward persons with disabilities. *American Journal of Occupational Therapy, 49,* 629–636.

Eddy, D. M. (1986). Before and after attitudes toward aging in a BSN program. *Journal of Gerontological Nursing, 12,* 30–34.

Eller, A. (2000). *Putting Pettigrew's reformulated model to the test: A reconceptualisation of the intergroup contact theory* (Study 5). Unpublished dissertation, University of Kent at Canterbury, UK.

Eller, A., & Abrams, D. (1999, December). *Direct and extended contact: Testing Pettigrew's (1998) and Wright et al's (1997) models.* Poster presented at the British Psychological Society London Conference, London, United Kingdom.

Eller, A., Abrams, D., & Randsley de Moura, G. (2000, June). *Intergroup contact between Mexicans and Americans: Can Pettigrew's (1998) model be applied to a real-world context?* Paper presented at the 3rd Jena Meeting on Intergroup Processes, Jena, Germany.

Eller, A., Abrams, D., & Wright, S. C. (2000). *Inter-ethnic contact in Mexico and the United States: Testing previous models.* Manuscript in preparation.

Ellis, A. L., & Vasseur, R. B. (1993). Prior interpersonal contact with and attitudes towards gays and lesbians in an interviewing context. *Journal of Homosexuality, 25,* 31–45.

Emerton, R. G., & Rothman, G. (1978). Attitudes towards deafness: Hearing students at a hearing and deaf college. *American Annals of the Deaf, 123,* 588–593.

Ervin, K. S. (1993). *The relationship of personal contact, media exposure and racial/ ethnic self-esteem and sterotypes and racial prejudice.* Unpublished doctoral dissertation, Michigan State University, East Lansing, Michigan.

Eshel, Y., & Dicker, R. (1995). Congruence and incongruence in perceived ethnic acceptance among Israeli students. *Journal of Social Psychology, 135,* 251–262.

Esposito, B. G., & Peach, W. J. (1983). Changing attitudes of preschool children toward handicapped persons. *Exceptional Children, 49,* 361–363.

Esposito, B. G., & Reed, T. M. (1986). The effects of contact with handicapped persons on young children's attitudes. *Exceptional Children, 53,* 224–229.

Evans, J. H. (1976). Changing attitudes toward disabled persons: An experimental study. *Rehabilitation Counseling Bulletin, 19,* 572–579.

Felton, G. S. (1975). Changes in attitudes toward disabled persons among allied health paraprofessional trainees in an interdisciplinary setting. *Perceptual and Motor Skills, 40,* 118.

Fenrick, N. J., & Petersen, T. K. (1984). Developing positive changes in attitudes towards moderately/severely handicapped students through a peer tutoring program. *Education and Training of the Mentally Retarded, 19,* 83–90.

Fichten, C. S., & Amsel, R. (1986). Trait attributions about college students with a physical disability: Circumplex analyses and methodological issues. *Journal of Applied Social Psychology, 16,* 410–427.

Fichten, C. S., Amsel, R., Bourdon, C. V., & Creti, L. (1988). Interaction between college students with physical disabilities and their professors. *Journal of Applied Rehabilitation Counseling, 19,* 13–20.

Fichten, C. S., Tagalakis, V., & Amsel, R. (1989). Effects of cognitive modeling, affect, and contact on attitudes, thoughts, and feelings toward college students with physical disabilities. *Journal of the Multihandicapped Person, 2,* 119–137.

Finchilescu, G. (1988). Interracial contact in South Africa within the nursing context. *Journal of Applied Social Psychology, 18,* 1207–1221.

Florian, V., & Kehat, D. (1987). Changing high school students' attitudes toward disabled people. *Health and Social Work, 12,* 57–63.

Floyd, H. H. (1970). *Rejection: A study of attitudes toward the mentally ill in a community near a mental hospital.* Unpublished doctoral dissertation, University of Georgia, Athens, Georgia.

Foley, L. A. (1977). Personality characteristics and interracial contact as determinants of Black prejudice toward Whites. *Human Relations, 30,* 709–720.

Ford, W. S. (1973). Interracial public housing in a border city: Another look at the contact hypothesis. *American Journal of Sociology, 78,* 1426–1447.

Friedman, R. S. (1975). *The peer-to-peer program: A model project for the integration of severely physically handicapped youngsters with nondisabled peers.* New York State Education Dept., Albany Division of Drug and Health Education Services.

Friesen, E. W. (1966). *Nature and determinants of attitudes toward education and toward physically disabled persons in Colombia, Peru, and the United States.* Unpublished doctoral dissertation, Michigan State University, East Lansing, Michigan.

Furnham, A., & Gibbs, M. (1984). School children's attitudes towards the handicapped. *Journal of Adolescence, 7,* 99–117.

Furnham, A., & Pendred, J. (1983). Attitudes towards the mentally and physically disabled. *British Journal of Medical Psychology, 56,* 179–187.

Furuto, S. B. C. L., & Furuto, D. M. (1983). The effects of affective and cognitive treatment on attitude change toward ethnic minority groups. *International Journal of Intercultural Relations, 7,* 149–165.

Gaertner, S. L., Dovidio, J. F., Rust, M. C., Nier, J., A., Banker, B. S., Ward, C. M., et al. (1999). Reducing intergroup bias: Elements of intergroup cooperation. *Journal of Personality and Social Psychology, 76,* 388–402.

Gaertner, S. L., Rust, M. C., Dovidio, J. F., Bachman, B. A., & Anastasio, P. A. (1994). The contact hypothesis: The role of a common ingroup identity on reducing intergroup bias. *Small Group Research, 25,* 224–249.

Gardner, R. C., Kirby, D. M., & Arboleda, A. (1973). Ethnic stereotypes: A cross-cultural replication of their unitary dimensionality. *Journal of Social Psychology, 91,* 189–195.

Gardner, R. C., Kirby, D. M., Smythe, P. C., Dumas, G., Zelman, M., & Bramwell, J. R. (1974). Bicultural excursion programs: Their effects on students' stereotypes, attitudes and motivation. *Alberta Journal of Educational Research, 20,* 270–277.

Gardner, R. C., Taylor, D. M., & Santos, E. (1969). Ethnic stereotypes: The role of contact. *Philippine Journal of Psychology, 2,* 11–24.

Gelber, D. M. (1993). *Changing attitudes toward physically disabled persons: Effects on contact, acknowledgment of disability, and information exchange.* Unpublished doctoral dissertation, Hofstra University, Hempstead, New York.

Gelfand, S., & Ullmann, L. P. (1961). Attitude changes associated with psychiatric affiliation. *Nursing Research, 10,* 200–204.

Gentry, C. S. (1987). Social distance regarding male and female homosexuals. *Journal of Social Psychology, 127,* 199–208.

Gerbert, B., Sumser, J., & Maguire, B. T. (1991). The impact of who you know and where you live on opinions about AIDS and health care. *Social Science and Medicine, 32,* 677–681.

Gething, L. (1991). Generality vs. specificity of attitudes towards people with disabilities. *British Journal of Medical Psychology, 64,* 55–64.

Glass, J. C., Jr., & Trent, C. (1980). Changing ninth-graders attitudes toward older persons: Possibility and persistence through education. *Research on Aging, 2,* 499–512.

Glass, R. M., & Meckler, R. S. (1972). Preparing elementary teachers to instruct mildly handicapped children in regular classrooms: A summer workshop. *Exceptional Children, 39,* 152–156.

Glassner, B., & Owen, C. (1976). Variations in attitudes toward homosexuality. *Cornell Journal of Social Relations, 11,* 161–176.

Glock, C. Y., Wuthnow, R., Piliavin, J. A., & Spencer, M. (1975). *Adolescent Prejudice.* New York: Harper & Row.

Glover, R. J., & Smith, C. A. (1997). Racial attitudes of preschoolers: Age, race of examiner, and child-care setting. *Psychological Reports, 81,* 719–722.

Goldstein, M. W., & Simpkins, R. E. (1973). Attitude changes toward juvenile delinquents as a function of interpersonal contact. *Psychological Reports, 32,* 1220.

Gordon, S. K., & Hallauer, D. S. (1976). Impact of a friendly visiting program on attitudes of college students toward the aged: A pedagogical note. *The Gerontologist, 16,* 371–376.

Gosse, V. F., & Sheppard, G. (1979). Attitudes toward physically disabled persons: Do education and personal contact make a difference? *Canadian Counselor, 13,* 131–135.

Goto, S. G. (2000). *Becoming friends or remaining foes: An empirical test of a causal model of intergroup contact across two cultures.* Unpublished manuscript, Pomona College, Claremont, California.

Gottlieb, J., & Corman, L. (1975). Public attitudes toward mentally retarded children. *American Journal of Mental Deficiency, 80,* 72–80.

Grack, C., & Richman, C. L. (1996). Reducing general and specific heterosexism through cooperative contact. *Journal of Psychology and Human Sexuality, 8,* 59–68.

Graffi, S., & Minnes, P. M. (1988). Attitudes of primary school children toward the physical appearance and labels associated with Down syndrome. *American Journal on Mental Retardation, 93,* 28–35.

Grantham, E. V., & Block, M. J. (1983). Effect of extramural experiences on dental students' attitudes. *Journal of Dental Education, 47,* 681–684.

Gray, J. S., & Thompson, A. H. (1953). The ethnic prejudices of White and Negro college students. *Journal of Abnormal and Social Psychology, 48,* 311–313.

Green, A. L., & Stoneman, Z. (1989). Attitudes of mothers and fathers of nonhandicapped children. *Journal of Early Intervention, 13,* 292–304.

Greenland, K., & Brown, R. (1999). Categorization and intergroup anxiety in contact between British and Japanese nationals. *European Journal of Social Psychology, 29,* 503–521.

Gregory, D. (1997). Before and after the Americans with Disabilities Act: An analysis of attitude and knowledge of undergraduate music majors. *Journal of Music Therapy, 34,* 119–128.

Gronberg, G. W. (1982). *Attitude responses of nonhandicapped elementary students to specific information and contact with the handicapped.* Unpublished doctoral dissertation, University of Northern Colorado, Greely, Colorado.

Gruesser, M. J. (1950). Categorical valuations of Jews among Catholic parochial school children. *The Catholic University of America Studies in Sociology, 34,* 1–163.

Gundlach, R. H. (1950). Effects of on-the-job experience with Negroes upon the racial attitudes of White workers in union shops. *American Psychologist, 5,* 300.

Haddock, G., Zanna, M. P., & Esses, V. M. (1993). Assessing the structure of prejudicial attitudes: The case of attitudes toward homosexuals. *Journal of Personality and Social Psychology, 65,* 1105–1118.

Hale, N. M. (1998). Effects of age and interpersonal contact on stereotyping of the elderly. *Current Psychology: Developmental, Learning, Personality, Social, 17,* 28–47.

Hall, E. P. (1969). *An experimental study of the modification of attitudes toward the mentally retarded.* Unpublished doctoral dissertation, University of Alabama, Tuscaloosa, Alabama.

Hall, P. H. (1998). *An assessment of perceptions of attitudes of common ground students.* Unpublished doctoral dissertation, University of Minnesota, Minneapolis/St. Paul, Minnesota.

Hamblin, R. L. (1962). The dynamics of racial discrimination. *Social Problems, 10,* 103–121.

Hansen, G. L. (1982). Measuring prejudice against homosexuality (homosexism) among college students: A new scale. *Journal of Social Psychology, 117,* 233–236.

Harding, J., & Hogrefe, R. (1952). Attitudes of White department store employees toward Negro co-workers. *Journal of Social Issues, 8,* 18–28.

Haring, N. G., Stern, G. G., & Cruickshank, W. M. (1958). *Attitudes of educators toward exceptional children.* New York: Syracuse University Press.

Haring, T. G., Breen, C., Pitts-Conway, V., Lee, M., & Gaylord-Ross, R. (1987). Adolescent peer tutoring and special friend experiences. *Journal of the Association for Persons with Severe Handicaps, 12*, 280–286.

Harlan, H. H. (1942). Some factors affecting attitude toward Jews. *American Sociological Review, 7*, 816–827.

Harper, D. C., & Wacker, D. P. (1985). Children's attitudes toward disabled peers and the effects of mainstreaming. *Academic Psychology Bulletin, 7*, 87–98.

Harris, J., & Fiedler, C. M. (1988). Preadolescent attitudes toward the elderly: An analysis of race, gender and contact variables. *Adolescence, 23*, 335–340.

Hastings, R. P., Berry, M., & Whennell, S. (1998). Pediatric nursing and education students' attitude toward children with Rett syndrome: A pilot study (Letter to the editor). *Developmental Medicine and Child Neurology, 40*, 284–287.

Hastings, R. P., & Graham, S. (1995). Adolescents' perceptions of young people with severe learning difficulties: The effects of integration schemes and frequency of contact. *Educational Psychology, 15*, 149–159.

Hatanaka, H. K. (1982). *The effects of a short term training program on the racial attitudes of child welfare workers*. Unpublished doctoral dissertation, University of California, Los Angeles, California.

Hazzard, A. (1983). Children's experience with, knowledge of, and attitude toward diasabled persons. *Journal of Special Education, 17*, 131–139.

Hébert, M., Voyer, J. P., & Valois, D. (2000). Evaluation of the program "Prejudices ... I don't know of any!" among youth in senior high school. *Canadian Journal of Community Mental Health, 19*, 105–126.

Helmstetter, E., Peck, C. A., & Giangreco, M. F. (1994). Outcomes of interactions with peers with moderate or severe disabilities: A statewide survey of high school students. *Journal of the Association for Persons with Severe Handicaps, 19*, 263–276.

Herek, G. M. (1988). Heterosexuals' attitudes toward lesbians and gay men: Correlates and gender differences. *Journal of Sex Research, 25*, 451–477.

Herek, G. M. (1999). [*Contact and attitudes toward gays and lesbians*]. Unpublished raw data.

Herek, G. M., & Capitanio, J. P. (1996). "Some of my best friends": Intergroup contact, concealable stigma, and heterosexuals' attitudes toward gay men and lesbians. *Personality and Social Psychology Bulletin, 22*, 412–424.

Herek, G. M., & Capitanio, J. P. (1997). AIDS stigma and contact with persons with AIDS: Effects of direct and vicarious contact. *Journal of Applied Social Psychology, 27*, 1–36.

Herek, G. M., & Glunt, E. K. (1993). Interpersonal contact and heterosexuals' attitudes toward gay men: Results from a national survey. *Journal of Sex Research, 30*, 239–244.

Herman, S. N. (1970). *American students in Israel*. Ithaca, New York: Cornell University Press.

Hicks, J. M., & Spaner, F. E. (1962). Attitude change and mental hospital experience. *Journal of Abnormal and Social Psychology, 65*, 112–120.

Hill, P. B. (1984). Räumlich Nähe und soziale Distanz zu ethnischen Minderheiten (Spacial proximity and social distance from ethnic minorities). *Zeitschrift für Soziologie, 13*, 363–370.

Hillis, S. R. (1986). *Modification of the attitudes of non-handicapped children toward the handicapped through information-based and contact-based intervention.*

Unpublished doctoral dissertation, University of Wisconsin, Madison, Wisconsin.

Hillman, J. L., & Stricker, G. (1996). Predictors of college students' knowledge of and attitudes toward elderly sexuality: The relevance of grandparental contact. *Educational Gerontology, 22*, 539–555.

Hoeh, J. A., & Spuck, D. W. (1975). Effects of a three phase acculturation process on language skill development and social and personal attitudes of high school French students. *Foreign Language Annals, 8*, 221–226.

Hofman, J. E., & Zak, I. (1969). Interpersonal contact and attitude change in a cross-cultural situation. *Journal of Social Psychology, 78*, 165–171.

Holmes, E. P., Corrigan, P. W., Williams, P., Canar, J., & Kubiak, M. A. (1999). Changing attitudes about schizophrenia. *Schizophrenia Bulletin, 25*, 447–456.

Holtzman, W. H. (1956). Attitudes of college men toward non-segregation in Texas schools. *Public Opinion Quarterly, 20*, 559–569.

Holzberg, J. D., & Gewirtz, H. (1963). A method of altering attitudes toward mental illness. *Psychiatric Quarterly Supplement, 37*, 56–61.

Horenczyk, G., & Bekerman, Z. (1997). The effects of intercultural acquaintance and structured intergroup interaction on ingroup, outgroup, and reflected ingroup stereotypes. *International Journal of Intercultural Relations, 21*, 71–83.

Hortacsu, N. (2000). Intergroup relations in a changing political context: The case of veiled and unveiled university students in Turkey. *European Journal of Social Psychology, 30*, 733–744.

Hraba, J., Brinkman, R., & Gray-Ray, P. (1996). A comparison of Black and White prejudice. *Sociological Spectrum, 16*, 129–157.

Hughey, S. J. (1988). *Theology students' attitudes toward disabled people with reference to dogmatism, intolerance of ambiguity, and contact.* Unpublished doctoral dissertation, Fuller Theological Seminary, Pasadena, California.

Hunt, B., & Hunt, C. S. (2000). Attitudes toward people with disabilities: A comparison of undergraduate rehabilitation and business majors. *Rehabilitation Education, 14*, 269–283.

Hunt, C. L. (1960). Private integrated housing in a medium size nothern city. *Social Problems, 7*, 195–209.

Ibrahim, S. E. M. (1970). Interaction, perception, and attitudes of Arab students toward Americans. *Sociology and Social Research, 55*, 29–46.

Ichilov, O., & Even-Dar, S. (1984). Interethnic contacts in an alternative educational environment: The Israeli Shelf Project. *Journal of Youth and Adolescence, 13*, 145–161.

Iguchi, M. T., & Johnson, R. C. (1966). Attitudes of students associated with participation in a mental-hospital volunteer program. *Journal of Social Psychology, 68*, 107–111.

Ijaz, M. A. (1980). *Ethnic attitudes of elementary school children toward Blacks and East Indians and the effect of a cultural program on these attitudes.* Unpublished doctoral dissertation, University of Toronto, Toronto, Canada.

Ingamells, S., Goodwin, A. M., & John, C. (1996). The influence of psychiatric hospital and community residence labels on social rejection of the mentally ill. *British Journal of Clinical Psychology, 35*, 359–367.

Institut für Demographie: Österreichische Akademie der Wissenschaften. (1999). *Migration und Fremdenfeindlichkeit: Fakten, Meinungen und Einstellungen zu internationaler Migration, ausländischer Bevölkerung und staatlicher Ausländerpolitik in*

Österreich (Migration and hostility towards strangers: Facts, opinions, and attitudes about international migration, the foreign population, and state politics concerning foreigners). Austria: Lebhart & Münz.

Irish, D. P. (1952). Reactions of Caucasian residents to Japanese-American neighbors. *Journal of Social Issues, 8*, 10–17.

Islam, M. R., & Hewstone, M. (1993). Dimensions of contact as predictors of intergroup anxiety, perceived out-group variability, and out-group attitude: An integrative model. *Personality and Social Psychology Bulletin, 19*, 700–710.

Ivester, C., & King, K. (1977). Attitudes of adolescents toward the aged. *The Gerontologist, 17*, 85–89.

Jackman, M. R., & Crane, M. (1986). "Some of my best friends are Black . . .": Interracial friendship and Whites' racial attitudes. *Public Opinion Quarterly, 50*, 459–486.

Jacobson, C. K. (1977). Separatism, integrationism, and avoidance among Black, White, and Latin adolescents. *Social Forces, 55*, 1011–1027.

Jaffe, J. (1966). Attitudes of adolescents toward the mentally retarded. *American Journal of Mental Deficiency, 70*, 907–912. (See also Jaffe, 1967).

Jaffe, J. (1967). Attitudes and interpersonal contact: Relationships between contact with the mentally retarded and dimensions of attitude. *Journal of Counseling Psychology, 14*, 482–484. (See also Jaffe, 1966).

James, H. E. O. (1955). Personal contact in school and change in intergroup attitudes. *International Social Science Bulletin, 7*, 66–70.

James-Valutis, M. (1993). *The impact of racial attitudes and interracial contact on stereotypical perceptions*. Unpublished doctoral dissertation, University of Missouri, St. Louis, Missouri.

Jaques, M. E., Linkowski, D. C., & Sieka, F. L. (1970). Cultural attitudes toward disability: Denmark, Greece, and the United States. *International Journal of Social Psychiatry, 16*, 54–62.

Jeffries, V., & Ransford, H. E. (1969). Interracial social contact and middle-class White reactions to the Watts riot. *Social Problems, 16*, 312–324.

Johannsen, W. J., Redel, M. C., & Engel, R. G. (1964). Personality and attitudinal changes during psychiatric nursing affiliation. *Nursing Research, 13*, 342–345.

Johnson, D. W., & Johnson, R. T. (1985). Mainstreaming hearing-impaired students: The effect of effort in communicating on cooperation and interpersonal attraction. *Journal of Psychology, 119*, 31–44.

Johnson, M. K., & Marini, M. M. (1998). Bridging the racial divide in the United States: The effect of gender. *Social Psychology Quarterly, 61*, 247–258.

Johnson, R. T., & Johnson, D. W. (1981). Building friendships between handicapped and nonhandicapped students: Effects of cooperative and individualistic instruction. *American Educational Research Journal, 18*, 415–423.

Johnstone, T. V. (1992). *The relationship of contact and social distance to attitudes toward deaf and disabled persons*. Unpublished doctoral dissertation, Hofstra University, Hempstead, New York.

Jones, R. J. (1960). *The effects of inter-ethnic group contact in a desegregated hospital community*. Unpublished doctoral dissertation, The American University, Washington, DC.

Jones, T. W., Sowell, V. M., Jones, J. K., & Butler, L. G. (1981). Changing children's perceptions of handicapped people. *Exceptional Children, 47*, 365–368.

Kalson, L. (1976). M*A*S*H: A program of social interaction between institutionalized aged and adult mentally retarded persons. *The Gerontologist, 16,* 340–348.

Kamal, A. A., & Maruyama, G. (1990). Cross-cultural contact and attitudes of Qatari students in the United States. *International Journal of Intercultural Relations, 14,* 123–134.

Kanouse-Roberts, A. L. (1977). *A study of the interaction between a group of Jewish senior citizens and a group of Black adolescent girls classified as "delinquent."* Unpublished doctoral dissertation, Teachers College at Columbia University, New York.

Katz, Y. J., & Yochanan, A. B. (1988). Social interaction as a function of active intervention in an Israeli elementary school. *Journal of Social Psychology, 128,* 89–96.

Kelly, J. G., Ferson, J. E., & Holtzman, W. H. (1958). The measurement of attitudes toward the Negro in the South. *Journal of Social Psychology, 48,* 305–317.

Kephart, W. M. (1957). *Racial factors and urban law enforcement.* Philadelphia: University of Pennsylvania Press.

Kidwell, I. J., & Booth, A. (1977). Social distance and intergenerational relations. *The Gerontologist, 17,* 412–420.

Kierscht, M. S., & DuHoux, M. A. (1980). Preparing the mainstream: Changing children's attitudes toward the disabled. *School Psychology Review, 9,* 279–283.

Kirchler, E., &, Zani, B. (1995). Why don't they stay at home? Prejudices against ethnic minorities in Italy. *Journal of Community and Applied Social Psychology, 5.* 59–65. (See also Zani & Kirchler, 1995).

Kisabeth, K. L., & Richardson, D. B. (1985). Changing attitudes toward disabled individuals: The effects of one disabled person. *Therapeutic Recreation Journal, 19,* 24–33.

Kish, G. B., & Hood, R. (1974). Voluntary activity promotes more realistic conceptions of the mentally ill by college students. *Journal of Community Psychology, 2,* 30–32.

Kishi, G. S., & Meyer, L. H. (1994). What children report and remember: A six-year follow-up of the effects of social contact between peers with and without severe disabilities. *Journal of the Association for Persons with Severe Handicaps, 19,* 277–289.

Kleinman, C. S. (1983). *Changes in attitudes toward mental illness by student nurses from various ethnic groups.* Unpublished doctoral dissertation, Florida Institute of Technology, Melbourne, Florida.

Knox, V. J., Gekoski, W. L., & Johnson, E. A. (1986). Contact with and perceptions of the elderly. *The Gerontologist, 26,* 309–313.

Knussen, C., & Niven, C. A. (1999). HIV/AIDS and health care workers: Contact with patients and attitudes towards them. *Psychology and Health, 14,* 367–378.

Kobe, F. H., & Mulick, J. A. (1995). Attitudes toward mental retardation and eugenics: The role of formal education and experience. *Journal of Developmental and Physical Disabilities, 7,* 1–9.

Kocarnik, R. A., & Ponzetti, J. J. (1986). The influence of intergenerational contact on child care participants' attitudes toward the elderly. *Child Care Quarterly, 15,* 244–250.

Koslin, S. C., Amarel, M., & Ames, N. (1969). A distance measure of racial attitudes in primary grade children: An exploratory study. *Psychology in the Schools, 6,* 382–385.

Kosmitzki, C. (1996). The reaffirmation of cultural identity in cross-cultural encounters. *Personality and Social Psychology Bulletin, 22,* 238–248.

Krajewski, J., & Flaherty, T. (2000). Attitudes of high school students toward individuals with mental retardation. *Mental Retardation, 38,* 154–162.

Kuelker, E. (1996). *Helping and stigmatization of persons with mental disorders.* Unpublished doctoral dissertation, University of Manitoba, Winnipeg, Manitoba, Canada.

Kulik, J. A., Martin, R. A., & Scheibe, K. E. (1969). Effects of mental hospital volunteer work on students' conceptions of mental illness. *Journal of Clinical Psychology, 25,* 326–329.

Kurtzweil, P. L. (1995). *The influence of life experience and social desirability on the development and measurement of White racial identity attitudes.* Unpublished doctoral dissertation, University of Alabama, Tuscaloosa, Alabama.

Ladd, G. W., Munson, H .L., & Miller, J. K. (1984). Social integration of deaf adolescents in secondary-level mainstreamed programs. *Exceptional Children, 50,* 420–428.

Lambert, D. J., Dellmann-Jenkins, M., & Fruit, D. (1990). Planning for contact between the generations: An effective approach. *The Gerontologist, 30,* 553–556.

Lance, L. M. (1987). The effects of interaction with gay persons on attitudes toward homosexuality. *Human Relations, 40,* 329–336.

Lance, L. M. (1992). Changes in homophobic views as related to interaction with gay persons: A study in the reduction of tensions. *International Journal of Group Tensions, 22,* 291–299.

Lance, L. M. (1994). Do reductions in homophobia from heterosexual interactions with gay persons continue?: A study of social contact theory of intergroup tensions. *International Journal of Group Tensions, 24,* 423–434.

Landis, D., Brislin, R. W., & Hulgus, J. F. (1985). Attributional training versus contact in acculturative learning: A laboratory study. *Journal of Applied Social Psychology, 15,* 466–482.

Larsen, L. F. C. (1997). *Parental beliefs concerning racism and sexism.* Unpublished doctoral dissertation, St. Louis University, St. Louis, Missouri.

Lazar, A. L., Gensley, J. T., & Orpet, R. E. (1971). Changing attitudes of young mentally gifted children toward handicapped persons. *Exceptional Children, 37,* 600–602.

Leach, R. H. (1990). *The effect of contact on attitudes toward individuals with disabilities.* Unpublished doctoral dissertation, Florida State University, Tallahassee, Florida.

Leonard, E. W. (1964). Attitude change in a college program of foreign study and travel. *Educational Record, 45,* 173–181.

Lepore, L., & Brown, R. (1997). Category and stereotype activation: Is prejudice inevitable? *Journal of Personality and Social Psychology, 72,* 275–287.

Lessing, E. E., Barbera, L., & Arnold, B. (1976). Teaching nuns' perceptions of White and Black pupils as a function of authoritarianism and other factors. *Community Mental Health Journal, 12,* 182–191.

LeUnes, A., Christensen, L., & Wilkerson, D. (1975). Institutional tour effects on attitudes related to mental retardation. *American Journal of Mental Deficiency, 79,* 732–735.

Levine, D. U., Fiddmont, N. S., & New, J. E. (1969). *Interracial attitudes and contact among Black and White students in a metropolitan area*. Unpublished manuscript.

Levinson, D. J. (1954). The intergroup relations workshop: Its psychological aims and effects. *Journal of Psychology, 38*, 103–126.

Levinson, D. J., & Schermerhorn, R. A. (1951). Emotional–attitudinal effects of an intergroup relations workshop on its members. *Journal of Psychology, 31*, 243–256.

Levy, J. M., Jessop, D. J., Rimmerman, A., & Levy, P. H. (1993). Attitudes of executives in Fortune 500 corporations toward the employability of persons with severe disabilities: Industrial and service corporations. *Journal of Applied Rehabilitation Counseling, 24*, 19–31.

Lewis, I. L., & Cleveland, S. E. (1966). Nursing students' attitudinal changes following a psychiatric affiliation. *Journal of Psychiatric Nursing, 4*, 223–231.

Lewis, M. R., & Frey, N. C. (1988). Changing attitudes toward parents of the chronically mentally ill. *Psychosocial Rehabilitaion Journal, 11*, 21–31.

Leyser, Y., & Abrams, P. D. (1983). A shift to the positive: An effective programme for changing pre-service teachers' attitudes toward the disabled. *Educational Review, 35*, 35–43.

Leyser, Y., Cumblad, C., & Strickman, D. (1986). Direct intervention to modify attitudes toward the handicapped by community volunteers: The Learning about Handicaps Programme. *Educational Review, 38*, 229–236.

Leyser, Y., & Price S. (1985). Improving attitudes of gifted children toward the handicapped. *Education, 105*, 432–437.

Li, W. L., & Yu, L. (1974). Interpersonal contact and racial prejudice: A comparative study of American and Chinese Students. *Sociological Quarterly, 15*, 559–566.

Liebkind, K., Haaramo, J., & Jasinskaja-Lahti, I. (2000). Effects of contact and personality on intergroup attitudes of different professionals. *Journal of Community and Applied Social Psychology, 10*, 171–181.

Link, B. G., & Cullen, F. T. (1986). Contact with the mentally ill and perception of how dangerous they are. *Journal of Health and Social Behavior, 27*, 289–303.

Lombardi, D. N. (1963). Factors affecting changes in attitudes toward Negroes among high school students. *Journal of Negro Education, 32*, 129–136.

Lombroso, D., Tyano, S., & Apter, A. (1976). Attitudes of the Israeli adolescent to the mentally ill and their treatment. *Israel Annals of Psychiatry and Related Disciplines, 14*, 120–131.

London, L. H., & Linney, J. A. (1993). *Kids' college: Enhancing children's understanding and acceptance of cultural diversity*. Unpublished manuscript, Loyola University Chicago.

Loomis, C. P., & Schuler, E. A. (1948). Acculturation of foreign students in the United States. *Applied Anthropology, 7*, 17–34.

Lopes, D. (2000). [*The impact of Black neighbourhood on stereotypes and emotions*]. Unpublished raw data.

Lopez, G. E. (1993). *The effect of group contact and curriculum on White, Asian American and African American students' attitudes*. Unpublished doctoral dissertation, University of Michigan, Ann Arbor, Michigan.

Luiz, D., & Krige, P. (1981). The effect of social contact between South African white and colored adolescent girls. *Journal of Social Psychology, 113*, 153–158. (See also Luiz and Krige, 1985).

Luiz, D., & Krige, P. (1985). The effect of social contact between South African white and colored adolescent girls: A follow-up study. *Journal of Social Psychology, 125*, 407–408. (See also Luiz and Krige, 1981).

MacKenzie, B. K. (1948). The importance of contact in determining attitudes toward Negroes. *Journal of Abnormal and Social Psychology, 43*, 417–441.

MacLean, D., & Gannon, P. M. (1995). Measuring attitudes toward disability: The Interaction with Disabled Persons Scale revisited. *Journal of Social Behavior and Personality, 10*, 791–806.

Malla, A., & Shaw, T. (1987). Attitudes towards mental illness: The influence of education and experience. *International Journal of Social Psychiatry, 33*, 33–41.

Maluso, D. (1992). *Interventions to lessen racist prejudice and discrimination among college students*. Unpublished doctoral dissertation, University of Rhode Island, Kingston, Rhode Island.

Mann, J. H. (1959). The effect of inter-racial contact on sociometric choices and perceptions. *Journal of Social Psychology, 50*, 143–152. (See also Mann, 1960).

Mann, J. H. (1960). The differential nature of prejudice reduction. *Journal of Social Psychology, 52*, 339–343. (See also Mann, 1959).

Maoz, I. (2000). An experiment in peace: Reconciliation-aimed workshops of Jewish–Israeli and Palestinian youth. *Journal of Peace Research, 37*, 721–736.

Maras, P., & Brown, R. (1996). Effects of contact on children's attitudes toward disability: A longitudinal study. *Journal of Applied Social Psychology, 26*, 2113–2134.

Marin, G. (1984). Stereotyping Hispanics: The differential effect of research method, label, and degree of contact. *International Journal of Intercultural Relations, 8*, 17–27.

Marin, G., & Salazar, J. M. (1985). Determinants of hetero- and autostereotypes: Distance, level of contact, and socioeconomic development in seven nations. *Journal of Cross-Cultural Psychology, 16*, 403–422.

Marion, P. B. (1980). Relationships of student characteristics and experiences with attitude changes in a program of study abroad. *Journal of College Student Personnel, 21*, 58–64.

Marks, M. (1992). *Beliefs, contact, and attitudes toward homeless persons of health care students and practitioners*. Unpublished doctoral dissertation, Hofstra University, Hempstead, New York.

Martin, S. (2000). *Untersuchung des Zusmmenhanges von Auslaenderfeindlichkeit und deutsch-nationaler Identitaet* (Investigation of the link between hostility toward foreigners and German national identity). Unpublished dissertation, Department of Psychology, Philipps University, Marburg, Germany.

Marx, G. T. (1967). *Protest and prejudice*. New York: Harper & Row.

Masson, C. N., & Verkuyten, M. (1993). Prejudice, ethnic identity, contact and ethnic group preferences among Dutch young adolescents. *Journal of Applied Social Psychology, 23*, 156–168.

Mathisen, J. H. (2000). *Stigma busting: Does strategic contact with individuals with severe mental illness reduce negative attitudes in an adolescent population?*. Unpublished doctoral dissertation, Adler School of Professional Psychology, Chicago, Illinois.

Maurice, W. L., Klonoff, H., Miles, J. E., & Krell, R. (1975). Medical student change during a psychiatry clerkship: Evaluation of a program. *Journal of Medical Education, 50*, 181–189.

Maxmen, J. S. (1979). Student attitude changes during "psychiatric medicine" clerkships. *General Hospital Psychiatry, 1,* 98–103.

McClenahan, C., Cairns, E., Dunn, S., & Morgan, V. (1996). Intergroup friendships: Integrated and desegregated schools in Northern Ireland. *Journal of Social Psychology, 136,* 549–558.

McConkey, R., McCormack, B., & Naughton, M. (1983). A national survey of young people's perceptions of mental handicap. *Journal of Mental Deficiency Research, 27,* 171–183.

McCrady, R. E., & McCrady, J. B. (1976). Effect of direct exposure to foreign target groups on descriptive stereotypes held by American students. *Social Behavior and Personality, 4,* 233–239.

McDonald, S., Birnbrauer, J. S., & Swerissen, H. (1987). The effect of an integration program on teacher and student attitudes to mentally-handicapped children. *Australian Psychologist, 22,* 313–322.

McGuigan, F. J. (1959). Further study of psychological changes related to intercultural experiences. *Psychological Reports, 5,* 244–248.

McKirnan, D. J., & Hamayan, E. V. (1984). Speech norms and attitudes toward outgroup members: A test of a model in a bicultural context. *Journal of Language and Social Psychology, 3,* 21–38.

McRainey, G. (1981). *Teacher–pupil contact as a factor in the development of positive teacher attitudes toward handicapped students.* Unpublished doctoral dissertation, George Peabody College for Teachers of Vanderbilt University, Nashville, Tennessee.

Meer, B., & Freedman, E. (1966). The impact of Negro neighbors on White home owners. *Social Forces, 45,* 11–19.

Merkwan, J. V., & Smith, T. B. (1999). Tolerance and racial identity among foreign sojourners: Testing the contact hypothesis. *Psychological Reports, 85,* 170.

Meshel, D. S. (1997). *The contact hypothesis and the effects of intergenerational contact on adolescents' attitudes and stereotypes toward older people.* Unpublished doctoral dissertation, Texas Tech University, Lubbock, Texas.

Meyer, M. M., Hassanein, R. S., & Bahr, R. T. (1980). A comparison of attitudes toward the aged held by professional nurses. *Journal of Nursing Scholarship, 12,* 62–66.

Milem, J. F. (1992). *The impact of college on students' racial attitudes and levels of racial awareness and acceptance.* Unpublished doctoral dissertation, University of California, Los Angeles, California.

Miller, J. M., Rivas, L., & Boivin, M. (1998). *Correlations between ethnocentrism and spiritualness among Indiana Wesleyan students.* Unpublished manuscript.

Millham, J., San Miguel, C., & Kellogg, R. (1976). A factor-analytic conceptualization of attitudes toward male and female homosexuals. *Journal of Homosexuality, 2,* 3–10.

Mills, R. B., Vermette, V., & Malley-Morrison, K. (1998). Judgments about elder abuse and college students' relationship with grandparents. *Gerontology and Geriatrics Education, 19,* 17–30.

Moeschl, T. P. (1978). *Attitude assessment across generations.* Unpublished doctoral dissertation, Virginia Commonwealth University, Richmond, Virginia.

Mohr, J. J., & Rochlen, A. B. (1999). Measuring attitudes regarding bisexuality in lesbian, gay male and heterosexual populations. *Journal of Counseling Psychology, 46,* 353–369.

Monroe, J. D., & Howe, C. E. (1971). The effects of integration and social class on the acceptance of retarded adolescents. *Education and Training of the Mentally Retarded, 6*, 20–24.
Morin, S. F. (1974). Educational programs as a means of changing attitudes toward gay people. *Homosexual Counseling Journal, 1*, 160–165.
Morris, K. D. (1964). Behavioral change: A concomitant of attitude change in nursing students. *Nursing Research, 13*, 132–138.
Morris, R. T., & Jeffries, V. (1968). Violence next door. *Social Forces, 46*, 352–358.
Mosher-Ashley, P. M., & Ball, P. (1999). Attitudes of college students toward elderly persons and their perceptions of themselves at age 75. *Educational Gerontology, 25*, 89–102.
Most, T., Weisel, A., & Tur-Kaspa, H. (1999). Contact with students with hearing impairments and the evaluation of speech intelligibility and personal qualities. *Journal of Special Education, 33*, 103–111.
Murphy, B. M., Black, P., Duffy, M., Kieran, J., & Mallon, J. (1993). Attitudes towards the mentally ill in Ireland. *Irish Journal of Psychological Medicine, 10*, 75–79.
Murphy-Russell, S., Die, A. H., & Walker, J. L. (1986). Changing attitudes toward the elderly: The impact of three methods of attitude change. *Educational Gerontology, 12*, 241–251.
Mussen, P. H. (1950). Some personality and social factors related to changes in children's attitudes toward Negroes. *Journal of Abnormal and Social Psychology, 45*, 423–441.
Nabuzoka, D., & Rønning, J. A. (1997). Social acceptance of children with intellectual disabilities in an integrated school setting in Zambia: A pilot study. *International Journal of Disability, Development, and Education, 44*, 105–115.
Naor, M., & Milgram, R. M. (1980). Two preservice strategies for preparing regular class teachers for mainstreaming. *Exceptional Children, 47*, 126–129.
Narukawa, Y. (1995). A multidimensional study of public attitudes toward persons with mental retardation. *Japanese Journal of Special Education, 32*, 11–19.
Nash, D. (1976). The personal consequences of a year of study abroad. *Journal of Higher Education, 47*, 191–203.
Naus, P. J. (1973). Some correlates of attitudes towards old people. *International Journal of Aging and Human Development, 4*, 229–243.
Neprash, J. A. (1953). Minority group contacts and social distance. *Phylon, 14*, 207–212.
Nesdale, D., & Todd, P. (1998). Intergroup ratio and the contact hypotheses. *Journal of Applied Social Psychology, 28*, 1196–1217.
Nesdale, D., & Todd, P. (2000). Effect of contact on intercultural acceptance: A field study. *International Journal of Intercultural Relations, 24*, 341–360.
Neto, F. (2000). Identité ethnique et acculutration chez des adolescents timorais vivant au Portugal (Ethnic identity and acculturation among Timorese adolescents living in Portugal). *Cahiers Internationaux de Psychologie Sociale, 46*, 62–74.
Newberry, M. K., & Parish, T. S. (1987). Enhancement of attitudes toward handicapped children through social interactions. *Journal of Social Psychology, 127*, 59–62.
Newswanger, J. F. (1996). The relationship between White racial identity attitudes and the experience of having a Black college roommate. *Journal of College Student Development, 37*, 536–542.

Ng, S. H., Liu, J. H., Weatherall, A., & Loong, C. S. F. (1997). Younger adults' communication experiences and contact with elders and peers. *Human Communication Research, 24*, 82–108.

Nieuwoudt, J. M., & Thom, D. P. (1980). Houdingsverandering teenoor die bejaarde deur eksistensiele kontak (Attitude change towards the elderly by existential contact). *South African Journal of Psychology, 10*, 72–76.

Nishi-Strattner, M., & Myers, J. E. (1983). Attitudes towards the elderly: An intergenerational examination. *Educational Gerontology, 9*, 389–397.

Noels, K. A., & Clément, R. (1996). Communicating across cultures: Social determinants and acculturative consequences. *Canadian Journal of Behavioural Science, 28*, 214–228.

Nosse, L. J. (1993). Effect of direct contact on students' ratings of adults with impairments. *College Student Journal, 27*, 396–400.

Nosse, L. J., & Gavin, K. J. (1991). Influence of direct contact on college students' attitude toward adults with mental handicaps. *College Student Journal, 25*, 201–206.

Oaker, G., & Brown, R. (1986). Intergroup relations in a hospital setting: A further test of social identity theory. *Human Relations, 39*, 767–778.

Ogedengbe, R. O. (1993). Prior contacts and perceptions of previously mentally disturbed patients. *International Journal of Nursing Studies, 30*, 247–259.

Olejnik, A. B., & LaRue, A. A. (1981). Changes in adolescents' perceptions of the aged: The effects of intergenerational contact. *Educational Gerontology, 6*, 339–351.

Pagtolun-An, I. G., & Clair, J. M. (1986). An experimental study of attitudes toward homosexuals. *Deviant Behavior, 7*, 121–135.

Palmerton, K. E., & Frumkin, R. M. (1969). Type of contact as a factor in attitudes of college counselors toward the physically disabled. *Perceptual and Motor Skills, 28*, 489–490.

Paris, M. J. (1991). *Attitudes toward the physically disabled among medical students and health-care professionals.* Unpublished doctoral dissertation, California School of Professional Psychology, Berkeley/Alameda, California.

Parker, W. M., Moore, M. A., & Neimeyer, G. J. (1998). Altering White racial identity and interracial comfort through multicultural training. *Journal of Counseling and Development, 76*, 302–310.

Patchen, M. (1982). *Black–White contact in schools: Its social and academic effects.* West Lafayette, IN: Purdue University Press. (See also Patchen, 1983 and Patchen et al., 1977).

Patchen, M. (1983). Students' own racial attitudes and those of peers of both races, as related to interracial behaviors. *Sociology and Social Research, 68*, 59–77. (See also Patchen, 1982 and Patchen et al., 1977).

Patchen, M., Davidson, J. D., Hofmann, G., & Brown, W. R. (1977). Determinants of students' interracial behavior and opinion change. *Sociology of Education, 50*, 55–75. (See also Patchen, 1982 and Patchen, 1983).

Penn, D. L., Guynan, K., Daily, T., Spaulding, W. D., Garbin, C. P., & Sullivan, M. (1994). Dispelling the stigma of schizophrenia: What sort of information is best? *Schizophrenia Bulletin, 20*, 567–574.

Peterson, G. F. (1974). Factors related to the attitudes of nonretarded children toward their EMR peers. *American Journal of Mental Deficiency, 79*, 412–416.

Petrangelo, G. J. (1976). *Attitudes of non-disabled college students toward their disabled classmates as a function of educational contact*. Unpublished doctoral dissertation, University of Northern Colorado, Greeley, Colorado.

Pettigrew, T. (1997). Generalized intergroup contact effects on prejudice. *Personality and Social Psychology Bulletin, 23*, 173–185.

Petzel, T. (2000). *Studies on authoritarianism*. Unpublished doctoral dissertation, Philipps University Marburg, Germany.

Phillips, D. L. (1963). Rejection: A possible consequence of seeking help for mental disorders. *American Sociological Review, 28*, 963–972.

Phinney, J. S., Ferguson, D. L., & Tate, J. D. (1997). Intergroup attitudes among ethnic minority adolescents: A causal model. *Child Development, 68*, 955–969.

Pinquart, M., Wenzel, S., & Sörensen, S. (2000). Changes in attitudes among children and elderly adults in intergenerational group work. *Educational Gerontology, 26*, 523–540.

Pleck, J. H., O'Donnell, L., O'Donnell, C., & Snarey, J. (1988). AIDS-phobia, contact with AIDS, and AIDS-related job stress in hospital workers. *Journal of Homosexuality, 15*, 41–54.

Porter, K., & O'Connor, N. (1978). Changing attitudes of university students to old people. *Educational Gerontology, 3*, 139–148.

Prather, J. H., & Chovan, W. L. (1984). Normal peers' reactions toward autistic children following a tutoring experience. *Psychological Reports, 55*, 887–892.

Preston, J. D., & Robinson, J. W. (1974). On modification of interracial interaction. *American Sociological Review, 39*, 283–285. (See also Robinson & Preston, 1976).

Price, F. S. (2000). *Intercultural contact, ethnocentrism, and the mediating role of epistemology*. Unpublished doctoral dissertation, University of Melbourne, Australia.

Proller, N. L. (1989). The effects of an adoptive grandparent program on youth and elderly participants. *Journal of Children in Contemporary Society, 20*, 195–203.

Pryer, M. W., Distefano M. K., Jr., & Marr, L. W. (1969). Attitude changes in psychiatric attendants following experience and training. *Mental Hygiene, 53*, 253–257.

Rabushka, A. (1969). Integration in a multi-racial institution: Ethnic attitudes among Chinese and Malay students at the University of Malaya. *Race, 11*, 53–63.

Radcliffe, A. (1972). *A Guttman facet analysis of the racial attitudes of Black and White adults toward the opposite race*. Unpublished doctoral dissertation, Michigan State University, East Lansing, Michigan.

Ralph, D. E. (1968). Attitudes toward mental illness among two groups of college students in a neuropsychiatric hospital setting. *Journal of Consulting and Clinical Psychology, 32*, 98.

Rapier, J., Adelson, R., Carey, R., & Croke, K. (1972). Changes in children's attitudes toward the physically handicapped. *Exceptional Children, 39*, 219–223.

Read, J., & Law, A. (1999). The relationship of causal beliefs and contact with users of mental health services to attitudes to the "mentally ill." *International Journal of Social Psychiatry, 45*, 216–229.

Reed, J. S. (1980). Getting to know you: The contact hypothesis applied to the sectional beliefs and attitudes of White southerners. *Social Forces, 59*, 123–135.

Reigrotski, E., & Anderson, N. (1959). National stereotypes and foreign contacts. *Public Opinion Quarterly, 23*, 515–528.

Reinsch, S., & Tobis, J. S. (1991). Intergenerational relations: Pre-med students at senior centers. *Archives of Gerontology and Geriatrics, 13,* 211–224.

Rich, P. E., Myrick, R. D., & Campbell, C. (1983). Changing children's perceptions of the elderly. *Educational Gerontology, 9,* 483–491.

Rich, Y., Kedem, P., & Shlesinger, A. (1995). Enhancing intergroup relations among children: A field test of the Miller-Brewer Model. *International Journal of Intercultural Relations, 19,* 539–553.

Rimmerman, A. (1998). Factors relating to attitudes of Israeli corporate executives toward the employability of persons with intellectual disability. *Journal of Intellectual and Developmental Disability, 23,* 245–254.

Rimmerman, A., Hozmi, B., & Duvdevany, I. (2000). Contact and attitudes toward individuals with disabilities among students tutoring children with developmental disabilities. *Journal of Intellectual and Developmental Disability, 25,* 13–18.

Riordan, C. (1987). Intergroup contact in small cities. *International Journal of Intercultural Relations, 11,* 143–154.

Robbins, I., Cooper, A., & Bender, M. P. (1992). The relationship between knowledge, attitudes and degree of contact with AIDS and HIV. *Journal of Advanced Nursing, 17,* 198–203.

Roberts, A. E. (1988). Racism sent and received: Americans and Vietnamese view one another. *Research in Race and Ethnic Relations, 5,* 75–97.

Robinson, J. W., Jr., & Preston, J. D. (1976). Equal-status contact and modification of racial prejudice: A reexamination of the contact hypothesis. *Social Forces, 54,* 911–924. (See also Preston & Robinson, 1974).

Robinson, P. J. (1987). *The relationship between favorable or unfavorable contact on the social distance attitudes of residence hall students toward residential subgroups.* Unpublished doctoral dissertation, Iowa State University, Ames, Iowa.

Rønning, J. A., & Nabuzoka, D. (1993). Promoting social interaction and status of children with intellectual disabilities in Zambia. *Journal of Special Education, 27,* 277–305.

Rooney-Rebeck, P., & Jason, L. (1986). Prevention of prejudice in elementary school students. *Journal of Primary Prevention, 7,* 63–73.

Roper, P. A. (1990). Special Olympics volunteers' perceptions of people with mental retardation. *Education and Training in Mental Retardation, 25,* 164–175.

Rose, A. M., Atelsek, F. J., & McDonald, L. R. (1953). Neighborhood reaction to isolated Negro residents: An alternative to invasion and succession. *American Sociological Review, 18,* 497–507.

Rose, P. I. (1961). Small-town Jews and their neighbours in the United States. *Jewish Journal of Sociology, 3,* 174–191.

Rosenblith, J. F. (1949). A replication of "some roots of prejudice." *Journal of Abnormal and Social Psychology, 44,* 470–489.

Rosencranz, H. A., & McNevin, T. E. (1969). A factor analysis of attitudes toward the aged. *The Gerontologist, 9,* 55–59.

Rowlett, J. D. (1981). *Attitudes of peers toward physically limited students in university resident halls.* Unpublished doctoral dissertation, Kansas State University, Manhattan, Kansas.

Rusalem, H. (1967). Engineering changes in public attitudes toward a severely disabled group. *Journal of Rehabilitation, 33,* 26–27.

Rusinko, W. T., Johnson, K. W., & Hornung, C. A. (1978). The importance of police contact in the formulation of youths' attitudes toward police. *Journal of Criminal Justice, 6,* 53–67.

Sadler, M. S., & Blair, I. (1999, June). *Are intergroup attitudes affective?: It depends on group and contact.* Poster session presented at the annual convention of the American Psychological Society, Denver, Colorado.

Sakaris, L. M. (2000). *Factors associated with the attitudes and expectations of teachers toward the homeless student.* Unpublished doctoral dissertation, Hofstra University, Hempstead, New York.

Salter, C. A., & Teger, A. I. (1975). Change in attitudes toward other nations as a function of the type of international contact. *Sociometry, 38,* 213–222.

San Miguel, C. L., & Millham, J. (1976). The role of cognitive and situational variables in aggression toward homosexuals. *Journal of Homosexuality, 2,* 11–27.

Sandberg, L. D. (1982). Attitudes of nonhandicapped elementary school students toward school-aged trainable mentally retarded students. *Education and Training of the Mentally Retarded, 17,* 30–34.

Sayler, R. I. (1969). *An exploration of race prejudice in college students and interracial contact.* Unpublished doctoral dissertation, University of Washington, Seattle, Washington.

Scarberry, N. C., Ratcliff, C. D., & Lord, C. G. (1996, June). *The effects of multiple group membership on Allport's contact hypothesis.* Poster presented at the 8th Annual Convention of the American Psychological Society, San Francisco, California.

Scheibe, K. E. (1965). College students spend eight weeks in mental hospital: A case report. *Psychotherapy: Theory, Research, and Practice, 2,* 117–120.

Schneider, S. (1994). *Vorurteile gegenüber ethnischen Minderheiten in Ost und West* (Ethnic prejudice in East and West Germany). Unpublished diploma thesis, Department of Psychology, University of Bochum, Bochum, Germany.

Schneider, W., & Lewis, I. A. (1984). The straight story on homosexuality and gay rights. *Public Opinion, 6,* 16–20, 59–60.

Schwarzwald, J., Fridel, S., & Hoffman, M. (1985). Carry-over of contact effects from acquainted to unacquainted targets. *Journal of Multilingual and Multicultural Development, 6,* 297–311.

Seefeldt, C. (1987). The effects of preschoolers' visits to a nursing home. *The Gerontologist, 27,* 228–232.

Segal, B. E. (1965). Contact, compliance, and distance among Jewish and non-Jewish undergraduates. *Social Problems, 13,* 66–74.

Sellin, D., & Mulchahay, R. (1965). The relationship of an institutional tour upon opinions about mental retardation. *American Journal of Mental Deficiency, 70,* 408–412.

Sellitz, C., Christ, J. R., Havel, J., & Cook, S. W. (1963). *Attitudes and social relations of foreign students in the United States.* Minneapolis: University of Minnesota Press.

Selznick, G. J., & Steinberg, S. (1969). *The tenacity of prejudice.* New York: Harper & Row.

Semmel, M. I., & Dickson, S. (1966). Connotative reactions of college students to disability labels. *Exceptional Children, 32,* 443–450.

Sewell, W. H., & Davidsen, O. M. (1956). The adjustment of Scandinavian students. *Journal of Social Issues, 12,* 9–19.

Shafer, M. S., Larus Rice, M., Metzler, H. M. D., & Haring, M. (1989). A survey of nondisabled employees' attitudes toward supported employees with mental retardation. *Journal of the Association for Persons with Severe Handicaps, 14*, 137–146.

Sheare, J. B. (1974). Social acceptance of EMR adolescents in integrated programs. *American Journal of Mental Deficiency, 78*, 678–682.

Sheehan, D. S. (1980). A study of attitude change in desegregated intermediate schools. *Sociology of Education, 53*, 51–59.

Shera, W., & Delva-Tauiliili, J. (1996). Changing MSW students' attitudes towards the severely mentally ill. *Community Mental Health Journal, 32*, 159–169.

Sherif, M., Harvey, O. J., White, B. J., Hood, W. R., & Sherif, C. W. (1961). *Intergroup conflict and cooperation: The Robbers Cave experiment*. Norman, OK: The University Book Exchange.

Shibuya, Y. (2000). Examination of the contact hypothesis: Intercultural attitudes among Japanese company-wives in England. *Japanese Journal of Social Psychology, 15*, 200–211.

Shoemake, A. F., & Rowland, V. T. (1993). Do laboratory experiences change college students' attitudes toward the elderly? *Educational Gerontology, 19*, 295–309.

Sigelman, L., & Welch, S. (1991). *Black Americans' views of racial inequality: The dream deferred*. New York: Cambridge University Press.

Siller, J., & Chipman, A. (1964). Factorial structure and correlates of the Attitudes Toward Disabled Personal Scale. *Educational and Psychological Measurement, 24*, 831–840.

Simon, A. (1995). Some correlates of individuals' attitudes toward lesbians. *Journal of Homosexuality, 29*, 89–103.

Simoni, J. M. (1996). Pathways to prejudice: Predicting students' heterosexist attitudes with demographics, self-esteem, and contact with lesbians and gay men. *Journal of College Student Development, 37*, 68–78.

Simpson, R. L., Parrish, N. E., & Cook, J. J. (1976). Modification of attitudes of regular class children towards the handicapped for the purpose of achieving integration. *Contemporary Educational Psychology, 1*, 46–51.

Singer, D. (1966). *Interracial attitudes of Negro and White fifth-grade children in segregated and unsegregated schools*. Unpublished doctoral dissertation, Teachers College of Columbia University, New York.

Slavin, R. E. (1979). Effects of biracial learning teams on cross-racial friendships. *Journal of Educational Psychology, 71*, 381–387.

Slavin, R. E., & Madden, N. A. (1979). School practices that improve race relations. *American Educational Research Journal, 16*, 169–180.

Slininger, D., Sherrill, C., & Jankowski, C. M. (2000). Children's attitudes toward peers with severe disabilities: Revisiting contact theory. *Adapted Physical Activity Quarterly, 17*, 176–196.

Smith, C. B. (1994). Back and to the future: The intergroup contact hypothesis revisited. *Sociological Inquiry, 64*, 438–455.

Smith, H. P. (1955). Do intercultural experiences affect attitudes? *Journal of Abnormal and Social Psychology, 51*, 469–477.

Smith, J. J. (1969). Psychiatric hospital experience and attitudes toward "mental illness." *Journal of Consulting and Clinical Psychology, 33*, 302–306.

Smith, T. W. (2000). *Taking America's Pulse II: NCCJ's 2000 survey of intergroup relations in the United States*. New York: National Conference for Community and Justice.
Smith-Castro, V. (2000). *Acculturation and psychological adaptation: Effects of acculturation on self-esteem among Black and White adolescents in Costa Rica*. Unpublished doctoral dissertation, Department of Psychology, Philipps University, Marburg, Germany.
Spangenberg, J., & Nel, E. M. (1983). The effects of equal-status contact on ethnic attitudes. *Journal of Social Psychology, 121*, 173–180.
Sparling, J. W., & Rogers, J. C. (1985). Intergenerational intervention: A reciprocal service delivery system for preschoolers, adolescents, and older persons. *Educational Gerontology, 11*, 41–55.
Stager, S. F., & Young, R. D. (1981). Intergroup contact and social outcomes for mainstreamed EMR adolescents. *American Journal of Mental Deficiency, 85*, 497–503.
Stainback, W. C., Stainback, S. B., & Dedrick, C. V. L. (1984). Teachers' attitudes toward integration of severely handicapped students into regular schools. *Teacher Education, 19*, 21–27.
Stangor, C., Jonas, K., Stroebe, W., & Hewstone, M. (1996). Influence of student exchange on national stereotypes, attitudes and perceived group variability. *European Journal of Social Psychology, 26*, 663–675.
Starr, P. D., & Roberts, A. E. (1982). Attitudes toward new Americans: Perceptions of Indo-Chinese in nine cities. *Research in Race and Ethnic Relations, 3*, 165–187.
Stephan, W. G., & Rosenfield, D. (1978a). Effects of desegregation on race relations and self-esteem. *Journal of Educational Psychology, 70*, 670–679.
Stephan, W. G., & Rosenfield, D. (1978b). Effects of desegregation on racial attitudes. *Journal of Personality and Social Psychology, 36*, 795–804.
Stephan, W. G., Diaz-Loving, R., & Duran, A. (2000). Integrated threat theory and intercultural attitudes: Mexico and the United States. *Journal of Cross-Cultural Psychology, 31*, 240–249.
Stephan W. G., & Stephan, C. W. (1985). Intergroup anxiety. *Journal of Social Issues, 41*, 157–175.
Stephan, W. G., & Stephan, C. W. (1989). Antecedents of intergroup anxiety in Asian-Americans and Hispanic-Americans. *International Journal of Intercultural Relations, 13*, 203–219.
Stewart, C. C. (1988). Modification of student attitudes toward disabled peers. *Adapted Physical Activity Quarterly, 5*, 44–48.
Stohl, C. (1985). The A.M.I.G.O. project: A multicultural intergroup opportunity. *International Journal of Intercultural Relations, 9*, 151–175.
Stouffer, S. A., Suchman, E. A., DeVinney, L. C., Star, S. A., & Williams, R. M., Jr. (1949). *The American soldier: Adjustment during army life. Vol. 1*. Princeton, NJ: Princeton University Press.
Strauch, J. D. (1970). Social contact as a variable in the expressed attitudes of normal adolescents toward EMR pupils. *Exceptional Children, 36*, 495–500.
Strauch, J. D., Chester, P. N., & Rucker, C. N. (1970). Teacher aide attitudes toward the mentally retarded. *The Training School Bulletin, 67*, 15–19.
Strohmer, D. C., Grand, S. A., & Purcell, M. J. (1984). Attitudes toward persons with a disability: An examination of demographic factors, social context, and specific disablility. *Rehabilitation Psychology, 29*, 131–145.

Surace, S. J., & Seeman, M. (1967). Some correlates of civil rights activism. *Social Forces, 46*, 197–207.

Tait, K., & Purdie, N. (2000). Attitudes toward disability: Teacher education for inclusive environments in an Australian univeristy. *International Journal of Disability, Development, and Education, 47*, 25–38.

Taylor, S. M., & Dear, M. J. (1981). Scaling community attitudes toward the mentally ill. *Schizophrenia Bulletin, 7*, 225–240.

Thomas, S. A., Foreman, P. E., & Remenyi, A. G. (1985). The effects of previous contact with physical disability upon Australian children's attitudes toward people with physical disabilities. *International Journal of Rehabilitation Research, 8*, 69–70.

Thompson, L. (1993). The impact of negotiation on intergroup relations. *Journal of Experimental Social Psychology, 29*, 304–325.

Togonu-Bickersteth, F., & Odebiyi, A. I. (1985). Prior contacts and perception of the deaf by the non-deaf in Nigeria. *Social Behavior and Personality, 13*, 43–53.

Towles-Schwen, T., & Fazio, R. H. (1999). *On the origins of racial attitudes: Correlates of childhood experiences.* Unpublished manuscript, Indiana University, Bloomington, Indiana.

Trent, C., Glass, J. C., & Crockett, J. (1979). Changing adolescent 4-H Club members' attitudes toward the aged. *Educational Gerontology, 4*, 33–48.

Triandis, H. C., & Vassiliou, V. (1967). Frequency of contact and stereotyping. *Journal of Personality and Social Psychology, 7*, 316–328.

Tropp, L. (2000). *The psychological impact of prejudice: Implications for intergroup contact.* Unpublished manuscript, Boston College, Chestnut Hill, Massachusetts.

Tropp, L. R., & Stout, A. M. (1999). [*Contact experiences and expectations for cross-group interactions among Asians, Latinos, and Whites*]. Unpublished raw data.

Trubowitz, J. (1969). *Changing the racial attitudes of children: The effects of an activity group program in New York City schools.* New York: Frederick A. Praeger.

Trute, B., & Loewen, A. (1978). Public attitude toward the mentally ill as a function of prior personal experience. *Social Psychiatry, 13*, 79–84.

Trute, B., Tefft, B., & Segall, A. (1989). Social rejection of the mentally ill: A replication study of public attitude. *Social Psychiatry and Psychiatric Epidemiology, 24*, 69–76.

Tsukashima, R. T. (1986). A test of competing contact hypotheses in the study of Black anti-Semitic beliefs. *Contemporary Jewry, 7*, 1–17. (See also Tsukashima & Montero, 1976).

Tsukashima, R. T., & Montero, D. (1976). The contact hypothesis: Social and economic contact and generational changes in the study of Black anti-Semitism. *Social Forces, 55*, 149–165. (See also Tsukashima, 1986).

Tuckman, J., & Lorge, I. (1958). Attitude toward aging of individuals with experiences with the aged. *Journal of Genetic Psychology, 92*, 199–204.

Turman, J. A., & Holtzman, W. H. (1955). Attitudes of White and Negro teachers toward non-segregation in the classroom. *Journal of Social Psychology, 42*, 61–70.

Van Den Berghe, P. L. (1962). Race attitudes in Durban, South Africa. *Journal of Social Psychology, 57*, 55–72.

Van Dick, R., & Wagner, U. (1995). *Ergebnissse einer Befragung von Zivildienstleistenden (Results of a questionnaire study among men doing their civil service).* Unpublished manuscript, Department of Psychology Philipps University, Marburg, Germany.

Van Dick, R., Wagner, U., Pettigrew, T., Christ, O., Petzel, T., Smith-Castro, V., et al. (2000). *Contact hypothesis revisited: The role of perceived importance*. Manuscript submitted for publication.

Van Dyk, A. C. (1990). Voorspellers van etniese houdings in 'n noue kontaksituasie (Determinants of ethnic attitudes in a close contact situation). *South African Journal of Psychology, 20*, 206–214.

Van Ossenbruggen, R. (1999). *Racisme in de europese gemeenschap: Secundaire analyses van het Eurobarometerbestand 1997*. Unpublished manuscript, University of Amsterdam, Amsterdam, The Netherlands.

Van Weerden-Dijkstra, J. R. (1972). The attitude of the population toward the mentally ill. *Psychiatria Neurologia Neurochirurgia, 72*, 95–106.

Verkuyten, M., & Masson, K. (1995). "New racism," self-esteem, and ethnic relations among minority and majority youth in the Netherlands. *Social Behavior and Personality, 23*, 137–154.

Voeltz, L. M. (1980). Children's attitudes toward handicapped peers. *American Journal of Mental Deficiency, 84*, 455–464.

Vornberg, J. A., & Grant, R. T. (1976). Adolescent cultural acquaintance experiences and ethnic group attitudes. *Adolescence, 11*, 601–608.

Wagner, U., Hewstone, M., & Machleit, U. (1989). Contact and prejudice between Germans and Turks: A correlational study. *Human Relations, 42*, 561–574.

Walsh, J. E. (1971). Instruction in psychiatric nursing, level of anxiety, and direction of attitude change toward the mentally ill. *Nursing Research, 20*, 522–529.

Ward, C. R., Duquin, M. E., & Streetman, H. (1998). Effects of intergenerational massage on future caregivers' attitudes toward aging, the elderly, and caring for the elderly. *Educational Gerontology, 24*, 35–46.

Ward, C. R., & Rana-Deuba, A. (2000). Home and host culture influences on sojourner adjustment. *International Journal of Intercultural Relations, 24*, 291–306.

Webster, S. W. (1961). The influence of interracial contact on social acceptance in a newly integrated school. *Journal of Educational Psychology, 52*, 292–296.

Weigert, K. M. (1976). Intergroup contact and attitudes about a third group: A survey of Black soldiers' perceptions. *International Journal of Group Tensions, 6*, 110–124.

Weinberg, N. (1978). Modifying social stereotypes of the physically disabled. *Rehabilitation Counseling Bulletin, 22*, 114–124.

Weis, C. B., & Dain, R. N. (1979). Ego development and sex attitudes in heterosexual and homosexual men and women. *Archives of Sexual Behavior, 8*, 341–356.

Weisel, A. (1988). Contact with mainstreamed disabled children and attitudes towards disability: A multi-dimensional analysis. *Educational Psychology, 8*, 161–168.

Weiss, H. (1987). On the significance of personal contact to Jews. In W. Bergmann (Ed.), *Error without trial: Psychological research on anti-Semitism* (pp. 449–455). Berlin, Germany: de Gruyter.

Weller, L., & Grunes, S. (1988). Does contact with the mentally ill affect nurses' attitudes to mental illness? *British Journal of Medical Psychology, 61*, 277–284.

Werrbach, G. B., & DePoy, E. (1993). Social work students' interest in working with persons with serious mental illness. *Journal of Social Work Education, 26*, 200–211.

Whaley, A. L. (1997). Ethnic and racial differences in perceptions of dangerousness of persons with mental illness. *Psychiatric Services, 48*, 1328–1330.

Whitley, B. E. (1990). The relationship of heterosexuals' attributions for the causes of homosexuality to attitudes toward lesbians and gay men. *Personality and Social Psychology Bulletin, 16*, 369–377.

Williams, E. (1972). *Effects of intergroup discussion on social distance and personal space of Black and White students*. Unpublished doctoral dissertation, University of Texas, Austin, Texas.

Williams, R. M. (1964). *Strangers next door: Ethnic relations in American communities*. Englewood Cliffs, New Jersey: Prentice-Hall.

Wilner, D. M, Walkley, R. P., & Cook, S. W. (1955). *Human relations in interracial housing: A study of the contact hypothesis*. Minneapolis, Minnesota: University of Minnesota Press.

Wilson, D., & Lavelle, S. (1990). Interracial friendship in a Zimbabwean primary school. *Journal of Social Psychology, 130*, 111–113.

Wilson, T. C. (1984). Urbanism and racial attitudes: A test of some urban theories. *Urban Affairs Quarterly, 20*, 201–209.

Wilson, T. C. (1996). Prejudice reduction or self-selection? A test of the contact hypothesis. *Sociological Spectrum, 16*, 43–60.

With, J., & Rabbie, J. M. (1985). Racist attitudes about intimate relationships between Blacks and Whites in The Netherlands. *Gedrag – Tijdschrift voor Psychologie, 13*, 10–28.

Wolsko, C., Park, B., Judd, C. M., & Bachelor, J. (2000). *Intergroup contact: Effects on evaluative responses and stereotype change*. Unpublished manuscript, University of Colorado, Boulder, Colorado.

Wood, E. P. (1990). *A study of racial attitudes of some White university students: Theoretical foundations for developing change programs*. Unpublished doctoral dissertation, University of Missouri, Kansas City, Missouri.

Wood, P. B., & Sonleitner, N. (1996). The effect of childhood interracial contact on adult anti-Black prejudice. *International Journal of Intercultural Relations, 20*, 1–17.

Works, E. (1961). The prejudice–interaction hypothesis from the point of view of the Negro minority group. *American Journal of Sociology, 67*, 47–52.

Wright, F. H., & Klein, R. A. (1966). Attitudes of hospital personnel and the community regarding mental illness. *Journal of Counseling Psychology, 13*, 106–107.

Wright, S. C., & Tropp, L. R. (2000). *Language of instruction and contact effects: Bilingual education and intergroup attitudes*. Manuscript submitted for publication.

Yeakley, A. M. (1998). *The nature of prejudice change: Positive and negative change processes arising from intergroup contact experiences*. Unpublished doctoral dissertation, University of Michigan, Ann Arbor, Michigan.

Yinon, Y. (1975). Authoritarianism and prejudice among married couples with similar or different ethnic origin in Israel. *Journal of Marriage and the Family, 37*, 214–220.

Young, K. (1998). *The impact of cross-group friendship on intergroup attitudes: A longitudinal study*. Unpublished undergraduate thesis, University of California, Santa Cruz, California.

Yum, J. O., & Wang, G. (1983). Interethnic perception and the communication behavior among five ethnic groups in Hawaii. *International Journal of Intercultural Relations, 7*, 285–308.

Zakay, D. (1985). The influence of information and daily contact on children's attitudes towards aphasic children. *British Journal of Educational Psychology, 55*, 1–10.

Zani, B., & Kirchler, E. (1995). Pregiudizi ed emozioni nei rapporti interetnici (Prejudice and emotion in interethnic relations). *Giornale Italiano di Psicologia, 22*, 65–85. (See also Kirchler & Zani, 1995).

Zentralarchiv für empirische Soczialforschung an der Universität zu Köln (1996). *Daten und Codebuch der Allgemeinen Bevölkerungsumfrage der Sozialwissenschaften (ALLBUS)*. Köln: ZA.

Zeul, C. R., & Humphrey, C. R. (1971). The integration of Black residents in suburban neighborhoods: A reexamination of the contact hypothesis. *Social Problems, 18*, 462–474.

☐ Note

1 All reference information applies through to December 2000, the cut-off date for the meta-analysis. Some of the then-unpublished references have likely been published since that time and the interested reader is encouraged to check on their current status in the PSYCINFO database.

APPENDIX B

☐ Item Wordings for Variables Used in Analyses of German Survey Data[1]

Chapter 3 Items (2002 and 2004 GFE Surveys)

Positive Contact Items (2002: $\alpha = .76$; 2004: $\alpha = .76$)

- How often have you had an interesting conversation with a foreigner – often, sometimes, seldom, or never?
- How often has a foreigner helped you – often, sometimes, seldom, or never?
- How many of your good friends and acquaintances are foreigners – none, few, many, very many?

Prejudice Against Resident Foreigners (2002: $r = +.58$; 2004: $r = +.59$)

- Too many foreigners live in Germany – completely agree, tend to agree, tend not to agree, don't agree at all.
- Foreigners should go back to their home country if jobs become scarce – completely agree, tend to agree, tend not to agree, don't agree at all.

Prejudice Against the Homeless (2002: $r = +.46$; 2004: $r = +.44$)

- Begging homeless people should be removed – completely agree, tend to agree, tend not to agree, don't agree at all.
- I find homeless people in the cities unpleasant – completely agree, tend to agree, tend not to agree, don't agree at all.

Prejudice Against Gay Men and Lesbians (2002: $r = +.52$; 2004: $r = +.56$)

- Marriages between two women and two men should be permitted – completely agree, tend to agree, tend not to agree, don't agree at all. [Reverse-scored item]
- It is disgusting when Gays kiss in public – completely agree, tend to agree, tend not to agree, don't agree at all.

Chapter 10 Items (2002 and 2004 GFE Surveys)

Foreign Population Percentage by District

Calculated from census data.

Prejudice Norm by District

- Which opinion do your friends or acquaintances have – mostly pro-immigrants, mostly against the immigrants, equally many support as reject?

[The average response from this item of all respondents in a district was determined for each German district.]

Positive Intergroup Contact

The same three items as listed for Chapter 3 above.

Negative Intergroup Contact

- How often has a foreigner pestered you – often, sometimes, seldom, or never?

Economic Predictors (Analyzed as Single-Item Measures)

- Please indicate how many of the things you wish to buy you can actually afford – all of them, nearly all of them, few, or none of them?

- How would you generally judge the current economic situation in Germany? Is it in your opinion – very good, rather good, rather poor, or very poor?
- If you compare the economic situation of the Germans with that of the foreigners living in Germany, how do the Germans fare by comparison – better, roughly the same, or worse?

Political Inefficacy (2002: $\alpha = .71$; 2004: $\alpha = .73$)

- People like myself don't have any influence over the government – doesn't apply at all, fully applies, tends not to apply, tends to apply, or fully applies.
- Political engagement makes no sense for me.
- I can influence German development as an individual. [Reverse-scored item]

Political Conservatism

- Thinking of your own political view, would you classify yourself as left, somewhat left, in the middle, somewhat right, or right?

European Identity (2002: $r = +.54$; 2004: $r = +.54$)

- I am proud to be a European – not proud at all, somewhat not proud, somewhat proud, or very proud.
- How much do you feel like a European – not at all, not much, somewhat, or very much?

German Identity (2002: $r = +.60$; 2004: $r = +.60$)

- I am proud to be a German – not proud at all, rather not proud, rather proud, or very proud.
- How much do you feel like a German – not at all, not much, somewhat, very much?

Authoritarianism (2002: $\alpha = .75$; 2004: $\alpha = .75$)

- Crime should be punished more severely – completely disagree, tend to disagree, tend to agree, completely agree.

- To ensure law and order, you should move more sternly against outsiders and troublemakers.
- Two of the most important characteristics should be obedience and respect for one's superiors.

Social Dominance Orientation (2002: $\alpha = .61$; 2004: $\alpha = .62$)

- Groups at the bottom of our society should stay there – don't agree at all, tend not to agree, tend to agree, completely agree.
- Some groups in the population are worth less than others.
- Some population groups are more useful than others.

Prejudice Against Foreigners Residing in Germany* (2002: $\alpha = +.84$; 2004: $r = +.59$)

- Foreigners enrich German culture – completely agree, tend to agree, tend not to agree, don't agree at all. [Reverse-scored item]
- Foreigners have jobs that we Germans should have.
- Foreigners living in Germany are a financial strain on the social welfare system.
- Foreigners living in Germany should choose their spouses from among those from their own country.
- There are too many foreigners living in Germany.**
- When jobs become scarce, foreigners who live in Germany should return to their home country.**

Individual Threat (2004: $\alpha = .85$)

- Foreigners living here threaten *my* personal freedom and rights; ... *my* personal economic situation; ... *my* personal way of life; ... *my* personal security – doesn't apply at all, tends not to apply, tends to apply, applies entirely.

Collective Threat (2004: $\alpha = .85$)

- Foreigners living here threaten *our* freedom and rights; ... *our* prosperity; ... *our* culture; and ... *our* security – doesn't apply at all, tends not to apply, tends to apply, applies entirely.

[* All six items were used to assess prejudice against foreigners in the 2002 survey. **Only the last two items comprise the prejudice against foreigners measure in the 2004 survey.]

Chapter 12 Items (2004 GFE Survey)

Positive Intergroup Contact ($\alpha = .76$)

- How often have you had an interesting conversation with a foreigner – never, seldom, sometimes, often?
- How often has a foreigner helped you – never, seldom, sometimes, often?
- Now think about encounters with foreigners in Germany. How often have you experienced the following feelings: satisfied and cheerful – never, sometimes, often, or very often?

Negative Intergroup Contact ($\alpha = .78$)

- How often has a foreigner pestered you – never, sometimes, often, or very often?
- Now think about encounters with foreigners in Germany. How often have you experienced the following feelings: angry, irritated and fearful – never, sometimes, often, or very often?

Three Conditions of Contact (Analyzed as Single-Item Measures)

- How would you judge the contacts you have with foreigners living here in Germany: superficial, on an equal footing, and voluntary? – does not apply at all, tends not to apply, tends to apply, fully applies.

Individual Threat

The same four items listed for Chapter 10 above.

Collective Threat

The same four items listed for Chapter 10 above.

Prejudice Against Resident Foreigners

The same two items listed for Chapter 3 above.

Authoritarianism

The same three items listed for Chapter 10 above.

Political Conservatism

- Many people use the terms "left" and "right" to describe different political views. On a scale from left to right, where would you place your own political views on this scale – left, somewhat left, exactly in the middle, somewhat right, right?

Chapter 13 Items (2004 GFE Survey)

Foreigners in Neighborhood

- How many foreigners are living in your neighborhood – many, rather many, rather few, none?

Neighborhood Contact with Foreigners

- How often do you have any personal contact with foreigners living in your neighborhood – frequently, sometimes, rarely, or never?

Authoritarianism Scale

The same three items as listed for Chapter 10 above.

Foreign Friends

- How many of your good friends and acquaintances are foreigners – none, few, many, very many?

Political Conservatism

The same item as listed for Chapter 12 above.

Anti-Muslim Prejudice ($\alpha = .75$)

- Muslim culture fits well in our Western World – agree completely, tend to agree, tend to disagree, completely disagree. [Reverse-scored item]
- With so many Muslims living here in Germany, I sometimes feel like a stranger in my own country – completely disagree, tend to disagree, tend to agree, agree completely.
- Muslim migration to Germany should be prohibited – completely disagree, tend to disagree, tend to agree, agree completely.
- I am more mistrustful of Muslim people – completely disagree, tend to disagree, tend to agree, agree completely.
- The many mosques in Germany prove that Islam wants to enlarge its power here – completely disagree, tend to disagree, tend to agree, agree completely.

☐ Note

1 The authors wish to thank Professor Ulrich Wagner of Philipps University, Marburg, Germany, for his careful translations of these items from their original German to English.

REFERENCES

Aberson, C. L., & Haag, S. C. (2007). Contact, perspective taking, and anxiety as predictors of stereotype endorsement, explicit attitudes, and implicit attitudes. *Group Processes and Intergroup Relations, 10*, 179–201.

Aberson, C. L., Porter, M. K., & Gaffney, A. M. (2008). Friendships influence Hispanic students' implicit attitudes toward White non-Hispanics relative to African Americans. *Hispanic Journal of Behavioral Sciences, 30*, 544–556.

Aberson, C., Shoemaker, C., & Tomolillo, C. (2004). Implicit bias and contact: The role of interethnic friendships. *Journal of Social Psychology, 144*, 335–347.

Aboud, F. E. (1988). *Children and prejudice*. New York: Blackwell.

Aboud, F. E. (2005). The development of prejudice in childhood and adolescence. In J. F. Dovidio, P. Glick, & L. A. Rudman (Eds.), *On the nature of prejudice: Fifty years after Allport* (pp. 310–326). Malden, MA: Blackwell.

Aboud, F. E., & Levy, S. R. (2000). Interventions to reduce prejudice and discrimination in children and adolescents. In S. Oskamp (Ed.), *Reducing prejudice and discrimination* (pp. 269–293). Mahwah, NJ: Lawrence Erlbaum Associates.

Aboud, F. E., Mendelson, M. J., & Purdy, K. T. (2003). Cross-race peer relations and friendship quality. *International Journal of Behavioral Development, 27*, 165–173.

Aboud, F. E., & Sankar, J. (2007). Friendship and identity in a language-integrated school. *International Journal of Behavioral Development, 31*, 445–453.

Adesokan, A., Van Dick, R., Ullrich, J., & Tropp, L. R. (in press). Diversity beliefs as a moderator of the contact–prejudice relationship. *Social Psychology*.

Adorno, T. W., Frenkel-Brunswik, E., Levinson, D. J., & Sanford, R. N. (1950). *The authoritarian personality*. New York: Harper & Row.

Ajzen, I., & Fishbein, M. (1980). *Understanding attitudes and predicting social behaviour*. Englewood Cliffs, NJ: Prentice-Hall.

Akinola, M., & Mendes, W. B. (2008, January). *Vigilance and intergroup interactions*. Symposium paper presented at the annual meeting of the Society for Personality and Social Psychology, Albuquerque, New Mexico.

Alesina, A., & La Ferrara, E. (2002). Who trusts others? *Journal of Public Economics, 85*, 207–234.

Alexander, L., & Tredoux, C. (2010). The spaces between us: A spatial analysis of informal segregation at a South African university campus. *Journal of Social Issues, 66*, 367–386.

Alexander, M. G., Brewer, M. B., & Livingston, R. W. (2005). Putting stereotype content in context: Image theory and interethnic stereotypes. *Personality and Social Psychology Bulletin, 31*, 781–794.

Allport, G. W. (1954). *The nature of prejudice*. Reading, MA: Addison-Wesley.

Allport, G. W., & Kramer, B. M. (1946). Some roots of prejudice. *Journal of Psychology, 22*, 9–39.

Altemeyer, B. (1981). *Right-wing authoritarianism*. Winnipeg, Canada: University of Manitoba Press.

Altemeyer, B. (1988). *Enemies of freedom: Understanding right-wing authoritarianism*. San Francisco: Jossey-Bass.

Altemeyer, B. (1996). *The authoritarian specter*. Cambridge, MA: Harvard University Press.
Alvaro, E. M., & Crano, W. D. (1997). Indirect minority influence: Evidence for leniency in source evaluation and counter argumentation. *Journal of Personality and Social Psychology, 72*, 949–964.
Amir, Y. (1969). Contact hypothesis in ethnic relations. *Psychological Bulletin, 71*, 319–342.
Amir, Y. (1976). The role of intergroup contact in change of prejudice and race relations. In P. Katz & D. A. Taylor (Eds.), *Towards the elimination of racism* (pp. 245–308). New York: Pergamon.
Amir, Y., & Ben-Ari, R. (1985). International tourism, ethnic contact, and attitude change. *Journal of Social Issues, 41*, 105–115.
Amsel, R., & Fichten, C. S. (1988). Effects of contact on thoughts about interaction with students who have a physical disability. *Journal of Rehabilitation, 54*, 61–65.
Araragi, C. (1983). The effect of the jigsaw learning method on children's academic performance and learning attitude. *Japanese Journal of Educational Psychology, 31*, 102–112.
Aron, A., & McLaughlin-Volpe, T. (2001). Including others in the self: Extensions to own and partner's group memberships. In C. Sedikides & M. Brewer (Eds.), *Individual self, relational self, collective self* (pp. 89–108). New York: Psychology Press.
Aron, A., McLaughlin-Volpe, T., Mashek, D., Lewandowski, G., Wright, S. C., & Aron, E. N. (2004). Including others in the self. *European Review of Social Psychology, 15*, 101–132.
Aronson, E. (1997). The theory of cognitive dissonance: The evolution and vicissitudes of an idea. In C. McGarty, S. Haslam, & S. Alexander (Eds.), *The message of social psychology: Perspectives on mind in society* (pp. 20–35). Malden, MA: Blackwell.
Aronson, E., & Bridgeman, D. (1979). Jigsaw groups and the desegregated classroom: In pursuit of common goals. *Personality and Social Psychology Bulletin, 5*, 438–446.
Aronson, E., & Gonzalez, A. (1988). Desegregation, jigsaw, and the Mexican-American experience. In P. A. Katz & D. A. Taylor (Eds.), *Eliminating racism: Profiles in controversy* (pp. 301–314). New York: Plenum Press.
Aronson, E., & Patnoe, S. (1997). *The Jigsaw Classroom: Building cooperation in the classroom* (2nd ed.) New York: Addison-Wesley-Longman.
Aronson, E., Stephan, C., Sikes, J., Blaney, N., & Snapp, M. (1978). *The Jigsaw Classroom*. Beverly Hills, CA: Sage.
Asbrock, F., Christ, O., Hewstone, M., Pettigrew, T. F., & Wagner, U. (under review). *Comparing the secondary transfer effect of direct and extended intergroup contact: The generalization of positive attitudes and its limitations*. Psychology Department, Philipps University, Marburg, Germany.
Asher, S. R., Singleton, L. C., & Taylor, A. R. (1982). *Acceptance versus friendship: A longitudinal study of racial integration*. Paper presented at the annual meeting of the American Educational Research Association, New York.
Ashmore, R. D., & Del Boca, F. K. (1981). Conceptual approaches to stereotypes and stereotyping. In D. L. Hamilton (Ed.), *Cognitive processes in stereotyping and intergroup behavior* (pp. 1–35). Hillsdale, NJ: Lawrence Erlbaum Associates.

Auerbach, D. N., & Levenson, R. L. (1977). Second impressions: Attitude change in college students toward the elderly. *The Gerontologist, 17,* 362–366.
Baker, P. E. (1934). *Negro–White adjustment.* New York: Association Press.
Ballard, M., Corman, L., Gottlieb, J., & Kaufman, M. J. (1977). Improving the social status of mainstreamed retarded children. *Journal of Educational Psychology, 69,* 605–611.
Banks, J. A. (1995). Multicultural education and the modification of students' racial attitudes. In W. D. Hawley & A. W. Jackson (Eds.), *Towards a common destiny: Improving race and ethnic relations in America* (pp. 315–339). San Francisco: Jossey-Bass.
Batson, C. D., Ahmad, N., & Stocks, E. L. (2004). Benefits and liabilities of empathy-induced altruism. In A. G. Miller (Ed.), *The social psychology of good and evil* (pp. 359–385). New York: Guilford Press.
Batson, C. D., Early, S., & Salvarani, G. (1997a). Perspective taking: Imagining how another feels versus imagining how you would feel. *Personality and Social Psychology Bulletin, 23,* 751–758.
Batson, C. D., Lishner, D. A., Cook, J., & Sawyer, S. (2005). Similarity and nurturance: Two possible sources of empathy for strangers. *Basic and Applied Social Psychology, 27,* 15–25.
Batson, C. D., Polycarpou, M. P., Harmon-Jones, E., Imhoff, H. J., Mitchener, E. C., Bednar, L. I., et al. (1997b). Empathy and attitudes: Can feeling for a member of a stigmatized group improve feelings toward the group? *Journal of Personality and Social Psychology, 72,* 105–118.
Beaton, A., Francine, T., Clayton, S., & Perrino, A. (2003). L'impact de valeurs conservatrices et de préjugés racistes sur l'ouverture à l'immigration [The impact of conservative values and racist prejudices on the opening of immigration]. *Revue Canadienne des Sciences du Comportement, 35,* 229–237.
Begg, C. B. (1994). Publication bias. In H. Cooper & L. V. Hedges (Eds.), *The handbook of research synthesis* (pp. 399–409). New York: Sage.
Berry, J. W. (2006). Mutual attitudes among immigrants and ethnocultural groups in Canada. *International Journal of Intercultural Relations, 30,* 719–734.
Berry, J. W. (2009). A critique of critical acculturation. *International Journal of Intercultural Relations, 33,* 361–371.
Bettencourt, B. A., Brewer, M. B., Rogers-Croak, M., & Miller, N. (1992). Cooperation and the reduction of intergroup bias: The role of reward structure and social orientation. *Journal of Experimental Social Psychology, 28,* 301–319.
Bigler, R. S., & Liben, L. S. (1993). A cognitive-developmental approach to racial stereotyping and reconstructive memory in Euro-American children. *Child Development, 64,* 1507–1518.
Binder, J., Zagefka, H., Brown, R., Funke, F., Kessler, T., Mummendey, A., et al. (2009). Does contact reduce prejudice or does prejudice reduce contact? A longitudinal test of the contact hypothesis amongst majority and minority groups in three European countries. *Journal of Personality and Social Psychology, 96,* 843–856.
Blake, D. (2003). Environmental determinants of racial attitudes among White Canadians. *Canadian Journal of Political Science, 36,* 491–509.
Blanchard, F., Lilly, T., & Vaughn, L. A. (1991). Reducing the expression of racial prejudice. *Psychological Science, 2,* 101–105.

Blascovich., J., Mendes, W. B., Hunter, S. B., Lickel, B., & Kowai-Bell, N. (2001). Perceiver threat in social interactions with stigmatized others. *Journal of Personality and Social Psychology, 80*, 253–267.

Blau, P., & Schwartz, J. (1997). *Crosscutting social circles: Testing a macrostructural theory of intergroup relations*. New Brunswick: Transaction.

Blumer, H. (1958). Race prejudice as a sense of group position. *Pacific Sociological Review, 1,* 3–7.

Bobo, L. D. (1999). Prejudice as group position: Microfoundations of a sociological approach to racism and intergroup relations. *Journal of Social Issues, 55,* 445–472.

Bobo, L. D., & Fox, C. (2003). Race, racism, and discrimination: Bridging problems, methods, and theory in social psychological research. *Social Psychology Quarterly, 66*, 319–332.

Bonilla-Silva, E. (2003). *Racism without racists: Color-blind racism and the persistence of racial inequality in the United States*. Lanham, MD: Rowman & Littlefield.

Bornman, E., & Mynhardt, J. C. (1991). Social identity and intergroup contact in South Africa with specific reference to work situation. *Genetic, Social, and General Psychology Monographs, 117,* 437–462.

Bornstein, R. F. (1989). Exposure and affect: Overview and meta-analysis of research, 1968–1987. *Psychological Bulletin, 106,* 263–289.

Brameld, T. (1946). *Minority problems in the public schools*. New York: Harper.

Breckler, S. J., & Wiggins, E. C. (1989). Affect versus evaluation in the structure of attitudes. *Journal of Experimental Social Psychology, 25,* 253–271.

Brewer, M. B. (1999). The psychology of prejudice: Ingroup love or outgroup hate? *Journal of Social Issues, 55,* 429–444.

Brewer, M. B. (2008). Deprovincialization: Social identity complexity and outgroup acceptance. In U. Wagner, L. R. Tropp, G. Finchilescu, & C. Tredoux (Eds.), *Emerging research directions for improving intergroup relations: Building on the legacy of Thomas F. Pettigrew* (pp. 160–176). Oxford, UK: Blackwell.

Brewer, M. B., & Campbell, D. T. (1976). *Ethnocentrism and intergroup attitudes: East African evidence*. Beverly Hills, CA: Sage.

Brewer, M. B., & Kramer, R. M. (1985). The psychology of intergroup attitudes and behavior. *Annual Review of Psychology, 36,* 219–243.

Brewer, M. B., & Miller, N. (1984). Beyond the contact hypothesis: Theoretical perspectives on desegregation. In N. Miller & M. B. Brewer (Eds.), *Groups in contact: The psychology of desegregation* (pp. 291–302). Orlando, FL: Academic Press.

Brigham, J. C. (1993). College students' racial attitudes. *Journal of Applied Social Psychology, 23,* 1933–1967.

Brophy, I. N. (1945). The luxury of anti-Negro prejudice. *Public Opinion Quarterly, 9,* 456–466.

Brown, K. T., Brown, T. N., Jackson, J. S., Sellers, R. M., & Manuel, W. J. (2003). Teammates on and off the field? Interracial contact and the racial attitudes of White intercollegiate student athletes. *Journal of Applied Social Psychology, 33,* 1379–1403.

Brown, R., Eller, A., Leeds, S., & Stace, K. (2007). Intergroup contact and intergroup attitudes: A longitudinal study. *European Journal of Social Psychology, 37,* 692–703.

Brown, R., & Hewstone, M. (2005). An integrative theory of intergroup contact. *Advances in Experimental Social Psychology, 37,* 255–343.
Brown, R., Maras, P., Masser, B., Vivian, J., & Hewstone, M. (2001). Life on the ocean wave: Testing some intergroup hypotheses in a naturalistic setting. *Group Processes and Intergroup Relations, 4,* 81–97.
Brown, R., & Turner, J. C. (1981). Interpersonal and intergroup behavior. In J. C. Turner & H. Giles (Eds.), *Intergroup behavior* (pp. 33–65). Chicago: University of Chicago Press.
Brown, R., Vivian, J., & Hewstone, M. (1999). Changing attitudes through intergroup contact: The effects of group membership salience. *European Journal of Social Psychology, 29,* 741–764.
Bullock, C. S. (1978). Contact theory and racial tolerance among high school students. *School Review, 86,* 187–216.
Burns, J. (2007, May). *Race and trust in a segmented society.* Paper presented at the Conference on Global Studies of Discrimination, Princeton University.
Burns, P., & Gimpel, J. (2000). Economic insecurity, prejudicial stereotypes, public opinion on immigration policy. *Political Science Quarterly, 115,* 201–225.
Butler, J. S., & Wilson, K. L. (1978). *The American Soldier* revisited: Race relations and the military. *Social Science Quarterly, 59,* 451–467.
Butz, D. A., & Plant, E. A. (2006). Perceiving outgroup members as unresponsive: Implications for approach-related emotions, intentions, and behavior. *Journal of Personality and Social Psychology, 91,* 1066–1079.
Caditz, J. (1975). Ambivalence towards integration: The sequence of response to six interracial situations. *Sociological Quarterly, 16,* 16–32.
Carlson, J. S., & Widaman, K. E. (1988). The effects of study abroad during college on attitudes toward other cultures. *International Journal of Intercultural Relations, 12,* 1–17.
Caspi, A. (1984). Contact hypothesis and inter-age attitudes: A field study of cross-age contact. *Social Psychology Quarterly, 47,* 74–80.
Cehajic, S., & Brown, R. (2010). Silencing the past. *Social Psychology and Personality Science, 1,* 190–196.
Chang, H. (1973). Attitudes of Chinese students in the United States. *Sociology and Social Research, 58,* 66–77.
Christ, O., Hewstone, M., Tausch, N., Wagner, U., Voci, A, Hughes, J., et al. (in press). Direct contact as a moderator of extended contact effects: Cross-sectional and longitudinal impact on outgroup attitudes, behavioral intentions, and attitude certainty. *Personality and Social Psychology Bulletin.*
Christ, O., Ullrich, J., & Wagner, U. (2008, July). *The joint effects of positive and negative intergroup contact on attitudes and attitude strength.* Paper presented at the general meeting of the European Association of Experimental Social Psychology, Opatija, Croatia.
Chu, D., & Griffey, D. (1985). The contact theory of racial integration: The case of sport. *Sociology of Sport Journal, 2,* 323–333.
Citrin, J., Green, D., Muste, C., & Wong, C. (1997). Public opinion toward immigration reform: The role of economic motivations. *Journal of Politics, 59,* 858–881.
Clack, B., Dixon, J., & Tredoux, C. (2005). Eating together apart: Patterns of segregation in a multi-ethnic cafeteria. *Journal of Community and Applied Social Psychology, 15,* 1–16.

Clark, M. L., & Ayers, M. (1992). Friendship similarity during early adolescence: Gender and racial patterns. *Journal of Psychology: Interdisciplinary and Applied, 126,* 393–405.

Clement, R., Gardner, R. C., & Smythe, P. C. (1977). Inter-ethnic contact: Attitudinal consequences. *Canadian Journal of Behavioral Science, 9,* 205–215.

Clunies-Ross, G., & O'Meara, K. (1989). Changing the attitudes of students toward peers with disabilities. *Australian Psychologist, 24,* 273–284.

Cohen, E. G. (1982). Expectation states and interracial interaction in school settings. *Annual Review of Sociology, 8,* 209–235.

Conover, T. (2006, March). The checkpoint. *The Atlantic Magazine.* Retrieved October 17, 2010, from http://www.theatlantic.com/magazine/archive/2006/03/the-checkpoint/4604/

Cook, S. W. (1962). The systematic analysis of socially significant events: A strategy for social research. *Journal of Social Issues, 18,* 66–84.

Cook, S. W. (1978). Interpersonal and attitudinal outcomes in cooperating interracial groups. *Journal of Research and Development in Education, 12,* 97–113.

Cook, S. W. (1984). Cooperative interaction in multiethnic contexts. In N. Miller & M. B. Brewer (Eds.), *Groups in contact: The psychology of desegregation* (pp. 155–185). Orlando, FL: Academic Press.

Cook, S. W., & Sellitz, C. (1955). Some factors which influence the attitudinal outcomes of personal contact. *International Social Science Bulletin, 7,* 51–58.

Cook, T. D., Cooper, H., Cordray, D. F., Hartman, H., Hedges, L. V., Light, R. J., et al. (1992). Some generic issues and problems for meta-analysis. In T. D. Cook, H. Cooper, D. S. Cordray, H. Hartman, L. V. Hedges, R. J. Light, et al. (Eds.), *Meta-analysis for explanation: A casebook* (pp. 283–320). New York: Sage.

Copans, L. (2000, October 26). Jews and Arabs cooperate to face flood despite woes. *Laredo Morning Times,* p. 15A.

Corkalo, D., Ajdukovic, D., Weinstein, H. M., Stover, E., Djipa, D., & Biro, M. (2004). Neighbors again? Intercommunity relations after ethnic cleansing. In E. Stover & H. M. Weinstein (Eds.), *My neighbor, my enemy: Justice and community in the aftermath of mass atrocity* (pp. 143–161). New York: Cambridge University Press.

Correll, J., Park, B., & Smith, J. A. (2008). Colorblind and multicultural prejudice reduction strategies in high-conflict situations. *Group Processes and Intergroup Relations, 11,* 471–491.

Corrigan, P. W., Watson, A. C., & Ottati, V. (2003). From whence comes mental illness stigma? *International Journal of Social Psychiatry, 49,* 142–157.

Coursol, A., & Wagner, E. E. (1986). Effect of positive findings on submission and acceptance rates: A note on meta-analysis bias. *Professional Psychology, 17,* 136–137.

Crain, R. L., & Weisman, C. S. (1972). *Discrimination, personality, and achievement.* New York: Seminar Press.

Crisp, R. J., & Abrams, D. (2008). Improving intergroup attitudes and reducing stereotype threat: An integrated contact model. *European Review of Social Psychology, 19,* 242–284.

Crisp, R. J., Stone, C. H., & Hall, N. R. (2006). Recategorization and subgroup identification: Predicting and preventing threats from common ingroups. *Personality and Social Psychology Bulletin, 32,* 230–243.

Crites, S. L., Fabrigar, L. R., & Petty, R. E. (1994). Measuring the affective and cognitive properties of attitudes: Conceptual and methodological issues. *Personality and Social Psychology Bulletin, 20,* 619–634.

Crocker, J., Major, B., & Steele, C. (1998). Social stigma. In D. T. Gilbert, S. T. Fiske, & G. Lindzey (Eds.), *The handbook of social psychology* (Vol. 2, pp. 504–553). New York: McGraw-Hill.

Crowne, D. P., & Marlowe, D. (1960). A new scale of social desirability independent of psychopathology. *Journal of Consulting Psychology, 24,* 349–354.

Crystal, D. S., Killen, M., & Ruck, M. (2008). It is who you know that counts: Intergroup contact and judgments about race-based exclusion. *British Journal of Developmental Psychology, 26,* 51–70.

Cuddy, A. J. C., Norton, M. I., & Fiske, S. T. (2005). This old stereotype: The pervasiveness and persistence of the elderly stereotype. *Journal of Social Issues, 61,* 267–285.

Cunningham, W. A., Nezlek, J. B., & Banaji, M. R. (2004). Implicit and explicit ethnocentrism: Revisiting the ideologies of prejudice. *Personality and Social Psychology Bulletin, 30,* 1332–1346.

Damico, S. B., Bell-Nathaniel, A., & Green, C. (1981). Effects of school organizational structure on interracial friendships in middle schools. *Journal of Education Research, 74,* 388–393.

Darby, J. P. (1986). *Intimidation and the control of conflict in Northern Ireland.* Dublin: Gill & Macmillan.

Dasgupta, N., & Rivera, L. M. (2008). When social context matters: The influence of long-term contact and short-term exposure to admired outgroup members on implciit attitudes and behavioral intentions. *Social Cognition, 26,* 112–123.

Davies, K., Tropp, L. R., Aron, A., Pettigrew, T. F., & Wright, S. C. (2011). Cross-group friendships and intergroup attitudes: A meta-analytic review. *Personality and Social Psychology Review.*

Davis, M. H. (1983). Measuring individual differences in empathy: Evidence for a multidimensional approach. *Journal of Personality and Social Psychology, 44,* 113–126.

Dawkins, C. (2008). Reflections on diversity and social capital: A critique of Robert Putnam's "*E pluribus unum*: Diversity and community in the twenty-first century: The 2006 John Skytte prize lecture." *Housing Policy Debate, 19,* 208–217.

De Houwer, J. (2007). A conceptual and theoretical analysis of evaluative conditioning. *Spanish Journal of Psychology, 10,* 230–241.

De Houwer, J., Thomas, S., & Baeyens, F. (2001). Associative learning of likes and dislikes: A review of 25 years of research on human evaluative conditioning. *Psychological Bulletin, 127,* 853–869.

Delgado, G. (2003). *Multiracial formations: New instruments for social change. A report prepared for the Annie E. Casey Foundation.* Oakland, CA: Applied Research Center.

Dellman-Jenkins, M., Lambert, D., & Fruit, D. (1991). Fostering preschoolers' prosocial behaviors toward the elderly: The effect of an intergenerational program. *Educational Gerontology, 17,* 21–32.

Desforges, D. M., Lord, C. G., Ramsey, S. L., Mason, J. A., Van Leeuwen, M. D., West, S. C., et al. (1991). Effects of structured cooperative contact on changing negative attitudes toward stigmatized social groups. *Journal of Personality and Social Psychology, 60,* 531–544.

De Tezanos-Pinto, P., Brown, R., & Bratt, C. (2010). What will the others think? Ingroup norms as a mediator of intergroup contact. *British Journal of Social Psychology, 49,* 507–523.

Deutsch, K. W. (1966). *Nationalism and social communication: An inquiry into the foundations of nationalism.* Cambridge, MA: MIT Press.

Deutsch, M., & Collins, M. (1951). *Interracial housing: A psychological evaluation of a social experiment.* Minneapolis: University of Minnesota Press.

Devine, P. G., & Vasquez, K. A. (1998). The rocky road to positive intergroup relations. In J. L. Eberhardt & S. T. Fiske (Eds.), *Confronting racism: The problem and the response* (pp. 234–262). Thousand Oaks, CA: Sage.

Dhont, K., Cornelis, I., & Van Hiel, A. (2010). Interracial public–police contact: Relationships with police officers' racial and work-related attitudes and behavior. *International Journal of Intercultural Relations, 34,* 551–560.

Dhont, K., Roets, A., & Van Hiel, A. (under review-a). *Opening closed minds: The combined effects of intergroup contact and need for closure on prejudice.* Ghent University, Ghent, Belgium.

Dhont, K., & Van Hiel, A. (2009). We must not be enemies: Interracial contact and the reduction of prejudice among authoritarians. *Personality and Individual Differences, 46,* 172–177.

Dhont, K., Van Hiel, A., & Roets, A. (under review-b). *Longitudinal intergroup effects on prejudice and essentialism: Using self-reports and observer ratings.* Ghent University, Ghent, Belgium.

Dickersin, K. (1997). How important is publication bias? A synthesis of available data. *AIDS Education and Prevention, 9* (Suppl. A), 15–21.

Dickersin, K., Min, Y. I., & Meinert, C. L. (1992). Factors influencing the publication of research results: Follow up of applications submitted to two institutional review boards. *Journal of the American Medical Association, 267,* 867–872.

Dihn, K. T., & Bond, M. A. (2008). The other side of acculturation: Changes among host individuals and communities in their adaptation to immigrant populations. *American Journal of Community Psychology, 42,* 283–285.

Dijker, A. J. (1987). Emotional reactions to ethnic minorities. *European Journal of Social Psychology, 17,* 305–325.

Dion, K. L. (2002). The social psychology of perceived prejudice and discrimination. *Canadian Psychology, 43,* 1–10.

Dixon, J. (2006). The ties that bind and those that don't: Toward reconciling group threat and contact theories of prejudice. *Social Forces, 84,* 2179–2204.

Dixon, J. A., & Durrheim, K. L. (2003). Contact and the ecology of racial division: Some varieties of informal segregation. *British Journal of Social Psychology, 43,* 1–23.

Dixon, J. A., Durrheim, K. L., & Tredoux, C. G. (2005). Beyond the optimal strategy: A "reality check" for the contact hypothesis. *American Psychologist, 60,* 697–711.

Dixon, J. A., Durrheim, K. L., & Tredoux, C. G. (2007). Intergroup contact and attitudes toward the principle and practice of racial equality. *Psychological Science, 18,* 867–872.

Dixon, J., Durrheim, K., Tredoux. C., Tropp, L., Clack, B., & Eaton, L. (2010a). A paradox of integration? Interracial contact, prejudice reduction and perceptions of racial discrimination. *Journal of Social Issues, 66,* 401–416.

Dixon, J., Durrheim, K., Tredoux. C., Tropp, L., Clack, B., Eaton, L., et al. (2010b). Challenging the stubborn core of opposition to equality: Racial contact and policy attitudes. *Political Psychology*, 31, 831–855.
Dixon, J., Tropp, L. R., Durrheim, K., & Tredoux, C. (2010c). "Let them eat harmony": Prejudice reduction strategies and attitudes of historically disadvantaged groups. *Current Directions in Psychological Science*, 19, 76–80.
Dovidio, J. F., Brigham, J. C., Johnson, B. T., & Gaertner, S. L. (1996). Stereotyping, prejudice, and discrimination: Another look. In C. N. Macrae, C. Stangor, & M. Hewstone (Eds.), *Stereotypes and stereotyping* (pp. 276–319). New York: Guilford Press.
Dovidio, J. F., Esses, V. M., Beach, K. R., & Gaertner, S. L. (2002a). The role of affect in determining intergroup behavior: The case of willingness to engage in intergroup contact. In D. M. Mackie & E. R. Smith (Eds.), *From prejudice to intergroup emotions: Differentiated reactions to social groups* (pp. 153–171). New York: Psychology Press.
Dovidio, J. F., & Gaertner, S. L. (1981). The effects of race, status, and ability on helping behavior. *Social Psychology Quarterly*, 44, 192–203.
Dovidio, J. F., Gaertner, S. L., & Kafati, G. (2000). Group identity and intergroup relations: The Common Ingroup Identity Model. In S. Thye, E. J. Lawler, M. Macy, & H. Walker (Eds.), *Advances in group processes* (pp. 1–35). Stamford, CT: JAI Press.
Dovidio, J. F., Gaertner, S. L., & Saguy, T. (2009). Commonality and the complexity of "we": Social attitudes and social change. *Personality and Social Psychology Review*, 13, 3–20.
Dovidio, J. F., Kawakami, K., & Gaertner, S. L. (2002b). Implicit and explicit prejudice and interracial interaction. *Journal of Personality and Social Psychology*, 82, 62–68.
Dovidio, J. F., Kawakami, K., Johnson, C., Johnson, B., & Howard, A. (1997). On the nature of prejudice: Automatic and controlled processes. *Journal of Experimental Social Psychology*, 33, 510–540.
Doyle, A. B., & Aboud, F. E. (1995). A longitudinal study of White children's racial prejudice as a social-cognitive development. *Merrill-Palmer Quarterly*, 41, 209–228.
Draguns, J. G. (2004). Interethnic relations in the Baltic states: Between confrontation and integration. In Y. T. Lee, C. McAuley, F. Moghaddam, & S. Worchel (Eds.), *The psychology of ethnic and cultural conflict* (pp. 175–192). Westport, CT: Praeger.
Drake, S. C., & Cayton, H. R. (1962). *Black metropolis*. New York: Harper & Row.
Duan, C., & Hill, C. (1996). The current state of empathy research. *Journal of Counseling Psychology*, 43, 261–274.
DuBois, D. L., & Hirsch, B. J. (1990). School and neighborhood friendship patterns of blacks and whites in early adolescence. *Child Development*, 61, 524–536.
Duckitt, J. (2001). A dual-process cognitive-motivational theory of ideology and prejudice. In M. P. Zanna (Ed.), *Advances in experimental social psychology* (pp. 41–113). San Diego, CA: Academic Press.
Duckitt, J. (2004). The cultural basis of ethnocentrism: Comparing White Afrikaners and European New Zealanders. In Y. T. Lee, C. McAuley, F. Moghaddam, & S. Worchel (Eds.), *The psychology of ethnic and cultural conflict* (pp. 155–173). Westport, CN: Praeger.

Duckitt, J., Callaghan, J., & Wagner, C. (2005). Group identification and outgroup attitudes in four South African ethnic groups: A multidimensional approach. *Personality and Social Psychology Bulletin, 31*, 633–646.

Dunton, B. C., & Fazio, R. H. (1997). Categorization by race: The impact of automatic and controlled components of racial prejudice. *Journal of Experimental Social Psychology, 33*, 451–470.

Durrheim, K., & Dixon, J. (2010). Racial contact and change in South Africa. *Journal of Social Issues, 66*, 273–288.

Dustmann, C., & Preston, I. (2001). Attitudes to ethnic minorities, ethnic context and location decisions. *Economic Journal, 111*, 353–373.

Duval, S. J., & Tweedie, R. L. (2000a). A nonparametric "trim and fill" method of accounting for publication bias in meta-analysis. *Journal of the American Statistical Association, 95*, 89–98.

Duval, S. J., & Tweedie, R. L. (2000b). Trim and fill: A simple funnel-plot-based method of testing and adjusting for publication bias in meta-analysis. *Biometrics, 56*, 455–463.

Eagly, A. H., & Chaiken, S. (1993). *The psychology of attitudes*. Fort Worth, TX: Harcourt Brace Jovanovich.

Easterbrook, P. J., Berlin, J. A., Gopalan, R., & Mathews, D. R. (1991). Publication bias in clinical research. *Lancet, 337*, 867–872.

Echebarria-Echabe, A., & Fernandez-Guede, E. (2006). Effect of terrorism on attitudes and ideological orientation. *European Journal of Social Psychology, 36*, 259–265.

Edmonds, C., & Killen, M. (2009). Do adolescents' perceptions of parental racial attitudes relate to their intergroup contact and cross-race relationships? *Group Processes and Intergroup Relations, 12*, 5–21.

Edwards, K., & von Hippel, W. (1995). Hearts and minds: The priority of affective versus cognitive factors in person perception. *Personality and Social Psychology Bulletin, 21*, 996–1011.

Eggins, R. A., Haslam, S. A., & Reynolds, K. J. (2002). Social identity and negotiation: Subgroup representation and superordinate consensus. *Personality and Social Psychology Bulletin, 28*, 887–899.

Eibach, R. P., & Ehrlinger, J. (2006). "Keep your eyes on the Prize": Reference points and racial differences in assessing progress toward equality. *Personality and Social Psychology Bulletin, 32*, 66–77.

Eller, A., & Abrams, D. (2003). "Gringos" in Mexico: Cross-sectional and longitudinal effects of language school-promoted contact on intergroup bias. *Group Processes and Intergroup Relations, 6*, 55–75.

Eller, A., & Abrams, D. (2004). Come together: Longitudinal comparisons of Pettigrew's reformulated intergroup contact model and the common ingroup identity model in Anglo-French and Mexican-American contexts. *European Journal of Social Psychology, 34*, 229–256.

Eller, A., Abrams, D., & Gómez, A. (under review). *When the direct route is blocked: The extended contact pathway to improving intergroup relations*. Psychology Department, University of Aberdeen, Scotland.

Ellison, C., & Powers, D. (1994). The contact hypothesis and racial attitudes among Black Americans. *Social Science Quarterly, 75*, 385–400.

Emerson, M. O., Kimbro, R. T., & Yancey, G. (2002). Contact theory extended: The

effects of prior racial contact on current social ties. *Social Science Quarterly, 83*, 745–761.
Ensari, N. K., & Miller, N. (2002). The out-group must not be so bad after all: The effects of disclosure, typicality, and salience on intergroup bias. *Journal of Personality and Social Psychology, 83*, 313–329.
Epstein, J. L. (1986). Friendship selection: Developmental and environmental influences. In E. C. Mueller & C. R. Cooper (Eds.), *Process and outcome in peer relationships* (pp. 129–160). Orlando, FL: Academic Press.
Espenshade, T., & Hempstead, K. (1996). Contemporary American attitudes toward U.S. immigration. *International Migration Review, 30*, 535–570.
Esses, V. M., & Dovidio, J. F. (2002). The role of emotions in determining willingness to engage in intergroup contact. *Personality and Social Psychology Bulletin, 28*, 1202–1214.
Esses, V. M., Dovidio, J., Jackson, L., & Armstrong, T. (2001). The immigration dilemma: The role of perceived group competition, ethnic prejudice, and national identity. *Journal of Social Issues, 57*, 389–412.
Esses, V. M., Haddock, G., & Zanna, M. P. (1993). Values, stereotypes, and emotions as determinants of intergroup attitudes. In D. Mackie & D. Hamilton (Eds.), *Affect, cognition, and stereotyping: Interactive processes in group perception* (pp. 137–166). San Diego, CA: Academic Press.
Feagin, J. R. (1991). The continuing significance of race: Anti-Black discrimination in public places. *American Sociological Review, 56*, 101–116.
Fehr, B. (2004). A prototype model of intimacy interactions in same-sex friendships. In D. J. Mashek & A. Aron (Eds.), *Handbook of closeness and intimacy* (pp. 9–26). Mahwah, NJ: Lawrence Erlbaum Associates.
Fenrick, N. J., & Petersen, T. K. (1984). Developing positive changes in attitudes towards moderately/severely handicapped students through a peer tutoring program. *Education and Training of the Mentally Retarded, 19*, 83–90.
Festinger, L., & Kelley, H. (1951). *Changing attitudes through social contact*. Ann Arbor, MI: Research Center for Group Dynamics, Institute for Social Research, University of Michigan.
Fetzer, J. (2000a). Economic self-interest or cultural marginality: Anti-immigration sentiment and nativist political movements in France, Germany and the U.S.A. *Journal of Ethnic and Migration Studies, 26*, 5–23.
Fetzer, J. (2000b). *Public attitudes toward immigration in the United States, France, and Germany*. New York: Cambridge University Press.
Finchilescu, G. (2010). Intergroup anxiety in inter-racial interaction: The role of prejudice and meta-stereotypes. *Journal of Social Issues, 66*, 334–351.
Fine, G. (1979). The Pinkston settlement: An historical and social psychological investigation of the contact hypothesis. *Phylon, 40*, 229–242.
Finlay, K., & Stephan, W. G. (2000). Reducing prejudice: The effects of empathy on intergroup attitudes. *Journal of Applied Social Psychology, 30*, 1720–1737.
Fishbein, H. D. (1996). *Peer prejudice and discrimination: Evolutionary, cultural, and developmental dynamics*. Boulder, CO: Westview Press.
Fiske, S. T., Cuddy, A. J., Glick, P., & Xu, J. (2002). A model of (often mixed) stereotype content: Competence and warmth respectively follow from perceived status and competition. *Journal of Personality and Social Psychology, 82*, 878–902.

Fiske, S. T., & Neuberg, S. L. (1999). The continuum model: Ten years later. In S. Chaiken & Y. Trope (Eds.), *Dual-process theories in social psychology* (pp. 231–254). New York: Guilford Press.

Forbes, H. (1997). *Ethnic conflict: Commerce, culture and the contact hypothesis.* New Haven, CT: Yale University Press.

Forbes, H. (2004). Ethnic conflict and the contact hypothesis. In Y. T. Lee, C. McAuley, F. Moghaddam, & S. Worchel (Eds.), *The psychology of ethnic and cultural conflict* (pp. 69–88). New York: Praeger.

Ford, W. S. (1986). Favorable intergroup contact may not reduce prejudice: Inconclusive journal evidence, 1960–1984. *Sociology and Social Research, 70,* 256–258.

Forman, T., & Rodriguez, M. (2003). *Intergroup contact and Latinos' racial attitudes: Revisiting the contact hypothesis.* Unpublished manuscript, University of Illinois at Chicago.

Foster, D., & Finchilescu, G. (1986). Contact in a "non-contact" society: The case of South Africa. In M. Hewstone & R. Brown (Eds.), *Contact and conflict in intergroup encounters* (pp. 119–136). Oxford, UK: Blackwell.

Frey, F. E., & Tropp, L. R. (2006). Being seen as individuals versus as group members: Extending research on metaperception to intergroup contexts. *Personality and Social Psychology Review, 10,* 265–280.

Friedman, R. S. (1975). *The Peer-Peer Program: A model project for the integration of severely physically handicapped youngsters with nondisabled peers.* New York: New York State Education Dept., Albany Division of Drug and Health Education Services.

Fritz, M. S., & MacKinnon, D. P. (2007). Required sample size to detect the mediated effect. *Psychological Science, 18,* 233–239.

Fujioka, Y. (1999). Television portrayals and African-American stereotypes: Examination of television effects when direct contact is lacking. *Journalism and Mass Communication Quarterly, 76,* 52–75.

Gaertner, S. L., & Dovidio, J. F. (2000). *Reducing intergroup bias: The common ingroup identity model.* Philadelphia, PA: Psychology Press.

Gaertner, S. L., Dovidio, J. F., & Bachman, B. A. (1996). Revisiting the contact hypothesis: The induction of a common ingroup identity. *International Journal of Intercultural Relations, 20,* 271–290.

Gaertner, S. L., Mann, J., Murrell, A., & Dovidio, J. F. (1989). Reducing intergroup bias: The benefits of recategorization. *Journal of Personality and Social Psychology, 57,* 239–249.

Gaertner, S. L., Rust, M. C., Dovidio, J. F., Bachman, B. A., & Anastasio, P. A. (1994). The contact hypothesis: The role of a common ingroup identity on reducing intergroup bias. *Small Groups Research, 25,* 224–249.

Galinsky, A. D., & Moskowitz, G. B. (2000). Perspective-taking: Decreasing stereotype expression, stereotype accessibility, and in-group favoritism. *Journal of Personality and Social Psychology, 78,* 708–724.

Gallup Organization (2001). *Black–White relations in the United States: 2001 update.* Washington, DC: Gallup Organization.

Gelman, A., Park, D., Shor, B., Bafumi, J., & Cortina, J. (2008). *Red state, blue state, rich state, poor state.* Princeton, NJ: Princeton University Press.

Gerbert, B., Sumser, J., & Maguire, B. T. (1991). The impact of who you know and where you live on opinions about AIDS and health care. *Social Science and Medicine, 32,* 677–681.

Gesthuizen, M., Van der Meer, T., & Scheepers, P. (2008). Ethnic diversity and social capital in Europe: Tests of Putnam's thesis in European countries. *Scandinavian Political Studies, 32*, 121–142.

Gibson, J. L. (2004). *Overcoming apartheid: Can truth reconcile a divided nation?* New York: Russell Sage Foundation.

Gibson, J. L. (2006). Do strong group identities fuel intolerance. Evidence from the South African case. *Political Psychology, 27*, 665–705.

Gibson, J. L., & Claassen, C. (2010). Racial reconciliation in South Africa: Interracial contact and changes over time. *Journal of Social Issues, 66*, 255–272.

Glass, G. V. J., McCaw, B., & Smith, M. L. (1981). *Meta-analysis in social research.* Beverly Hills, CA: Sage.

Goffman, E. (1963). *Stigma: Notes on the management of spoiled identity.* New York: Simon & Schuster.

Gómez, A., & Huici, C. (2008). Vicarious intergroup contact and role of authorities in prejudice reduction. *Spanish Journal of Psychology, 11*, 103–114.

Gómez, A., Tropp, L. R., & Fernandez, S. (in press). When extended contact opens the door to future contact: Testing the effects of extended contact on intergroup attitudes and expectancies among minority and majority groups. *Group Processes and Intergroup Relations.*

Goodman, M. E. (1952). *Race awareness in young children.* Cambridge, Massachusetts.

Gordijn, E. H., Hindriks, I., Koomen, W., Dijksterhuis, A., & Knippenberg, A. V. (2004). Consequences of stereotype suppression and internal suppression motivation. A self-regulatory approach. *Personality and Social Psychology Bulletin, 30*, 212–224.

Graves, S. B. (1999). Television and prejudice reduction: When does television as a vicarious experience make a difference? *Journal of Social Issues, 55*, 707–727.

Green, C. W., Adams, A. F., & Turner, C. W. (1988). Development and validation of the School Interracial Climate Survey. *American Journal of Community Psychology, 16*, 241–259.

Greenland, K., & Brown, R. (1999). Categorization and intergroup anxiety in contact between British and Japanese nationals. *European Journal of Social Psychology, 29*, 503–521.

Greenwald, A. G., McGhee, D. E., & Schwartz, J. L. K. (1998). Measuring individual differences in implicit cognition: The Implicit Associations Test. *Journal of Personality and Social Psychology, 74*, 1464–1480.

Gudykunst, W. B. (1985). A model of uncertainty reduction in intercultural encounters. *Journal of Language and Social Psychology, 4*, 79–97.

Gudykunst, W. B. (1986). Ethnicity, types of relationship, and intraethnic and interethnic uncertainty reduction. In Y. Y. Kim (Ed.), *Interethnic communication* (pp. 201–244). Thousand Oaks, CA: Sage.

Gudykunst, W. B., & Hammer, M. R. (1988). Strangers and hosts: An uncertainty reduction based theory of intercultural adaptation. In Y. Y. Kim & W. B. Gudykunst (Eds.), *Cross-cultural adaptation: Current approaches* (pp. 106–139). Thousand Oaks, CA: Sage.

Guinier, L., & Torres, G. (2002). *The miner's canary: Enlisting race, resisting power, transforming democracy.* Cambridge, MA: Harvard University Press.

Ha, S. (2008). *Multiracial friendship networks and public attitudes toward immigration in the U.S.* Unpublished paper, Yale University.

Haddock, G., Zanna, M. P., & Esses, V. M. (1993). Assessing the structure of prejudicial attitudes: The case of attitudes towards homosexuals. *Journal of Personality and Social Psychology, 65,* 1105–1118.
Hallinan, M. T., & Smith, S. S. (1985). The effects of classroom racial composition on students' interracial friendliness. *Social Psychology Quarterly, 48,* 3–16.
Hallinan, M. T., & Teixeira, R. A. (1987). Opportunities and constraints: Black–White differences in the formation of interracial friendships. *Child Development, 58,* 1358–1371.
Hamberger, J., & Hewstone, M. (1997). Inter-ethnic contact as a predictor of blatant and subtle prejudice: Tests of a model in four West European nations. *British Journal of Social Psychology, 36,* 173–190.
Hamilton, D. L. (1981). Stereotyping and intergroup behavior: Some thoughts on the cognitive approach. In D. L. Hamilton (Ed.), *Cognitive processes in stereotyping and intergroup behavior* (pp. 333–353). Hillsdale, NJ: Lawrence Erlbaum Associates.
Hamilton, D. L., Stroessner, S. J., & Driscoll, D. M. (1994). Social cognition and the study of stereotyping. In P. G. Devine, D. L. Hamilton, & T. M. Ostrom (Eds.), *Social cognition: Impact on social psychology* (pp. 291–321). San Diego, CA: Academic Press.
Harmon-Jones, E., & Allen, J. J. B. (2001). The role of affect in the mere exposure effect: Evidence from physiological and individual differences approaches. *Personality and Social Psychology Bulletin, 27,* 889–898.
Harrington, H. J., & Miller, N. (1992). Research and theory in intergroup relations: Issues of consensus and controversy. In J. Lynch, C. Modgil, & S. Modgil (Eds.), *Cultural diversity and the schools* (Vol. 2, pp. 159–178). London: Falmer.
Harwood, J., Hewstone, M., Paolini, S., & Voci, A. (2005). Grandparent–grandchild contact and attitudes toward older adults: Moderator and mediator effects. *Personality and Social Psychology Bulletin, 31,* 393–406.
Harwood, J., Raman, P., & Hewstone, M. (2006). The family and communication dynamics of group salience. *Journal of Family Communication, 6,* 181–200.
Hatanaka, H. K. (1982). *The effects of a short term training program on the racial attitudes of child welfare workers.* Doctoral dissertation, University of California, Los Angeles, California.
Hayes, B., & Dowds, L. (2006). Social contact, cultural marginality, or economic self-interest? Attitudes towards immigrants in Northern Ireland. *Journal of Ethnic and Migration Studies, 32,* 455–476.
Hebl, M. R., & Dovidio, J. F. (2005). Promoting the "social" in the examination of social stigmas. *Personality and Social Psychology Review, 9,* 156–182.
Hedges, L. V. (1994). Fixed effects models. In H. Cooper & L. V. Hedges (Eds.), *The handbook of research synthesis* (pp. 285–299). New York: Russell Sage Foundation.
Hedges, L. V., & Olkin, I. (1985). *Statistical methods for meta-analysis.* New York: Academic Press.
Heider, F. (1958). *The psychology of interpersonal relations.* New York: Wiley.
Heitmeyer, W. (2002). *Deutsche Zustände, Folge 1* [The German situation, Part 1]. Frankfurt, Germany: Suhrkamp Verlag.
Heitmeyer, W. (2003). *Deutsche Zustände, Folge 2* [The German situation, Part 2]. Frankfurt, Germany: Suhrkamp Verlag.

Heitmeyer, W. (2005). *Deutsche Zustände, Folge 3* [The German situation, Part 3]. Frankfurt, Germany: Suhrkamp Verlag.
Henninger, D. (2007, August 16). The death of diversity. *Wall Street Journal*, A 10.
Henry, P. J., & Hardin, C. D. (2006). The contact hypothesis revisited: Status bias in the reduction of implicit prejudice in the United States and Lebanon. *Psychological Science, 17*, 862–868.
Herek, G. M. (1988). Heterosexuals' attitudes toward lesbians and gay men: Correlates and gender differences. *Journal of Sex Research, 25*, 451–477.
Herek, G. M. (2002). Gender gaps in public opinion about lesbians and gay men. *Public Opinion Quarterly, 66*, 40–66.
Herek, G. M. (2003). Why tell if you're not asked? Self-disclosure, intergroup contact, and heterosexuals' attitudes toward lesbians and gay men. In L. Garnets & D. C. Kimmel (Eds.), *Psychological perspectives on lesbian, gay, and bisexual experiences* (2nd ed., pp. 270–298). New York: Columbia University Press.
Herek, G. M., & Capitanio, J. P. (1996). "Some of my best friends": Intergroup contact, concealable stigma, and heterosexuals' attitudes toward gay men and lesbians. *Personality and Social Psychology Bulletin, 22*, 412–424.
Herek, G. M., & Capitanio, J. P. (1997). AIDS stigma and contact with persons with AIDS: Effects of direct and vicarious contact. *Journal of Applied Social Psychology, 27*, 1–36.
Herek, G. M., & Gonzalez-Rivera, M. (2006). Attitudes toward homosexuality among U.S. residents of Mexican descent. *Journal of Sex Research, 43*, 122–135.
Hewstone, M. (2003). Intergroup contact: Panacea for prejudice? *Psychologist, 16*, 352–355.
Hewstone, M., & Brown, R. (1986). *Contact and conflict in intergroup encounters.* Oxford: Blackwell.
Hewstone, M., Cairns, E., Voci, A., Hamberger, J., & Niens, U. (2006). Intergroup contact, forgiveness, and experience of "The Troubles" in Northern Ireland. *Journal of Social Issues, 62*, 99–120.
Hewstone, M., Cairns, E., Voci, A., Paolini, S, McLernon, F., Crisp, R. J., et al. (2005). Intergroup contact in a divided society: Challenging segregation in Northern Ireland. In D. Abrams, J. M. Marques, & M. A. Hogg (Eds.), *The social psychology of inclusion and exclusion* (pp. 265–292). Philadelphia, PA: Psychology Press.
Hewstone, M., Kenworthy, J., Tausch, N., Popan, J., Psaltis, C., & Schmid, K. (2008, August). *Generalized effects of intergroup contact: Replications and extensions of Pettigrew (1997).* Paper presented at the EAESP-SPSSI small group meeting on *Intergroup contact: Recent advancements in basic and applied research*, Philipps University, Marburg, Germany.
Hiner, N. R. (1990). History of education for the 1990s and beyond: The case for academic imperialism. *History of Education Quarterly, 30*, 137–160.
Hirschfeld, L. A. (1996). *Race in the making: Cognition, culture, and the child's construction of human kinds.* Cambridge, MA: MIT Press.
Hodson, G. (2008). Interracial prison contact: The pros for (social dominant) cons. *British Journal of Social Psychology, 47*, 325–351.
Hodson, G., Harry, H., & Mitchell, A. (2009). Independent benefits of contact and friendship on attitudes toward homosexuals among authoritarians and highly identified heterosexuals. *European Journal of Social Psychology, 35*, 509–525.

Hogg, M. A., & Reid, S. A. (2006). Social identity, self-categorization, and the communication of group norms. *Communication Theory, 16,* 7–30.

Holmes, E. P., Corrigan, P. W., Williams, P., Canar, J., & Kubiak, A. A. (1999). Changing attitudes about schizophrenia. *Schizophrenia Bulletin, 25,* 447–456.

Holtman, Z., Louw, J., Tredoux, C. G., & Carney, T. (2005). Prejudice and social contact in South Africa: A study of integrated schools ten years after apartheid. *South African Journal of Psychology, 33,* 473–493.

Holzberg, J. D., & Gewitz, H. (1963). A method of altering attitudes toward mental illness. *Psychoanalytic Quarterly Supplement, 37,* 56–61.

Homans, G. C. (1950). *The human group.* New York: Harcourt, Brace & World.

Hood, III, M. V., & Morris, I. (2000). Brother, can you spare a dime? Racial / ethnic context and the Anglo vote on Proposition 187. *Social Science Quarterly, 81,* 194–207.

Hopkins, N., Reicher, S., & Levine, M. (1997). On the parallels between social cognition and the 'new racism'. *British Journal of Social Psychology, 36,* 305–329.

Horn, S. (2003). Adolescents' reasoning about exclusion from social groups. *Developmental Psychology, 39,* 11–84.

Hornsey, M. J., & Hogg, M. A. (2000). Subgroup relations: A comparison of mutual intergroup differentiation and common ingroup identity models of prejudice reduction. *Personality and Social Psychology Bulletin, 26,* 242–256.

Hummert, M. L. (1990). Multiple stereotypes of elderly and young adults: A comparison of structure and evaluations. *Psychology and Aging, 5,* 182–193.

Hunt, M., Jackson, P., Powell, B., & Steelman, L. (2000). Color-blind: The treatment of race and ethnicity in social psychology. *Social Psychology Quarterly, 63,* 352–364.

Hyers, L. L., & Swim, J. K. (1998). A comparison of the experiences of dominant and minority group members during an intergroup encounter. *Group Processes and Intergroup Relations, 1,* 143–163.

Ibrahim, H. (1970). Recreation preference and temperament. *Research Quarterly, 41,* 145–155.

Irish, D. P. (1952). Reactions of Caucasian residents to Japanese-American neighbors. *Journal of Social Issues, 8,* 10–17.

Islam, M. R., & Hewstone, M. (1993). Dimensions of contact as predictors of intergroup anxiety, perceived out-group variability, and out-group attitude: An integrative model. *Personality and Social Psychology Bulletin, 19,* 700–710.

Jackman, M. R. (1973). Education and prejudice or education and response-set? *American Sociological Review, 38,* 327–339.

Jackman, M. R. (2005). Rejection or inclusion of outgroups? In J. F. Dovidio, P. Glick, & L. A. Rudman (Eds.), *On the nature of prejudice: Fifty years after Allport* (pp. 89–105). Oxford, UK: Blackwell.

Jackman, M. R., & Crane, M. (1986). Some of my best friends are black . . .: Interracial friendship and whites' racial attitudes. *Public Opinion Quarterly, 50,* 459–486.

Jackson, J. W. (1993). Contact theory of intergroup hostility: A review and evaluation of the theoretical and empirical literature. *International Journal of Group Tensions, 23,* 43–65.

Jackson, J., Brown, K., Brown, T., & Marks, B. (2001). Contemporary immigration policy orientations among dominant-group members in western Europe. *Journal of Social Issues, 57,* 431–456.

Jackson, L., & Esses, V. (2000). Effects of perceived economic competition in people's willingness to empower immigrants. *Group Processes and Intergroup Relations, 3,* 419–435.
Jeffries, V., & Ransford, H. E. (1969). Interracial social contact and middle-class White reactions to the Watts riot. *Social Problems, 16,* 312–324.
Johnson, B. T. (1993). *DSTAT: Software for the meta-analytic review of research literatures.* Hillsdale, NJ: Lawrence Erlbaum Associates.
Johnson, B. T., & Eagly, A. H. (2000). Quantitative synthesis of social psychological research. In H. T. Reis & C. M. Judd (Eds.), *Handbook of research methods in social psychology* (pp. 496–528). Cambridge, MA: Cambridge University Press.
Johnson, D. W., & Johnson, R. T. (1984). Mainstreaming hearing-impaired students: The effect of effort in communicating on cooperation and interpersonal attraction. *Journal of Psychology, 119,* 31–44.
Johnson, D. W., Johnson, R. T., & Maruyama, G. M. (1983). Interdependence and interpersonal attraction among heterogeneous and homogeneous individuals: A theoretical formulation and a meta-analysis of the research. *Review of Educational Research, 53,* 5–54.
Johnson, M. K., & Marini, M. M. (1998). Bridging the racial divide in the United States: The effect of gender. *Social Psychology Quarterly, 61,* 247–258.
Johnson, R. T., & Johnson, D. W. (1981). Building friendship between handicapped and non-handicapped students: Effects of cooperative and individualistic instruction. *American Educational Research Journal, 18,* 415–423.
Johnston, L., & Hewstone, M. (1992). Cognitive models of stereotype change: III. Subtyping and the perceived typicality of disconfirming group members. *Journal of Experimental Social Psychology, 28,* 360–386.
Jones, E. E., Farina, A., Hastorf, A. H., Markus, H., Miller, D. T., Scott, R. A., et al. (1984). *Social stigma: The psychology of marked relationships.* New York: Freeman.
Joseph, S., Weatherall, K., & Stringer, M. (1997). Attributions for unemployment in Northern Ireland: Does it make a difference what your name is? *Irish Journal of Psychology, 18,* 341–348.
Joyner, K., & Kao, G. (2000). School racial composition and adolescent racial homophily. *Social Science Quarterly, 81,* 810–825.
Kalev, A., Dobbin, F., & Kelly, E. (2006). Best practices or best guesses? Assessing the efficacy of corporate affirmative action and diversity policies. *American Sociological Review, 71,* 589–617.
Kalin, R. (1996). Ethnic attitudes as a function of ethnic presence. *Canadian Journal of Behavioural Science, 28,* 171–179.
Kamal, A. A., & Maruyama, G. (1990). Cross-cultural contact and attitudes of Qatari students in the United States. *International Journal of Intercultural Relations, 14,* 123–134.
Katz, I., & Hass, R. G. (1988). Racial ambivalence and American value conflict. *Journal of Personality and Social Psychology, 55,* 893–905.
Katz, P. A., & Zalk, S. R. (1978). Modification of children's racial attitudes. *Developmental Psychology, 14,* 447–461.
Kearney, E. (2007). Demographic diversity in sports teams: A model of successful social integration? *Zeitschrift für Sozialpsychologie, 38,* 85–94.
Kephart, W. M. (1957). *Racial factors and urban law enforcement.* Philadelphia: University of Pennsylvania Press.

Kessler, A., & Freeman, G. (2005). Public opinion in the EU on immigration from outside the community. *Journal of Common Market Studies, 43*, 825–850.

Khmelkov, V. T., & Hallinan, M. T. (1999). Organizational effects on race relations in schools. *Journal of Social Issues, 55*, 627–645.

Killen, M., Crystal, D., & Ruck, M. (2007a). The social developmental benefits of intergroup contact for children and adolescents. In E. Frankenberg & G. Orfield (Eds.), *Realizing the promise of diversity in American schools* (pp. 57–73). Charlottesville, VA: University of Virginia Press.

Killen, M., Henning, A., Kelly, M. C., Crystal, D., & Ruck, M. (2007b). Evaluations of interracial peer encounters by majority and minority U.S. children and adolescents. *International Journal of Behavioral Development, 31*, 491–500.

Kim, Y. Y., & Gudykunst, W. B. (1988). *Cross-cultural adaptation: Current approaches.* Thousand Oaks, CA: Sage.

Kinder, D. R., & Sanders, L. M. (1996). *Divided by color: Racial politics and democratic ideals.* Chicago: University of Chicago Press.

Kluegel, J., & Bobo, L. (2001). Perceived group discrimination and policy attitudes. In A. O'Connor, C. Tilly, & L. Bobo (Eds.), *Urban inequality: Evidence from four cities* (pp. 163–213). New York: Russell Sage Foundation.

Koschate, M. J., & Van Dick, R. (under review). *A multilevel test of Allport's contact conditions.*

Kramer, B. M. (1950). *Residential contact as a determinant of attitudes toward Negroes.* Unpublished doctoral dissertation, Harvard University.

Krueger, J. (1996). Personal beliefs and cultural stereotypes about racial characteristics. *Journal of Personality and Social Psychology, 71*, 536–548.

Kunovich, R. M., & Hodson, R. (2002). Ethnic diversity, segregation, and inequality: A structural model of ethnic prejudice in Bosnia and Croatia. *Sociological Quarterly, 43*, 185–212.

Landis, D., Hope, R. O., & Day, H. R. (1984). Training for desegregation in the military. In M. B. Brewer & N. Miller (Eds.), *Groups in contact: The psychology of desegregation* (pp. 258–278). Orlando, FL: Academic Press.

Lane, K. A., Banaji, M. R., Nosek, B. A., & Greenwald, A. G. (2007). Understanding and using the Implicit Association Test: IV: Procedures and validity. In B. Wittenbrink & N. Schwarz (Eds.), *Implicit measures of attitudes: Procedures and controversies* (pp. 59–102). New York: Guilford Press.

Leach, C. W., Snider, N., & Iyer, A. (2002). Poisoning the consciences of the fortunate: The experience of relative advantage and support for social equality. In I. Walker & H. J. Smith (Eds.), *Relative deprivation: Specification, development, and integration* (pp. 136–163). New York: Cambridge University Press.

Lee, A. M., & Humphrey, N. D. (1968). *Race riot, Detroit 1943.* New York: Octagon Books.

Lee, A. Y. (2001). The mere exposure effect: An uncertainty reduction explanation revisited. *Personality and Social Psychology Bulletin, 27*, 1255–1266.

Lee, C. M., & Gudykunst, W. B. (2001). Attraction in initial interethnic interactions. *International Journal of Intercultural Relations, 25*, 373–387.

Lett, H. A. (1945). Techniques for achieving interracial cooperation. *Proceedings of the Institute on Race Relations and Community Organization.* Chicago, IL: University of Chicago and the American Council on Race Relations.

Levin, J., & Rabrenovic, G. (2004). Preventing ethnic violence: The role of interdependence. In Y. T. Lee, C. McAuley, F. Moghaddam, & S. Worchel

(Eds), *The psychology of ethnic and cultural conflict* (pp. 251–271). Westport, CT: Praeger.
Levin, S., Van Laar, C., & Sidanius, J. (2003). The effects of ingroup and outgroup friendships on ethnic attitudes in college: A longitudinal study. *Group Processes and Intergroup Relations, 6,* 76–92.
Levine, R. A., & Campbell, D. (1972). *Ethnocentrism: Theories of conflict, ethnic attitudes, and group behavior.* New York: Wiley.
Levy, J. M., Jessop, D. J., Rimmerman, A., & Levy, P. H. (1993). Attitudes of executives in Fortune 500 corporations toward the employability of persons with severe disabilities: Industrial and service corporations. *Journal of Applied Rehabilitation Counseling, 24,* 19–31.
Lewin, K. (1951). *Field theory in social science: Selected theoretical papers.* New York: Harper & Row.
Light, R. J., & Pillemer, D. B. (1984). *Summing up: The science of reviewing research.* Cambridge, MA: Harvard University Press.
Link, B. G., & Cullen, F. T. (1986). Contact with the mentally ill and perceptions of how dangerous they are. *Journal of Health and Social Behavior, 27,* 289–303.
Lipsey, M. W., & Wilson, D. B. (1993). The efficacy of psychological, educational, and behavioral treatment: Confirmation from meta-analysis. *American Psychologist, 48,* 1181–1209.
Lipsey, M. W., & Wilson, D. B. (2001). *Practical meta-analysis.* Thousand Oaks, CA: Sage.
Little, R. J. A., & Rubin, D. B. (1987). *Statistical analysis with missing data.* New York: Wiley.
Livingston, R. W., Brewer, M. B., & Alexander, M. G. (2004). *Images, emotions, and prejudice: Qualitative differences in the nature of Black and White racial attitudes.* Paper presented at the annual meeting of the Society for Personality and Social Psychology, Austin, Texas.
Longshore, D., & Wellisch, J. (1981). *The impact of the Emergency School Aid Act on human relations in desegregated elementary schools.* Paper presented at the annual meeting of the American Sociological Association, Toronto, Canada.
Luedtke, A. (2005). European integration, public opinion, and immigration policy: Testing the impact of national identity. *European Union Politics, 6,* 83–112.
Luiz, D., & Krige, P. (1985). The effect of social contact between South African White and colored adolescent girls: A follow-up study. *Journal of Social Psychology, 125,* 407–408.
MacKenzie, B. K. (1948). The importance of contact in determining attitudes toward Negroes. *Journal of Abnormal and Social Psychology, 43,* 417–441.
Mackie, D. M., & Hamilton, D. L. (1993) (Eds.). *Affect, cognition, and stereotyping: Interactive processes in group perception.* San Diego, CA: Academic Press.
Mackie, D. M., & Smith, E. R. (1998). Intergroup relations: Insights from a theoretically integrative approach. *Psychological Review, 105,* 499–529.
Maddens, B., Billiet, J., & Beerten, R. (2000). National identity and the attitude towards foreigners in multi-national states: The case of Belgium. *Journal of Ethnic and Migration Studies, 26,* 45–60.
Maddux, W. M., & Galinsky, A. D. (2009). Cultural borders and mental barriers: The relationship between living abroad and creativity. *Journal of Personality and Social Psychology, 96,* 1047–1061.

Malecki, C. K., & Demaray, M. K. (2002). Measuring perceived social support: Development of the child and adolescent social support scale (CASSS). *Psychology in the Schools, 39*, 1–118.

Mallett, R. K., Huntsinger, J. R., Sinclair, J. R., & Swim, J. K. (2008a). Seeing through their eyes: When majority group members take collective action on behalf of an outgroup. *Group Processes and Intergroup Relations, 11*, 451–470.

Mallett, R. K., Wagner, D. E., & Harrison, P. R. (in press). Understanding the intergroup forecasting error. In L. R. Tropp & R. K. Mallett (Eds.), *Moving beyond prejudice reduction: Pathways to positive intergroup relations*. Washington, DC: American Psychological Association.

Mallett, R. K., & Wilson, T. D. (2010). Increasing positive intergroup contact. *Journal of Experimental Social Psychology, 46*, 382–387.

Mallett, R. K., Wilson, T. D., & Gilbert, D. T. (2008b). Expect the unexpected: Failure to anticipate similarities leads to an intergroup forecasting error. *Journal of Personality and Social Psychology, 94*, 265–277.

Maoz, I. (2000). Multiple conflicts and competing agendas: A framework for conceptualizing structured encounters between groups in conflict – the case of the coexistence project of Jews and Palestinians in Israel. *Peace and Conflict, 6*, 135–156.

Maras, P., & Brown, R. (1996). Effects of contact on children's attitudes toward disability: A longitudinal study. *Journal of Applied Social Psychology, 26*, 2113–2134.

Martin, R., & Hewstone, M. (2008). Majority versus minority influence, message processing and attitude change: The source–context–elaboration model. *Advances in Experimental Social Psychology, 40*, 237–326.

Massey, D. S., & Denton, N. A. (1993). *American apartheid: Segregation and the making of the underclass*. Cambridge, MA: Harvard University Press.

Mathews, D. R., & Prothro, J. W. (1966). *Negroes and the new southern politics*. New York: Harcourt, Brace & World.

Mayda, A. (2006). Who is against immigration? A cross-country investigation of individual attitudes toward immigrants. *Review of Economics and Statistics, 88*, 510–530.

Mazziotta, A., Mummendey, A., Wright, S. C., & Jung, M. (2010, June). *Vicarious intergroup contact as a tool to improve intergroup relations*. Paper presented at the biennial meeting of the Society for the Psychological Study of Social Issues, New Orleans, Louisiana.

McCauley, C., Plummer, M., Moskalenko, S., & Mordkoff, J. T. (2001). The exposure index: A measure of intergroup contact. *Peace and Conflict, 7*, 321–336.

McCauley, C., Worchel, S., Moghaddam, F., & Lee, Y. (2004). Contact and identity in intergroup relations. In Y. Lee, C. McCauley, F. Moghaddam, & S. Worchel (Eds.), *The psychology of ethnic and cultural conflict* (pp. 309–326). Westport, CT: Praeger.

McClelland, K., & Linnander, E. (2006). The role of contact and information in racial attitude change among White college students. *Sociological Inquiry, 76*, 81–115.

McClenahan, C., Cairns, E., Dunn, S., & Morgan, V. (1996). Intergroup friendships: Integrated and desegregated schools in Northern Ireland. *Journal of Social Psychology, 136*, 549–558.

McClendon, M. J. (1974). Interracial contact and the reduction of prejudice. *Sociological Focus*, 7, 47–65.
McConahay, J. B., Hardee, B. B., & Batts, V. (1981). Has racism declined in America? It depends on who is asking and what is asked. *Journal of Conflict Resolution*, 25, 563–579.
McConnell, A. R., & Leibold, J. M. (2001). Relations among the implicit association test, discriminatory behavior, and explicit measures of racial attitudes. *Journal of Experimental Social Psychology*, 37, 435–442.
McFarland, S. (2010). Authoritarianism, social dominance and other roots of generalized prejudice. *Political Psychology*, 31(3), 453–477.
McGarry, J., & O'Leary, B. (1995). *Explaining Northern Ireland: Broken images*. Oxford, UK: Blackwell.
McGarty, C., & de la Haye, A. M. (1997). Stereotype formation: Beyond illusory correlation. In R. Spears, P. J. Oakes, N. Ellemers, & S. A. Haslam (Eds.), *The social psychology of stereotyping and social life* (pp.144–170). Oxford, UK: Blackwell.
McGinnis, S. P. (1990). *Descriptive and evaluative components of stereotypes of computer programmers and their determinants*. Unpublished doctoral dissertation, City University of New York.
McGuire, W. J. (1960a). Cognitive consistency and attitude change. *Journal of Abnormal and Social Psychology*, 60, 345–353.
McGuire, W. J. (1960b). A syllogistic analysis of cognitive relationships. In M. J. Rosenberg, C. I. Hovland, W. J. McGuire, R. P. Abelson, & J. W. Brehm (Eds.), *Attitude organization and change: An analysis of consistency among attitude components* (pp. 65–111). New Haven, CT: Yale University Press.
McGuire, W. J., McGuire, C. V., Child, P., & Fujioka, T. (1978). Salience of ethnicity in the spontaneous self-concept as a function of one's ethnic distinctiveness in the social environment. *Journal of Personality and Social Psychology*, 36, 511–520.
McKay, S., & Pittam, J. (1993). Determinants of Anglo-Australian stereotypes of the Vietnamese in Australia. *Australian Journal of Psychology*, 45, 17–23.
McLaughlin-Volpe, T., Aron, A., Wright, S. C., & Reis, H. T. (2000). *Intergroup social interaction and intergroup prejudice: Quantity versus quality*. Unpublished manuscript, State University of New York, Stony Brook.
Mendoza-Denton, R., Downey, G., Purdie, V. J., Davis, A., & Pietrzak, J. (2002). Sensitivity to status-based rejection: Implications for African American students' college experience. *Journal of Personality and Social Psychology*, 83, 896–918.
Mendoza-Denton, R., Page-Gould, E., & Pietrzak, J. (2006). Mechanisms for coping with status-based rejection expectations. In S. Levin & C. Van Laar (Eds.), *Stigma and group inequality: Social psychological perspectives* (pp.151–169). Mahwah, NJ: Lawrence Erlbaum Associates.
Migacheva, K., & Tropp, L. R. (2008, August). Responses to intergroup contact and metaperceptions among Black and White American youth. Paper presented at the EAESP-SPSSI small group meeting on *Intergroup contact: Recent advancements in basic and applied research*, Philipps University, Marburg, Germany.
Migacheva, K., Tropp, L. R., & Crocker, J. (2011). Focusing beyond the self: Goal orientations in intergroup relations. In L. R. Tropp & R. Mallett (Eds.), *Moving beyond prejudice reduction: Pathways to positive intergroup relations*. Washington, DC: American Psychological Association.

Milgram, S. (1974). *Obedience to authority: An experimental view*. New York: Harper & Row.

Miller, D. A., Smith, E. R., & Mackie, D. M. (2004). Effects of intergroup contact and political predispositions on prejudice: The role of intergroup emotions. *Group Processes and Intergroup Relations, 7*, 221–237.

Miller, N. (2002). Personalization and the promise of contact theory. *Journal of Social Issues, 58*, 387–410.

Miller, N., Brewer, M. B., & Edwards, K. (1985). Cooperative interaction in desegregated settings: A laboratory analogue. *Journal of Social Issues, 41*, 63–79.

Minard, R. D. (1952). Race relations in the Pocahontas coal field. *Journal of Social Issues, 8*, 29–44.

Molina, L. E., & Wittig, M. A. (2006). Relative importance of contact conditions in explaining prejudice reduction in a classroom context: Separate and equal? *Journal of Social Issues, 62*, 489–509.

Molina, L. E., Wittig, M. A., & Giang, M. T. (2004). Mutual acculturation and social categorization: A comparison of two perspectives in intergroup bias. *Group Processes and Intergroup Relations, 7*, 239–265.

Monteith, M., & Spicer C. V. (2000). Contents and correlates of Whites' and Blacks' racial attitudes. *Journal of Experimental Social Psychology, 36*, 125–154.

Moreland, R. L., & Zajonc, R. B. (1977). Is stimulus recognition a necessary condition for the occurrence of exposure effects? *Journal of Personality and Social Psychology, 35*, 191–199.

Moreno, K. N., & Bodenhausen, G. V. (1999). Resisting stereotype change: The role of motivation and attentional capacity in defending social beliefs. *Group Processes and Intergroup Relations, 2*, 5–16.

Morrison, E. W., & Herlihy, J. M. (1992). Becoming the best place to work: Managing diversity at American Express travel related services. In S. E. Jackson & Associates (Eds.), *Diversity in the workplace: Human resources initiatives* (pp. 203–226). New York: Guilford Press.

Mosteller, F., & Colditz, G. A. (1996). Understanding research synthesis (meta-analysis). *Annual Review of Public Health, 17*, 1–23.

Mulder, M., & Krahn, H. (2005). Individual- and community-level determinants of support for immigration and cultural diversity in Canada. *Canadian Journal of Sociology and Anthropology, 42*, 421–444.

Mummendey, A., & Wenzel, M. (1999). Social discrimination and tolerance in intergroup relations: Reactions to intergroup difference. *Personality and Social Psychology Review, 3*, 158–174.

Mutz, D. C. (2002). Cross-cutting social networks: Testing democratic theory in practice. *American Political Science Review, 96*, 111–126.

Nagda, B. A. (2006). Breaking barriers, crossing borders, building bridges: Communication processes in intergroup dialogues. *Journal of Social Issues, 62*, 553–576.

Nash, D. (1976). The personal consequences of a year of study abroad. *Journal of Higher Education, 47*, 191–203.

National Conference for Community and Justice (2000). *Taking America's pulse: NCCJ's survey of intergroup relations in the United States*. New York: NCCJ.

Niens, U., Cairns, E., & Hewstone, M. (2002). Contact and conflict in Ireland. In O. Hargie & D. Dickson (Eds.), *Researching the Troubles: Social science perspectives* on the Northern Ireland conflict (pp. 123–140). Edinburgh, Scotland: Mainstream Publishing.

Oaker, G., & Brown, R. (1986). Intergroup relations in a hospital setting: A further test of social identity theory. *Human Relations, 39,* 767–778.

Oberschall, A. (2001). From ethnic cooperation to violence and war in Yugoslavia. In D. Chirot & M. E. P. Seligman (Eds.), *Ethnopolitical warfare: Causes, consequences, and possible solutions* (pp. 119–150). Washington, DC: American Psychological Association.

Oliner, P. M. (2004). *Saving the forsaken: Religious culture and the rescue of Jews in Nazi Europe.* New Haven, CT: Yale University Press.

Oliner, S. P., & Oliner, P. M. (1988). *The altruistic personality: Rescuers of Jews in Nazi Europe.* New York: Free Press.

Oliver, J. E., & Wong, J. (2003). Intergroup prejudice in multiethnic settings. *American Journal of Political Science, 47,* 567–582.

Olson, J. M., & Stone, J. (2005). The influence of behavior on attitudes. In D. Albarracín, B. T. Johnson, & M. P. Zanna (Eds.), *The handbook of attitudes* (pp. 223–271). Mahwah, NJ: Lawrence Erlbaum Associates.

Operario, D., & Fiske, S. T. (2001). Causes and consequences of stereotypes in organizations. In M. London (Ed.), *How people evaluate others in organizations* (pp. 45–62). Mahwah, NJ: Lawrence Erlbaum Associates.

Orfield, G., & Lee, C. (2006). *Racial transformation and the changing nature of segregation.* A report of the Civil Rights Project, Harvard University.

Orfield, G., & Lee, C. (2007). *Historic reversals, accelerating resegregation, and the need for new integration strategies.* A report of the Civil Rights Project, University of California, Los Angeles.

Osgood, C. E., Suci, G. J., & Tannenbaum, P. H. (1957). *The measurement of meaning.* Urbana, IL: University of Illinois Press.

Ostrom, T. M. (1969). The relationship between the affective, behavioral, and cognitive components of attitude. *Journal of Experimental Social Psychology, 5,* 12–30.

Ostrom, T. M., Skowronski, J. J., & Nowak, A. (1994). The cognitive foundation of attitudes: It's a wonderful construct. In P. G. Devine, D. L. Hamilton, & T. M. Ostrom (Eds.), *Social cognition: Impact on social psychology* (pp. 195–258). New York: Academic Press.

Page-Gould, E., Mendoza-Denton, R., Alegre, J. M., & Siy, J. O. (2010). Understanding the impact of cross-group friendship on interactions with novel outgroup members. *Journal of Personality and Social Psychology, 98,* 775–793.

Page-Gould, E., Mendoza-Denton, R., & Tropp, L. R. (2008). With a little help from my cross-group friend: Reducing anxiety in intergroup contexts through cross-group friendship. *Journal of Personality and Social Psychology, 95,* 1080–1094.

Palmer, D. (1996). Determinants of Canadian attitudes toward immigration: More than just racism? *Canadian Journal of Behavioural Science, 28,* 180–192.

Paluck, E. L., & Green, D. P. (2009). Prejudice reduction: What works? A review and assessment of research and practice. *Annual Review of Psychology, 60,* 339–367.

Pantoja, A. (2006). Against the tide? Core American values and attitudes toward U.S. immigration policy in the mid-1990s. *Journal of Ethnic and Migration Studies, 32,* 515–531.

Paolini, S., Hewstone, M., Cairns, E., & Voci, A. (2004). Effects of direct and indirect cross-group friendships on judgments of Catholics and Protestants in

Northern Ireland: The mediating role of an anxiety-reduction mechanism. *Personality and Social Psychology Bulletin, 30,* 770–786.
Parker, J. H. (1968). The interaction of Negroes and Whites in an integrated church setting. *Social Forces, 46,* 359–366.
Patchen, M. (1982). *Black–White contact in schools.* West Lafayette, IN: Purdue University Press.
Patchen, M. (1999). *Diversity and unity: Relations between racial and ethnic groups.* Chicago, IL: Nelson-Hall.
Patchen, M., Davidson, J. D., Hofmann, G., & Brown, W. R. (1977). Determinants of students' interracial behavior and opinion change. *Sociology of Education, 50,* 55–75.
Penn, D. L., Guynan, K., Daily, T., Spaulding, W. D., Garbin, C. P., & Sullivan, M. (1994). Dispelling the stigma of schizophrenia: What sort of information is best? *Schizophrenia Bulletin, 20,* 567–577.
Pettigrew, T. F. (1959). Regional differences in anti-Negro prejudice. *Journal of Abnormal and Social Psychology, 59,* 28–36.
Pettigrew, T. F. (1961). Social psychology and desegregation research. *American Psychologist, 16,* 105–112.
Pettigrew, T. F. (1964). *A Profile of the Negro American.* New York: Van Nostrand.
Pettigrew, T. F. (1971). *Racially separate or together?* New York: McGraw-Hill.
Pettigrew, T. F. (1979). The ultimate attribution error: Extending Allport's cognitive analysis of prejudice. *Personality and Social Psychology Bulletin, 5,* 461–476.
Pettigrew, T. F. (1986). The contact hypothesis revisited. In M. Hewstone & R. Brown (Eds.), *Contact and conflict in intergroup encounters* (pp. 169–195). Oxford, UK: Blackwell.
Pettigrew, T. F. (1991). The importance of cumulative effects: A neglected emphasis of Sherif's work. In D. Granberg & G. Sarup (Eds.), *Social judgment and intergroup relations: Essays in honor of Muzafer Sherif* (pp. 89–103). New York: Springer-Verlag.
Pettigrew, T. F. (1996). *How to think like a social scientist.* New York: Harper-Collins.
Pettigrew, T. F. (1997a). Generalized intergroup contact effects on prejudice. *Personality and Social Psychology Bulletin, 23,* 173–185.
Pettigrew, T. F. (1997b). The affective component of prejudice: Empirical support of the new view. In S. A. Tuch & J. K. Martin (Eds.), *Racial attitudes in the 1990s: Continuity and change* (pp. 76–90). Westport, CT: Praeger.
Pettigrew, T. F. (1998). Intergroup contact theory. *Annual Review of Psychology, 49,* 65–85.
Pettigrew, T. F. (2000). Systematizing the predictors of prejudice. In D. Sears, J. Sidanius, & L. D. Bobo (Eds.), *Racialized politics: The debate about racism in America* (pp. 280–301). Chicago, IL: University of Chicago Press.
Pettigrew, T. F. (2004a). The social science study of American race relations in the 20th century. In C. S. Crandall & M. Schaller (Eds.), *The social psychology of prejudice: Historical and contemporary issues* (pp. 1–32). Seattle, WA: Lewinian Press.
Pettigrew, T. F. (2004b). Ethnocentrism. In K. Kempf-Leonard (Ed.), *Encyclopedia of social measurement* (pp. 827–831). San Diego, CA: Academic Press.
Pettigrew, T. F. (2004c). Intergroup contact: Theory, research, and new perspectives. In J. A. Banks & C. A. M. Banks (Eds.), *Handbook of research on multicultural education* (2nd ed., pp. 770–781). San Francisco, CA: Jossey-Bass.

Pettigrew, T. F. (2006). Commentary: The advantages of multi-level approaches. *Journal of Social Issues, 62,* 615–620.
Pettigrew, T. F. (2007a). European attitudes toward immigrants. In J. Peacock & P. Thornton (Eds.), *Identity matters: How ethnic and sectarian allegiances both prevent and promote collective violence* (pp. 99–119). New York: Berghahn Books.
Pettigrew, T. F. (2007b). Social identity matters: Predicting prejudice and violence in Western Europe. In J. Peacock & P. Thornton (Eds.), *Identity matters: How ethnic and sectarian allegiances both prevent and promote collective violence* (pp. 34–48). New York: Berghahn Books.
Pettigrew, T. F. (2007c). Still a long way to go: American Black–White relations today. In G. Adams, M. Biernat, N. R. Branscombe, C. S. Crandall, and L. S. Wrightsman (Eds.), *Commemorating Brown: The social psychology of racism and discrimination* (pp. 45–61). Washington, DC: American Psychological Association.
Pettigrew, T. F. (2008). Future directions for intergroup contact theory and research. *International Journal of Intercultural Relations, 32,* 187–199.
Pettigrew, T. F. (2009). Contact's secondary transfer effect: Do intergroup contact effects spread to non-participating outgroups? *Social Psychology, 40,* 55–65.
Pettigrew, T. F., Christ, O., Wagner, U., Meertens, R., van Dick, R., & Zick, A. (2007a). Relative deprivation and intergroup prejudice. *Journal of Social Issues, 64,* 385–401.
Pettigrew, T. F., & Cramer, M. R. (1959). The demography of desegregation. *Journal of Social Issues, 15,* 61–71.
Pettigrew, T. F., & Meertens, R. W. (1995). Subtle and blatant prejudice in Western Europe. *European Journal of Social Psychology, 57,* 57–75.
Pettigrew, T. F., Stellmacher, J., Christ, O., & Wagner, U. (under review). *How and why does authoritarianism predict prejudice? The mediators of a global phenomenon.*
Pettigrew, T. F., & Tropp, L. R. (2000). Does intergroup contact reduce prejudice? Recent meta-analytic findings. In S. Oskamp (Ed.), *Reducing prejudice and discrimination: The Claremont Symposium on Applied Social Psychology* (pp. 93–114). Mahwah, NJ: Lawrence Erlbaum Associates.
Pettigrew, T. F., & Tropp, L. R. (2006). A meta-analytic test of intergroup contact theory. *Journal of Personality and Social Psychology, 90,* 751–783.
Pettigrew, T. F., & Tropp, L. R. (2008). How does intergroup contact reduce prejudice? Meta-analytic tests of three mediators. *European Journal of Social Psychology, 38,* 922–934.
Pettigrew, T. F., Wagner, U., & Christ, O. (2007b). Who opposes immigration? Comparing German results with those of North America. *DuBois Review, 4,* 19–39.
Pettigrew, T. F., Wagner, U., & Christ, O. (2010). Population ratios and prejudice: Modeling both contact and threat effects. *Journal of Ethnic and Migration Studies, 36,* 635–650.
Pettigrew, T. F., Wagner, U., Christ, O. & Stellmacher, J. (2007c). Direct and indirect intergroup contact effects on prejudice: A normative interpretation. *International Journal of Intercultural Relations, 31,* 41–425.
Pew Research Center (2006). *America's immigration quandary: No consensus on immigration problem or proposed fixes.* Washington, DC: Pew Research Center. Retrieved March 21, 2007, from http://www.pewhispanic.org/files/reports/63.pdf

Pinel, E. C. (1999). Stigma consciousness: The psychological legacy of social stereotypes. *Journal of Personality and Social Psychology, 76,* 114–128.
Pinel, E. C. (2002). Stigma consciousness in intergroup contexts: The power of conviction. *Journal of Experimental Social Psychology, 38,* 178–185.
Plant, E. A. (2004). Responses to interracial interactions over time. *Personality and Social Psychology Bulletin, 30,* 1458–1471.
Plant, E. A., Butz, D. A., & Tartakovsky, M. (2008). Interethnic interactions: Expectancies, emotions, and behavioral intentions. *Group Processes and Intergroup Relations, 11,* 555–574,
Plant, E. A., & Devine, P. G. (1998). Internal and external motivation to respond without prejudice. *Journal of Personality and Social Psychology, 75,* 811–832.
Plant, E. A., & Devine, P. G. (2003). The antecedents and implications of interracial anxiety. *Personality and Social Psychology Bulletin, 29,* 790–801.
Poore, A. G., Gagne, F., Barlow, K. M., Taylor, J. E., & Wright, S. C. (2002). Contact and the person–group discrimination discrepancy in an Inuit community. *Journal of Psychology, 136,* 371–382.
Popan, J. R., Kenworthy, J. B., Frame, M. C., Lyons, P. A., & Snuggs, S. J. (2010). Political groups in contact: The role of attributions for outgroup attitudes in reducing antipathy. *European Journal of Social Psychology, 40,* 86–104.
Porter, J. D. R. (1971). *Black child, White child: The development of racial attitudes.* Cambridge, MA: Harvard University Press.
Powers, D. A., & Ellison, C. G. (1995). Interracial contact and Black racial attitudes: The contact hypothesis and selectivity bias. *Social Forces, 74,* 205–226.
Preacher, K. J., & Hayes, A. F. (2004). SPSS and SAS procedures for estimating indirect effects in simple mediation models. *Behavior Research Methods, Instruments, and Computers, 36,* 717–731.
Preacher, K. J., & Leonardelli, G. J. (2006). Calculation for the Sobel test: An interaction calculation tool for mediation tests. Retrieved August 21, 2006, from http://www.psych.ku/preacher/sobel
Premack, S. L., & Hunter, J. E. (1988). Individual unionization decisions. *Psychological Bulletin, 103,* 223–234.
Prewitt, K. (1968). Political efficacy. In D. L. Sills (Ed.), *International encyclopedia of the social sciences* (Vol. 12. pp. 225–228). New York: Macmillan/Free Press.
Pruett, S. R., & Chan, F. (2006). The development and psychometric validation of the disability attitude implicit association test. *Rehabilitation Psychology, 51,* 202–213.
Putnam, R. (2007). *E pluribus unum*: Diversity and community in the twenty-first century: The 2006 John Skytte prize lecture. *Scandinavian Political Studies, 30,* 137–174.
Quinn, D. (2006). Concealable versus conspicuous stigmatized identities. In S. Levin & C. Van Laar (Eds.), *Stigma and group inequality: Social psychological perspectives* (pp. 83–103). Mahwah, NJ: Lawrence Erlbaum Associates.
Rabushka, A. (1970). Affective, cognitive, and behavioral consistency of Chinese–Malay interracial attitudes. *Journal of Social Psychology, 82,* 35–41.
Raudenbush, S. W. (1994). Random effects models. In H. Cooper & L. V. Hedges (Eds.), *Handbook of research synthesis* (pp. 301–321). New York: Russell Sage Foundation.
Ray, J. J. (1983). Racial attitudes and the contact hypothesis. *Journal of Social Psychology, 119,* 3–10.

Reagans, R. (1998). Differences in social differences: Examining third party effects on relational stability. *Social Networks, 20,* 143–157.
Reicher, S. (2007). Rethinking the paradigm of prejudice. *South African Journal of Psychology, 35,* 412–432.
Reis, H. J., & Shaver, P. (1988). Intimacy as an interpersonal process. In S. Duck, D. F. Hay, S. E. Hobfell, W. Ickes, & B. M. Montgomery (Eds.), *Handbook of personal relationships: Theory, research and interventions* (pp. 367–389). Oxford, UK: Wiley.
Reitzes, D. C. (1953). The role of organizational structures: Union versus neighborhood in a tension situation. *Journal of Social Issues, 9,* 37–44.
Rhodes, G., Halberstadt, J., & Brajkovich, G. (2001). Generalization of mere exposure effects to averaged composite faces. *Social Cognition, 19,* 57–70.
Richeson, J. A., & Nussbaum, R. J. (2004). The impact of multiculturalism versus color-blindness on racial bias. *Journal of Experimental Social Psychology, 40,* 417–423.
Richeson, J. A., & Shelton, J. N. (2007). Negotiating interracial interactions: Costs, consequences, and possibilities. *Current Directions in Psychological Science, 16,* 316–320.
Riek, B. M., Mania, E. W., & Gaertner, S. L. (2006). Intergroup threat and outgroup attitudes: A meta-analytic review. *Personality and Social Psychology Review, 10,* 336–353.
Riley, R. T., & Pettigrew, T. F. (1976). Dramatic events and attitude change. *Journal of Personality and Social Psychology, 34,* 1004–1015.
Riordan, C. (1978). Equal-status interracial contact: A review and revision of the concept. *International Journal of Intercultural Relations, 2,* 161–185.
Riordan, C., & Ruggiero, J. (1980). Producing equal-status interracial interaction: A replication. *Social Psychology Quarterly, 43,* 131–136.
Robbins, I., Cooper, A., & Bender, M. P. (1992). The relationship between knowledge, attitudes and degree of contact with AIDS and HIV. *Journal of Advanced Nursing, 17,* 198–203.
Robinson, J. W., & Preston, J. D. (1976). Equal status contact and modification of racial prejudice: A reexamination of the contact hypothesis. *Social Forces, 54,* 911–924.
Roccato, M., & Ricolfi, L. (2005). On the correlation between right-wing authoritarianism and social dominance orientation. *Basic and Applied Social Psychology, 27,* 187–200.
Rodriguez, J., & Gurin, P. (1990). The relationships of intergroup contact to social identity and political consciousness. *Hispanic Journal of Behavioral Sciences, 20,* 235–255.
Rogers, M., Hennigan, K., Bowman, C., & Miller, N. (1984). Intergroup acceptance in classroom and playground settings. In N. Miller & M. B. Brewer (Eds.), *Groups in contact: The psychology of desegregation* (pp. 187–212). Orlando, FL: Academic Press.
Rohmann, A., Florack, A., & Piontkowski, U. (2006). The role of discordant acculturation attitudes in perceived threat: An analysis of host and immigrant attitudes in Germany. *International Journal of Intercultural Relations, 30,* 683–702.
Rojahn, K., & Pettigrew, T. F. (1992). Memory for schema-relevant information: A meta-analytic resolution. *British Journal of Social Psychology, 31,* 81–109.

Ronning, J. A., & Nabuzoka, D. (1993). Promoting social interaction and status of children with intellectual disabilities in Zambia. *Journal of Special Education, 27,* 277–305.

Rooney-Rebeck, P., & Jason, L. (1986). Prevention of prejudice in elementary school students. *Journal of Primary Prevention, 7,* 63–73.

Rosenthal, R. (1991). *Meta-analytic procedures for social research.* Newbury Park, CA: Sage.

Rosenthal, R. (1995). Writing meta-analytic reviews. *Psychological Bulletin, 118,* 183–192.

Ross, L., & Nisbett, R. (1991). *The person and the situation.* New York: McGraw-Hill.

Ross, M. H. (1998). Review of *Ethnic conflict: Commerce, culture, and the contact thesis. Canadian Journal of Political Science, 31,* 393–395.

Rothbart, M. (1996). Category-exemplar dynamics and stereotype change. *International Journal of Intercultural Relations, 20,* 305–321.

Rothbart, M., & John, O. P. (1985). Social categorization and behavioral episodes: A cognitive analysis of the effects of intergroup contact. *Journal of Social Issues, 41,* 81–104.

Rothbart, M., & John, O. P. (1993). Intergroup relations and stereotype change: A social-cognitive analysis and some longitudinal findings. In P. M. Sniderman, P. E. Tetlock, & E. G. Carmines (Eds.), *Prejudice, politics and the American dilemma* (pp. 32–59). Stanford, CA: Stanford University Press.

Rothbart, M., & Lewis, S. H. (1994). Cognitive processes and intergroup relations: A historical perspective. In P. G. Devine, D. L. Hamilton, & T. M. Ostrom (Eds.), *Social cognition: Impact on social psychology* (pp. 347–382). San Diego, CA: Academic Press.

Rothbart, M., Sriram, N., & Davis-Stitt, C. (1996). The retrieval of typical and atypical category members. *Journal of Experimental Social Psychology, 32,* 309–336.

Rothwell, J. T. (2009). *Trust in diverse, integrated cities: A revisionist perspective.* Unpublished paper, Woodrow Wilson School of Public and International Affairs, Princeton University, New Jersey.

Rotton, J., Foos, P. W., Van Meek, L., & Levitt, M. (1995). Publication practices and the file drawer problem: A survey of published authors. *Journal of Social Behavior and Personality, 10,* 1–13.

Rudman, L. A., Greenwald, A. G., Mellott, D. S., & Schwartz, J. L. K. (1999). Measuring the automatic components of prejudice: Flexibility and generality of the Implicit Association Test. *Social Cognition, 17,* 437–465.

Saguy, T., Tausch, N., Dovidio, J. F., & Pratto, F. (2009). The irony of harmony: Intergroup contact can produce false expectations for equality. *Psychological Science, 20,* 114–121.

Saguy, T., Tausch, N., Dovidio, J. F., Pratto, F., & Singh, P. (in press). Tension and harmony in intergroup relations. In M. Mikulincer & P. R. Shaver (Eds.), *Understanding and reducing aggression, violence, and their consequences.* Washington, DC: American Psychological Association.

Saucier, D. A., Miller, C. T., & Doucet, N. (2005). Differences in helping Whites and Blacks: A meta-analysis. *Personality and Social Psychology Review, 9,* 2–16.

Schiappa, E., Gregg, P., & Hewes, D. E. (2005). The parasocial contact hypothesis. *Communication Monographs, 72,* 92–115.

Schiappa, E., Gregg, P., & Hewes, D. E. (2006). Can one TV show make a difference? Will and Grace and the parasocial contact hypothesis. *Journal of Homosexuality, 51,* 15–37.

Schlueter, E., & Scheepers, P. (2010). The relationship between outgroup size and anti-outgroup attitudes: A theoretical synthesis and empirical test of group threat and intergroup contact theory. *Social Science Research, 39,* 285–295.

Schofield, J. W. (1978). School desegregation and intergroup attitudes. In D. Bar-Tal & L. Saxe (Eds.), *Social psychology of education: Theory and research* (pp. 330–363). Washington, DC: Halsted Press.

Schofield, J. W. (1979). The impact of positively structured contact on intergroup behavior: Does it last under adverse conditions? *Social Psychology Quarterly, 42,* 280–284.

Schofield, J. W. (1989). *Black and White in school: Trust, tension, or tolerance?* New York: Teachers College Press.

Schofield, J. W. (1995). Improving intergroup relations among students. In J. A. Banks & C. A. McGee Banks (Eds.), *Handbook of research on multicultural education* (pp. 635–646). New York: Macmillan.

Schofield, J. W., & Eurich-Fulcer, R. (2001). When and how school desegregation improves intergroup relations. In R. Brown & S. L. Gaertner (Eds.), *Blackwell handbook of social psychology: Intergroup processes* (pp. 475–494). Malden, MA: Blackwell.

Schofield, J. W., & Sagar, H. A. (1977). Peer interaction patterns in an integrated middle school. *Social Psychology Quarterly, 40,* 130–138.

Schofield, J. W., & Sagar, H. A. (1979). The social context of learning in an interracial school. In R. Rist (Ed.), *Inside desegregated schools* (pp. 155–199). San Francisco, CA: Academic Press.

Searles, R., & Williams, Jr., S. A. (1962). Negro college students' participation in sit-ins. *Social Forces, 40,* 215–220.

Sears, D. O. (1986). College sophomores in the laboratory: Influences of a narrow data base on social psychology's view of human nature. *Journal of Personality and Social Psychology, 51,* 515–530.

Sechrist, G. B., & Stangor, C. (2001). Perceived consensus influences intergroup behavior and stereotype accessibility. *Journal of Personality and Social Psychology, 80,* 645–654.

Seefeldt, C. (1987). The effects of preschoolers' visits to a nursing home. *The Gerontologist, 27,* 228–232.

Shadish, W. R. (1996). Meta-analysis and the exploration of causal mediating processes: A primer of examples, methods, and issues. *Psychological Methods, 1,* 47–65.

Shadish, W. R., Doherty, M., & Montgomery, L. M. (1989). How many studies are in the file drawer? An estimate from the family/marital psychotherapy literature. *Clinical Psychology Review, 9,* 589–603.

Shelton, J. N. (2000). A reconceptualization of how we study issues of racial prejudice. *Personality and Social Psychology Review, 4,* 374–390.

Shelton, J. N. (2003). Interpersonal concerns in social encounters between majority and minority group members. *Group Processes and Intergroup Relations, 6,* 171–185.

Shelton, J. N., & Richeson, J. A. (2005). Intergroup contact and pluralistic ignorance. *Journal of Personality and Social Psychology, 88,* 91–107.

Shelton, J. N., & Richeson, J. A. (2006). Ethnic minorities' racial attitudes and contact experiences with White people. *Cultural Diversity and Ethnic Minority Psychology, 12*, 149–164.

Shelton, J. N., Richeson, J. A., Salvatore, J., & Trawalter, S. (2005). Ironic effects of racial bias during interracial interactions. *Psychological Science, 16*, 397–402.

Shelton, J. N., Richeson, J. A., & Vorauer, J. D. (2006). Threatened identities and interethnic interactions. *European Review of Social Psychology, 17*, 321–358.

Sherif, M. (1936). *The psychology of social norms*. Oxford, UK: Harper.

Sherif, M. (1966). *In common predicament*. Boston, MA: Houghton Mifflin.

Sherif, M., Harvey, O. J., White, J. B., Hood, W. R., & Sherif, C. W. (1961). *Intergroup conflict and cooperation: The Robbers Cave experiment*. Norman, OK: University of Oklahoma Book Exchange.

Shook, N. J., & Fazio, R. H. (2008). Interracial roommate relationships: An experimental field test of the contact hypothesis. *Psychological Science, 19*, 717–723.

Short, R. (2004). Justice, politics, and prejudice regarding immigration attitudes. *Current Research in Social Psychology, 9*, 193–208. Retrieved March 21, 2007, from http://www.uiowa.edu/~grpproc/crisp/crisp.9.14.html

Shrum, W., Cheek, N. H., & Hunter, S. M. (1988). Friendship in school: Gender and racial homophily. *Sociology of Education, 61*, 227–239.

Sidanius, J., Levin, S., Van Laar, C., & Sears, D. O. (2008). *The diversity challenge: Social identity and intergroup relations on the college campus*. New York: Russell Sage Foundation.

Sidanius, J., & Pratto, F. (1999). *Social dominance: An intergroup theory of social hierarchy and oppression*. Cambridge, MA: Cambridge University Press.

Sidanius, J., Van Laar, C., Levin, S., & Sinclair, S. (2004). Ethnic enclaves and the dynamics of social identity on the college campus: The good, the bad, and the ugly. *Journal of Personality and Social Psychology, 87*, 96–110.

Sigelman, L., & Welch, S. (1991). *Black Americans' views of racial inequality: The dream deferred*. Cambridge, UK: Cambridge University Press.

Sigelman, L., & Welch, S. (1993). The contact hypothesis revisited: Black–White interaction and positive racial attitudes. *Social Forces, 71*, 781–795.

Simon, A. (1995). Some correlates of individuals' attitudes toward lesbians. *Journal of Homosexuality, 29*, 89–103.

Simon, B., & Klandermans, B. (2001). Politicized collective identity: A social-psychological analysis. *American Psychologist, 56*, 319–331.

Simon, B., & Ruhe, D. (2008). Identity and politicization among Turkish migrants in Germany: The role of dual identification. *Journal of Personality and Social Psychology, 95*, 1354–1366.

Sims, V. M., & Patrick, J. R. (1936). Attitude toward the Negro of northern and southern college students. *Journal of Social Psychology, 7*, 192–204.

Slavin, R. E. (1979). Effects of biracial learning teams on cross-racial friendships. *Journal of Educational Psychology, 71*, 381–387.

Slavin, R. E. (1983). *Cooperative learning*. New York: Longman.

Slavin, R. E. (1985). Cooperative learning: Applying contact theory in desegregated schools. *Journal of Social Issues, 41*, 45–62.

Slavin, R. E., & Cooper, R. (2000). Improving intergroup relations: Lessons learned from cooperative learning programs. *Journal of Social Issues, 55*, 647–663.

Smith, E. R. (1993). Social identity and social emotions: Toward new conceptualizations of prejudice. In D. Mackie & D. Hamilton (Eds.), *Affect, cognition, and*

stereotyping: Interactive processes in group perception (pp. 137–166). San Diego, CA: Academic Press.
Smith, H. P. (1955). Do intercultural experiences affect attitudes? *Journal of Abnormal and Social Psychology, 51*, 469–477.
Smith, H., & Pettigrew, T. F. (2011). Relative deprivation and mobilization for social change: A meta-analytic test. Unpublished paper, Sonoma State University, Rohnert Park, California.
Smith, T. W. (2002). Measuring inter-racial friendships. *Social Science Research, 31*, 576–593.
Sobel, M. E. (1982). Asymptotic intervals for indirect effects in structural equations models. In S. Leinhart (Ed.), *Sociological methodology* (pp. 290–312). San Francisco, CA: Jossey-Bass.
Sommer, B. (1987). The file drawer effect and publication rates in menstrual cycle research. *Psychology of Women Quarterly, 11*, 233–242.
Sommers, S. R. (2006). On racial diversity and group decision making: Identifying multiple effects of racial composition on jury deliberations. *Journal of Personality and Social Psychology, 90*, 597–612.
Sommers, S. R., Warp, L. S., & Mahoney, C. C. (2008). Cognitive effects of racial diversity: White individuals' information processing in heterogeneous groups. *Journal of Experimental Social Psychology, 44*, 1129–1136.
Southwell, P., & Everest, M. J. (1998). The electoral consequences of alienation: Non-voting and protest voting in the 1992 presidential race. *Social Science Journal, 35*, 43–51.
Spangenberg, J., & Nel, E. M. (1983). The effects of equal-status contact on ethnic attitudes. *Journal of Social Psychology, 121*, 173–180.
Spencer-Rodgers, J., & McGovern, T. (2002). Attitudes toward the culturally different: The role of intercultural communication barriers, affective responses, consensual stereotypes, and perceived threat. *International Journal of Intercultural Relations, 26*, 609–631.
Stangor, C., Jonas, K., Stroebe, W., & Hewstone, M. (1996). Influence of student exchange on national stereotypes, attitudes and perceived group variability. *European Journal of Social Psychology, 26*, 663–675.
Stangor, C., Sullivan, L. A., & Ford, T. E. (1991). Affective and cognitive determinants of prejudice. *Social Cognition, 9*, 359–380.
Stearns, E., Buchmann, C., & Bonneau, K. (2009). Interracial friendships in the transition to college: Do birds of a feather flock together once they leave the nest? *Sociology of Education, 82*, 173–195.
Steele, C. (1997). A threat in the air: How stereotypes shape the intellectual identities and performance of women and African Americans. *American Psychologist, 52*, 613–629.
Stein, R., Post, S., & Rinden, A. (2000). Reconciling context and contact effects on racial attitudes. *Political Research Quarterly, 53*, 285–303.
Stephan, W. G. (1987). The contact hypothesis in intergroup relations. In C. Hendrick (Ed.), *Review of personality and social psychology: Group processes and intergroup relations* (Vol. 9, pp. 13–40). Newbury Park, CA: Sage.
Stephan, W. G., Boniecki, K. A., Ybarra, O., Bettencourt, A., Ervin, K. S., Jackson, L. A., et al. (2002). The role of threats in the racial attitudes of Blacks and Whites. *Personality and Social Psychology Bulletin, 28*, 1242–1254.

Stephan, W. G., & Stephan, C. W. (1984). The role of ignorance in intergroup relations. In N. Miller & M. B. Brewer (Eds.), *Groups in contact: The psychology of desegregation* (pp. 229–255). Orlando, FL: Academic Press.

Stephan, W. G., & Stephan, C. W. (1985). Intergroup anxiety. *Journal of Social Issues, 41,* 157–175.

Stephan, W. G., Stephan, C. W., & Gudykunst, W. B. (1999). Anxiety in intergroup relations: A comparison of anxiety/uncertainty management theory and integrated threat theory. *International Journal of Intercultural Relations, 23,* 613–628.

Stephan, W. G., Ybarra, O., & Morrison, K. R. (2009). Intergroup threat theory. In T. D. Nelson (Ed.), *Handbook of prejudice, stereotyping, and discrimination* (pp. 43–59). New York: Psychology Press.

Sterne, J. A. C., & Egger, M. (2000). High false positive rates for trim and fill method. *British Journal of Medicine.* Retrieved February 5, 2004, from http://bmj.com/cgi/eletters/320/7249/1574#EL1

Stolle, D., Soroka, S., & Johnson, R. (2008). When does diversity erode trust? Neighborhood diversity, interpersonal trust, and mediating effect of social interactions. *Political Studies, 56,* 57–75.

Stouffer, S. A., Schuman, E. A., DeVinney, L. C., Star, S. A., & Williams, Jr., R. M. (1949). *The American soldier: Adjustment during army life* (Vol. 1). Princeton, NJ: Princeton University Press.

Sumner, W. G. (1906). *Folkways.* New York: Ginn.

Swart, H., Hewstone, M., Christ, O., & Voci, A. (2010). The impact of cross-group friendships in South Africa: Affective mediators and multi-group comparisons. *Journal of Social Issues, 66,* 309–333.

Swim, J. K., Hyers, L. L., Cohen, L. L., & Ferguson, M. J. (2001). Everyday sexism: Evidence for its incidence, nature, and psychological impact from three diary studies. *Journal of Social Issues, 57,* 31–53.

Swim, J. K., Hyers, L. L., Cohen, L. L., Fitzgerald, D. C., & Bylsma, W. H. (2003). African American colleges students' experiences with everyday racism: Characteristics of and responses to these incidents. *Journal of Black Psychology, 29,* 38–67.

Tajfel, H. (1970). Experiments in intergroup discrimination. *Scientific American, 223,* 96–102.

Talaska, C. A., Fiske, S. T., & Chaiken, S. (2008). Legitimating racial discrimination: Emotions, not beliefs, best predict discrimination in a meta-analysis. *Social Justice Research, 21,* 263–296.

Tam, T. (2006). *The impact of intergroup contact on Catholic–Protestant relations in Northern Ireland: A focus on affective and empathetic psychological processes.* Doctoral dissertation, Oxford University, Oxford, UK.

Tam, T., Hewstone, M., Harwood, J., Voci, A., & Kenworthy, J. (2006). Intergroup contact and grandparent–grandchild communication: The effects of self-disclosure on implicit and explicit biases against older people. *Group Processes and Intergroup Relations, 9,* 413–429.

Tam, T., Hewstone, M., Kenworthy, J. B., Cairns, E., Marinetti, C., Geddes, L., et al. (2008). Postconflict reconciliation: Intergroup forgiveness and implicit biases in Northern Ireland. *Journal of Social Issues, 64,* 303–320.

Tatum, B. D. (1997). *Why are all the Black kids sitting together in the cafeteria?* New York: Basic Books.

Tausch, N., Hewstone, M., Kenworthy, J., Cairns, E., & Christ, O. (2007a). Cross-community contact, perceived status differences, and intergroup attitudes in Northern Ireland: The mediating roles of individual-level vs. group-level threats and the moderating role of social identification. *Political Psychology, 28*, 53–61.

Tausch, N., Hewstone, M., Kenworthy, J. B., Psaltis, C., Schmid, K., Popan, J. R., et al. (2010). Secondary transfer effects of intergroup contact: Alternative accounts and underlying processes. *Journal of Personality and Social Psychology, 99*, 282–302.

Tausch, N., Tam, T., Hewstone, M., Kenworthy, J., & Cairns, E. (2007b). Individual-level and group-level mediators of contact effects in Northern Ireland: The moderating role of social identification. *British Journal of Social Psychology, 46*, 541–556.

Taylor, M. (1998). How White attitudes vary with the racial composition of local populations: Numbers count. *American Sociological Review, 63*, 512–535.

Towles-Schwen, T., & Fazio, R. H. (2006). Automatically activated racial attitudes as predictors of the success of interracial roommate relationships. *Journal of Experimental Social Psychology, 42*, 698–705.

Trail, T. E., Shelton, J. N., & West, T. V. (2009). Interracial roommate relationships: negotiating daily interactions. *Personality and Social Psychology Bulletin, 35*, 671–684.

Trawalter, S., & Richeson, J. A. (2008). Let's talk about race, baby! When Whites' and Blacks' interracial contact experiences diverge. *Journal of Experimental Social Psychology, 44*, 1214–1217.

Tredoux, C., & Dixon, J. A. (2009). Mapping the multiple contexts of racial isolation: The case of Long Street, Cape Town. *Urban Studies, 46*, 761–777.

Tredoux, C., & Finchilescu, G. (2010). Mediators of the contact–prejudice relationship amongst South African students on four university campuses. *Journal of Social Issues, 66*, 289–308.

Triandis, H. C. (1994). *Culture and social behavior.* New York: McGraw-Hill.

Tropp, L. R. (2003). The psychological impact of prejudice: Implications for intergroup contact. *Group Processes and Intergroup Relations, 6*, 131–149.

Tropp, L. R. (2006). Stigma and intergroup contact among members of minority and majority status groups. In S. Levin & C. Van Laar (Eds.), *Stigma and group inequality: Social psychological perspectives* (pp. 171–191). Mahwah, NJ: Lawrence Erlbaum Associates.

Tropp, L. R. (2007). Perceived discrimination and interracial contact: Predicting interracial closeness among Black and White Americans. *Social Psychology Quarterly, 70*, 70–81.

Tropp, L. R. (2008). The role of trust in intergroup contact: Its significance and implications for improving relations between groups. In U. Wagner, L. R. Tropp, G. Finchilescu, & C. Tredoux (Eds.), *Improving intergroup relations: Building on the legacy of Thomas F. Pettigrew* (pp. 91–106). Malden, MA: Blackwell.

Tropp, L. R., & Bianchi, R. A. (2006). Valuing diversity and interest in intergroup contact. *Journal of Social Issues, 62*, 533–551.

Tropp, L. R., & Bianchi, R. A. (2007). Interpreting references to group membership in context: Feelings about intergroup contact depending on who says what to whom. *European Journal of Social Psychology, 37*, 153–170.

Tropp, L. R., & Pettigrew, T. F. (2004). Intergroup contact and the central role of affect in intergroup prejudice. In C. W. Leach & L. Tiedens (Eds.), *Social life of emotion* (pp. 246–269). Cambridge, UK: Cambridge University Press.

Tropp, L. R. & Pettigrew, T. F. (2005a). Differential relationships between intergroup contact and affective and cognitive dimensions of prejudice. *Personality and Social Psychology Bulletin, 31*, 1145–1158.

Tropp, L. R., & Pettigrew, T. F. (2005b). Relationships between intergroup contact and prejudice among minority and majority status groups. *Psychological Science, 16*, 651–653.

Turiel, E. (1983). *The development of social knowledge: Morality and convention.* Cambridge, UK: Cambridge University Press.

Turner, R. N., Hewstone, M., & Voci, A. (2007). Reducing explicit and implicit outgroup prejudice via direct and extended contact: The mediating role of self-disclosure and intergroup anxiety. *Journal of Personality and Social Psychology, 93*, 369–388.

Turner, R. N., Hewstone, M., Voci, A., & Vonofakou, C. (2008). A test of the extended intergroup contact hypothesis: The mediating role of intergroup anxiety, perceived ingroup and outgroup norms, and inclusion of the outgroup in the self. *Journal of Personality and Social Psychology, 95*, 843–860.

Uslaner, E. M. (in press). Trust, diversity, and segregation. *Comparative Sociology*.

Uslaner, E. M. (2011). Does diversity drive down trust? In P. Selle & S. Prakash (Eds.), *Civil society, the state of social capital, theory, evidence, policy*. London, UK: Routledge.

Van Dick, R., Wagner, U., Pettigrew, T. F., Christ, O., Wolf, C., Petzel, T., et al. (2004). The role of perceived importance in intergroup contact. *Journal of Personality and Social Psychology, 87*, 211–227.

Van Dyk, A. C. (1990). Voorspellers van etniese houdings in 'n noue kontaksituasie [Determinants of ethnic attitudes in a close contact situation]. *South African Journal of Psychology, 20*, 206–214.

Van Houten, P. (1998). Review of *Ethnic conflict: Commerce, culture, and the contact thesis*. *Journal of Interdisciplinary History, 29*, 93–94.

Van Laar, C., Levin. S., & Sidanius, J. (2008). Ingroup and outgroup contact: A longitudinal study of the effects of cross-ethnic friendships, dates, roommate relationships and participation in segregated organizations. In U. Wagner, L. R. Tropp, G. Finchilescu, & C. Tredoux (Eds.), *Improving intergroup relations: Building on the legacy of Thomas F. Pettigrew* (pp. 127–142). Oxford, UK: Blackwell.

Van Laar, C., Levin, S., Sinclair, S., & Sidanius, J. (2005). The effect of university roommate contact on ethnic attitudes and behavior. *Journal of Experimental Social Psychology, 41*, 329–345.

Van Oudenhoven, J. P., Groenewoud, J. T., & Hewstone, M. (1996). Cooperation, ethnic salience and generalization of interethnic attitudes. *European Journal of Social Psychology, 26*, 649–661.

Varshney, A. (2002). *Ethnic conflict and civil life: Hindus and Muslims in India*. New Haven, CT: Yale University Press.

Vescio, T. K., Sechrist, G. B., & Paolucci, M. P. (2003). Perspective taking and prejudice reduction: The mediational role of empathy arousal and situational attributions. *European Journal of Social Psychology, 33*, 455–472.

Vevea, J. L., & Hedges, L. V. (1995). A general linear model for estimating effect size in the presence of publication bias. *Psychometrika, 60*, 419–435.

Voci, A., & Hewstone, M. (2003). Intergroup contact and prejudice toward immigrants in Italy: The mediational role of anxiety and the moderational role of group salience. *Group Processes and Intergroup Relations, 6*, 37–54.

Vollhardt, J. (2010). Enhanced external and culturally sensitive attributions after extended intercultural contact. *British Journal of Social Psychology, 49*, 363–383.

Vorauer, J. D. (2006). An information search model of evaluative concerns in intergroup interaction. *Psychological Review, 113*, 862–886.

Vorauer, J. D., Main, K. J., & O'Connell, G. B. (1998). How do individuals expect to be viewed by members of lower status groups? Content and implications of meta-stereotypes. *Journal of Personality and Social Psychology, 75*, 917–937.

Wagner, U., & Christ, O. (2007). Intergroup aggression and emotion: A framework and first data. In M. Gollwitzer & G. Steffgen (Eds.), *Emotions and aggressive behavior* (pp.133–148). Goettingen, Germany: Hogrefe & Huber.

Wagner, U., Christ, O., & Pettigrew, T. F. (2008). Prejudice and group-related behavior in Germany. *Journal of Social Issues, 64*, 403–416.

Wagner, U., Christ, O., Pettigrew, T. F., Stellmacher, J., & Wolf, H. (2006). Prejudice and minority proportion: Contact instead of threat effects. *Social Psychology Quarterly, 69*, 380–390.

Wagner, U., Hewstone, M., & Machleit, U. (1989). Contact and prejudice between Germans and Turks: A correlational study. *Human Relations, 42*, 561–574.

Wagner, U., & Machleit, U. (1986). "Gastarbeiter" in the Federal Republic of Germany: Contact between Germans and migrant populations. In M. Hewstone & R. Brown (Eds.), *Contact and conflict in intergroup encounters* (pp. 59–78). Oxford, UK: Basil Blackwell.

Wagner, U., Van Dick, R., Pettigrew, T. F., & Christ, O. (2003). Ethnic prejudice in East and West Germany: The explanatory power of intergroup contact. *Group Processes and Intergroup Relations, 6*, 22–36.

Wagner, U., & Zick, A. (1995). The relation of formal education to ethnic prejudice: Its reliability, validity, and explanation. *European Journal of Social Psychology, 25*, 41–56.

Walker, I., & Crogan, M. (1998). Academic performance, prejudice, and the jigsaw classroom: New pieces to the puzzle. *Journal of Community and Applied Social Psychology, 8*, 381–393.

Walker, I., & Pettigrew, T. F. (1984). Relative deprivation theory: An overview and conceptual critique. *British Journal of Social Psychology, 23*, 301–310.

Walker, I., & Smith, H. (2002) (Eds.). *Relative deprivation: Specification, development, and integration.* New York: Cambridge University Press.

Walther, E. (2002). Guilt by mere association: Evaluative conditioning and the spreading attitude effect. *Journal of Personality and Social Psychology, 82*, 919–934.

Ward, C., & Masgoret, A. (2006). An integrative model of attitudes toward immigrants. *International Journal of Intercultural Relations, 30*, 671–682.

Watts, W. A., & Holt, L. E. (1970). Logical relationships among beliefs and timing as factors in persuasion. *Journal of Personality and Social Psychology, 16*, 571–582.

Weber, R., & Crocker, J. (1983). Cognitive processes in the revision of stereotype beliefs. *Journal of Personality and Social Psychology, 45*, 961–977.

Webster, S. W. (1961). The influence of interracial contact on social acceptance in a newly integrated school. *Journal of Educational Psychology, 52*, 292–296.

Weigert, K. M. (1976). Intergroup contact and attitudes about third-group: A survey of Black soldiers' perceptions. *International Journal of Group Tensions, 6*, 110–124.

Weller, L., & Grunes, S. (1988). Does contact with the mentally ill affect nurses' attitudes to mental illness? *British Journal of Medical Psychology, 61*, 277–284.

Wellisch, J. B., Marcus, A., MacQueen, A., & Duck, G. (1976). An in-depth study of Emergency School Aid Act (ESAA) Schools: 1974–1975. Washington, DC: System Development Corportation.

Werth, J. L., & Lord. C. G. (1992). Previous conceptions of the typical group member and the contact hypothesis. *Basic and Applied Social Psychology, 13*, 351–369.

West, T. V., Pearson, A. R., Dovidio, J. F., Shelton, J. N., & Trail, T. E. (2009a). Superordinate identity and intergroup roommate friendship development. *Journal of Experimental Social Psychology, 45*, 1266–1272.

West, T. V., Shelton, J. N., & Trail, T. E. (2009b). Relational anxiety in interracial interactions. *Psychological Science, 20*, 289–292.

Wilder, D. A. (1984). Intergroup contact: The typical member and the exception to the rule. *Journal of Experimental Social Psychology, 20*, 177–194.

Wilder, D. A. (1986). Cognitive factors affecting the success of intergroup contact. In S. W. Worchel & W. G. Austin (Eds.), *Psychology of intergroup relations* (pp. 49–66). Chicago, IL: Nelson-Hall.

Wilder, D. A. (1993). The role of anxiety in facilitating stereotypic judgments of outgroup behavior. In D. M. Mackie & D. L. Hamilton (Eds.), *Affect, cognition and stereotyping: Interactive processes in group perception* (pp. 87–109). San Diego, CA: Academic Press.

Wilder, D. A., & Shapiro, P. (1989). Effects of anxiety on impression formation in a group context: An anxiety-assimilation hypothesis. *Journal of Experimental Social Psychology, 25*, 481–499.

Wilder, D. A., & Thompson, J. (1980). Intergroup contact with independent manipulations on in-group and out-group interaction. *Journal of Personality and Social Psychology, 38*, 589–603.

Wildschut, T., & Insko, C. A. (2007). Explanations of interindividual–intergroup discontinuity: A review of the evidence. *European Review of Social Psychology, 18*, 175–211.

Williams, Jr., R. M. (1947). *The reduction of intergroup tensions*. New York: Social Science Research Council.

Wilner, D. M., Walkley, R. P., & Cook, S. W. (1955). *Human relations in interracial housing: A study of the contact hypothesis*. Minneapolis, MN: University of Minnesota Press.

Wilson, D. B. (2002). SPSS macros for performing meta-analytic analyses. Retrieved February 16, 2004, from http://mason.gmu.edu/~dwilsonb/ma.html

Wilson, T. C. (1996). Prejudice reduction or self-selection? A test of the contact hypothesis. *Sociological Spectrum, 16*, 43–60.

Wilson, W. J. (1999). *The bridge over the racial divide: Rising inequality and coalition politics*. Berkeley, CA: University of California Press.

Wolsko, C., Park, B. Judd, C. M., & Bachelor, J. (2003). Intergroup contact: Effects on group evaluations and perceived variability. *Group Processes and Intergroup Relations, 6*, 93–110.

Wolsko, C., Park, B., Judd, C. M., & Wittenbrink, B. (2000). Framing interethnic ideology: Effects of multicultural and color-blind perspectives in judgement of groups and individuals. *Journal of Personality and Social Psychology, 78*, 635–654.
Wood, P. B., & Sonleitner, N. (1996). The effect of childhood interracial contact on adult antiblack prejudice. *International Journal of Intercultural Relations, 20*, 1–17.
Wood, W., Lundgren, S., Ouellette, J. A., Busceme, S., & Blackstone, T. (1994). Minority influence: A meta-analytic review of social influence processes. *Psychological Bulletin, 115*, 323–345.
Works, E. (1961). The prejudice-interaction hypothesis from the point of view of the Negro minority group. *American Journal of Sociology, 67*, 47–52.
Wright, S. C., Aron, A., & Brody, S. M. (2008). Extended contact and including others in the self: Building on the Allport/Pettigrew legacy. In U. Wagner, L. R. Tropp, G. Finchilescu, & C. Tredoux (Eds.), *Improving intergroup relations: Building on the legacy of Thomas F. Pettigrew* (pp. 143–159). Malden, MA: Blackwell.
Wright, S. C., Aron, A., McLaughlin-Volpe, T., & Ropp, S. A. (1997). The extended contact effect. *Journal of Personality and Social Psychology, 73*, 73–90.
Wright, S. C., Aron, A., & Tropp, L. R. (2002). Including others (and groups) in the self: Self-expansion and intergroup relations. In J. P. Forgas & K. D. Williams (Eds.), *The social self: Cognitive, interpersonal and intergroup perspectives* (pp. 343–363). Philadelphia, PA: Psychology Press.
Wright, S. C., Brody, S. A., & Aron, A. (2005). Intergroup contact: Still our best hope for reducing prejudice. In C. S. Crandall & M. Schaller (Eds.), *The social psychology of prejudice: Historical perspectives* (pp. 115–142). Seattle, WA: Lewinian Press.
Wright, S. C., & Lubensky, M. (2009). The struggle for social equality: Collective action vs. prejudice reduction. In S. Demoulin, J. P. Leyens, & J. F. Dovidio (Eds.), *Intergroup misunderstandings: Impact of divergent social realities* (pp. 291–310). New York: Psychology Press.
Wright, S. C., & Taylor, D. M. (1998). Responding to tokenism: Individual action in the face of collective injustice. *Personality and Social Psychology Bulletin, 28*, 647–667.
Wright, S. C., & Taylor, D. M. (1999). Success under tokenism: Co-option of the newcomer and the prevention of collective protest. *British Journal of Social Psychology, 38*, 369–396.
Wright, S. C., & Tropp, L. R. (2002). Collective action in response to disadvantage: Intergroup perceptions, social identification, and social change. In I. Walker & H. Smith (Eds.), *Relative deprivation: Specification, development, and integration* (pp. 200–236). Cambridge, MA: Cambridge University Press.
Wright, S. C., & Tropp, L. R. (2005). Language and intergroup contact: Investigating the impact of bilingual instruction on children's intergroup attitudes. *Group Processes and Intergroup Relations, 8*, 309–328.
Wright, S. C., & Van der Zande, C. C. (1999). *Bicultural friends: When cross-group friendships cause improved intergroup attitudes*. Paper presented at the annual meeting of the Society for Experimental Social Psychology, St. Louis, Missouri.
Wright, S. C., Van der Zande, C. C., Ropp, S. A., Tropp, L. R., Zanna, M., Aron, A., et al. (2000). *Cross-group friendships and intergroup attitudes: Experimental evidence for a causal direction*. Unpublished manuscript, University of California, Santa Cruz.

Yarrow, M. R., Campbell, J. D., & Yarrow, L. J. (1958). Acquisition of new norms: A study of racial desegregation. *Journal of Social Issues, 14*, 8–28.

Yinon, Y. (1975). Authoritarianism and prejudice among married couples with similar or different ethnic origin in Israel. *Journal of Marriage and the Family, 37*, 214–220.

Zagefka, H., Gonzalez, R., Brown, R., & Manzi, J. (under review). *To know you is to love you?: Longitudinal effects of intergroup contact and knowledge on intergroup anxiety and prejudice among indigenous and non-indigenous Chileans.* Psychology Department, Pacifica Universidad Catolica de Chile.

Zajonc, R. B. (1968). Attitudinal effects of exposure. *Journal of Personality and Social Psychology, 9*, 1–27.

Zajonc, R. B. (1980). Feeling and thinking: Preferences need no inferences. *American Psychologist, 35*, 151–175.

Zajonc, R. B., & Rajecki, D. W. (1969). Exposure and affect: A field experiment. *Psychonomic Science, 17*, 216–217.

Zanna, M. P., & Rempel, J. K. (1988). Attitudes: A new look at an old concept. In D. Bar Tal & A. Kruglanski (Eds.), *The social psychology of knowledge* (pp. 315–334). Cambridge, UK: Cambridge University Press.

Zebrowitz, L. A., White, B., & Wieneke, K. (2008). Mere exposure and racial prejudice: Exposure to other-race faces increases liking for strangers of that race. *Social Cognition, 26*, 259–275.

Zick, A. (1997). *Vorurteile und Rassismus: Eine sozialpsychologische Analyse.* [Prejudice and racism: A social psychological analysis]. Muenster, Germany: Waxmann.

Zick, A., Wolf, C., Kuepper, B., Davidov, E., Schmidt, P., & Heitmeyer, W. (2008). The syndrome of group-focused enmity: The interrelation of prejudices tested with multiple cross-sectional and panel data. *Journal of Social Issues, 64*, 363–383.

Zinn, H. (1964). *SNCC, the new abolitionists.* Boston: Beacon Press.

AUTHOR INDEX

A

Aberson, C. L., 110, 118, 170
Aboud, F. E., 57, 58, 123, 125, 127, 128
Abrams, D., 22, 37, 44, 46, 118, 120, 142, 156, 209
Adams, A. F., 70
Adesokan, A., 93
Adorno, T. W., 29, 34, 153
Ahmad, N., 82
Ajdukovic, D., 71
Ajzen, I., 112
Akinola, M., 110, 170
Alegre, J. M., 91, 125
Alesina, A., 166
Alexander, L., 169
Alexander, M. G., 136, 139, 141
Allen, J. J. B., 68
Allport, G. W., 5, 6, 8, 29, 34, 55, 61, 64, 67, 70, 71, 75, 79, 80, 88, 131, 137, 138, 145, 169, 194, 201, 202
Altemeyer, B., 153
Alvaro, E. M., 43
Amir, Y., 14, 31, 56, 64, 71
Amsel, R., 9
Anastasio, P. A., 74
Araragi, C., 63
Armstrong, T., 151
Aron, A., 22, 92, 93, 100, 106, 115, 116, 118, 119, 120, 121, 123, 124, 125
Aron, E. N., 93
Aronson, E., 63, 91, 169
Asbrock, F., 42
Asher, S. R., 127
Ashmore, R. D., 97
Auerbach, D. N., 187
Ayers, M., 125

B

Bachelor, J., 101, 109
Bachman, B. A., 74
Baeyens, F., 44
Bafumi, J., 179
Baker, P. E., 2, 3
Ballard, M., 52
Banaji, M. R., 34, 118

Banks, J. A., 58
Barlow, K. M., 173, 176
Batson, C. D., 82, 108
Batts, V., 106
Beach, K. R., 101, 105, 108, 112
Beaton, A., 152
Bednar, L. I., 82
Beerten, R., 154
Begg, C. B., 19
Bell-Nathaniel, A., 59
Ben-Ari, R., 56
Bender, M. P., 88
Berlin, J. A., 19
Berry, J. W., 89, 216
Bettencourt, A., 81
Bettencourt, B. A., 73
Bianchi, R. A., 72, 75, 93, 207, 208
Bigler, R. S., 57
Billiet, J., 154
Binder, J., 6, 13, 22, 27, 35, 38, 86, 87, 118, 209
Biro, M., 71
Blackstone, T., 43, 44
Blake, D., 2, 149, 151, 152
Blanchard, F., 88, 92
Blaney, N., 63
Blascovich, J., 81, 85, 86
Blau, P., 136
Blumer, H., 132
Bobo, L. D., 132, 136, 141
Bodenhausen, G. V., 109
Bond, M. A., 89
Boniecki, K. A., 81
Bonilla-Silva, E., 124, 136
Bonneau, K., 120, 127, 128
Bornman, E., 8
Bornstein, R. F., 68
Bowman, C., 128
Brajkovich, G., 68
Brameld, T., 3
Bratt, C., 88, 93, 128
Breckler, S. J., 97
Brewer, M. B., 34, 62, 63, 73, 85, 93, 94, 136, 139, 141
Bridgeman, D., 91
Brigham, J. C., 98, 101, 106
Brody, S. M., 22, 92, 93, 115, 120, 124

Brophy, I. N., 4, 5
Brown, K., 148, 149, 154, 155
Brown, K. T., 91
Brown, R., 6, 10, 13, 22, 27, 32, 35, 38, 52, 57, 73, 74, 75, 86, 87, 88, 90, 93, 99, 117, 118, 125, 126, 128, 138, 163, 187, 201, 206, 209
Brown, T., 148, 149, 154, 155
Brown, T. N., 91
Brown, W. R., 121
Buchmann, C., 120, 127, 128
Bullock, C. S., 117
Burns, J., 171
Burns, P., 148, 149, 151, 152
Busceme, S., 43, 44
Butler, J. S., 22, 35, 87, 91, 135
Butz, D. A., 72, 89, 90, 91
Bylsma, W. H., 132, 168

C

Caditz, J., 35
Cairns, E., 51, 81, 93, 100, 110, 118, 119, 120, 156, 162, 163, 165, 170
Callaghan, J., 94
Campbell, D., 3
Campbell, D. T., 94
Campbell, J. D., 63
Canar, J., 88
Capitanio, J. P., 9, 22, 52, 93, 100, 118
Carlson, J. S., 56
Carney, T., 170
Caspi, A., 9, 53
Cayton, H. R., 4
Cehajic, S., 163
Chaiken, S., 11, 97, 100, 108, 112, 203
Chan, F., 110, 170
Chang, H., 8
Cheek, N. H., 125
Child, P., 132
Christ, O., 22, 35, 40, 42, 57, 87, 92, 93, 97, 99, 109, 120, 121, 126, 146, 150, 152, 162, 163, 170, 171, 179, 185, 195, 196, 209, 211, 213
Chu, D., 62
Citrin, J., 147, 148, 149, 151, 152
Claassen, C., 170, 175
Clack, B., 51, 111, 112, 170, 172, 173, 174, 177
Clark, M. L., 125
Clayton, S., 152
Clement, R., 35, 40, 46
Clunies-Ross, G., 51
Cohen, E. G., 62, 72, 139, 141

Cohen, L. L., 132, 168
Colditz, G. A., 17
Collins, M., 7
Conover, T., 185
Cook, J., 82
Cook, S. W., 7, 9, 13, 33, 64, 70, 72, 118, 126
Cook, T. D., 17
Cooper, A., 88
Cooper, H., 17
Cooper, R., 169
Copans, L., 1
Cordray, D. F., 17
Corkalo, D., 71
Corman, L., 52
Cornelis, I., 196
Correll, J., 90
Corrigan, P. W., 54, 88
Cortina, J., 179
Coursol, A., 19, 87
Crain, R. L., 2, 59, 68
Cramer, M. R., 147
Crane, M., 110, 111, 116, 117, 124, 125, 171, 172
Crano, W. D., 43
Crisp, R. J., 75, 142, 162
Crites, S. L., 101
Crocker, J., 32, 88, 132
Crogan, M., 63, 64
Crowne, D. P., 47
Crystal, D. S., 57, 58, 108, 127, 170
Cuddy, A. J. C., 42, 54
Cullen, F. T., 22
Cunningham, W. A., 34

D

Daily, T., 54
Damico, S. B., 59
Darby, J. P., 162
Dasgupta, N., 110
Davidov, E., 34, 54
Davidson, J. D., 121
Davies, K., 121, 125
Davis, A., 118
Davis, M. H., 79
Davis-Sitt, C., 98
Dawkins, C., 164, 183
Day, H. R., 63
de Houwer, J., 44
de la Haye, A. M., 9, 161
de Tezanos-Pinto, P., 88, 93, 128
Del Boca, F. K., 97
Delgado, G., 178

Dellman-Jenkins, M., 53
Demaray, M. K., 59
Denton, N. A., 126
Desforges, D. M., 9
Deutsch, K. W., 180
Deutsch, M., 7
Devine, P. G., 23, 72, 74, 92, 125, 131, 133, 141, 168, 182
DeVinney, L. C., 6
Dhont, K., 6, 13, 22, 38, 47, 83, 87, 118, 196, 212
Dickersin, K., 19, 87
Dihn, K. T., 89
Dijker, A. J., 99
Dijksterhuis, A., 42
Dion, K. L., 176
Dixon, J., 51, 111, 112, 147, 170, 172, 173, 174, 175, 177
Dixon, J. A., 110, 168, 169, 170, 171, 183
Djipa, D., 71
Dobbin, F., 64
Doherty, M., 20
Doucet, N., 113
Dovidio, J. F., 74, 93, 101, 105, 108, 109, 112, 113, 125, 127, 141, 151, 173, 207
Dowds, L., 147, 148, 149 151, 156, 171
Downey, G., 118
Doyle, A. B., 57
Draguns, J. G., 180
Drake, S. C., 4
Driscoll, D. M., 98
Duan, C., 79
DuBois, D. L., 126, 127
Duck, G., 63
Duckitt, J., 94, 153, 183
Dunn, S., 162
Dunton, B. C., 23
Durrheim, K. L., 51, 110, 111, 168, 169, 170, 171, 172, 173, 174, 175, 177, 183
Dustmann, C., 147
Duval, S. J., 20

E

Eagly, A. H., 15, 16, 17, 97, 100
Early, S., 108
Easterbrook, P. J., 19
Eaton, L., 51, 111, 170, 172, 173, 174, 177
Echebarria-Echabe, A., 45
Edmonds, C., 92, 127
Edwards, K., 73, 99
Egger, M., 20
Eggins, R. A., 75

Ehrlinger, J., 132, 136
Eibach, R. P., 132, 136
Eller, A., 22, 37, 44, 46, 74, 118, 120, 156, 209
Ellison, C. G., 22, 35, 57, 87, 131, 132, 173
Emerson, M. O., 59, 120
Ensari, N. K., 75, 120
Epstein, J. L., 127
Ervin, K. S., 81
Espenshade, T., 149, 151, 152
Esses, V. M., 97, 99, 101, 105, 106, 108, 112, 118, 151, 153, 203
Eurich-Fulcer, R., 62
Everest, M. J., 152

F

Fabrigar, L. R., 101
Farina, A., 132
Fazio, R. H., 23, 24, 27
Feagin, J. R., 136
Fehr, B., 120
Fenrick, N. J., 52
Ferguson, M. J., 132
Fernandez, S., 92
Fernandez-Guede, E., 45
Festinger, L., 156, 179
Fetzer, J., 147, 148, 149, 150, 156, 171
Fichten, C. S., 9
Finchilescu, G., 11, 62, 139, 142, 170
Fine, G., 9
Finlay, K., 108
Fishbein, H. D., 127
Fishbein, M., 112
Fiske, S. T., 11, 42, 54, 73, 108, 109, 112, 203
Fitzgerald, D. C., 132, 168
Florack, A., 155
Foos, P. W., 20
Forbes, H., 14, 178, 179, 180, 183, 196, 197
Ford, T. E., 11, 97, 99, 106, 108, 127, 203
Ford, W. S., 14, 97
Forman, T., 135
Foster, D., 11, 62, 138
Fox, C., 136
Frame, M. C., 171
Francine, T., 152
Freeman, G., 147, 148, 149, 150, 151, 152, 154
Frenkel-Brunswik, E., 29, 34, 153
Frey, F. E., 75, 88, 91, 93, 128, 142
Friedman, R. S., 65
Fritz, M. S., 79, 87
Fruit, D., 53
Fujioka, T., 132

Author Index

Fujioka, Y., 93
Funke, F., 6, 13, 22, 27, 35, 38, 86, 87, 118, 209

G

Gaertner, S. L., 74, 93, 101, 105, 108, 109, 112, 113, 125, 141, 198
Gaffney, A. M., 110, 170
Gagne, F., 173, 176
Galinsky, A. D., 83, 90
Gallup Organization, 136
Garbin, C. P., 54
Gardner, R. C., 35, 40, 46
Geddes, L., 110, 162, 170
Gelman, A., 179
Gerbert, B., 112
Gesthuizen, M., 165
Gewitz, H., 53
Giang, M. T., 72, 208
Gibson, J. L., 170, 175
Gilbert, D. T., 91
Gimpel, J., 148, 149, 151, 152
Glass, G. V. J., 19
Glick, P., 42, 54
Goffman, E., 132
Gómez, A., 92, 93, 118, 120, 209
Gonzalez, A., 63, 169
Gonzalez, R., 90
Gonzalez-Rivera, M., 52
Goodman, M. E., 57
Gopalan, R., 19
Gordijn, E. H., 42
Gottlieb, J., 52
Graves, S. B., 93
Green, C., 59
Green, C. W., 70
Green, D., 147, 148, 149, 151, 152
Green, D. P., 49
Greenland, K., 187
Greenwald, A. G., 109, 118
Gregg, P., 93
Griffey, D., 62
Groenewoud, J. T., 74, 75
Grunes, S., 53
Gudykunst, W. B., 54, 81, 89
Guinier, L., 178
Gurin, P., 173
Guynan, K., 54

H

Ha, S., 36, 148, 149, 151, 152, 155, 156
Haag, S. C., 110

Haddock, G., 97, 99, 101, 105, 106, 118, 203
Halberstadt, J., 68
Hall, N. R., 75
Hallinan, M. T., 59, 125, 126, 128
Hamberger, J., 51, 115, 120, 162, 163, 165
Hamilton, D. L., 45, 98, 99, 100
Hammer, M. R., 89
Hardee, B. B., 106
Hardin, C. D., 110, 170
Harmon-Jones, E., 68, 82
Harrington, H. J., 13, 73
Harrison, P. R., 128
Harry, H., 212
Hartman, H., 17
Harvey, O. J., 9, 62
Harwood, J., 53, 85, 120
Haslam, S. A., 75
Hass, R. G., 97, 106
Hastorf, A. H., 132
Hatanaka, H. K., 88
Hayes, A. F., 83
Hayes, B., 147, 148, 149, 151, 156, 171
Hebl, M. R., 207
Hedges, L. V., 17, 20, 84, 95
Heider, F., 120
Heitmeyer, W., 34, 39, 45, 146, 157, 186, 188
Hempstead, K., 149, 151, 152
Hennigan, K., 128
Henning, A., 58
Henninger, D., 164
Henry, P. J., 110, 170
Herek, G. M., 9, 22, 52, 93, 100, 118
Herlihy, J. M., 64
Hewes, D. E., 93
Hewstone, M., 2, 9, 10, 32, 35, 36, 37, 42, 43, 51, 53, 56, 57, 72, 73, 74, 75, 81, 82, 85, 87, 92, 93, 99, 100, 110, 115, 118, 119, 120, 125, 126, 138, 156, 162, 163, 165, 166, 170, 201, 206, 209, 216
Hill, C., 79
Hindriks, I., 42
Hiner, N. R., 59
Hirsch, B. J., 126, 127
Hirschfeld, L. A., 57
Hodson, G., 83, 212
Hodson, R., 179
Hofmann, G., 121
Hogg, M. A., 74, 75, 127, 216
Holmes, E. P., 88
Holt, L. E., 42
Holtman, Z., 170
Holzberg, J. D., 53

Homans, G. C., 68
Hood, III, M. V., 147, 148, 149, 151, 152
Hood, W. R., 9, 62
Hope, R. O., 63
Hopkins, N., 14
Horn, S., 127
Hornsey, M. J., 74, 75, 216
Howard, A., 109
Hughes, J., 120, 163, 209
Huici, C., 93
Hummert, M. L., 54
Humphrey, N. D., 1
Hunt, M., 131
Hunter, J. E., 79
Hunter, S. B., 81, 85, 86
Hunter, S. M., 125
Huntsinger, J. R., 83, 175
Hyers, L. L., 131, 132, 168

I

Ibrahim, H., 56
Imhoff, H. J., 82
Insko, C. A., 179
Irish, D. P., 87
Islam, M. R., 51, 56, 75, 93
Iyer, A., 132

J

Jackman, M. R., 110, 111, 116, 117, 124, 125, 150, 171, 172
Jackson, J. S., 91, 148, 149, 154, 155
Jackson, J. W., 3, 13, 97
Jackson, L., 151, 153
Jackson, L. A., 81
Jackson, P., 131
Jason, L., 113
Jeffries, V., 111
Jessop. D. J., 112
John, O. P., 14, 31, 88, 97, 98, 99, 104
Johnson, B., 109
Johnson, B. T., 15, 16, 17, 84, 101
Johnson, C., 109
Johnson, D. W., 62, 63, 113
Johnson, M. K., 121
Johnson, R., 166
Johnson, R. T., 62, 63, 113
Johnston, L., 32
Jonas, K., 56, 57
Jones, E. E., 132
Joseph, S., 111, 116, 170
Joyner, K., 126

Judd, C. M., 90, 101, 109
Jung, M., 93

K

Kafati, G., 141
Kalev, A., 64
Kalin, R., 147
Kamal, A. A., 56
Kao, G., 126
Katz, I., 97, 106
Katz, P. A., 57
Kaufman, M. J., 52
Kawakami, K., 109
Kearney, E., 62
Kelley, H., 156, 179
Kelly, E., 64
Kelly, M. C., 58
Kenworthy, J., 36, 37, 53, 72, 120, 162
Kenworthy, J. B., 36, 37, 110, 162, 170, 171
Kephart, W. M., 4
Kessler, A., 147, 148, 149, 150, 151, 152, 154
Kessler, T., 6, 13, 22, 27, 35, 38, 86, 87, 118, 209
Khmelkov, V. T., 59, 126
Killen, M., 57, 58, 92, 108, 127, 170
Kim, Y, Y., 89
Kimbro, R. T., 59, 120
Kinder, D.R., 106
Klandermans, B., 175
Kluegel, J., 136
Knippenberg, A. V., 42
Koomen, W., 42
Koschate, M. J., 70, 71
Kowai-Bell, N., 81, 85, 86
Krahn, H., 147, 148, 149, 151
Kramer, B. M., 5, 6, 8
Kramer, R. M., 62
Krige, P., 51
Krueger, J., 142
Kubiak, A. A., 88
Kuepper, B., 34, 45
Kunovich, R. M., 179

L

La Ferrara, E., 166
Lambert, D., 53
Landis, D., 63
Lane, K. A., 118
Leach, C. W., 132
Lee, A. M., 1
Lee, A. Y., 68

Lee, C., 126, 169
Lee, C. M., 89
Lee, Y., 71
Leeds, S., 74
Leibold, J. M., 109
Leonardelli, G. J., 83
Lett, H. A., 3
Levenson, R. L., 187
Levin, J., 180
Levin, S., 6, 13, 22, 27, 35, 38, 39, 44, 86, 87, 94, 100, 118, 119, 142, 156, 209
Levine, M., 14
Levine, R. A., 3
Levinson, D. J., 29, 34, 153
Levitt, M., 20
Levy, J. M., 112
Levy, P. H., 112
Levy, S. R., 58
Lewandowski, G., 93
Lewin, K., 32
Lewis, S. H., 98
Liben, L. S., 57
Lickel, B., 81, 85, 86
Light, R. J., 17, 19
Lilly, T., 88, 92
Link, B. G., 22
Linnander, E., 45
Lipsey, M. W., 16, 17, 20
Lishner, 82
Little, R. J. A., 188
Livingston, R. W., 136, 139, 141
Longshore, D., 63
Lord, C. G., 9
Louw, J., 170
Lubensky, M., 173, 174, 178
Luedtke, A., 154
Luiz, D., 51
Lundgren, S., 43, 44
Lyons, P. A., 171

M

Machleit, U., 9
MacKenzie, B. K., 8
Mackie, D. M., 99, 100, 101, 109
MacKinnon, D. P., 79, 87
MacQueen, A., 63
Maddens, B., 154
Maddux, W. M., 90
Maguire, B. T., 112
Mahoney, C. C., 91
Main, K. J., 93, 131, 142
Major, B., 132

Malecki, C. K., 59
Mallett, R. K., 83, 91, 128, 175
Mania, E. W., 198
Mann, J., 74
Manuel, W. J., 91
Manzi, J., 90
Maoz, I., 51
Maras, P., 32, 52, 75, 117
Marcus, A., 63
Marinetti, C., 110, 162, 170
Marini, M. M., 121
Marks, B., 148, 149, 154, 155
Markus, H., 132
Marlowe, D., 47
Martin, R., 43
Maruyama, G., 56
Maruyama, G. M., 62, 63
Masgoret, A., 156
Mashek, D., 93
Mason, J. A., 9
Masser, B., 32, 75
Massey, D. S., 126
Mathews, D. R., 19, 177
Mayda, A., 148, 149, 155
Mazziotta, A., 93
McCauley, C., 71, 113
McCaw, B., 19
McClelland, K., 45
McClenahan, C., 162
McClendon, M. J., 14
McConahay, J. B., 106
McConnell, A. R., 109
McFarland, S., 83, 153
McGarry, J., 9, 162, 178
McGarty, C., 9, 161
McGhee, D. E., 109
McGinnis, S. P., 9
McGovern, T., 89
McGuire, C. V., 132
McGuire, W. J., 42, 132
McKay, S., 9
McLaughlin-Volpe, T., 92, 93, 100, 106, 116, 119, 120, 121, 123, 125
McLernon, F., 162
Meertens, R., 150, 152, 171
Meertens, R. W., 152
Meinert, C. L., 19
Mellott, D. S., 118
Mendelson, M. J., 57, 123, 125, 127
Mendes, W. B., 81, 85, 86, 110, 170
Mendoza-Denton, R., 22, 75, 81, 85, 86, 91, 118, 124, 125, 142, 207

Migacheva, K., 88, 92, 128
Milgram, S., 32
Miller, C. T., 113
Miller, D. A., 101, 109
Miller, D. T., 132
Miller, N., 13, 63, 73, 74, 75, 85, 120, 128
Min, Y. I., 19
Minard, R. D., 29, 92, 147
Mitchell, A., 212
Mitchener, E. C., 82
Moghaddam, F., 71
Molina, L. E., 70, 71, 72, 208
Monteith, M., 136
Montgomery, L. M., 20
Mordkoff, J. T., 113
Moreland, R. L., 68
Moreno, K. N., 109
Morgan, V., 162
Morris, I., 147, 148, 150, 151, 152
Morrison, E. W., 64
Morrison, K. R., 197
Moskalenko, S., 113
Moskowitz, G. B., 83
Mosteller, E., 17
Mulder, M., 147, 148, 149, 151
Mummendey, A., 6, 13, 22, 27, 35, 38, 86, 87, 93, 118, 209, 216
Murrell, A., 74
Muste, C., 147, 148, 149, 151, 152
Mutz, D. C., 2, 171
Mynhardt, J. C., 8

N

Nabuzoka, D., 52
Nagda, B. A., 75, 176
Nash, D., 187
National Conference for Community and Justice, 134
Nel, E. M., 120
Neuberg, S. L., 73
Nezlek, J. B., 34
Niens, U., 51, 162, 163, 165
Nisbett, R., 32
Norton, M. I., 54
Nosek, B. A., 118
Nowak, A., 97
Nussbaum, R. J., 90

O

Oaker, G., 93
Oberschall, A., 1
O'Connell, G. B., 93, 131, 142
O'Leary, B., 9, 162, 178
Oliner, P. M., 1, 2, 34, 115
Oliner, S. P., 1, 2, 34, 115
Oliver, J. E., 49
Olkin, I., 17, 84, 95
Olson, J. M., 90
O'Meara, K., 51
Operario, D., 109
Orfield, G., 126, 169
Osgood, C. E., 102, 106
Ostrom, T. M., 97
Ottati, V., 54
Ouelette, J. A., 43, 44

P

Page-Gould, E., 22, 75, 81, 85, 86, 91, 118, 124, 125, 142, 207
Palmer, D., 148, 149, 151
Paluck, E. L., 49
Pantoja, A., 147, 148, 151
Paolini, S., 53, 81, 85, 93, 100, 118, 119, 120, 156, 162, 163
Paolucci, M. P., 83
Park, B., 90, 101, 109
Park, D., 179
Parker, J. H., 64
Patchen, M., 13, 14, 55, 59, 62, 63, 121, 128
Patnoe, S., 63, 91, 169
Patrick, J. R., 4
Pearson, A. R., 127
Penn, D. L., 54
Perrino, A., 152
Petersen, T. K., 52
Pettigrew, T. F., 6, 8, 9, 10, 13, 14, 21, 22, 33, 34, 35, 36, 39, 40, 41, 42, 43, 44, 46, 54, 57, 64, 67, 68, 74, 78, 79, 81, 87, 88, 92, 93, 94, 95, 97, 98, 99, 100, 101, 104, 105, 108, 109, 111, 115, 117, 118, 120, 121, 123, 125, 126, 129, 131, 133, 135, 136, 137, 138, 139, 140, 146, 147, 150, 152, 154, 169, 170, 171, 172, 176, 177, 179, 183, 196, 201, 209, 210, 211, 212, 213, 216
Petty, R. E., 101
Petzel, T., 22, 35, 87, 93, 109, 121
Pew Research Center, 147, 150, 151, 152
Pietrzak, J., 75, 118
Pillemer, D. B., 19
Pinel, E. C., 75, 132
Piontkowski, U., 155
Pittam, J., 9

Plant, E. A., 23, 72, 89, 90, 91, 92, 125, 131, 141
Plummer, M., 113
Polycarpou, M. P., 82
Poore, A. G., 173, 176
Popan, J., 36, 37, 72
Popan, J. R., 36, 37, 171
Porter, J. D. R., 57
Porter, M. K., 110, 170
Post, S., 147, 148, 154
Powell, B., 131
Powers, D. A., 22, 35, 57, 87, 131, 132, 173
Pratto, F., 132, 153, 173
Preacher, K. J., 83
Premack, S. L., 79
Preston, I., 147
Preston, J. D., 11, 62, 72, 132, 139, 141, 187, 208
Prewitt, K., 152
Prothro, J. W., 177
Pruett, S. R., 110, 170
Psaltis, C., 36, 37, 72
Purdie, V. J., 118
Purdy, K. T., 57, 123, 125, 127
Putnam, R., 94, 164, 165, 166, 196, 197

Q

Quinn, D., 52

R

Rabrenovic, G., 180
Rabushka, A., 51
Rajecki, D. W., 68
Raman, P., 53
Ramsey, S. L., 9
Ransford, H. E., 111
Raudenbush, S. W., 17
Ray, J. J., 9, 161
Reagans, R., 127
Reicher, S., 14, 110, 173
Reid, S. A., 127
Reis, H. J., 120
Reis, H. T., 100, 106, 116, 119, 121
Reitzes, D. C., 30, 147
Rempel, J. K., 97, 101, 108
Reynolds, K. J., 75
Rhodes, G., 68
Richeson, J. A., 72, 90, 138, 142, 168, 207
Ricolfi, L., 153
Riek, B. M., 198
Riley, R. T., 43

Rimmerman, A., 112
Rinden, A., 147, 148, 154
Riordan, C., 9, 14, 61, 62, 97, 132, 139, 208
Rivera, L. M., 110
Robbins, I., 88
Robinson, J. W., 11, 62, 72, 132, 139, 141, 187, 208
Roccato, M., 153
Rodriguez, J., 173
Rodriguez, M., 135
Roets, A., 6, 13, 22, 38, 47, 83, 87, 118
Rogers, M., 128
Rogers-Croak, M., 73
Rohmann, A., 155
Rojahn, K., 98
Ronning, J. A., 52
Rooney-Rebeck, P., 113
Ropp, S. A., 92, 115, 118, 120
Rosenthal, R., 15, 17, 19, 105, 134, 187
Ross, L., 32
Ross, M. H., 180
Rothbart, M., 14, 31, 88, 97, 98, 99, 104
Rothwell, J. T., 166
Rotton, J., 20
Rubin, D. B., 188
Ruck, M., 57, 58, 108, 127, 170
Rudman, L. A., 118
Ruggiero, J., 62
Ruhe, D., 176
Rust, M. C., 74

S

Sagar, H. A., 112
Saguy, T., 74, 173
Salvarani, G., 108
Salvatore, J., 207
Sanders, L. M., 106
Sanford, R. N., 29, 34, 153
Sankar, J., 127, 128
Saucier, D. A., 113
Sawyer, S., 82
Scheepers, P., 165, 199
Schiappa, E., 93
Schlueter, E., 199
Schmid, K., 36, 37, 72
Schmidt, P., 34, 45
Schofield, J. W., 59, 62, 63, 112, 113, 126, 128
Schuman, E. A., 6
Schwartz, J., 136
Schwartz, J. L. K., 109, 118
Scott, R. A., 132
Searles, R., 177

Author Index 301

Sears, D. O., 6, 13, 27, 35, 38, 39, 86, 94, 118, 209
Sears, R., 49, 58
Sechrist, G. B., 83, 127
Seefeldt, C., 53, 186
Sellers, R. M., 91
Sellitz, C., 72
Shadish, W. R., 20, 79, 86
Shapiro, P., 86
Shaver, P., 120
Shelton, J. N., 72, 127, 131, 133, 138, 142, 168, 182, 207, 209
Sherif, C. W., 9, 62
Sherif, M., 9, 55, 62, 70, 87, 209, 213
Shoemaker, C., 110, 118, 170
Shook, N. J., 23, 27
Shor, B., 179
Short, R., 152
Shrum, W., 125
Sidanius, J., 6, 13, 22, 27, 35, 38, 39, 44, 86, 87, 94, 100, 118, 119, 132, 142, 153, 156, 209
Sigelman, L., 9, 131, 134, 135, 136
Sikes, J., 63
Simon, A., 120
Simon, B., 175, 176
Sims, V. M., 4
Sinclair, J. R., 83, 175
Sinclair, S., 13, 27, 38, 44
Singh, P., 173
Singleton, L. C., 127
Siy, J. O., 91, 125
Skowronski, J. J., 97
Slavin, R. E., 63, 91, 169
Smith, E. R., 97, 99, 100, 101, 109
Smith, H., 150, 175, 176
Smith, H. P., 187
Smith, J. A., 90
Smith, M. L., 19
Smith, S. S., 126
Smith, T. W., 124, 125
Smythe, P. C., 35, 40, 46
Snapp, M., 63
Snider, N., 132
Snuggs, S. J., 171
Sobel, M. E., 83
Sommer, B., 20
Sommers, S. R., 91
Sonleiter, N., 58
Soroka, S., 166
Southwell, P., 152
Spangenberg, J., 120

Spaulding, W. D., 54
Spencer-Rodgers, J., 89
Spicer, C. V., 136
Sriram, N., 98
Stace, K., 74
Stangor, C., 11, 56, 57, 97, 99, 106, 108, 127, 203
Star, S. A., 6
Stearns, E., 120, 127, 128
Steele, C., 132, 142
Steelman, L., 131
Stein, R., 147, 148, 154
Stellmacher, J., 57, 92, 126, 196, 211
Stephan, C. W., 4, 23, 54, 63, 80, 81, 88, 89, 105, 131, 155, 185
Stephan, W. G., 4, 14, 23, 54, 80, 81, 87, 88, 89, 105, 108, 131, 155, 185, 197
Sterne, J. A. C., 20
Stocks, E. L., 82
Stolle, D., 166
Stone, C. H., 75
Stone, J., 90
Stouffer, S. A., 6
Stover, E., 71
Stringer, M., 111, 116, 170
Stroebe, W., 56, 57
Stroessner, S. J., 98
Suci, G. J., 102, 106
Sullivan, L. A., 11, 97, 99, 106, 108, 127, 203
Sullivan, M., 54
Sumner, W. G., 3, 94
Sumser, J., 112
Swart, H., 170
Swim, J. K., 83, 131, 132, 168, 175

T

Tajfel, H., 83
Talaska, C. A., 11, 108, 112, 203
Tam, T., 53, 110, 120, 162, 170
Tannenbaum, P. H., 102, 106
Tartakovsky, M., 90
Tatum, B. D., 128
Tausch, N., 36, 37, 72, 120, 162, 163, 173, 209
Taylor, A. R., 127
Taylor, D. M., 173
Taylor, J. E., 173, 176
Taylor, M., 147
Teixeira, R. A., 125, 126 128
Thomas, S., 44
Thompson, J., 94, 123, 157
Tomolillo, C., 110, 118, 170
Torres, G., 178

Author Index

Towles-Schwen, T., 23
Trail, T. E., 127, 207, 209
Trawalter, S., 207
Tredoux, C., 51, 110, 111, 112, 142, 168, 169, 170, 171, 172, 173, 174, 177, 183
Tredoux, C. G., 170
Triandis, H. C., 89
Tropp, L. R., 8, 9, 13, 21, 22, 44, 51, 54, 67, 72, 74, 75, 78, 79, 81, 85, 86, 88, 91, 92, 93, 95, 100, 101, 104, 105, 106, 111, 115, 116, 118, 120, 121, 123, 124, 125, 128, 131, 133, 134, 135, 136, 137, 139, 140, 141, 142, 165, 168, 169, 170, 172, 173, 174, 176, 177, 182, 187, 207, 208
Turiel, E., 127
Turner, C. W., 70
Turner, J. C., 74
Turner, R. N., 82, 85, 92, 110, 120, 170
Tweedie, R. L., 20

U

Ullrich, J., 93, 185, 195
Uslaner, E. M., 166

V

Van der Meer, T., 165
Van der Zande, C. C., 22, 115, 118
Van Dick, R., 22, 35, 70, 71, 87, 93, 109, 121, 150, 152, 171, 179, 213
Van Dyk, A. C., 68
Van Hiel, A., 6, 13, 22, 38, 47, 83, 87, 118, 196, 212
Van Houten, P., 180
Van Laar, C., 6, 13, 22, 27, 35, 38, 39, 44, 86, 87, 94, 100, 118, 119, 142, 156, 209
Van Leeuwen, M. D., 9
Van Meek, L., 20
Van Oudenhoven, J. P., 74, 75
Varshney, A., 180
Vasquez, K. A., 72, 74, 131, 133, 141, 168, 182
Vaughn, L. A., 88, 92
Vescio, T. K., 83
Vevea, J. L., 20
Vivian, J., 32, 74, 75, 99, 126
Voci, A., 32, 51, 53, 74, 81, 82, 85, 92, 93, 100, 110, 118, 119, 120, 126, 156, 162, 163, 165, 170, 209
Vollhardt, J., 108, 111, 116, 170
Von Hippel, W., 99
Vonofakou, C., 92
Vorauer, J. D., 72, 93, 131, 142, 207

W

Wagner, C., 94
Wagner, D. E., 128
Wagner, E. E., 19, 87
Wagner, U., 9, 22, 35, 40, 42, 57, 87, 92, 93, 97, 99, 109, 120, 121, 126, 146, 150, 152, 163, 171, 179, 185, 195, 196, 209, 211, 213
Walker, I., 63, 64, 150, 175, 176
Walkley, R. P., 7
Walther, E., 44, 45
Ward, C., 156
Warp, L. S., 91
Watson, A. C., 54
Watts, W. A., 42
Weatherall, K., 111, 116, 170
Weber, R., 32
Webster, S. W., 117, 121
Weigert, K. M., 34
Weinstein, H. M., 71
Weisman, C. S., 2, 59, 68
Welch, S., 9, 131, 134, 135, 136
Weller, L., 53
Wellisch, J. B., 63
Wenzel, M., 216
Werth, J. L., 9
West, T. V., 127, 207, 209
White, B., 68, 91
White, J. B., 9, 62
Widaman, K. E., 56
Wieneke, K., 68, 91
Wiggins, E. C., 97
Wilder, D. A., 32, 75, 86, 94, 98, 99, 109, 123, 157
Wildschut, T., 179
Williams, P., 88
Williams, Jr., R. M., 5, 6, 64
Williams, Jr., S. A., 177
Wilner, D. M., 7
Wilson, D. B., 16, 17, 20, 67, 104, 135, 140
Wilson, K. L., 22, 35, 87, 91, 135
Wilson, T. C., 22, 35, 87
Wilson, T. D., 91, 128
Wilson, W. J., 178
Wittenbrink, B., 90
Wittig, M. A., 70, 71, 72, 208
Wolf, C., 22, 34, 35, 45, 87, 93, 109, 121
Wolf, H., 126, 196
Wolsko, C., 90, 101, 109
Wong, C., 147, 148, 149, 151, 152
Wong, J., 49
Wood, P. B., 58

Wood, W., 43, 44
Worchel, S., 71
Works, E., 7
Wright, S. C., 22, 92, 93, 100, 106, 115, 116, 118, 119, 120, 121, 124, 125, 128, 173, 174, 176, 178

X

Xu, J., 42, 54

Y

Yancey, G., 59, 120
Yarrow, L. J., 63

Yarrow, M. R., 63
Ybarra, O., 81, 197
Yinon, Y., 117

Z

Zagefka, H., 6, 13, 22, 27, 35, 38, 86, 87, 90, 118, 209
Zajonc, R. B., 68, 91, 101, 202
Zalk, S. R., 57
Zanna, M. P., 97, 99, 101, 105, 106, 108, 115, 118, 203
Zebrowitz, L. A., 68, 91
Zick, A., 34, 45, 150, 152, 171, 179
Zinn, H., 173

SUBJECT INDEX

Abortion, 43
Acquaintance potential, 72
Adolescents, 58, 59–60
Affective measures, 104–105, 106–108
Affective outcomes, 100–109
Affective processes, 11, 31, 42, 44–45, 88, 89, 97, 99–100, 203
Affective ties, 100, 101
Age, 36, 40, 49, 52, 54, 57–58, 133, 135, 146, 147, 148, 157, 159, 187–188, 191, 192, 193, 202, 204, 211
Aggregate level of analysis, 179–180, 182
AIDS, 9, 112
Anxiety, 11, 23, 24, 38, 44, 54, 77, 78, 79, 81, 82, 83, 84, 85–86, 87, 89, 90, 92, 93, 94, 118, 119, 120, 137, 138,142,162, 171, 187, 203, 205, 206, 207, 209
Apples-and-oranges problem, 134
Arab Israelis, 1, 174
Armed forces, see Military
Assimilation, 180, 215–216
Athletic teams, 55, 62, 91
Attitude
  behavior as precursor to attitude, 90–91
  multifaceted concept, 97
  strength, 195
Attitudes toward Blacks Scale, 106
Attribution bias, 108, 111, 170
Australia, 50, 63
Authoritarianism, 29, 45, 83, 146, 150, 153, 158, 159, 160, 183, 188–191, 192, 204, 209, 211–212
Authority support, 71

Balance theory, 120
Bangladesh, 51
Behavioral processes, 89, 90–92, 97, 112–113, 119–120, 123
Belgium, 7, 13, 154, 195
Beliefs, 11, 83, 100, 101, 102, 103, 104, 105, 106, 108, 113, 152, 203
Between-subject designs, 25
Bias
  attributional bias, 108, 111, 170
  cross-group friendship reports, 123–126

publication bias, 19–21, 87
sampling bias, 18–19
Bosnia, 1, 163, 215
Budget-cutting task, 118

Canada, 30, 35, 46, 147, 149, 151, 154, 166, 180
Canadian Inuits, 173, 177
Categorization, 29, 73–74, 98, 100
Causal direction, 6, 35, 40, 85–86, 87, 90, 211
Ceiling effect, 43, 54, 212
Checkpoints, 185
Children
  attitudes towards the elderly, 53–54, 186–187
  cross-group friendships, 127–128
  intergroup contact effects, 57–60, 169
Choice, 22–24
Civil Rights Movement, 29, 175, 177
Closeness, 119
Coal miners, 29
Cognitive measures, 104–105, 108
Cognitive outcomes, 100–109
Cognitive processes, 31, 42–44, 89, 97, 98–99
Collective guilt, 90
Collective threat, 44–45, 151–153, 155, 158, 159, 163, 171, 181, 188, 191, 193, 196, 198, 205, 207, 214
College roommate studies, 13, 23–24, 38–39, 46, 94, 126–127, 209, 213
College students, 49, 58, 187
Comfort, 52, 100, 102, 123
Common goals, 7, 61, 62, 64, 69, 75, 128, 202
Commonality, 127
Communication, 89
Compensatory policies, 112, 172
Competition over resources, 71
Compositional fallacy, 212
Computer programmers, 9
Contact effects, 6, 7, 10, 11, 13–60, 69, 72, 76, 80, 81, 90, 97, 102, 107, 112, 114, 121, 123, 129, 131–145, 170–171, 175–181, 185, 186–187, 196, 205
Contact settings, 54–57
Contextual variables, 75
Control groups, 25, 35, 52, 53, 56, 66

Subject Index 305

Cooperation, 61–63, 69, 70, 71, 76, 128
Cortisol response, 81, 118–119
Counter-ceiling effect, 43
Creativity, 90
Cross-group friendships, 11, 36, 37, 38, 57, 100, 105, 113, 114, 115–129, 142, 169, 204
  biases in reports, 123–126
  children, 127–128
  experimental studies, 118–119, 124
  generalization, 116–117
  indirect effects, 120
  inflated reports, 123–124, 125
  longitudinal studies, 118
  measurement, 120–123
  minority–majority relations, 141–143
  obstacles to, 126–128
  processes, 119–120
  situational features, 128
  sustaining, 127
Crowne–Marlowe scale of social desirability, 47
Cultural dissimilarities, 180
Cultural information, 88–90
Culture Assimilator program, 89
Cyprus, 36–37

Dartmouth College, 5
Decategorization, 73
Deprovincialization, 34
Desegregation, vii, 4, 30, 214
Detroit race riots, 1
Disability, 9, 51–52, 112, 113, 133
Discrimination, 3, 71, 132, 136–138, 141, 142–143, 168–169, 173, 175–177, 204, 214
Diversity, 164–167, 181
DSTAT, 84
Dual identity, 74, 176
Dummy variables, 103

Early contact experience, 59
East Germany, 179
Ecological fallacy, 212
Economic predictors, 146, 150–151
Education, 3, 36, 39, 111, 135, 146, 147, 149–150, 157, 159, 191, 192, 204–210, 214, 215, 216
Educational settings, 55, *see also* School settings
Elderly
  anti-immigration attitudes, 148
  attitudes towards, 9, 53–54, 186–187

Empathy, 11, 44, 77, 78, 79, 82–83, 84, 85–86, 87, 94, 171, 203, 205
Employment attitudes, 112
Equal status, 5, 6, 7, 8, 11, 61–62, 64, 69, 70, 72, 128, 132, 138–139, 174, 188, 193, 194, 208
Essentialist view, 83
Ethnic cleansing, 1
European identity, 154
Euthanasia, 43
Evaluative conditioning, 44
Expectation maximization algorithm, 188
Expectations, 72
Experiential predictors, 146, 156–157
Experimental studies, 22, 24, 118–119, 124, 137–138
Explicit prejudice, 109–110
Exposure, 45, 68, 202, 207

Facilitating conditions, 68, 76, 190
Fail-safe index, 19
Familiarity, 68
Field studies, 24
Fixed effects models, 17
Foreign exchanges, 56–57
French Canadians, 35, 40, 46
Friend-of-my-friend-is-my-friend, 120
Friendship potential, 117–118
Friendships, *see* Cross-group friendships

Gays, *see* Homosexuality
Gender, 147, 148–149, 157, 211
General linear models, 20–21
Generalization, 7, 29–47, 202
  across different levels of analysis, 30–32, 45–46
  across different situations, 32–33, 46
  affective and cognitive outcomes, 100–109
  affective processes, 44–45
  cognitive processes, 31, 42–44, 98
  cross-group friendships, 116–117
  inhibiting processes, 29
  irrationality of, 45–46
  psychological factors, 29, 31
  social norms, 29–30
  to entire outgroup, 30–32, 45–46
  to other outgroups, 33–45, 46
Gentrification, 165
Geographical differences, 50–51
Germany, 9, 13, 34, 36, 39–42, 43, 44, 56, 111, 146–147, 150, 155, 157–159, 179, 180, 187–189, 193, 213

Goals, 62, 69, 128
Group discrimination, 176
Group interdependence, 64, 180–181
Group membership salience, 73–75
Group relative deprivation, 150, 157, 176, 177, 182
Group status, 131–143, 204
    contact between minorities, 177–178
    cross-group friendships, 141–143
    majority status groups, 131–132, 133, 134
    minority–majority relations, 136–138
    minority status groups, 131, 133, 134, 207
    negative intergroup contact, 187
    optimal conditions for contact, 138–141
    perspective on group relationship, 132, 141
Guilt, 90
Gun control, 43

Harvard University, 5, 7
Herzegovina, 1, 163
Holocaust rescuers, 1–2, 34
Homeless, 40–42, 43, 44, 46, 153
Homosexuality, 9, 40–42, 43, 52–53
Housing, 7
Human Relations Movement, 3–4, 79–80

Identity predictors, 146, 154–155
Ideology, 43
Ignorance, 4, 80
Immigration attitudes, 36, 148–159, 171–172
Implicit Association Test (IAT), 118, 208
Implicit prejudice, 109–110
Income, 151
Indirect contact, 42, 44, 46, 92–93, 120, 129
Individual level of analysis, 179, 180, 182
Individual threat, 155, 158, 191, 193, 196, 198, 205
Ingroup, thinking less of, 94
Institutional support, 63–64, 69–70, 128
Intercultural communication, 89
Intergroup contact hypothesis (Allport), 8–10
Intergroup contact theory
    criticisms, 9–10, 161–183, 205
    historical development, 3–10
Interpersonal processes, 123
Inuits, 173, 177
Israel, 1, 174

Japan, 63
Jews, 1–2, 34, 39
Jigsaw classroom, 63, 169

King Jr., Dr. M. L., 43
Knowledge, 11, 77, 78, 79–80, 83, 84, 86, 87, 88, 90, 93–94, 171, 193, 195

Laboratory settings, 55
Leading-the-horse-to-water problem, 167–171
Lesbians, see Homosexuality
Levels of analysis, 17–18, 30–32, 146, 164, 168, 171, 178–181, 182, 205, 206, 208–209, 212–213
Liking, 68
Longitudinal studies, 37–39, 90, 118, 209

Macro-level analysis, 178–181, see also Levels of analysis
Madrid terrorist attacks, 45
Majority status groups, 131–132, 133, 134, see also Group status
Malaysia, 51
Measurement reliability, 25–26
Mediators and mediational analysis, 41, 78–79, 203, see also specific mediators
Mental disability, 51–52
Mental illness, 9, 53, 54
Merchant Marine, 4
Mere exposure effect, 68, see also Exposure
Meta-analysis, 14–27, 105, 201, 203
    group status effects, 132–136
    intergroup contact research, 14–27, 201, 203
    negative intergroup contact, 186–187
Meta-stereotypes, 93, 142
Methodology, 24–26
Micro-level analysis, 178–181, see also Levels of analysis
Middle East, 51
Military, 6–7, 34–35, 63, 91
Minority influence, 43–44
Minority–majority relations, 136–138
    cross-group friendships, 141–143
Minority status groups, 131, 133, 134, 207, see also Group status
Model of intergroup contact and threat, 196–200
Moderators, 39–42, 197, 202–203
    negative, 71–72
Modern Racism Scale, 106

Subject Index

Multiculturalism, 216
Multi-level analysis, 212–213, see also Levels of analysis
Muslims, 39–40, 46
Mutual friendships, 123

National identity, 146, 154, 159, 204
National pride, 154, 155
Necessary conditions, 68
Negative intergroup contact, 185, 186–187, 188, 189–190, 205–206
   age, 191, 192, 193
   attitude strength, 195
   counteracted by positive contact, 190, 195
   education, 191, 192
   equal status, 193, 194
   invoking conditions, 193–194
   quality of contact, 193–194
   special groups, 195–196
   substantive contact, 193, 194
   threat, 191, 192, 193, 196
   voluntary contact, 193, 194
Negative meta-stereotypes, 142, see also Meta-stereotypes
Negative moderating factors, 71–72
Negative secondary transfer effects, 44–45
Neighborhood contact, 210
Norms, 29–30, 33, 42, 44, 63, 70, 88, 90, 92–93, 111, 116, 126–128, 129, 146–147, 169, 203, 206, 213
Northern Ireland, 30, 37, 51, 119, 156, 162–163, 165

Objective features of contact, 72–73
Openness, 73
Optimal conditions for contact, 61–64, 68, 138–141
Organizational settings, 55, 64
Outcomes of intergroup contact, 100–109, 205, see also Contact effects

Palestinian West Bank checkpoint, 185
Parental influence, 127
Participant choice, 22–24
Passive contact, 56
Peer influences, 127
Peer socialization, 38
Peer tutoring, 113
Perceived percentage of foreigners, 197–199
Perceived threat, 137, 197
Percentage of the minority, 197–200

Personal finances, 151
Personal threat, see Individual threat
Personality, 29, 146, 153–154, 158
Perspective-taking, 83
Physical disability, 9, 51–52, see also Disability
Police, 4, 195–196
Policy, 110–112, 171–172, 181–182, 213–216
Political conservatism, 114, 152
Political inefficacy, 152
Political predictors, 146, 152
Political right, 152, 192
Political tolerance, 171
Population ratio, 146–147, 179, 196–200
Poverty, 150
Predictors of prejudice, 145–157, 204
Preferential policies, 112
Prejudice
   implicit/explicit, 109–110
   intercorrelations, 34
   norm, 146–147, see also Norms
   predictors, 145–157, 204
Primary transfer, 30–32
Prior contact, 46
Pro-Black and Anti-Black Attitudes scales, 106
Processes
   cross-group friendships, 119–120
   secondary transfer, 34, 42–45
Proximity, 2, 156, 166, 179
Psychological factors, 29, 31
Public housing, 7
Publication bias, 19–21, 87

Quality of contact, 54, 56, 111, 117, 135, 140, 172, 174, 193–194
Quality of research, 24–26, 67
Quasi-experimental studies, 24

Race-related discussions, 207
Race riots, 1
Racial climate, 70
Racial discrimination, 136–138, 142–143, see also Discrimination
Racial Resentment Scale, 106
Racial seating patterns, 168–169
Racial segregation, 29–30, 126, 168–169
Random designs, 22
Random effects models, 17, 79
Rebound effects, 42
Recategorization, 74
Recreational settings, 55

308 Subject Index

Re-fencing, 29, 31
Reicher effect, 173–178, 182
Rejection, 72
Relationship restructuring, 93–94
Relative deprivation, 177, see also Group relative deprivation
Reliability, 25–26
Religious communities, 64
Repeated contact, 91–92
Representativeness, 98
Residential settings, 55, see also Housing
Resource limitation, 71
Restructured relationships, 93–94
Reverse causal effect, 35, 211
Right-wing authoritarianism, 153, see also Authoritarianism
Robbers' Cave, 209

Salient categorization model, 32
Sampling bias, 18–19
Saturated path model, 85
Scatter plots, 19
School settings, 59–60, 62, 63, 70, 126, 128, 169
Seating segregation, 168–169
Secondary transfer effect, 33–45, 46, 156
    affective factors, 44–45
    cognitive factors, 42–44
    cross-sectional evidence, 36–37
    indirect contact, 42
    longitudinal evidence, 37–39
    moderators, 39–42
    negative effects, 44–45
    norms, 44
    time delay, 42–43
    underlying processes, 34, 42–45
Segregation, 29–30, 126, 165–169, 181–182, 206, 213, 214, 216
Selection processes, 209–211
Self-disclosure, 82–83, 120, 122–123
Self-selection, 6, 147
Settings, 54–57
Shared activities, 120
Similarity, 39
Situational norms, 127–128, see also Norms
Situations
    cross-group friendships, 128
    generalization, 32–33, 46
Sobel test, 41, 83, 158
Social capital, 164–167, 181
Social categorization, 74
Social change, 173–178, 182

Social context predictors, 146–147
Social Darwinism, 3
Social desirability, 46–47
Social dominance orientation, 153–154, 158
Social identity, 154
Social norms, 29–30, 128, see also Norms
Social policy, 171–172, 181–182, 213–216
Societal diversity, 164–167, 181
Societal norms, 127–128
Socio-location predictors, 146, 147–150
Soldiers, see Military
South Africa, 2, 8, 30, 51, 68, 71, 111–112, 142, 168–169, 170, 171, 173, 174–176
Spain, 45, 180
Sports teams, 55, 62, 91
Spreading attitude effect, 44, 45
Status equality, 61–62, 69, 128, 138–139, 193, 194
Steel mill workers, 30
Stereotype threat, 142
Stereotypes, 35, 42, 54, 83, 93, 98–99, 100, 101, 102, 103, 104, 106, 109, 142, 186
Stigma, 40, 46
Stimulus generalization gradient, 39, 46
Stress response, 23, 81, 118–119, 126
Structural equation models, 79, 86, 119, 197
Structured contact, 65–67
Subjectivity
    perception of contact situation, 208
    response to contact, 72–73
Summer camps, 62
Superordinate category, 74, 93, 206
Surveys, 24
Syllogistic attitude change, 42

Target groups, 51–54
Teams, 55, 62, 91
Terrorism, 44–45, 71
Threat, 11, 44–45, 81, 112, 137, 137, 146, 147, 152, 153, 155–156, 158, 159, 166, 167, 187, 191, 192, 193, 195, 196, 197, 198–199, 200, 206, see also Collective threat, Individual threat, Stereotype threat
Time delay, secondary transfer, 42–43
Time spent, 122–123
Tito, M., 215
Tourist settings, 56
Transfer effects, see Primary transfer; Secondary transfer effect
Travel settings, 56
Trim-and-fill technique, 20

Trust, 123, 164–167, 181
Typicality, 32

Ultimate attribution bias, 170
Unemployment, 150–151, 197
United States, 1, 2, 3, 8, 49, 50, 61, 63, 79, 137, 156, 169, 176–177
University of Alabama, 4
University of California Los Angeles (UCLA) college roommate studies, 13, 23–24, 38–39, 40, 46, 55, 94, 119, 142, 209

Vicarious contact, 92–93
Violence, 71

Within-subject designs, 25
Workplace, 4, 29–30, 70, 71

Yugoslavia, 1, 163